MW00896481

STUDY GUIDE TO THE BHAGAVADGĪTĀ

Study Guide to the Bhagavadgītā

With Practical Concordance

ॐ

Les Morgan

ISBN-13: 978-1482332728 (paper)
ISBN-10: 1482332728 (paper)

Front cover image: Viśvarūpa: The Cosmic Form of Kṛṣṇa (circa 1820)
This image was uploaded as a donation by the Brooklyn Museum to the Wikimedia Commons, and is considered to have no known copyright restrictions by the institutions of the Brooklyn Museum.
https://commons.wikimedia.org/wiki/File:Brooklyn_Museum_-_Vishvarupa_The_Cosmic_Form_of_Krishna.jpg

Cataloging data:
Study Guide to the Bhagavadgītā: With Practical Concordance
Morgan, Les (author)
In English and Sanskrit (romanized and Devanāgarī)
Includes bibliographical references. First Edition, 2017
6.14" x 9.21" (15.60 x 23.39 cm)

BISAC: RELIGION / Hinduism / Sacred Writings

Digital Edition 2017.9.15

ॐ

Dedicated to

Dr. Ram Karan Sharma

ॐ गं गणपतये नमः

Oṁ Gaṁ Gaṇapataye Namaḥ

ॐ कवीनामृषभाय नमः

Oṁ Kavīnāmṛṣbhāya Namaḥ

तद्विद्धि प्रणिपातेन परिप्रश्नेन सेवया ।
उपदेक्ष्यन्ति ते ज्ञानं ज्ञानिनस्तत्त्वदर्शिनः ॥

tad viddhi praṇipātena paripraśnena sevayā ।
upadekṣyanti te jñānaṁ jñāninas tattvadarśinaḥ ॥

Learn by showing respect, asking questions, and doing service.
People of wisdom, who see what is real, will teach you wisdom.

Bhagavadgītā 4.34

Contents

Introduction

The *Bhagavadgītā* is one of the most widely read spiritual masterpieces of India. I began to develop this *Study Guide* while editing Ram Karan Sharma's translation of the *Bhagavadgītā*.[1] I expanded the contents and added theme guides as study aids for group discussion.[2] Based on the Critical Edition, this reference guide can be used with any translation. The arrangement is designed for English readers who are studying the text closely.

The *Bhagavadgītā* has influenced such diverse figures as Mahātma Gandhi, Henry David Thoreau, Aldous Huxley, and C. G. Jung. It raises universal questions that are as important today as they were thousands of years ago. What is the right way to act in this world, balancing social duty with personal responsibility? Is there an eternal reality behind the ordinary reality of daily life? What is our relationship with the divine? The teaching takes place in a war zone. Arjuna, a great warrior, is troubled by the terrible battle he is about to fight. Kṛṣṇa, his friend and spiritual guide, consoles him with insights into the nature of duty.

The text deals with a wide range of topics, but The *Bhagavadgītā* is not arranged as a textbook. For the most part, it does not follow a linear, step-by-step teaching method that organizes ideas in a logical order, with foundational ideas presented first. On the contrary, the work is presented as a conversation between friends at a time of peak emotional stress. As with many Indian scriptures, the sequence of ideas is driven by questions, in this case asked by Arjuna, a man whose normal composure has been shattered by world events. As the tale begins, we find ourselves in a warrior's chariot stationed in a no man's land between two armies. First we must get our bearings, surveying both fronts, hearing the tumultuous sounds of the powerful forces that are about to fight to the death. Indeed, death hangs in the air all around us. Arjuna, a great leader who should be spearheading his troops into battle, is immobilized by doubt and grief. He slumps down and

---

[1] It was in February of 2011 that Dr. Sharma asked me to consider taking on the task of editing the manuscript he had prepared with Carol Pitts. I began work on the text in March of 2011. The book was published in 2015 as *Bhagavadgītā*, by Ram Karan Sharma, with Carol Pitts and Les Morgan. For general information on the *Bhagavadgītā*, see my Introduction in that volume. I completed the concordance work on July 4, 2017.

[2] One of my study groups is discussed in my book on translation issues. See Les Morgan, *Translating the Bhagavadgītā: A Workbook for Sanskrit Students* (2017).

drops his weapon. This is no time for classroom lectures! A more immediate and compelling intervention is needed, and that is exactly what his dear friend Kṛṣṇa provides.

To help you understand this great and complex scripture, the *Study Guide* is divided into several sections.

- The story of the *Bhagavadgītā* is part of an epic tale, and mentions many characters in passing. The sections on *Who's Who in the Bhagavadgītā* and *Epithets in the Bhagavadgītā* give background on the diverse cast.
- The *Sanskrit Concordance* shows where individual Sanskrit words appear in the text. If you want to follow a single term, this is the place to start. The concordance includes all words that appear in the Critical Edition of the text, with some suggested meanings. The section on *Concordancing Methodology* explains the organizational strategy.
- *Theme Guides* are collections of verses that can be read as a group to see how key ideas play out in the text. The *Theme Guides* point out important vocabulary, noting synonyms for concepts. If a specific word interests you, you can look it up in the *Sanskrit Concordance* to get more detail.

I am grateful to Peter Frentzel and Richard Schimpf for reviewing early drafts and making many helpful suggestions on content and format. They served with me on the editorial team for the Ram Karan Sharma translation. Hours of friendly wrangling with them over words gave me much joy.

Les Morgan
Pacifica, California, 2017

Who's Who in the *Bhagavadgītā*

The *Bhagavadgītā* is presented as a dialogue between Kṛṣṇa, who is an incarnation of God, and Arjuna, a great leader and warrior. Their conversation is being reported by Saṁjaya to King Dhṛtarāṣṭra. In addition to those four primary *dramatis personæ*, many others are mentioned in passing.

Abhimanyu — The son of Arjuna and Subhadrā. Mentioned in 1.6 and 1.18 by his epithet Saubhadra. He will be killed in the coming battle while fighting bravely against great odds.

Arjuna — Pāṇḍu's third and last son by Kuntī, but in fact fathered by Indra, the lord of the gods. He is an outstanding archer and a principal warrior of the Pāṇḍava army. He is a cousin of Duryodhana. His conversation with Kṛṣṇa, his cousin and chariot driver, forms the central narrative of the *Bhagavadgītā*. Arjuna means "white".

Aśvatthāmā — The son of Droṇa. He is an ally of Duryodhana, fighting on the Kaurava side. Droṇa gives up the fight after receiving a false report that Aśvatthāmā had been killed. Aśvatthāmā is the nom. sing. form of the masc. noun Aśvatthāman. Both forms of the name appear in different translations. Mentioned in verse 1.8.

Bharata — King Bharata was the common ancestor of both the Pāṇḍavas and the Kauravas, whose great internecine war is the subject of the *Mahābhārata*. He was the founder of the Bharata lineage. The term Bhārata ("descendant of Bharata") is a general term for all the family lines. The story of his birth is given in *MBh.* 1.62-69. He was the son of Śakuntalā and Duḥṣanta, who was a descendant of Pūru, in the Lunar Dynasty.

Bhīma — "The Terrible One", Pāṇḍu's second son by Kuntī, but actually fathered by the wind god. His prowess in battle is mentioned in 1.4, where he and his brother Arjuna set a standard as outstanding fighters (*bhīmārjunasamāḥ*). In 1.10 the Pāṇḍava army is described as "protected by Bhīma" (*bhīmābhirakṣitam*). Said to have an enormous appetite, he is referred to by his epithet "Wolf-belly" (Vṛkodara) in 1.15, where he is also said to be a doer of terrible deeds (*bhīmakarmā*). His conch Pauṇḍra is also mentioned in 1.15. Bhīma means "fearsome" or "terrific".

Bhīṣma — The first-born son of King Śantanu and Gaṅgā. An uncle of Pāṇḍu and Dhṛtarāṣṭra, he is the grand-uncle and beloved teacher of both the Pāṇḍavas and the Kauravas. Bhīṣma was Śantanu's lawful heir, but renounced his right to the kingship and swore permanent celibacy in order to ensure that his father's sons by Satyavatī would inherit the kingdom. For the first ten days of the eighteen-day battle, Bhīṣma was the supreme commander of the Kaurava forces. On the tenth day, Bhīṣma was mortally wounded after refusing to fight Śikhaṇḍī, whom he considered to be a woman, and Droṇa assumed command. Resting upon a bed of arrows, Bhīṣma remained alive for fifty-eight days, delaying his death so that it would occur during the auspicious "upper course" of the sun in the northern solstice (see verse 8.24). Bhīṣma is referred to as "the elder Kuru" (*kuruvṛddhaḥ*) and "grandfather" (*pitāmahaḥ*) in verse 1.12. Mentioned in verses 1.8, 10-12, 25; 2.4; 11.26, 34.

Bhūriśravas — Bhūriśravas was a warrior who fought on the side of the Kauravas. Referred to in verse 1.8 as Saumadatti (the son of Somadatta). Somadatta was king of the Bāhīkas.

Cekitāna — A Yādava prince allied with the Pāṇḍavas. Prince of the Kekaya people. The name means "highly intelligent". Mentioned in verse 1.5.

Citrāṅgada — The elder of Śantanu's two sons by Satyavatī. He is not mentioned in the *Bhagavadgītā.*

Dhṛṣṭaketu — The king of Cedi, allied with the Pāṇḍavas. The name means "bold leader". Mentioned in verse 1.5.

Dhṛṣṭadyumna — The Commander-in-chief of the Pāṇḍava army. He will kill Droṇa. Dhṛṣṭadyumna is the son of Drupada and the brother of Draupadī. Mentioned by name in verse 1.17 and by his epithet "Son of Drupada" (Drupadaputra) in verse 1.3.

Dhṛtarāṣṭra — The blind king who is the father of the Kauravas. He is the posthumous son of Vicitravīrya, in fact fathered by Vyāsa with Ambikā. His reign is under attack by the Pāṇḍavas, the sons of Dhṛtarāṣṭra's younger half-brother Pāṇḍu. After the battle, Pāṇḍu's son Yudhiṣṭhira will rule the devastated kingdom, but Dhṛtarāṣṭra will remain as the nominal king. The dramatic structure of the *Bhagavadgītā* is a story within a story. The frame story begins in verse 1.1 when Dhṛtarāṣṭra asks his minister, Saṁjaya, to give him a report on how things are going as his army prepares for battle with the Pāṇḍavas. The entire text of the *Bhagavadgītā* is then related by Saṁjaya to Dhṛtarāṣṭra. He is addressed as "Descendant Of Bharata" (Bhārata) in verses

1.24 and 2.10. He is addressed as "king" (*rāja*) in verses 11.9; 18.76, 77. He is addressed as "king" (*mahīpati*) in verse 1.21.

Draupadī — Co-wife of the Pāṇḍava brothers. Mentioned indirectly in 1.6 and 1.18 by references to the "sons of Draupadī".

Droṇa — The teacher of both the Kauravas and the Pāṇḍavas. Arjuna was his favorite pupil. After Bhīṣma allowed himself to be mortally wounded on the tenth day of the eighteen-day battle, Droṇa assumed command of the Kaurava forces. On the fifteenth day, after receiving a false report that his son Aśvatthāmā had been killed, Droṇa gave up the fight and was killed by Dhṛṣṭadyumna. Karṇa then assumed command of the Kaurava forces. Duryodhana addresses Droṇa as "teacher" (*ācārya*) in 1.2 and 1.3. Droṇa is mentioned by name in 1.25; 2.4; 11.26, 34.

Drupada — The king of Pāñcāla, the son of Pṛṣata. His name means "Whose feet are fast" or "Rapid-step". He is the father of Draupadī (co-wife of the Pāṇḍava brothers), Dhṛṣṭadyumna (chief of the Pāṇḍava army), and Śikhaṇḍī. Drupada is mentioned in verses 1.4 and 1.18. Dhṛṣṭadyumna is referred to as the "son of Drupada" in verse 1.3.

Duryodhana — A leading general of the Kauravas. He is the eldest son of Dhṛtarāṣṭra. Duryodhana is a cousin of Arjuna. At the opening of the text (verses 1.2-11), he delivers a report on the status of the armies as the battle is about to begin. His name literally means "Tough Fighter" or "Wicked Warrior". He will be killed by Bhīma. He is called Dhārtarāṣṭra, "Dhṛtarāṣṭra's son", in verse 1.23. He is referred to as "king" or "prince" (*rāja*) in verse 1.2.

Gaṅgā — The mother of Bhīṣma. She is not mentioned in the *Bhagavadgītā*.

Janaka — There was more than one king named Janaka, but the reference in verse 3.20 seems to be to a great philosopher-king, a member of the Kṣatriya class. In the *Rāmāyaṇa*, Janaka was the father of Sītā, the wife of the hero Rāma.

Jayadratha — The king of Sindhudeśa. He was the son-in-law of Dhṛtarāṣṭra. Jayadratha will be killed in the battle by Arjuna. Mentioned in 11.34.[3]

Karṇa — The name means "ear", possibly referring to the fact he was born wearing earrings and armor that would confer immortality on him. The eldest son of Kuntī, fathered by Sūrya, the sun god. He was abandoned by his mother at birth, and was brought up by a charioteer. He is referred to by his epithet "Son

[3] In the Critical Edition, Jayadratha is mentioned only in verse 11.34. Some manuscripts mention him in verse 1.8 as a variant reading for *tathaiva ca*.

of a charioteer" (*sūtaputra*) in verse 11.26. He is referred to by name in verses 1.8 and 11.34. He is a great ally of Duryodhana and a fierce enemy of Arjuna. After Droṇa gave up the fight on the fifteenth day, Karṇa assumed command of the Kaurava forces until he was killed by Arjuna on the seventeenth day.

Kāśirāja — The King of Kāśī, a Pāṇḍava ally. Kāśī refers to a region (modern Vārāṇasī) and its people. Mentioned in verses 1.5 and 1.17.

Kauravas — King Dhṛtarāṣṭra's Kaurava army is fighting their cousins, the Pāṇḍavas. Kuru was the common ancestor of the Kauravas and the Pāṇḍavas. Kaurava is a general term for all of the descendants of Kuru, but since King Dhṛtarāṣṭra belongs to the Kuru Dynasty the term Kaurava usually refers to his forces in particular.

Kṛpa — A warrior, the brother-in-law of Droṇa. The maternal uncle of Aśvatthāmā. The name (in feminine form, *kṛpā*) means "pity" or "compassion", referring to the fact that Krpa was found in a clump of grass as an infant and was adopted in an act of compassion.[4] Mentioned in verse 1.8.

Kṛṣṇa — A noted prince of the Vṛṣṇi clan who is serving as Arjuna's chariot driver. As the conversation between him and his cousin Arjuna develops, he reveals himself to be an incarnation of the Supreme Being. He is the son of Vasudeva and Devakī. Kṛṣṇa is also used as another name for Arjuna, and Arjuna and Kṛṣṇa are called "the two Kṛṣṇas".

Kuntī — The daughter of Śūra, she is the sister of Vasudeva (Kṛṣṇa's father, thus making her Kṛṣṇa's paternal aunt). Kuntī was the first wife of Pāṇḍu, and mother of the three eldest Pāṇḍava brothers. As a young woman she was granted a boon by a sage, empowering her to invoke the birth of a child by any god of her choice. Before marrying Pāṇḍu, Kuntī bore her son Karṇa by Sūrya (the sun god). After marrying Pāṇḍu, she bore Yudhiṣṭhira by Dharma (the god of righteousness), Bhīma by Vāyu (the wind god), and Arjuna by Indra (the lord of the gods). Kuntī was originally named Pṛthā. She was adopted by her father's childless cousin Kuntibhoja, and took the name Kuntī after him (Kuntibhoja is mentioned in 1.5). She is referred to in Arjuna's epithet Kaunteya, ("Son of Kuntī"), discussed on page 17.

Kuntibhoja — A cousin of Śūra. An ally of the Pāṇḍavas. The childless Kuntibhoja adopted Kuntī, who became Pāṇḍu's wife, the mother of Karṇa, Yudhiṣṭhira, Bhīma, and Arjuna. Mentioned in verse 1.5.

---

[4] Sargeant, p. 46.

Kuru — A descendant of Bharata, Kuru was the common ancestor of the Kauravas and the Pāṇḍavas. His name is used as a general term for all of his descendants and as the name of the royal dynasty to which Dhṛtarāṣṭra belongs. The battle itself takes place at the "field of Kuru" (*kurukṣetra*). Dhṛtarāṣṭra's Kaurava army is fighting the Pāṇḍava forces.

Madhu (a demon) — A demon who was slain by Viṣṇu. Kṛṣṇa's epithet Madhusūdana ("slayer of Madhu") refers to this incident.

Madhu (a patriarch) — A patriarch of the Yadu dynasty. One of Madhu's sons, Vṛṣṇi, was the founder of Kṛṣṇa's clan. Kṛṣṇa is referred to as a "Descendant of Madhu" (Mādhava) the first time he is mentioned in the *Bhagavadgītā* (in verse 1.14) and that epithet is used again in 1.37. The epithet involves a possible play on words, because the traditional interpretation of "Mādhava" as an epithet of Kṛṣṇa is that it refers to the "husband of Lakṣmī" (i.e., Viṣṇu).

Nakula — The fourth of the Pāṇḍava brothers, one of twin sons (Nakula and Sahadeva) born to Mādrī, the second wife of Pāṇḍu. The twins were in fact fathered by the two Aśvins, divine horsemen who draw the chariot of the sun. Nakula was the elder of the twins. Mentioned in verse 1.16.

Pāṇḍavas — The five Pāṇḍava brothers are the sons of Pāṇḍu. The five brothers are Yudhiṣṭhira, Bhīma, Arjuna, Nakula, and Sahadeva. The Pāṇḍavas are about to do battle with their cousins, the sons of Dhṛtarāṣṭra (the Kauravas).

Pāṇḍu — The younger half-brother of King Dhṛtarāṣṭra. Pāṇḍu is the posthumous son of Vicitravīrya, actually fathered by Vyāsa with Ambālikā. Pāṇḍu tooks two wives, Kuntī and Mādrī. Placed under a curse by a sage, he was unable to produce children, but he is the nominal father of the five Pāṇḍava brothers, all of whom were born through divine intervention. The Pāṇḍava army is confronting King Dhṛtarāṣṭra's Kaurava army.

Pūru — King Pūru was the second son of king Yayāti. Puru was the founder of the Paurava dynasty from which the Bhāratas and Kurus were descended. His elder brother was Yadu, founder of the Yādava line.

Purujit — Mentioned in verse 1.5. A Kunti prince, an ally of the Pāṇḍavas. Most translators treat Purujit and Kuntibhoja as two different warriors.[5] Other

---

[5] Those treating the words *purujit kuntibhojaś ca* as referring to two people include Ādidevānanda, p. 45; Edgerton, p. 3; Feuerstein and Feuerstein, p. 79; Hill, p. 100; Gambhīrānanda 1997, p. 12; Gambhīrānanda 1998, p. 33; Sampatkumaran, p. 6; Sargeant,

translators think that Purujit ("Conqueror of the Purus") is an epithet modifying Kuntibhoja.[6] Two translators treat Purujit as a name for the "King of Kāśi" (Kāśirāja).[7]

Sahadeva — The fifth of the Pāṇḍava brothers, one of twin sons (Nakula and Sahadeva) born to Mādrī, the second wife of Pāṇḍu. The twins were in fact fathered by the two Aśvins, divine horsemen who draw the chariot of the sun. Nakula was the elder of the twins. The name Sahadeva means "He who goes with god" or "He who is accompanied by the gods". Mentioned in verse 1.16.

Śaibya — Śaibya ("of the Śibi"). A king of the Śibi tribe or the family of Śibi. An ally of the Pāṇḍavas. Mentioned in verse 1.5.

Saṁjaya — Saṁjaya is a charioteer (*sūta*), a companion and counsellor to the blind king King Dhṛtarāṣṭra. Dhṛtarāṣṭra sent Saṁjaya on a mission to negotiate with the Pāṇḍavas, but the effort failed. The frame story begins in verse 1.1 when Dhṛtarāṣṭra asks Saṁjaya, who has the power of divine sight, to report what is happening on the battlefield. Saṁjaya is the son of Gavalgana.

Samitiṁjaya — Some translators think Samitiṁjaya ("Victorious in War") is the name of a warrior, while others consider it an epithet applied to Kṛpa, another warrior in the verse.[8] Mentioned in verse 1.8.

---

p. 43; Sivananda, p. 5; Swarupananda, p. 4; Tapasyananda, p. 16; Vireśwarānanda, p. 5; and Zaehner, p. 113. Hill (p. 100, note 9), Gotshalk (p. 141, note 10), and Sargeant (p. 43) say that Purujit and Kuntibhoja were brothers. Minor (p. 6) says that Purujit and Kuntibhoja were two brothers, sometimes taken as one.

[6] Sörensen (p. 568) says that, in most passages of the *MBh.*, Purujit seems to be another name of Kuntibhoja. Those treating *purujit kuntibhojaś ca* as referring to one person include Divanji (p. 89, entry # 2026) and Van Buitenen (1981, p. 69). Tilak (vol, 2, p. 853) also says Purujit Kuntibhoja refers to one person, the son of King Kuntibhoja, and that Kuntibhoja was his family name.

[7] Warrier (p. 7) and Marjanovic (p. 31) treat Purujit as describing the King of Kāśī.

[8] Most translators think *samitiṁjaya* is an epithet of Kṛpa, e.g., Divanji, p. 153, entry #3516; Edgerton, p. 4; Hill, p. 101; Sargeant, p. 46; Swarupananda, p. 5; Tapasyananda, p. 17; etc. Those who think Samitiṁjaya is the name of a warrior include Van Buitenen (1981, p. 69). Sörensen (p. 612) identifies Samitiṁjaya as the name of a warrior, one of the seven great chariot fighters of the Vṛṣṇi clan, and also as an epithet of Viṣṇu. The Critical Edition reading of *samitiṁjaya* is replaced by the variant *śalyo jayadrathaḥ* ("Śalya, Jayadratha") in the Kaśmir recension as shown in Marjanovic (p. 31). Minor (p. 8) adopts the variant *śalyo jayadrathaḥ* and notes issues with the reading. For the epithet *samitiṁjaya* meaning

Śantanu — King of the Kurus. Śantanu is not mentioned in the *Bhagavadgītā*. He fathered Bhīṣma by the river goddess Gaṅgā, and had two sons (Citrāṅgada and Vicitravīrya) by Satyavatī. Citrāṅgada died young and Vicitravīrya ascended to the throne. Vicitravīrya died before fathering children, but after his death, the sage Vyāsa (the son of the sage Parāśara with Satyavatī before her marriage to Śantanu) ensured the line of succession through the right of levirate, by fathering of the two princes, Dhṛtarāṣṭra and Pāṇḍu.

Sātyaki — A Vṛṣṇi warrior fighting on the side of the Pāṇḍavas, mentioned in verse 1.17. Referred to by his epithet Yuyudhāna ("Eager to fight") in verse 1.4.

Satyavatī — The mother of Vyāsa (by the sage Parāśara), and of Citrāṅgada and Vicitravīrya (by King Śantanu). She is not mentioned in the *Bhagavadgītā*.

Śikhaṇḍī — Mentioned in verse 1.17. Śikhaṇḍī was a warrior fighting on the Pāṇḍava side. Born as a girl (Śikhaṇḍinī) and miraculously changed to a man, he was considered to be the reincarnation of Ambā.[9] His presence in battle while acting as Arjuna's charioteer results in the death of Bhīṣma, who had taken a vow not to fight a woman or a eunuch. Bhīṣma refused to defend himself against Śikhaṇḍī, whom he thought of as a woman.

Subhadrā — Kṛṣṇa's sister, the second wife of Arjuna. Abhimanyu, the son of Arjuna and Subhadrā, is mentioned in verses 1.6 and 1.18.

Śūra — A Yādava king. The father of Vasudeva and Kuntī.

Uttamaujas — A warrior allied with the Pāṇḍavas. Mentioned in verse 1.6.

Vasudeva — The father of Balarāma, Kṛṣṇa, and Subhadrā. Kṛṣṇa is called "Son of Vasudeva" in 10.37.

Vikarṇa — A Kaurava warrior, the third son of King Dhṛtarāṣṭra. Mentioned in verse 1.8.

Virāṭa — King of the Matsyas. He gave shelter to the Pāṇḍavas, who lived incognito in his court during the thirteenth year of their exile. He fought on the side of the Pāṇḍavas during the Mahābharata war. Mentioned in 1.4 and 1.17.

Vṛṣṇi — A son of Madhu. Kṛṣṇa was a member of the Vṛṣṇi clan, and is addressed as a "descendant of Vṛṣṇi" in verses 1.41 and 3.36. The Vṛṣṇi clan is also mentioned in verse 10.37.

"victorious in war" used as a name of Viṣṇu in the *Viṣṇu Sahasranāma*, verse 52, see Sankaranarayanan, p. 106.

[9] *MBh.* 5.188-193.

Vyāsa — Name of the sage traditionally credited as the compiler of the Vedas as well as of the *Mahābhārata,* of which the *Bhagavadgītā* is a part. The name means editor, arranger, or compiler. He is the son of the sage Parāśara and Satyavatī. He fathered Dhṛtarāṣṭra, Pāṇḍu, and Vidura. Mentioned in verses 10.13, 37; 18.75.

Yādavas — The Yādavas, also called Yadus, are the descendants of Yadu. Kṛṣṇa is addressed as a descendant of Yadu in verse 11.41.

Yadu — An ancient king, Yadu was the eldest son of the great king Yayāti. Yadu was the founder of the Yādava lineage.

Yudhāmanyu — A warrior allied with the Pāṇḍavas. The name means "very brave". Mentioned in verse 1.6.

Yudhiṣṭhira — The eldest of the Pāṇḍava brothers, born of Kuntī and considered to be a son of Pāṇḍu, but actually fathered by the god Dharma. After the war, Yudhiṣṭhira ("Steady in Battle") will rule the devastated kingdom, but Dhṛtarāṣṭra will remain as the nominal king. Mentioned in verse 1.16.

Epithets in the *Bhagavadgītā*

The *Bhagavadgītā* makes frequent use of epithets or "nicknames" that are shorthand references that can be understood in context as referring to a specific person. An epithet is often a descriptive adjective or phrase based on a characteristic of the person being referred to. For example, both *śrī* (Illustrious) and *bhagavān* (Blessed One) are honorific epithets applied to gods, holy persons, and other respected people. When Kṛṣṇa speaks, his passages are prefaced with the statement, "The Illustrious Blessed One said" (*Śrībhagavān uvāca*). Bhagavan also is used as a vocative epithet for Kṛṣṇa in verses 10.14 and 10.17.[10]

It is difficult to draw the line between terms that have the full force of epithets and adjectives that are used in passing. A general rule is that if a person is addressed descriptively in the vocative case, the term used is an epithet. Descriptive terms that are applied infrequently without the force of epithets are not included in this section. For example, in verse 9.18, Kṛṣṇa says he is The Way (*gatiḥ*), The Witness (*sākṣī*), The Friend (*suhṛt*), etc., but constructions like that do not have the force of epithets. Similarly, Kṛṣṇa is identified with a wide range of beings and phenomena in passages connected with his revelation of divinity, but these things are not epithets because they are not used as substitute terms to identify Kṛṣṇa in other passages.[11]

Used for both Arjuna and Kṛṣṇa

Mahābāhu — Long-armed One. In Indian physiognomy, having long arms that reach down to the knees was considered an auspicious sign.[12] Apte's dictionary

---

[10] Bhagavan ("O Blessed One") is the vocative form of the nominative Bhagavān ("the Blessed One").

[11] E.g., he is identifed with Prajāpati, the *de facto* Creator of all Beings (the Lord of Creatures) in 11.39; Prajāpati himself is mentioned in 3.10.

[12] An example of long-arms that reach the knees as an iconographic detail for a military leader is given in the description of an image of Skandagupta in: B. N, Goswamy. *The Spirit of Indian Painting: Close Encounters with 100 Great Works 1100-1900.* (Allen Lane: 2014. [unpaginated electronic text]). URL https://books.google.com/books?id=J5E3BQAAQBAJ&pg=PT52&-

translates *mahābāhu* as "long-armed" or "powerful" and notes that it is used as an epithet of Viṣṇu.[13] The epithet was a common one for warriors, indicating a man of great personality and strength. Someone endowed with long arms reaching down to the knees was considered to have great physical, mental and spiritual powers. The similar epithet *ājānubāhu* ("having arms that reach to the knees") is also used to express the same idea, but is more clear that the length of the arms is the issue. Mahābāhu is often translated as Great-Armed One, Large-Armed One, or Mighty-armed One, but these do not exactly capture the detail as it was understood in Indian culture. Used to refer to Arjuna in 2.26, 68; 3.28, 43; 5.3, 6; 6.35; 7.5; 10.1; 14.5; 18.13. Used to refer to Kṛṣṇa in 6.38; 11.23; 18.1. Used to refer to Abhimanyu in 1.18 (*mahābāhuḥ*).

Mahātman — Great-souled One, Magnanimous-souled One, Great Self. Used to refer to Kṛṣṇa in 11.12, 11.20, 11.37, 11.50. Used to refer to Arjuna in 18.74. Used to refer to people of wisdom in 7.19; 8.15; 9.13 ("magnanimous souls", "great souls").

Used For Kṛṣṇa

Acyuta — The Unfallen One, The Imperishable One, i.e., immortal. Used in 1.21; 11.42; 18.73.

Ananta — Infinite, Unlimited. Used as an epithet in 11.37, where translators generally treat it as a modifier to the following epithet, *deveśa, q.v.*

Anantarūpa — One of Infinite (*ananta*) Forms (*rūpa*). Used as an epithet in 11.38; used as a description in 11.16.

Anantavīrya — One of Infinite (*ananta*) Power (*vīrya*). This may be included as an epithet if it is treated as a vocative in 11.40. For discussion see footnote for *anantavīryāmitavikramaḥ* on page 40.

Aprameya — Immeasurable One. Used as a description in 11.17, used with the sense of an epithet in 11.42.

Apratimaprabhāva — Incomparable Glory, One of Infinite Influence, One of Unequalled Power. Used in 11.43.

Arisūdana — Destroyer of Enemies. Used in 2.4.

---

dq=indian+iconography+lakshana+of+men+long+arms&hl=en&sa=X&ved=0CCcQ6AEwAGoVChMI-pjqwqTtxwIVEjGICh1fFw5T#v=onepage&q=long%20arms&f=false. Accessed September 10, 2015.

[13] Apte, p. 750, right column, entry for महा, compounded with –बाहु.

Bhagavān — Blessed One. See Śrībhagavān.

Bhūtabhāvana — Source of Beings, Creator of Beings. Used in 10.15. Kṛṣṇa refers to himself this way in 9.5. A related term is used as a description of *Brahman* in 8.3 (*bhūtabhāvodbhavakara*).

Bhuteśa — Lord of Beings. Used in 10.15.

Deva — God. Used in 11.15, 11.44, 11.45. Arjuna refers to Kṛṣṇa as *deva* without using the vocative in 11.11 and 11.14. Arjuna refers to Kṛṣṇa as *ādideva* (Primordial God) in 10.12 and 11.38.

Devadeva — God of Gods. Used in 10.15 and 11.13.

Devavara — Best of the Gods, Supreme God. Used in 11.31.

Deveśa — Lord of the Gods (*deva īśa*). Used in 11.25, 11.37, 11.45.

Govinda — Authorities do not agree on the derivation or meaning of the name Govinda. Hill notes a story of Kṛṣṇa "finding the earth (*go*)" but feels that the earlier use of *govid* meaning "finder of cows" as an epithet of Indra in the *Ṛgveda* is more probable.[14] A metaphysical interpretation is that it means the One who is aware of the activities of the organs of the body as their presiding deity.[15] Used in 1.32 and 2.9.

Hari — An epithet of uncertain etymology, possibly meaning "the tawny one." More devotional understandings of the name include "the remover of sin" or "the destroyer of evil." Hari was used to refer to fire, the sun, lightning, Agni, and Soma during the Vedic period, and later was commonly applied to Viṣṇu.[16] Used in 11.9 and 18.77.

Hṛṣīkeśa — Kṛṣṇa's epithet Hṛṣīkeśa can be translated in two different ways. In Indian tradition it is often understood to mean "Master of the senses" (*hṛṣīka* +

---

[14] Hill, p. 106, note 3. Sargeant (p. 70) translates it as "Chief of Cowherds" noting that the derivation is debated.

[15] Gambhīrānanda 1997, p. 24, note 1. For "Master of the organs" see Gambhīrānanda 1998, p. 51.

[16] Apte (p. 1023, entry for हरि, nominal form हरिः) devotes nearly two full columns to a broad range of uses with citations to Vedic and other literature. Minor (p. 336) notes a wide range of prior use for this epithet and concludes that in the context of the *BG* it does not necessarily imply a reference to Kṛṣṇa as an *avatara* of Viṣṇu although it is interpreted that way by many modern readers. The term is also used to refer to Vāyu, Indra, Brahmā, Yāma, and Śiva (though Hara, the destroyer, is Śiva's more common epithet).

īśa).[17] Some modern translators take it to mean "Bristling-hair" (*hṛṣī* + *keśa*).[18] Used in 1.15, 21, 24; 2.9, 10; 11.36; 18.1.

Īśam Īḍyam — Adorable Lord, Lord to be Praised. Used with the force of an epithet in 11.44.

Jagannivāsa — Refuge of the Worlds, Abode of the Universe. Used in 11.25, 11.37, 11.45.

Jagatpati — Lord of the Universe. Used in 10.15.

Janārdana — Motivator of Men, Rouser of Men. The verb *ard* has a range of meanings, including "to rouse" or "to agitate".[19] Used in 1.36, 39, 44; 3.1; 10.18; 11.51.

Kamalapatrākṣa — Lotus-petal-eyed One. Used in 11.2.

Keśava — He who has beautiful hair (*keśa*); long-haired. An alternate meaning is that He has slain demons such as Keśin.[20] Used in 1.31; 2.54; 3.1; 10.14; 11.35; 18.76.[21]

Keśiniṣūdana — Slayer of Keśin (a demon).[22] The name means "One with a Mane (*keśa*)" or "One Having Fine Hair". Keśin attacked Kṛṣṇa in the form of a horse. Kṛṣṇa killed him by thrusting his arm down the demon's throat. The demon Keśin can also be spelled as Keśī, the nominative form. Used in 18.1.

Kṛṣṇa — Kṛṣṇa is sometimes referred to simply by his ordinary name, either in the vocative ("O Kṛṣṇa", as in verses 1.28, 32, 41; 5.1; 6.34, 37, 39; 11.41; 17.1), or by direct reference to him ("Kṛṣṇa", as in verses 11.35; 18.75, 78).

---

[17] E.g., Divanji, p. 167, entry #3852, who translates it as "Lord of the sense-organs" and hence "the self", adding that it is used as a synonym of Viṣṇu with whom Śrī Kṛṣṇa is identified, and with whom the *ātman* is identical in essence.

[18] E.g., "Bristling Haired One" in Sargeant, p. 488. Hill (p. 103, note 1) says that while "Lord of the senses" is preferred by the oldest commentators, modern scholars prefer to derive it from *hṛiṣ-* and *keśa*, with the meaning "having strong, or upstanding, hair." For discussion of the alternatives also see Feuerstein and Feuerstein, p. 83, note 5.

[19] Apte, p. 152, entry for अर्द्.

[20] Gambhīrānanda 1997, p. 22, note 2. Gambhīrānanda provides a metaphysical etymology based on the components *ka*, *īśa*, and *vāti*. Meaning of the name is also discussed in Gambhīrānanda 1998, p. 50.

[21] Also used in an unnumbered prefatory verse to chapter thirteen that does not appear in the Critical Edition.

[22] Keśin was a *dānava*, a son of Dānu (*MBh.* 1.59.22). See *MBh.* 3.213 for a battle between Keśin and Indra. See Hill, p. 256, note 1.

Madhusūdana — Slayer of Madhu (a demon).[23] Used in 1.35; 2.1, 4; 6.33; 8.2.

Mādhava — A traditional interpretation of Mādhava as an epithet of Kṛṣṇa is that it means "husband of the goddess Lakṣmī". This is based on parsing Mādhava as a compound of *mā* — meaning Lakṣmī, the goddess of wealth, beauty, and prosperity — and *dhavaḥ*, husband.[24] An alternative interpretation is that it means "Descendant of Madhu".[25] Madhu was a patriarch of the Yadu dynasty. One of Madhu's sons, Vṛṣṇi, was the founder of Kṛṣṇa's clan. Used in 1.14 and 1.37.

Parameśvara — Supreme Lord. Used in 11.3. Also used in 13.27 to refer to God in a general statement.

Prabhu — Lord. Used in 11.4 and 14.21. Used by Kṛṣṇa self-referentially in 9.18 and 9.24. Used as a general term for God in 5.14.

Puruṣottama — The simple meaning is "best of men", but Kṛṣṇa gives it the sense of "Supreme *Puruṣa*" in verses 15.18-19 when he refers to himself using this term and explains that he is called *puruṣottama* because He transcends all perishable ones, and is superior even to the imperishable. Used as an epithet in 8.1; 10.15; 11.3.

Sahasrabāhu — Thousand-armed One. Used in 11.46.

Sakhā — Friend, comrade. Used in 11.41. Kṛṣṇa also refers to Arjuna as his friend (but not in the vocative case) in 4.3. Friendship as a model of relationship between Arjuna and Kṛṣṇa is also mentioned in 11.44.

Sarva — All. Used as a vocative epithet ("O All") in 11.40.

---

[23] Madhusūdana is an epithet of Viṣṇu. The story of Viṣṇu killing the demons Madhu and Kaiṭabha appears in *MBh.* 3.194. Other epithets of Viṣṇu used in that chapter include Acyuta, Hari, Keśava, Govinda, and Hṛṣikeśa. The two demons are mentioned elsewhere in the *MBh.*, including 5.128.49, 9.48.21, and 12.335.55-64 (which explains the origin of the demons and relates the story of their theft of the Vedas from Brahmā and their slaying by Viṣṇu). The two demons are shown in some standard iconographic representations of Viṣṇu as described in Stutley, p. 82.

[24] Chidbhavananda, p. 88.

[25] Sargeant, p. 52. Zaehner (p. 115) translates as "Madhu's scion". The genealogy of the Yādava people appears in *Viṣṇu Purāṇa*, book 4, chapter 11; see Wilson, vol. 4., p. 58.

Śrībhagavān — Both *śrī* (Illustrious) and *bhagavān* (Blessed One) are honorific epithets applied to gods, holy persons, and other respected people.[26] Bhagavan is used as a vocative epithet for Kṛṣṇa in 10.14 and 10.17.[27] The compound form Śrībhagavān is used to refer to Kṛṣṇa in nominative form in 2.2, 11, 55; 3.3, 37; 4.1, 5; 5.2; 6.1, 35, 40; 7.1; 8.3; 9.1; 10.1, 19; 11.5, 32, 47, 52; 12.2; 13.1; 14.1, 22; 15.1; 16.1; 17.2; 18.2.

Vārṣṇi — Scion of the Vṛṣṇi Dynasty, Member of the Vṛṣṇi Clan, Descendant of Vṛṣṇi (Vārṣṇeya). "The Vṛṣṇi" is a name for Kṛṣṇa's clan, which is within the Yādava lineage that was founded by the patriarch Yadu. Vṛṣṇi was the son of Yadu, and great-great-grandfather of Vasudeva, who was the father of Kṛṣṇa.[28] Vṛṣṇi literally means "potent". Used in 1.41 and 3.36. The Vṛṣṇi clan is also mentioned in 10.37.

Vāsudeva — Sometimes used as a patronymic meaning "Son of Vasudeva" (as in 10.37), and sometimes meaning "Omnipresent God" (as in 7.19, where Kṛṣṇa refers to himself using this epithet). Also used in 11.50 and 18.74. This epithet is never used in the vocative in this text.

Viṣṇu — Viṣṇu. Used as an epithet in 11.24 and 11.30. Kṛṣṇa refers to himself as Viṣṇu in 10.21, but in that case Viṣṇu is one of the Ādityas, a group of gods.

Viśvamūrti — Cosmic Form, Universal Form. Used in 11.46.

Viśvarūpa — Cosmic Form, Universal Form. Used in 11.16.

Viśveśvara — Lord of the Universe (*viśva* + *īśvara*). Used in 11.16.

Yādava — Descendant of Yadu, member of the Yadu lineage. Used in 11.41.

Yogeśvara — Lord of *Yoga* (*yoga* + *īśvara*). Used in 11.4; 18.75, 78. Mahāyogeśvara (Great Lord of *Yoga*) is used in 11.9.

Yogin — Practitioner of *yoga*. Used in the vocative to refer to Kṛṣṇa in 10.17.

Used for Arjuna

Anagha — Sinless One. Used in 3.3; 14.6; 15.20.

Bhārata — Descendant of Bharata, a member of the Bharata lineage. Bharata was the founding patriarch for both of the clans that were engaged in the great internecine war that provides the story line for the *Mahābhārata*. Bhārata is a

---

26 The history of the term and the complexity of its interpretation are discussed in Minor, pp. 28-9.

27 *Bhagavān* is the masc. nom. sing. form. *Bhagavan* is the masc. voc. sing. form.

28 Venkateswaran, p. 169; Hill, p. 200, note 5.

general term for all his family lines. The epithet is used 22 times in the text, always at the end of a half-verse, a very standardized pattern. Used to refer to Arjuna in 2.14, 18, 28, 30; 3.25; 4.7, 42; 7.27; 11.6; 13.2, 33; 14.3, 8-10; 15.19-20; 16.3; 17.3; 18.62. The epithet is also applied to King Dhṛtarāṣṭra in verses 1.24 and 2.10.

Bharatarṣabha — Bull of the Bharatas. "Bull" (*ṛṣabha*) was a common epithet for a hero, and is used to here to indicate excellence, the "best" of the Bharatas, always at the end of a half-verse, a very standardized pattern. Used in 3.41; 7.11, 16; 8.23; 13.26; 14.12; 18.36.

Bharatasattama — Best (*sattama*) of the Bharatas. Used in 18.4.

Bharataśreṣṭha — Best (*śreṣṭha*) of the Bharatas. Used in 17.12.

Dehabhṛtām Vara — Best (*vara*) of the Embodied (*dehabhṛtām*), Most Excellent of Beings. Used in 8.4.

Dhanaṁjaya — Winner of Wealth, Conqueror of Wealth, Master of Wealth. Used in 1.15; 2.48-49; 4.41; 7.7; 9.9; 10.37; 11.14; 12.9; 18.29, 72. Always used at the end of a half-verse, a very standardized pattern.

Dhanurdhara — The archer. Used in 18.78.

Guḍākeśa — Authorities do not agree on the derivation or meaning of the epithet Guḍākeśa. A traditional interpretation is that it means "Lord of sleep" (*guḍākā* + *īśa*).[29] If parsed as (*guḍā* + *keśa*) it may mean "Balled-hair" referring to a balled or bun-like hairstyle.[30] Used in 1.24; 2.9; 10.20; 11.7.

Kapidhvaja — Monkey-bannered. This term refers to the figure of a monkey appearing on the flag of Arjuna's chariot. Many commentators assume the monkey is Hanumān.[31] Used in 1.20.

Kaunteya — Son of Kuntī. The epithet Kaunteya ("Son of Kuntī") means the same thing as Pārtha ("Son of Pṛthā"). The epithet Kaunteya is used 25 times in the text. Used in 1.27; 2.14, 37, 60; 3.9, 39; 5.22; 6.35; 7.8; 8.6, 16; 9.7, 10, 23, 27, 31;

---

[29] For interpretation as "master of sleep" meaning that Arjuna was "ever alert" see Gambhīrānanda 1997, p. 20, note 2.

[30] Minor (p. 15) has a good note on the alternatives, concluding that the most likely meaning is *guḍa* meaning "ball" and *keśa* meaning "hair", suggesting an obvious hair style. Hill (p. 105, note 2) doubts the "lord of sleep" derivation, saying "there seems to be no good reason for applying such an epithet to Arjuna."

[31] In *MBh.* 3.150.15, Hanumān granted a boon to Bhīma, saying he would take the place of a flag on Arjuna's chariot (*vijayasya dhvajasthaḥ*). See Van Buitenen 1975, p. 509.

13.1, 31; 14.4, 7; 16.20, 22; 18.48, 50, 60. Yudhiṣṭhira is called *kuntīputra* ("son of Kuntī") in 1.16.

Kirīṭin — The Crowned One. Used as an epithet of Arjuna in 11.35.

Kurunandana — Joy of the Kurus, O Descendant of the Kurus, O Son of the Kurus. Used in 2.41; 6.43; 14.13. Both the Pāṇḍavas and the Kauravas are all collectively Sons of Kuru.

Kurupravīra — Foremost Kuru Hero, Great Hero of the Kurus. Used in 11.48.

Kurusattama — Best (*sattama*) of the Kurus. Used in 4.31.

Kuruśreṣṭha — Best (*śreṣṭha*) of the Kurus. Used in 10.19.

Pāṇḍava — Son of Pāṇḍu. Pāṇḍu was the father of the five Pāṇḍava brothers, including Arjuna. Pāṇḍu was the brother of the blind King Dhṛtarāṣṭra, to whom the events of the *Bhagavadgītā* are being recited. The war that is taking place is between the Pāṇḍavas (the "Sons of Pāṇḍu") and the Kauravas, the dynasty to which Dhṛtarāṣṭra belongs. Used as an epithet for Arjuna in 1.14, 20; 4.35; 6.2; 11.13, 55; 14.22; 16.5. Used to refer to the Pāṇḍavas collectively in 1.1, 2; 10.37.

Paraṁtapa — Literally, "Enemy-Burner" or "One who inflicts pain on the enemy", often translated as "Burner of the Enemy", "Scorcher of the Foe", "Destroyer of Enemies". Used in 2.3; 4.2, 5, 33; 7.27; 9.3; 10.40; 11.54; 18.41. Used as an epithet of Dhṛtarāṣṭra in 2.9.[32] In all cases, it appears at the end of a half-verse, a very standardized pattern

Pārtha — Son of Pṛthā. Pṛthā is another name for Kuntī, Arjuna's mother. Kuntī was the wife of Pāṇḍu. This is a very common epithet, used 42 times throughout the text, in 1.25-26; 2.3, 21, 32, 39, 42, 55, 72; 3.16, 22-23; 4.11, 33; 6.40; 7.1, 10; 8.8, 14, 19, 22, 27; 9.13, 32; 10.24; 11.5, 9; 12.7; 16.4, 6; 17.26, 28; 18.6, 30-35, 72, 74, 78.

Puruṣarṣabha — Bull (*ṛṣabha*) Among Men, Best of Men. Used in 2.15.

Puruṣavyāghra — Tiger (*vyāghra*) Among Men. Used in 18.4.

Savyasācin — Masterful Archer, Expert Bowman. Literally, "One who can shoot arrows with the left hand" (indicating an ambidextrous archer). Used in 11.33.

Tāta — Dear One. A term of affection used between seniors and juniors, taking the sense of "my son" or "my father" depending on context. Used in 6.40.

---

[32] The Critical Edition reads *evam uktvā hṛṣīkeśaṁ guḍākeśaḥ paraṁtapa,* ending the line with a vocative *paraṁtapa,* addressing Dhṛtarāṣṭra. Vulgate editions read *evam uktvā hṛṣīkeśaṁ guḍākeśaḥ paraṁtapaḥ,* ending the line with a nominative *paraṁtapaḥ,* agreeing with *guḍākeśaḥ* (Arjuna).

Used for Others

Ācārya — Teacher. Used in 1.2-3 to refer to Droṇa.

Aparājita — Undefeated. Used in 1.17 as an epithet of Sātyaki.

Dhārtarāṣṭra — Dhṛtarāṣṭra's son. Used in 1.23 to refer to Duryodhana.

Dvijottama — Highest of the twice-born, Most excellent of the twice-born. Applied to Droṇa in 1.7.

Kuntīputra — Son of Kuntī. In 1.16 this term is applied to Yudhiṣṭhira, the son of Kuntī by the god Dharma. Yudhiṣṭhira was the eldest of the Pāṇḍava princes. The epithet means the same thing as Kaunteya, which is used often to refer to Arjuna, Yudhiṣṭhira's younger brother.

Kuruvṛddha — The Oldest of the Kurus. Used to refer to Bhīṣma in 1.12.

Mahīpati — King, Lord of the Earth, Earth-ruler. An epithet applied to Dhṛtarāṣṭra by Saṁjaya in 1.21.

Pṛthivīpati — Lord of the Earth. Applied to Dhṛtarāṣṭra in 1.18.

Rāja — King, Royal. Applied in the vocative to Dhṛtarāṣṭra in 11.9; 18.76-77. Used descriptively of Duryodhana in verse 1.2 and of Yudhiṣṭhira in verse 1.16.

Saubhadra — Son of Subhadrā. Referring to Abhimanyu, the son of Arjuna and Subhadrā (Kṛṣṇa's sister), in verses 1.6 and 1.18.

Saumadatti — Son of Somadatta. Referring to Bhūriśravas in verse 1.8.

Sūtaputra — Son of a Charioteer. In 11.26 this epithet refers to Karṇa, the son of Kuntī, fathered by the sun god, but raised by a charioteer. He is a great ally of Duryodhana and a fierce enemy of Arjuna.

Vṛkodara — Wolf-belly. Endowed with a belly like that of a wolf. Epithet of Bhīma, who had an enormous appetite. Used in 1.15, where Bhīma is also referred to as a doer of "terrible actions" (*bhīmakarmā*).

Yuyudhāna — Eager to fight. An epithet for Sātyaki in verse 1.4.

Sanskrit Concordance

The concordance includes all words that appear in the Critical Edition of the text. Each entry is numbered to make referencing easy. The concordance is arranged to allow the reader to locate all references to a particular word regardless of grammatical form. To simplify lookups, some entries are based on a stem or base form of a word. Grouped entries of this type are in a slightly larger font and are marked with a vertical bar in the left margin. For example, the entry for the base word *deva* consolidates various case endings under one entry, cross-referencing related words. The entry for the compound word *devabhogān* does not have a vertical bar because it is a single grammatical form. A grouped entry with a vertical bar may also cover a word that has broad semantic range, a verbal root [√] where conjugated forms are shown, or where longer examples are used to make various uses more clear. The two types of format are shown in these examples:

842. **deva** "god". Also see *ādideva, devabhogān, devadatta, devadeva, devadvijaguruprājñapūjanam, devarṣi, devatā, devavara, devavratāḥ, devayajaḥ, deveśa, deveṣu, sahadeva, vāsudeva.*

- deva "O God". 11.15, 44, 45.
- devāḥ "the gods". 3.11, 12; 10.14; 11.52.
- devam "God". 11.11, 14.
- devān "the gods". 3.11; 7.23; 9.25; 11.15; 17.4.
- devānām "of the gods". 10.2, 22.

843. **devabhogān** "godly pleasures; the enjoyments of the gods". 9.20. Also see *deva, bhoga.*

Most Sanskrit words can be translated in multiple ways. The concordance is not a dictionary. The meanings shown in the concordance are for illustrative purposes only and are not exhaustive. Some entries include footnotes to specific translations that show a range of possible meanings. Some entries include grammatical details or other clarifying notes contained within [square brackets]. For the convenience of English readers, entries are shown in English alphabetical order. Since the concept of capitalization does not exist in Devanāgarī, generally I do not capitalize Sanskrit terms, with the exception of proper names and words that have special importance, e.g., *Brahman*.

The Devanāgarī alphabet has more letters than the English alphabet. Letters that do not exist in the English alphabet are transliterated using diacritical marks. To make the concordance easy to use, the sort order of words is as close to English as possible, but the correct diacritical marks are always shown. The sort order of Devanāgarī letters within each English letter group is shown in the following table:

English alphabet:	*Devanāgarī transliteration:*	*Devanāgarī alphabet*
A	a / ā / ai / au	अ / आ / ऐ / औ
B	b / bh	ब् / भ्
C	c / ch	च् / छ्
D	ḍ / ḍh / d / dh	ड् / ढ् / द् / ध्
E	e	ए
F	[not used]	[not used]
G	g / gh	ग् / घ्
H	h / ḥ	ह् / ◌ः
I	i / ī	इ / ई
J	j / jh	ज् / झ्
K	k / kh	क् / ख्
L	ḷ / ḹ / l	ऌ / ॡ / ल्
M	ṁ / m̐ / m	◌ं / ◌ँ / म्
N	ṅ / ñ / ṇ / n	ङ् / ञ् / ण् / न्
O	o	ओ
P	p / ph	प् / फ्
Q	[not used]	[not used]
R	ṛ / ṝ / r	ऋ / ॠ / र्
S	ś / ṣ / s	श् / ष् / स्
T	ṭ / ṭh / t / th	ट् / ठ् / त् / थ्
U	u / ū	उ / ऊ
V	v	व्
W	[not used]	[not used]
X	[not used]	[not used]
Y	y	य्
Z	[not used]	[not used]
apostrophe	'	ऽ

In this table, which follows the sort order of a Devanāgarī dictionary, sometimes letters with diacritical marks come before those without marks, but this is not always the case For example, the English letter "N" represents four different Devanāgarī letters, which appear in the Devanāgarī dictionary order ङ् (ṅ), ञ् (ñ), ण् (ṇ), and न् (n). In that case, the letter without the diacritical mark appears last. But in the case of the English letter "I", which represents two different vowels in Sanskrit, the dictionary order is इ (i) first, followed by ई (ī).

When looking in alphabetical lists, English readers tend to ignore vowel length and are more strongly affected by the consonant that follows the vowel. Here is an example of easy English reading order in which sorting by the short and long vowels in *dha* and *dhā* is less important than sorting by the order of the consonant following the vowel, which is less confusing for the non-specialist:

1. dhāma (abode)
2. dhanuḥ (bow)
3. dharma (righteousness, the natural order)
4. dhātā (one who upholds)

Here is an example in which the three sibilants of Sanskrit (ś, ṣ, s) are all sorted as the simple English "s":

1. śabda (sound)
2. sadoṣa (imperfect)
3. śama (peace)
4. samatā (equanimity)
5. ṣaṇmāsā (a group of six months)
6. śānti (peace)
7. smṛti (memory)
8. śruti (that which has been heard; revealed scripture)

A

अ = A. आ = Ā. ऐ = AI. औ = AU.

1. **ā** "to; up to". 8.16. [*ā brahmabhuvanāt,* where *ā* is used for a sense of inclusion. Also see *brahmabhuvanāt*].
2. **abhaktāya** "to a non-devotee; to one who is not devoted". 18.67. Also see *bhakta.*
3. **abhāṣata** "he said". 11.14. Also see *bhāṣase.* [Imperf. 3rd pers. sing. of √ *bhāṣ* "to speak".]
4. **abhāvaḥ** "non-existence". 2.16; 10.4. Also see *bhavaḥ.*
5. **abhavat** "it was". 1.13. Also see *bhavati.*
6. **abhāvayataḥ** "of a person not having spiritual devotion; of one who lacks faith". 2.66. Also see *bhāva.*
7. **abhayam** "fearlessness". 10.4; 16.1. Also see *bhaya, bhayābhaye.*
8. **abhibhavati** "it attacks; it overpowers; it overcomes". 1.40. Also see *abhibhūya, adharmābhibhavāt, bhavati.*
9. **abhibhūya** "having overpowered; after overcoming". 14.10. Also see *abhibhavati.*
10. **abhidhāsyati** "one who imparts; one who will narrate". 18.68. Also see *abhidhīyate.*
11. **abhidhīyate** "it is called; it is said to be; it is described as; it is considered to be". 13.1; 17.27; 18.11. Also see *abhidhāsyati, ucyate.*
12. **abhihitā** "has been presented; declared; narrated". 2.39.
13. **abhijānanti** "they know". 9.24. [*abhi* + √ *jñā*]
14. **abhijānāti** "one knows; is aware of; one recognizes". 4.14; 7.13, 25, 18.55. [*abhi* + √ *jñā*]
15. **abhijanavān** "of noble descent; born in a high family". 16.15.
16. **abhijāta** "born; born for; born to". Also see *jātāḥ.*
    - abhijātasya "to one who is born for". 16.3, 4.
    - abhijātaḥ "born for; endowed with". 16.5.
17. **abhijāyate** "it is born; it is produced". 2.62; 6.41; 13.23. Also see *jāyate.*
18. **abhikramanāśaḥ** "loss of effort; loss due to incomplete effort; waste of attempt; the destruction (*nāśaḥ*) of the beginning". 2.40.
19. **abhimānaḥ** "pride". 16.4. See *atimānaḥ* for alternate reading in the Critical Edition.

20. **abhimukhāḥ** "turning towards; facing toward". 11.28. Also see *mukha.*
21. **abhinandati** "one rejoices". 2.57.
22. **abhipravṛttaḥ** "engaged in (action); proceeding with (action)". 4.20. Also see √ *pravṛt.*
23. **abhirakṣantu** "protect on all sides". 1.11. Also see *rakṣ-.*
24. **abhirataḥ** "devoted to; engaged in". 18.45.
25. **abhisaṁdhāya** "after expecting; having aimed at". 17.12. Also see *anabhisaṁdhāya.*
26. **abhitaḥ** "all around; on all sides; near by; close". 5.26.
27. **abhivijvalanti** "flaming forth; burning all over intensely; emitting flames on all sides". 11.28. [*abhi* + *vi* + √ *jval.*]
28. **abhyadhikaḥ** "surpassing". 11.43. Also see *adhika.*
29. **abhyahanyanta** "were beaten; were struck". 1.13. [√ *han*]
30. **abhyarcya** "having worshipped; worshipping". 18.46.
31. **abhyāsa** "repeated practice; repetition; constant application (to anything)."[33] [√ *abhyas,* "to practice; to repeat; to perform repeatedly; to learn by practice".] Also see *abhyāsayoga, svādhyāyābhyasanam* (17.15).
    - abhyāsāt "(better) than practice; (superior) to practice" 12.12.; "by practice; from practice; due to habit; due to frequent repetition" 18.36.
    - abhyāse "in (constant) practice; (if you are unable) to practice[34]". 12.10.
    - abhyāsena "with practice; by practice; through practice". 6.35. [*abhyāsena tu kaunteya vairāgyeṇa ca gṛhyate* = "with practice (*abhyāsena*) and with dispasssion (*vairāgyeṇa*)..."; compare *YS* 1.12.]
    - pūrvābhyāsena "by previous practice". 6.44.
32. **abhyāsayoga** "the *yoga* of practice". Also see *abhyāsa, yoga.*
    - abhyāsayogayuktena "controlled by (constant) practice; engaged in the *yoga* of practice; disciplined by the practice of *yoga*; yoked by the *yoga* of practice". 8.8. Also see *yogayukta.*

---

[33] The importance of ongoing, habitual practice (*abhyāsa*) is also stressed in Patañjali's *Yogasūtra* 1.12: *abhyāsa-vairāgyābhyāṁ tan-nirodhaḥ* = "By practice and dispassion, restraint of those (fluctuations of the mind is achieved)."

[34] Translated with sense "to practice" by Gambhīrānanda 1997, p. 482.

- abhyāsayogena "by the method of constant practice[35]; through the *yoga* of practice[36]; by the practice of *yoga*". 12.9.

33. **abhyasūya** "angry with; jealous of; criticizing".
    - abhyasūyakāḥ "(those who) find fault; malicious people; jealous people; grumblers; detractors". 16.18.
    - abhyasūyantaḥ "showing disrespect; jealous of; showing ill-will". 3.32.
    - abhyasūyati "he finds fault; he is jealous of; he speaks evil of; he criticizes". 18.67.
34. **abhyutthānam** "rising up; ascendance; growth". 4.7.
35. **ābrahmabhuvanāt** "up to the world of Brahmā; from the region of Brahmā downwards[37]; down from the realm of Brahmā[38]". 8.16. Also see *loka, surendralokam, svargalokam.* [*ā brahmabhuvanāt*]
36. **abravīt** "he spoke; he said; he taught". 1.2, 28; 41. [√ *brū*]
37. **abuddhayaḥ** "those of inadequate understanding; one who is wanting in intelligence or the faculty of right perception". 7.24. Also see *akṛtabuddhitvāt, alpabuddhayaḥ, buddhi.*
38. **acala** "steady; stable; motionless; unmoving; unwavering; immovable; still". Also see *niścalā, calam, dhruva.*
    - acalā "stable; steady; immovable; one-pointed (in meditation)". 2.53.
    - acalaḥ "stable; steady; immovable". 2.24.
    - acalam "stable; immovable; still". 6.13; 12.3.
    - acalām "steady; steadfast; unwavering". 7.21.
    - acalena "steady; unmoving; motionless". 8.10.
39. **acalapratiṣṭham** "remains unchanged[39]; stays unmoved; that which has been immovably fixed[40]; well-established with stability; unmoving and stable". 2.70. Also see *pratiṣṭh-*.
40. **acāpalam** "freedom from fickleness". 16.2.

---

[35] Hill's (pp. 218-9) "by the method of constant practice" is simple and captures the core idea. Hill notes that Śaṅkara's commentary defines *abhyāsa* as "'withdrawing thought from all quarters, and fixing it again and again on some particular object.' It is the repetition that differentiates *abhyāsa* from the steady (*sthira, acala*) *samādhi*."

[36] Gambhīrānanda 1997, p. 481.

[37] Divanji, p. 27, entry #603.

[38] Ādidevānanda, p. 281.

[39] Gambhīrānanda 1998, p. 204.

[40] Divanji, p. 2, entry #38.

41. **ācar-** [*ā* + √ *car*]
    - ācaran "doing; acting; performing". 3.19.
    - ācarataḥ "doing; performing; undertaking". 4.23. [*yajñāyācarataḥ karma* = undertaking action for sacrifice]
    - ācarati "he does; he brings about; he behaves". 3.21; 16.22.
    - samācara "do; perform". 3.9, 19. [*ā* + *saṁ* + √ *car*]
    - samācaran "doing; performing". 3.26. [*ā* + *saṁ* + √ *car*]
42. **ācāra** "conduct; good conduct".
    - ācāraḥ"good conduct; prescribed course of behavior". 16.7.
    - kimācāraḥ "of what conduct?; of what kind of behavior?". 14.21.
    - mithyācāraḥ "a person with false behavior; a hypocrite". 3.6.
    - sudurācāraḥ "a person of very bad conduct". 9.30,
43. **acaram** "not moving; immobile; static; inanimate". 13.15. Also see *cara, carācara.*
44. **ācārya** "teacher".
    - ācārya "O Teacher!; O Mentor!". 1.3. [Addressing Droṇa.]
    - ācāryāḥ "teachers; mentors". 1.34.
    - ācāryam "teacher; mentor". 1.2. [Addressing Droṇa.]
    - ācāryān "teachers; mentors". 1.26.
    - ācāryopāsanaṁ "sitting close to the teacher; serving the teacher; showing respect for one's mentor". 13.7. Also see *āsana.*
45. **acchedyaḥ** "unassailable; not capable of being cut into pieces". 2.24.
46. **acetasaḥ** "foolish; not mindful; devoid of spiritual vision; deprived of wisdom; witless". 3.32; 15.11; 17.6.
47. **acintya** "inconceivable; cannot be thought of; beyond the reach of the mind". Also see *cintyaḥ.*
    - acintyaḥ "beyond the reach of the mind". 2.25.
    - acintyam "beyond the reach of the mind". 12.3.
48. **acintyarūpam** "one whose form is unthinkable; whose appearance is inconceivable". 8.9. Also see *rūpa.*
49. **acireṇa** "without delay; before long". 4.39. [*a* + *cira*] Also see *cira.*
50. **acyuta** "O Unfallen One, O Imperishable One". 1.21; 11.42; 18.73. [Used as an epithet.]
51. **adakṣiṇam** "without reverent gifts". 17.13.

52. **adambhitvam** "absence of deceit; honesty[41]; freedom from hypocrisy; unpretentiousness[42]; absence of ostentation[43]; free from the desire to appear as one is not[44]". 13.7. Also see *dambha.*
53. **ādarśaḥ** "a mirror". 3.38.
54. **ādatte** "it takes on; it receives". 5.15. Also see *datta.*
55. **adāhyaḥ** "that which cannot be burned; incombustible". 2.24.
56. **adbhutam** "wonderful; astonishing; inspiring". 11.20; 18.74, 76. Also see *atyadbhutam, anekādbhutadarśanam.*
57. **adeśakāle** "at the wrong place (*deśa*) and time (*kāla*); without regard to the appropriate place and time". 17.22. Also see *deśe, kāla.*
58. **adhaḥ** "downwards". 14.18; 15.2 (twice). Also see *adhaḥśākham.*
59. **adhaḥśākham** "with branches below". 15.1. Also see *adhaḥ, bahuśākhāḥ, śākhāḥ.*
60. **adhamām** "low". 16.20. Also see *narādham-.*
61. **adharma** "unrighteousness; injustice; breach of duty; lawlessness; conduct that is against the dictates of religion". Also see *adharmābhibhavāt, dharma.*
    - adharmaḥ "unrighteousness". 1.40.
    - adharmam "unrighteousness". 18.31, 32.
    - adharmasya "of unrighteousness". 4.7.
62. **adharmābhibhavāt** "overcome by injustice; by the prevalence of lawlessness". Also see *adharma, dharma, abhibhavati.* 1.41.
63. **ādhatsva** "fix (your mind); concentrate (your mind); focus". 12.8. Also see *ādhāya.* [Imp. 2nd pers. sing. of √ *dhā* with prefix *ā.*]

---

[41] See Apte, p. 37, entry for अदंभ as an adj., "honest, undeceitful" and अदंभः as a noun, "honesty, absence of deceit".

[42] Gambhīrānanda (1997, p. 521) translates Śaṅkara's commentary on the word as "upretentiousness—proclaiming one's own virtues is *dambhitvam*; the absence of that is *adambhitvam.*" Gambhīrānanda (1998, p. 716) translates Madhusūdana Sarasvati's commentary as "*Dambhitvam* means making a show of one's own virtues for gain, adoration, or fame."

[43] Ādidevānanda (pp. 434-5) translates it as "absence of ostentation", with Rāmānuja's commentary as "'Dambha' is the practice of Dharma for winning fame as a virtuous person; freedom from it is Adambhitva."

[44] Sivananda (p. 324) defines hypocrisy as "the desire to appear as what one is not". For example, a person "may have some virtues and a little theoretical knowledge derived from books. He pretends to be a liberated sage. This is religious hypocrisy."

64. **ādhāya** "having located". 5.10; 8.12. Also see *ādhatsva*. [*ā* + √ *dhā*]
65. **adhibhūta** "the deity presiding over the primary elements; that which pertains to (or presides over) the material". Also see *bhūta*.
    - adhibhūtam "that which pertains to the material; the presiding deity of the material realm". 8.1, 4.
    - sādhibhūtādhidaivam "along with the material and divine aspects". 7.30. Also see *adhidaiva*.
66. **adhidaiva** "that which pertains to (or presides over) the divine". Also see *daiva, deva*.
    - adhidaivam "what pertains to the divine; divinity". 8.1.
    - adhidaivatam "divinity". 8.4.
    - sādhibhūtādhidaivam "along with the material and divine aspects". 7.30.
67. **adhigacchati** "one attains; one reaches". 2.64, 71; 4.39; 5.6, 24; 6.15; 14.19; 18.49. Also see *gacchati, nigacchati, samadhigacchati*.
68. **adhika "greater; superior to".**
    - abhyadhikaḥ "surpassing; more excellent". 11.43.
    - adhikaḥ "superior to". 6.46 (three times).
    - nādhikam "not greater; not superior to". 6.22.
    - adhikataraḥ "greater". 12.5. [Nom. sing. of the masc. form of the comparative degree of the adj. *adhika*.]
69. **adhikāraḥ** "entitlement; qualification; right (to do something); claim (on something); jurisdiction". 2.47.[45]
70. **ādhipatyam** "supremacy; lordship". 2.8.
71. **adhiṣṭhānam** "substratum; basis; receptacle". 3.40; 18.14.
72. **adhiṣṭhāya** "sitting over; presiding over; controlling; availing (oneself) of". 4.6; 15.9.
73. **adhiyajñaḥ** "the presiding deity of sacrifice; the true object of worship; the basis of sacrifice". Also see *yajña*.
    - adhiyajñaḥ "the presiding deity of sacrifice; the true object of worship". 8.2, 4.
    - sādhiyajñam "along with the true object of worship; along with the ritualistic aspects". 7.30.

---

[45] For *adhikāra* ("entitlement") as a technical term in Mīmāṁsā see Van Buitenen 1981, p. 19. It covers all the properties that qualify a person to perform a certain act and obtain the reward of that performance.

74. **adhruvam** "transitory; impermanent; not fixed". 17.18. Also see *dhruva, calam.*

75. **āḍhyaḥ** "wealthy; rich". 16.15.

76. **adhyakṣa** "supervisor; overseer".
   - mayādhyakṣeṇa (*mayā adhyakṣeṇa*) "under my supervision; with me as overseer". 9.10.

77. **adhyātma** "pertaining to the spiritual self (*ātman*); spiritual".
   - adhyātmajñānanityatvam "the permanence of the knowledge of the self; constant focus on spiritual knowledge; cultivation of knowledge about the self". 13.11.
   - adhyātmam "that which pertains to the soul (*ātman*); relating to spirituality". 7.29; 8.1, 3 (defined).
   - adhyātmanityāḥ "well-grounded in spiritual wisdom; permanently devoted to the true self; always intent on that which pertains to the self". 15.5.
   - adhyātmasaṁjñitam "designated as spiritual; that which is known as *adhyātma*". 11.1.
   - adhyātmavidyā "the science of the self (*ātman*); knowledge of the soul (*ātman*); spiritual science". 10.32.
   - saṁnyasyādhyātmacetasā "by means of the mind filled with spiritual wisdom; by means of having the mind devoted to the (true) self". 3.30.

78. **adhyātmacetasā** "by means of the mind filled with spiritual wisdom; by means of having the mind devoted to the (true) self". 3.30.

79. **adhyātmajñānanityatvam** "the permanence of the knowledge of the self; constant focus on spiritual knowledge". 13.11. Also see *nitya, adhyātmanityāḥ.*

80. **adhyātmanityāḥ** "well-grounded in spiritual wisdom; permanently devoted to the true self; always intent on that which pertains to the self". 15.5. Also see *nitya, adhyātmajñānanityatvam.*

81. **adhyātmasaṁjñitam** "designated as spiritual; that which is known as *adhyātma*". 11.1.

82. **adhyātmavidyā** "the science (*vidyā*) of the self (*ātman*); knowledge of the soul (*ātman*); spiritual science". 10.32.

83. **adhyeṣyate** "one will study; one will recite". 18.70.

84. **ādi** "the beginning". Also see *ādya-, anādi-, bhūtādim, kalpādau.* Sometimes used with sense of "et cetera" or "firstly", as in *putradāragṛhādiṣu* (13.9).
   - ādau "in the beginning". 3.41; 4.4.

- ādiḥ "the beginning". 10.2, 20, 32; 15.3.
- ādim "the beginning". 11.16.

85. **ādideva** "primordial god; first of the gods". Also see *deva.*
    - ādidevam "primordial god; first of the gods". 10.12.
    - ādidevaḥ "primordial god; first of the gods". 11.38.
86. **ādikartre** "primordial creator; original creator; first creator". 11.37. Also see *kartā, kartāram.*
87. **āditya** "the sun (sing.); the Ādityas (pl.)". [The twelve Ādityas represent the months of the annual solar cycle.]
    - ādityagatam "proceeding from the sun; residing in the sun; solar". 15.12.
    - ādityānām ahaṁ viṣṇuḥ "of the Ādityas I am Viṣṇu". 10.21.
    - ādityavarṇam "the color of the sun; radiant like the sun". 8.9.
    - ādityavat "like the sun".5.16.
    - paśyādityān "behold the Ādityas". 11.6. Also see *paśya.*
    - rudrādityāḥ "the Rudras and the Ādityas".11.22.
88. **ādityavarṇam** "the color of the sun; radiant like the sun". 8.9. Also see *varṇa.*
89. **adrohaḥ** "freedom from hatred; absence of malice". 16.3. Also see *mitradrohe.*
90. **adṛṣṭapūrva** "not seen before; not previously seen". Also see *dṛṣṭapūrvam, dṛṣṭvā.*
    - adṛṣṭapūrvam "not seen before; not previously seen". 11.45.
    - adṛṣṭapūrvāṇi "not seen before; not previously seen". 11.6.
91. **adveṣṭā** "having no hatred". 12.13. Also see *dveṣa.*
92. **adya** "now; today". 4.3; 11.7; 16.13.
93. **ādyam** "the first; the primal; primordial". 8.28; 11.31, 47; 15.4. Also see *ādi.*
94. **ādyantavantaḥ** "having a beginning (*ādi*) and an end (*anta*); transient". 5.22. Also see *antavantaḥ, antavat.*
95. **āgacchet** "one should come to; one should fall into". 3.34. Also see *gacchati.*
96. **āgamāpāyinaḥ** "coming and going; transient". 2.14.
97. **āgatāḥ** "arrived at; come to; have attained". 4.10; 14.2.
98. **agatāsūn** "the living; those whose vital breath has not left the body". 2.11. Also see *agatāsūn.*
99. **agham** "sin; evil; that which is vile". 3.13. Also see *aghāyuḥ, anagha, pāpa.*
100. **aghāyuḥ** "whose life (*āyuḥ*) is sinful (*agha*); living a vile life". 3.16. Also see *agham, āyuḥ.*
101. **agni** "fire". Also see *vahniḥ, vibhāvasau.*
    - agnau "in fire". 15.12.

- agniḥ "fire". 4.37; 8.24; 9.16; 11.39.
- ātmasaṁyamayogāgnau "in the fire of the *yoga* of self-control; in the (internal) fire of yogic restraint; in the fire of the discipline of self-control". 4.27.
- brahmāgnau "in the fire of *Brahman*". 4.24, 25.
- dhūmenāgnir "fire with smoke". 18.48.
- indriyāgniṣu "in the fire of he senses; in the fire of the organs of sense and action". 4.26.
- jñānāgnidagdhakarmāṇam "one who has burned off his karma with the fire of knowledge".4.19. Also see *jñāna, karma*.
- jñānāgniḥ "the fire of knowledge". 4.37. Also see *jñāna*.
- niragniḥ "without fire; one who does not maintain a sacrificial fire". 6.1.
- saṁyamāgniṣu "in the fire of self-restraint; in the fire of discipline". 4.26.

102. **agre** "initially; in commencement". 18.37, 38, 39.
103. **āha** "he said". 1.21; 11.35. Also see *prāha, āhuḥ*.
104. **ahaḥ** "day". 8.17, 24. Also see *aharāgame, ahorātravidaḥ*.
105. **ahaitukam** "devoid of reason; aimless; having no purpose behind it". 18.22. Also see *hetu*.
106. **aham** "I". 1.22, 23; 2.4, 7, 12; 3.2, 23, 24, 27; 4.1, 5, 7, 11; 6.30, 33, 34; 7.2, 6, 8, 10, 11,[46] 12, 17, 21, 25, 26; 8.4, 14; 9.4, 7, 16 (eight times), 17, 19 (three times), 22, 24, 26, 29 (twice); 10.1, 2, 8, 11, 17, 20 (twice), 21 (twice), 23, 24, 25, 28, 29 (twice), 30 (twice), 31, 32 (twice), 33 (twice), 34, 35 (twice), 36 (twice), 37, 38, 39, 42; 11.23, 42, 44, 46, 48, 53, 54; 12.7; 14.3, 4, 27; 15.13, 14, 15 (three times), 18; 16.14 (three times), 19; 18.66, 70, 74, 75.
107. **ahaṁkāra** "ego; egoism; egotism; vanity". Also see *ahaṁkṛtaḥ, anahaṁkāraḥ, anahaṁvādī, dambhāhaṁkārasaṁyuktāḥ, nirahaṁkāraḥ, sāhaṁkāreṇa*. [(lit.) conviction that "I am the doer" or "I-making".]
    - ahaṁkāraḥ "ego; ego-sense[47]; the I-faculty[48]". 7.4; 13.5.

---

[46] In verse 7.11a, some Vulgate editions read *cāham* (*ca aham,* "and I"), but the Critical edition reads *asmi* ("I am").

[47] Warrier, p. 254 ("ego-sense"); p. 605 ("egoism").

[48] Edgerton, pp. 38, 65.

- ahaṁkāram "vanity; egoism[49]; egotism[50]". 16.18; 18.53. "egoistically".[51] [*ahaṁkāram āśritya*]" 18.59.
- ahaṁkārāt "out of vanity; due to ego; from egotism[52]; egotistically[53]". 18.58.

108. **ahaṁkāravimūḍhātmā** "a person whose mind is deluded by vanity (*ahaṁkāra*); he whose mind is deluded by egoism[54]; he whose soul is deluded by the I-faculty[55]; deluded by self-attribution[56]". 3.27. Also see *ahaṁkāra, ātman, √ mūḍh-.*

109. **ahaṁkṛtaḥ** "egoistic; egoized[57]; that which arises from the consciousness of having done a particular thing[58]". 18.17. Also see *ahaṁkāra.*

110. **āhāra** "food; diet". Also see *bhojana.*
    - āhāraḥ "food". 17.7.
    - āhārāḥ "foods". 17.8, 9.
    - nirāhārasya "of one who is abstaining from food". 2.59.
    - niyatāhārāḥ "those having a well-regulated diet; those who restrict their diet; those who eat prescribed food". 4.30.
    - yuktāhāravihārasya "one whose food and movements are regulated[59]; a person with balanced diet (*āhāra*) and regimens (*vihāra*)". 6.17. Also see *yukta.*

111. **aharāgame** "at (cosmic) daybreak; at the coming of day (*ahaḥ*)". 8.18, 19.

112. **ahatvā** "by not killing". 2.5. [Indec. past part. of √ *han* with prefix *a*; used with sense "by not slaying".] Also see *hatvā, -tvā.*

113. **āhave** "in the battle". 1.31.

---

[49] Warrier, p. 523.

[50] Edgerton, p. 78. Edgerton distinguishes egotism (*ahaṁkāram*) from "the I-faculty" (*ahaṁkāraḥ*).

[51] Warrier, p. 612.

[52] Sargeant, p. 719.

[53] Warrier, p. 611.

[54] Warrier, p. 121.

[55] Edgerton, p. 21.

[56] Van Buitenen 1981, p. 83.

[57] Edgerton, p. 84.

[58] Divanji, p. 23, entry #522.

[59] Gambhīrānanda 1998, p. 417.

114. **ahiṁsā** "non-injury; avoidance of harm; abstention from injury to living things; non-violence". 10.5; 13.7; 16.2; 17.14. Also see *hiṁsā.*

115. **ahitāḥ** "hostile; not favorably inclined; ill-wishers; enemies". 2.36; 16.9. Also see *hitam.*

116. **aho** "ah!; oh!". 1.45.

117. **āho** "is it so?; which?; whether (or)?". 17.1.

118. **ahorātravidaḥ** "knowers of day and night; those who know of days and nights[60]". 8.17. Also see *ahaḥ, rātri, –vid.*

119. **āhuḥ** "(they) say". 3.42; 4.19; 8.21; 10.13; 14.16; 16.8. Also see *prāhuḥ, āha.*

120. **aikāntikasya** "of absolute; of perfect". 14.27. [*sukhasyaikāntikasya* = of absolute happiness][61]

121. **airāvatam** "Airāvata". 10.27. [Name of the divine elephant who emerged from the churning of the ocean by the gods and the demons. Airāvata became the mount of Indra, the lord of the gods.]

122. **aiśvaram** "majestic; magnificent; grand; sovereign". 9.5 (*yogam aiśvaram*); 11.3 (*te rūpam aiśvaram,* "your form as *Īśvara*"), 11.8 (*yogam aiśvaram*), 11.9 (*paramaṁ rūpam aiśvaram,* "supreme form as *Īśvara*"). Also see *bhogaiśvarya, īśvara.*

123. **aja** "unborn; beginningless".
   - ajaḥ "unborn".2.20; 4.6.
   - ajam "unborn". 2.21; 7.25; 10.3, 12.

124. **ajānantaḥ** "not knowing; ignorant; unaware". 7.24; 9.11; 13.25. [*a* + √ *jñā*]

125. **ajānatā** "knowing; ignorant of". 11.41. [*a* + √ *jñā*]

126. **ajasram** "ceaselessly; forever; always". 16.19.

127. **ajñānajam** "arising from ignorance". 10.11; 14.8.

128. **ajñānam** "ignorance". 5.16; 13.11; 14.16, 17; 16.4.

129. **ajñānām** "of the ignorant". 3.26.

130. **ajñānasaṁbhūtam** "born of ignorance". 4.42.

131. **ajñānasaṁmohaḥ** "the delusion of ignorance". 18.72. Also see *moha, saṁmoha.*

---

[60] Van Buitenen 1981, p. 103.

[61] The word *aikāntikasya* is listed as *ekāntikasya* by some translators in vocabularies. The commentaries by Śaṅkara, Rāmānuja, and Madhusūdana Sarasvati all comment on it as *aikāntikasya. BG* 14.27 is cited as a usage example for the word *aikāntika* in Apte, p. 317, entry for ऐकांतिक. For commentators see Warrier, p. 488; Ādidevānanda, p. 480; Gambhīrānanda 1998, p. 773.

132. **ajñānavimohitāḥ** "those who are deluded by ignorance". 16.15. Also see *mohita, √ muh, vimohayati.*

133. **ajñānenāvṛtam** "covered by ignorance". 5.15. Also see *āvṛtam.*

134. **ajñaḥ** "ignorant". 4.40.

135. **ājyam** "ghee; clarified butter'. 9.16.

136. **akalmaṣam** "free from sin; free of blemish". 6.27. Also see *kalmaṣa.*

137. **akāraḥ** "The letter 'A' (अ)". 10.33.

138. **akarma** "inaction; non-action". Also see *akarmakṛt, karma.*
- akarma "inaction". 4.16, 18.
- akarmaṇaḥ "(better than) inaction; without action". 3.8 (twice).
- akarmaṇaḥ "of inaction". 4.17.
- akarmaṇi "(attachment) to inaction, in inaction; in inaction". 2.47; 4.18.

139. **akarmakṛt** "A non-doer of action". 3.5. Also see *akartāram, akarma.*

140. **akartāram** "a non-doer". 4.13; 13.29. Also see *akarmakṛt, kartāram, kartṛtvam, kāryakāraṇakartṛtve.*

141. **akārya** "what ought not to be done". Also see *kārya-.*
- kāryākāryavyavasthitau "in determining what to do and what not to do; distinguishing what should and should not be done; distinguishing between duties and violations of duty". 16.24. Also see *vyavasthita.*
- kāryākārye "what ought to be done and what ought not to be done". 18.30.
- kāryaṁ cākāryam "what ought to be done and what ought not to be done". 18.31.

142. **ākāśa** "space; the sky; ether".
- ākāśam "space". 13.32.
- ākāśasthitaḥ "abiding in space; residing in space". 9.6. Also see *sthita.*

143. **akhila** "entire; whole".
- akhilam "the entire; the whole" 7.29; 15.12.
- karmākhilam "all action; action in its entirety; actions in their totality". 4.33. Also see *karma.*

144. **ākhyāhi** "tell; explain; inform". 11.31.

145. **ākhyātam** "has been told; explained; expounded". 18.63.

146. **akīrti** "infamy". Also see *kīrti.*
- akīrtiḥ "infamy". 2.34.
- akīrtim "infamy". 2.34.

147. **akīrtikaram** "that which will cause infamy; defaming". 2.2. Also see *kīrti.*

148. **akledyaḥ** "that which cannot become wet". 2.24. Also see *kledayanti.*

149. **akriyaḥ** "not performing action; one who does not do the prescribed acts". 6.1.

150. **akrodhaḥ** "absence of anger". 16.2. Also see *krodha.*

151. **akṛta** "not done; not performed; wrongly done; not cultivated; immature". Also see *kṛta.*

- akṛtabuddhitvāt "due to imperfect understanding; not possessed of a gifted intellect". 18.16. Also see *buddhi, abuddhayaḥ, alpabuddhayaḥ,*
- akṛtātmānaḥ "those who do not have self-control; not possessed of a refined nature". 15.11. Also see *ātman.*
- akṛtena "by non-performance of action; by abstention from action". 3.18. Also see *kṛtena.*

152. **akṛtātmānaḥ** [*akṛta-ātmānaḥ*] "men whose self is unperfected[62]; those who have not mastered themselves[63]; ones who lack self-control[64]; those of unrefined minds[65]; those who are not possessed of a gifted soul". 15.11. Also see *ātman.*

153. **akṛtsnavidaḥ** "those who do not know the All; those who do not know the whole truth; those who do not have a comprehensive view; those who are not aware of the entirety; those ignorant of the universal aspect thereof; those who don't see 'the big picture'". 3.29. Also see *kṛtsnavid, –vid.*

154. **akṣara** "imperishable; indestructible; unalterable". Also see *akṣara* ("syllable"); *kṣara.*

- akṣaraḥ "the imperishable". 8.21; 15.16 (twice).
- akṣaram "the imperishable". 8.3, 11; 11.18, 37; 12.1, 3.
- akṣarāt "than the imperishable; beyond the imperishable". 15.18.
- brahmākṣarasamudbhavam "originating in the imperisable *Brahman*; the Veda is risen from the imperishable; *Brahman* arises from the imperishable". 3.15.

155. **akṣara** "a letter of the alphabet; a syllable". Also see *akṣara* ("imperishable"); *kṣara* ("perishable").

- akṣarāṇām "of letters; among syllables". 10.33.
- ekam akṣaram "one syllable". 10.25.

---

[62] Zaehner, p. 365.

[63] Van Buitenen 1981, p. 131.

[64] Gambhīrānanda 1997, pp. 603-4. The commentary by Śaṅkara gives a range of possible interpretations.

[65] Ādidevānanda, p. 493.

- om ity ekākṣaraṁ "'om', thus, the single-syllable (ॐ)". 8.13.

156. **akṣaya** "indestructible". Also see *kṣaya*.
    - akṣayam "indestructible". 5.21.
    - evākṣayaḥ (*eva akṣayaḥ*) "alone imperishable". 10.33.
157. **akurvata** "they did". 1.1. [√ *kṛ*]
158. **akuśalam** "disagreeable; unfavorable; inauspicious". 18.10. Also see *kuśale*.
159. **alābha** "loss". 2.38. [*lābhālābhau* = gain (*lābha*) and loss (*alābha*)]
160. **alasaḥ** "indolent; lazy; idle". 18.28. Also see *nidrālasyapramādottham, pramādālasyanidrābhiḥ*.
161. **aloluptvam** "the quality of non-greediness; freedom from greed". 16.2.
162. **alpabuddhayaḥ** "those of small intelligence; mean-minded ones". 16.9. Also see *abuddhayaḥ, akṛtabuddhitvāt, alpamedhasām, buddhi*.
163. **alpam** "little; small; limited; insufficient; trivial". 18.22. Also see *svalpam*.
164. **alpamedhasām** "of those who have little intelligence; of those who are of poor intellect". 7.23. Also see *alpabuddhayaḥ, medhā*.
165. **amalān** "pure; spotless; without impurity". 14.14. Also see *malena, nirmalam, nirmalatvāt*.
166. **amānitvam** "absence of egotism; freedom from conceit". 13.7. Also see *atimānitā*.
167. **āmarṣa** "impatience; non-forebearance; not bearing things patiently, intolerance".[66]
    - harṣāmarṣabhayodvegaiḥ "(free) from agitation (*udvega*) caused by delight (*harṣa*), intolerance (*āmarṣa*), and fear (*bhaya*)" *or* "(free) from delight (*harṣa*), intolerance (*āmarṣa*), fear (*bhaya*), and agitation (*udvega*)". 12.15. Also see *harṣa, bhaya*.
168. **āmaya** "disease; sickness". See *anāmayam, duḥkhaśokāmayapradāḥ*.
169. **ambhas** "water".
    - ambhasā "by water". 5.10.
    - ambhasi "in water". 2.67.
170. **ambuvegāḥ** "torrents of water; streams of rushing water". 11.28. Also see *vegam*.
171. **amedhyam** "impure; unfit for being used in a sacrifice". 17.10.

---

[66] Apte, p. 222, entry for *āmarṣaḥ* (आमरषः) lists "anger, wrath, impatience" with note to see *amarṣa* (अमरष), which is defined as "not enduring or bearing" (p. 136). *Marṣa* (मर्षः, p. 745) is endurance, forebearance, or patience.

172. **amī** "these; those (yonder)". 11.21, 26, 28.

173. **amitavikramaḥ** "unlimited in power". 11.40. [Some translators consider this word to be part of a larger compound. See footnote for *anantavīryāmitavikramaḥ.*]

174. **amla** "sour". 17.9. See *kaṭvamlalavaṇātyuṣṇatīkṣṇarūkṣavidāhinaḥ.*

175. **amṛta** "immortality; ambrosia; the nectar of immortality of the gods; the residue or leavings of a sacrifice[67]". Also see *mṛtyu.*

- amṛtam "immortality; ambrosia; nectar". 9.19; 10.18; 13.12; 14.20.
- amṛtasya "of the immortal". 14.27.
- amṛtatvāya "for immortality". 2.15.
- amṛtodbhavam "born from (the ocean of) ambrosial nectar". 10.27. Also see *-udbhava.*
- amṛtopamam "like ambrosia". 18.37, 38.
- dharmyāmṛtam "the nectar of righteousness; ambrosial virtue; true immortality; this immortal law; this elixir of Law[68]". 12.20.
- yajñaśiṣṭāmṛtabhujaḥ "one who experiences immortality from the remnants of the sacrifice; one who eats the nectar of the remnants of the sacrifice (i.e., the remnants of the food offered at a sacrifice)".[69] 4.31. Also see *yajñaśiṣṭa.*

176. **aṁśa** "a particle; a part; a fraction".

- aṁśaḥ "a particle; a part". 15.7.
- ekāṁśena "with a single (*eka*) part (*aṁśa*)". 10.42. Also see *eka-.*
- tejoṁśasaṁbhavam "originates (*saṁbhavam*) from a fraction (*aṁśa*) of my splendor (*tejas*)". 10.41. Also see *tejas, saṁbhavam.*

177. **aṁśumān** "radiant, shining". 10.21.

178. **amūḍhāḥ** "undeluded; unconfused". 15.5. Also see √ *muh.*

179. **amutra** "there; in that world; in the other world". 6.40.

180. **anabhiṣvaṅgaḥ** "freedom from too much attachment; absence of clinging". 13.9.

---

[67] For "residue or leavings of a sacrifice (यज्ञशेष)" see Apte, p. 138, entry for अमृतं, meaning 7 (as a noun).

[68] Van Buitenen 1981, p. 123.

[69] Divanji, p. 118, entry #2714, glosses this as "One who eats the nectar of, i.e., the remnant of the food offered at, a sacrifice."

181. **anabhisaṁdhāya** "without having aiming at; without expecting; without ulterior motives". 17.25. [√ *dhā* with the prefixes *an*, *abhi*, and *saṁ* collectively conveying a negative sense.] Also see *abhisaṁdhāya*.

182. **anabhisnehaḥ** "non-desirous; free from attachment". 2.57.

183. **anādī** "(both are) without a beginning (*ādi*); beginningless". 13.19.

184. **anādim** "without a beginning (*ādi*); beginningless". 10.3.

185. **anādimadhyāntam** "having no beginning (*ādi*), middle (*madhya*), or end (*anta*)". 11.19.

186. **anādimat** "having no beginning (*ādi*)". 13.12.

187. **anāditvāt** "due to having no beginning (*ādi*); because it is without a beginning". 13.31.

188. **anagha** "O sinless one". 3.3; 14.6; 15.20. Also see *agham*. [Epithet of Arjuna.]

189. **anahaṁkāraḥ** "freedom from ego; absence of I-faculty[70]; absence of egotism[71]; absence-of-ego-sense[72]". 13.8. Also see *anahaṁvādī, ahaṁkāra, nirahaṁkāraḥ*.

190. **anahaṁvādī** "one who is not egotistic". 18.26. Also see *anahaṁkāraḥ, nirahaṁkāraḥ, ahaṁkāra, vādinaḥ*.

191. **anala** "fire". Also see *agni*.
  - analaḥ "fire". 7.4.
  - dīptānalārkadyutim "blazing like the fiery radiance of the sun; having the splendor of a blazing fire and the sun; shining like glowing fire or the sun". 11.17.
  - duṣpūreṇānalena "by insatiable fire; fire that is difficult to quench". 3.39.
  - kālānalasaṁnibhāni "like the fire of destruction (at the dissolution of the worlds); like the fire of time". 11.25.

192. **anāmayam** "beyond ills (metaphorical); free of ailments; free from disease; healthy; salutary". Also see *duḥkhaśokāmayapradāḥ*.
  - anāmayam "beyond ills; beyond evil". 2.51. [*padaṁ gacchanty anāmayam* = "they go to the realm beyond all ills", speaking of the state of liberation.]
  - anāmayam "salutary; free from morbidity[73]; free from evil[74]". 14.6. [Describing *sattva guṇa*.]

---

[70] Edgerton, p. 65.

[71] Divanji, p. 7, entry #162.

[72] Feuerstein and Feuerstein, p. 255.

[73] Ādidevānanda, p. 465.

[74] Swarupananda, p. 311.

193. **ananta** "without end; endless; infinite".

- ananta "O Endless One; O Infinite". 11.37.
- anantaḥ "Ananta". 10.29. [Ananta is the name of a semi-divine thousand-headed cobra.] Also see *nāgānām*.
- anantāḥ "endless". 2.41.
- anantam "endless; infinite". 11.11, 47.

194. **anantabāhum** "having innumerable hands". 11.19. Also see *bāhu*.

195. **anantaram** "without delay; at once; immediately". 12.12. Also see *antaram, tadanantaram*.

196. **anantarūpa** "having infinite forms; unlimited forms". Also see *rūpa*.

- anantarūpa "O one possessing infinite forms; O one who has unlimited forms". 11.38.
- anantarūpam "having infinite forms; having unlimited forms". 11.16.

197. **anantavijayam** "Infinite Victory; Unending Victory". 1.16. [The name of Yudhiṣṭhira's conch.] Also see *vijaya*.

198. **anantavīryam** "endowed with infinite power; possessed of inexhaustible strength". 11.19. Also see *vīryavān*.

199. **anantavīryāmitavikramaḥ** "infinite power and immeasurable might". 11.40.[75] Also see *vīryavān*.

200. **ananyabhāk** "not devoted to any other object of devotion; not devoted to anything else; with one-minded focus (on Me)". 9.30.

201. **ananyacetāḥ** "one who thinks of nothing else; one whose mind has no other object (of devotion)". 8.14. Also see *ananyamanasaḥ, mayyāsaktamanāḥ, manas, manmanāḥ*.

---

[75] Edgerton (p. 59) divides *anantavīrya* and *amitavikramaḥ* as a vocative with a separate nominative ("O Thou of infinite might, Thy prowess is unmeasured") and provides a note (p. 98, note 8 for Chapter XI) saying that it seems better to him to take *anantavīrya* as a separate vocative, as does Rāmānuja, rather than as part of the following compound, as does Śaṅkara. Divanji lists *anantavīrya* (page 6, entry #136) as a vocative for "One who is possessed of inexhaustible strength" and lists *amitavikramaḥ* separately (page 15, entry #340) as nominative singular for "One whose strength is beyond measure". Sargeant (p. 492) follows Śaṅkara and interprets *anantavīryāmitavikramaḥ* as a *karmadhāraya* compound ("infinite, heroic, boundless, might") with all members having the same case, and translates it as, "You are infinite valor and boundless might."

202. **ananyāḥ** "excluding all else[76]; one-pointed; without another (focus); non-separate[77]". 9.22.

203. **ananyamanasaḥ** "single-minded ones; whose minds are not on anything else". 9.13. Also see *ananyacetāḥ, manas, manmanāḥ, mayyāsaktamanāḥ.*

204. **ananyayā** "by single-minded (devotion); by having no other object in view". 8.22; 11.54.

205. **ananyayogena** "without means of another discipline; without using another *yoga*; by the *yoga* consisting of concentration on only one ideal". 13.10.

206. **ananyena** "with single-minded (practice)". 12.6. Also see *anyena.*

207. **anapekṣaḥ** "one who has no longing for anything; having no expectations". 12.16.

208. **anapekṣya** "overlooking; without looking to; without considering; without a regard for; disregarding". 18.25.

209. **anārambhāt** "by non-initiation (of action); from non-commencement". 3.4. Also see *ārambh-.*

210. **anāryajuṣṭam** (*anārya-juṣṭam*) "adopted by inferior people; not befitting an *Āryan*". 2.2.

211. **anāśinaḥ** "indestructible; imperishable; immortal". 2.18. Also see *avināśi, avināśinam.*

212. **anaśnataḥ** (*an-aśnataḥ*) "one who does not eat (enough)". 6.16. Also see *atyaśnataḥ,* √ *aś.*

213. **anāśritaḥ** "one who is not dependent on another; one who is detached; independent". 6.1. Also see *āśrita, śritāḥ.*

214. **anasūya** "without disrespect; without disputing; not scoffing; not sneering; not spiteful; not envious; not jealous; free from malice".

- anasūyaḥ "not disrespectful; free from malice; filled with belief[78]". 18.71.
- anasūyantaḥ "not disrespectful; free from malice; without disputing[79]". 3.31.

---

[76] Ādidevānanda, p. 310.

[77] Śaṅkara's commentary (Gambhīrānanda 1997, p. 388) interprets *ananyāḥ* as meaning "becoming non-different (from Me)." Swarupananda (p. 210) says that here *ananyāḥ* may mean "non-separate" in the sense of looking on the Supreme Being as not separate from their own self, but also giving "without any other (thought)" as a possibility.

[78] Van Buitenen 1981, p. 145.

[79] Van Buitenen 1981, p. 85.

- anasūyave "to one who is respectful; to one who is not disrespectful; to one without faultfinding attitude; who do not demur[80]". 9.1.

215. **anātmanaḥ** [*an-ātmanaḥ*] "for the man who has not mastered himself; for he who is not self-possessed; of one whose self is not; of the not-self; of the unrestrained; for one who has not conquered his self". 6.6. Also see *ātman.*
216. **anavalokayan** "not looking (at)". 6.13.
217. **anavāptam** "not gained; not acquired". 3.22. Also see *avāpt-.*
218. **anāvṛttim** "non-return; non-rebirth". 8.23, 26. Also see *āvṛttim.*
219. **anayoḥ** "of these two; both of these". 2.16.
220. **aneka** "not one; many; various". See *aneka-, divyānekodyatāyudham.*
221. **anekabāhūdaravaktranetram** "endowed with many arms, bellies, mouths [or faces], and eyes". 11.16. Also see *bahu, udara, vaktra, netra.*
222. **anekacittavibhrāntāḥ** "bewildered with multiple thoughts; confused by too many concerns[81]". 16.16.
223. **anekādbhutadarśanam** "with many astonishing aspects; one who puts on diverse wonderful appearances[82]". 11.10. Also see *adbhutam.*
224. **anekadhā** "in numerous ways; in many forms". 11.13.
225. **anekadivyābharaṇam** "(adorned) with numerous divine ornaments". 11.10. Also see *divya.*
226. **anekajanmasaṁsiddhaḥ** "perfected after several lifetimes; one who has become an adept after many births". 6.45. Also see *janma, saṁsiddh-.*
227. **anekavaktranayanam** "endowed with many mouths [or faces] and eyes". 11.10. Also see *vaktra, nayana, netra.*
228. **anekavarṇam** "many-colored; having many complexions; (lit.) not a single color". 11.24. Also see *varṇa.*
229. **anena** "by this; with this". 3.10, 11; 9.10; 11.8.
230. **aṅgāni** "limbs". 2.58.
231. **anicchan** "not inclined; unwilling". 3.36. [*an* + √ *iṣ*]
232. **aniketaḥ** "not having a fixed abode; not attached to home; at home anywhere". 12.19.
233. **anirdeśyam** "inexplicable; inexpressible; undefinable; that which cannot be referred to by speech[83]". 12.3. Also see *nirdeśaḥ.*

---

[80] Van Buitenen 1981, p. 105.

[81] Van Buitenen 1981, p. 133.

[82] Divanji, p. 8, entry #220.

[83] Divanji, p. 8, entry #181.

234. **anirviṇṇacetasā** "with undismayed mind; without losing heart". 6.23.

235. **aniṣṭam** "not wished for; that which is undesirable". 18.12. Also see *iṣṭa, iṣṭāniṣṭopapattiṣu.*

236. **anīśvaram** "godless; without a Lord (*īśvara*)". 16.8. Also see *Īśvara.*

237. **anitya** "not eternal; transient; ephemeral"

- anityāḥ "not eternal". 2.14.
- anityam "not eternal". 9.33.

238. **aṇīyāṁsam** "more minute; smaller; more subtle". 8.9. [*aṇor aṇīyāṁsam* = subtler than the atom]

239. **anna** "food". Also see √ *aś.*

- annam "food". 15.14.
- annasaṁbhavaḥ "the source of food (is from rain); the origin of food (is due to rain); food is produced (by rain); food is brought into being (by rain)". 3.14. Also see *saṁbhava.*
- annāt "from food". 3.14.
- asṛṣṭānnam "without distributing food; with no food offered". 17.13.

240. **aṇoḥ** "than an atom". 8.9. [*aṇor aṇīyāṁsam* = subtler than the atom]

241. **anta** "end".

- antaḥ "the essence; the final truth; the end". 2.16.
- antaḥ "end". 10.19, 20, 32, 40; 15.3.
- antaḥ "inside". 13.15. [Ind. adv.]
- antam "the end". 11.16.
- ante "at the end". 7.19; 8.6.

242. **antagatam** "terminated; come to an end". 7.28.

243. **antaḥśarīrastham** "dwelling deep within the body". 17.6. Also see *śarīra.*

244. **antaḥsthāni** "residing within". 8.22. Also see *matsthāni, prakṛtisthāni, sthānam.*

245. **antaḥsukhaḥ** "inward happiness; one who finds happiness within oneself". 5.24. Also see *sukham.*

246. **antakāle** "at the final time; at the time of death". 2.72; 8.5. Also see *kāla.*

247. **antaram** "intervening space or difference". Also see *anantaram, tadanantaram.*

- antaram "central area (between space and earth, i.e., the atmosphere)". 11.20.
- antaram "distinction; difference". 13.34.
- antare "in the space between (the eyebrows)". 5.27.

248. **antarārāmaḥ** "inner joy (*ārāma*); delight (*ārāma*) within; one who has interior contentment; one who is at ease with himself". 5.24. Also see *indriyārāmaḥ*, √ *ram-*.

249. **antarātmanā** "with the inner soul; with the heart". 6.47. [*mad-gatenāntarātmanā*] Also see *ātman, pravyathitāntarātmā*.

250. **antarjyotiḥ** "inner light". 5.24. Also see *jyoti*.

251. **antavantaḥ** "perishable; ephemeral; likely to end". 2.18. Also see *ādyantavantaḥ, antavat*.

252. **antavat** "perishable; ephemeral; likely to end". 7.23. Also see *ādyantavantaḥ, antavantaḥ*.

253. **antike** "in proximity; in nearness; very close". 13.15.

254. **anubandha** "result, effect, consequence". Also see *bandham* ("binding"). Also see *karmānubandhīni*.

- anubandham "end result; consequence". 18.25.
- anubandhe "in result; in consequence". 18.39.

255. **anucintayan** "thinking over; contemplating; meditating on". 8.8. Also see *cintayantaḥ, paricintayan*.

256. **anudarśana** "contemplation; insight".

- janmamṛtyujarāvyādhiduḥkhadoṣānudarśanam "contemplation (*anu-darśana*) of the fault (*doṣa*) consisting of the miseries (*duḥkha*) of birth (*janma*), death (*mṛtyu*), old age (*jarā*), and disease (*vyādhi*)". 13.8.

257. **anudvegakaram** "inoffensive [speech]; that which does not cause perturbation". 17.15. Also see *vegam*.

258. **anudvignamanāḥ** "one whose mind is not troubled; not perturbed mentally; not distressed". 2.56. Also see *-manāḥ, manas, vigna*.

259. **anugraha** "grace; favor; blessing".

- madanugrahāya "for the stake of bestowing grace (*anugraha*) on me; as a favor to me; in order to bless me". 11.1.

260. **anukampārtham** "for the sake of bestowing grace; out of compassion". 10.11. [*anukampā + artham*]

261. **anumantā** "permitter; consenter; approver; one who expresses approval of another's act". 13.22.

262. **anupakāriṇe** "to one from whom no return service is expected; to one who will not serve in return". 17.20.

263. **anupaśyāmi** "I see; I perceive; I realize; I foresee; I anticipate". 1.31. Also see *paśyāmi*.

264. **anupaśyanti** "they see; they perceive; they realize". 15.10. Also see *paśyanti.*

265. **anupaśyati** "one sees; one perceives; one realizes". 13.30; 14.19. Also see *paśyati.*

266. **anuprapannā** "depending on; after taking shelter in". 9.21. Also see *prapannam.*

267. **anurajyate** "it is delighted; it rejoices; it is very glad; it is flooded with love[84]". 11.36 [*anu* + √ *rañj*]

268. **anuṣajjate** "one clings; one is attached". 6.4; 18.10. [*anu* + √ *sañj*]

269. **anusaṁtatāni** "extended; stretched forth; proliferating". 15.2.

270. **anuśāsitāram** "governor; regulator; director". 8.9.

271. **anusmara** "meditate on; remember". 8.7.

272. **anusmaran** "meditating on; remembering". 8.13. Also see *smaran.*

273. **anusmaret** "one meditates on; one who remembers". 8.9. Also see *smarati.*

274. **anuśocanti** "they grieve; they are sorry for; they repent". 2.11. Also see √ *śuc.*

275. **anuśocitum** "to grieve; to be sorry for; to worry". 2.25. Also see √ *śuc.*

276. **anuśuśruma** "we have heard traditionally; we have heard repeatedly". 1.44. Also see *aśuśrūṣave.*

277. **anutiṣṭhanti** "they follow; they abide by (my teaching)". 3.31, 32. Also see *tiṣṭh-.*

278. **anuttama** "having nothing superior; unsurpassed; unexcelled; supreme; highest". Also see *uttama.*
   - anuttamām "supreme; unsurpassed". 7.18.
   - anuttamam "supreme; unsurpassed". 7.24.

279. **anuvartante** "they follow". 3.23; 4.11. See *vartmānuvartante.*

280. **anuvartate** "it follows; one follows". 3.21.

281. **anuvartayati** "one follows; one causes to turn (the wheel)". 3.16.

282. **anuvidhīyate** "it obeys; it follows; it is guided by; (the mind) is allowed to indulge (in the senses)". 2.67. Also see *vidhīyate.*

283. **anvaśocaḥ** "have worried about; become sorry for". 2.11. Also see √ *śuc.*

284. **anviccha** "seek for; try to find; desire". 2.49. [*anu* + √ *iṣ*]

285. **anvita** "accompanied by; endowed with; possessing". [ifc.] See *bhāvasamanvitāḥ* (10.8); *dambhamānamadānvitāḥ* (16.10); *dhanamānamadānvitāḥ* (16.17); *dhṛtyutsāhasamanvitaḥ* (18.26); *guṇānvitam* (15.10); *harṣaśokānvitaḥ* (18.27); *kāmarāgabalānvitāḥ* (17.5); *śraddhayānvitāḥ* (9.23; 17.1).

---

[84] Van Buitenen 1981, p. 117.

286. **anyadevatāḥ** "other gods". Also see *devatā*.

- anyadevatāḥ "other gods". 7.20.
- anyadevatā "other gods". 9.23. [Shown in many Vulgate editions as part of a compound: *anyadevatābhaktāḥ*, ("devotees of other gods"), but shown divided as *anyadevatā bhaktāḥ* in the Critical Edition.]

287. **anya** "another; other".

- anyaḥ "another; other". 2.29 (twice); 4.31; 6.39; 8.20; 11.43; 15.17; 16.15; 18.69.
- anyam "another; other". 14.19.
- anyām "another; other". 7.5.
- anyān "others". 11.34.
- anyāni "others". 2.22.
- anyat "another; other". 2.31, 42; 7.2, 7; 11.7; 16.8.
- anyayā "by the other". 8.26. [*anyayāvartate* = by the other path one returns]
- anye "others". 1.9; 4.26 (twice); 9.15; 13.24, 25; 17.4.
- anyebhya "from others". 13.25.
- anyena "by another". 11.47, 48. Also see *ananyena*.

288. **anyathā** "otherwise; contrary; opposed". 13.11. Also see *ayathāvat, yathā*.

289. **anyatra** "elsewhere". 3.9.

290. **anyāyena** "unjustly; by unjustified means". 16.12.

291. **anyena** "by another". 11.47, 48. [*tvad anyena* = by other than you] Also see *ananyena*.

292. √ **āp** "to obtain; to acquire". See *āpnoti, āpnuvanti, āpnuyām, āptum, avāp-, prāpnu-, prāps-, prāptaḥ, prāpya-, aprāpya*.

293. **āpaḥ** "waters". 2.23, 70; 7.4.

294. **apahṛtacetasām** "whose thoughts are carried away". 2.44.

295. **apahṛtajñānāḥ** "those whose knowledge (*jñāna*) has been carried away". 7.15. [*māyayāpahṛtajñānāḥ*]

296. **apaiśunam** "not backbiting; not speaking maliciously about someone who is not present; not having a tendency to disclose the faults of others; not slandering; loyalty". 16.2.

297. **apalāyanam** "not flying away from; not avoiding (battle)". 18.43.

298. **apāna** "the downward breath; the eliminative breath". Also see *prāṇa*.

- apāne juhvati prāṇaṁ prāṇe 'pānaṁ tathāpare । prāṇāpānagatī ruddhvā prāṇāyāmaparāyaṇāḥ ॥ "Still others, after being absorbed in the practice of restraining the flow of *apāna* and *prāṇa*, offer as a sacrifice the joining of *prāṇa* into *apāna* and *apāna* into *prāṇa*.". 4.29. Also see *parāyaṇa*.

- prāṇāpānagatī "the movement of the upward and downward breaths". 4.29.
- prāṇāpānasamāyuktaḥ "accompanied by the life force (*prāṇa*) and eliminative wind (*apāna*); united with the upward and downward breaths". 15.14. Also see *yukta*.
- prāṇāpānau "the inhaling and exhaling breaths; the upward and downward breaths". 5.27.

299. **apanudyāt** "it would remove; it would dispel". 2.8.

300. **āpanna** "fallen into; reduced to; gone to".

- āpannāḥ "fallen into; gone to". 16.20.
- āpannam "fallen into; gone to". 7.24.

301. **aparājitaḥ** "undefeated; unconquered". 1.17. [Used as an epithet of Sātyaki.]

302. **apara** "other". Also see *paraḥ, ātmaparadeheṣu*.

- aparā "lower; inferior; gross [as opposed to subtle]". 7.5. [*apareyam* = *aparā* + *iyam*]
- aparam "other". 6.22.
- aparam "later [birth]; not previous; subsequent". 4.4.
- aparān "others". 16.14.
- aparāṇi "others". 2.22.
- apare "others; some". 4.25 (twice); 27, 28, 29, 30; 13.24; 18.3.

303. **aparasparasaṁbhūtam** "it has not come to be by mutual causal law[85]; not produced by the interdependence of causes[86]; arising without mutual union (of God and Nature)[87]; born of sexual union[88]; born of mutual union[89]". 16.8. Also see *parasparam*.

---

[85] Zaehner, p. 371. Zaehner adds a note that Śaṅkara's interpretation that "its sole origin is the union of the sexes" seems to be an interpretation of *paraspara-saṁbhūtam* rather than of *a-paraspara-saṁbhūtam*.

[86] Van Buitenen 1981, p. 133.

[87] Sharma, Morgan and Pitts, p. 280.

[88] Tapasyananda, p. 399.

[89] Gambhīrānanda 1997, p. 622.

304. **aparigraha** "non-acceptance of gifts; non-grasping; non-possessiveness; free from acquisitiveness".
   - aparigrahaḥ "one who does not accept gifts; free from possessiveness". 6.10.
   - tyaktasarvaparigrahaḥ "one who has given up accepting all kinds of gifts; one who has given up all need to possess; one who has renounced all possessions". 4.21.
   - parigraham "greed; acceptance of gifts" 18.53.

305. **aparihārye** "in the inevitable; in the unavoidable". 2.27.

306. **aparimeyām** "immeasurable". 16.11.

307. **aparyāptam** "more than sufficient, unlimited, boundless" *or* "insufficient, incomplete". 1.10.[90]
   - aparyāptam "more than sufficient, unlimited, boundless" *or* "insufficient, incomplete". 1.10.
   - paryāptam "limited; just barely sufficient; sufficient". 1.10.

308. **apaśyat** "he saw". 1.26; 11.13. Also see *paśyati.*

309. **apātrebhyaḥ** "to undeserving people; to unworthy recipients; to those who are not fit persons for a gift". 17.22. Also see *pātre.*

310. **apāvṛtam** "open; opened out". 2.32. Also see *āvṛta.*

311. **aphalākāṅkṣibhiḥ** "by those who do not long for fruits; by those who do not desire rewards; by those who do not covet fruits". 17.11, 17. Also see √ *kāṅkṣ, phala, phalākāṅkṣī.*

312. **aphalaprepsunā** "by a person free from desire for fruits". 18.23. Also see *phala.*

313. **api** "also; and; moreover; even; even though; even if; then". 1.27, 35 (twice), 38; 2.5, 8, 16, 26, 29, 31, 34, 40, 59, 60, 72; 3.5, 8, 20, 31, 33, 36; 4.6 (twice), 13, 15, 16, 17, 20, 22, 30, 36; 5.4, 5, 7, 9, 11; 6.9, 22, 25, 31, 44 (twice), 46, 47; 7.3, 23, 30; 8.6; 9.15, 23 (twice), 25, 29, 30, 32 (twice); 10.37, 39; 11.2, 26, 29, 32, 34, 37, 39, 41, 42,

---

[90] The adjective *aparyāpta* is ambiguous because it can mean either "not sufficient", "unlimited", or "unable to do its work; incompetent" (Apte, p. 101, entry for अपर्याप्त). The noun *aparyāptiḥ* means "insufficiency" (Apte, p. 101, entry for अपर्याप्तिः). The word *paryāptam* is also ambiguous and can mean either sufficient or equal. Various translators have grappled with this ambiguity. Tilak (pp. 854-5) discusses the words in detail and concludes that in this verse *aparyāpta* means *unlimited* or *boundless* and *paryāpta* means *limited.* Divanji defines *aparyāpta* as *incomplete* or *insufficient* (p. 12, entry #269) and defines *paryāpta* as *sufficient* (p. 86, entry #1957). Sargeant (p. 48) notes the ambiguity, citing a paper by Van Buitenen on the matter.

43, 52; 12.1, 10 (twice), 11; 13.2, 17, 19, 22, 23, 25, 31; 14.2; 15.8, 10, 11, 18; 16.7, 13, 14; 17.7, 10, 12; 18.6, 17, 19, 43, 44, 48, 56, 60, 71 (twice). [Meaning of the particle *api* depends on context.]

314. **āpnoti** "one attains; one obtains". 2.70; 3.19; 4.21; 5.12; 18.47, 50. [√ *āp*] Also see *avāpnoti*.

315. **āpnuvanti** "they attain; they incur; they are subjected to (rebirth)". 8.15. [√ *āp*] Also see *prāpnuvanti*.

316. **āpnuyām** "I should attain; I may reach (the highest goal)". 3.2. [√ *āp*] Also see *prāpnuyāt*.

317. **apohanam** "(their) loss; (their) removal; reasoning faculty[91]". 15.15.

318. **apradāya** "without offering; without having given". 3.12.

319. **aprakāśaḥ** "absence of light; absence of illumination; unenlightenment". 14.13. Also see √ *prakāś*.

320. **aprameya** "immeasurable". Also see *pramāṇam*.

- aprameyam "immeasurable". 11.17.
- aprameyam "the Immeasurable One". 11.42. [Used with the effect of an epithet.]
- aprameyasya "of immeasurable". 2.18.

321. **aprāpya** "without attaining; without having acquired". 6.37; 9.3; 16.20. Also see *prāpya*. [*a* + *pra* + √ *āp*]

322. **apratīkāram** "without fighting back; unresisting; not retaliating". 1.46.

323. **apratimaprabhāva** "O Incomparable Glory; O One of Infinite Influence; O One Whose Prowess is Unparalleled". 11.43. Also see *prabhāva*, *yatprabhāvaḥ*.

324. **apratiṣṭha** "without a foundation; without support; unstable". Also see *pratiṣṭh-*.

- **apratiṣṭhaḥ** "without a foundation; without support; unstable". 6.38.
- **apratiṣṭham** "without a foundation; without support; unstable". 16.8.

325. **apravṛttiḥ** "inactivity; indolence; lack of striving". 14.13. Also see √ *pravṛt*.

326. **apriyam** "unliked; unfavorable; unpleasant". 5.20. Also see *priyam*, *tulya-priyāpriyaḥ*.

327. **apsu** "in water". 7.8.

328. **āptum** "to attain; to obtain; to acquire". 5.6; 12.9. [√ *āp*] Also see *avāptum*.

---

[91] Some translators take *apohanam* in the sense of loss or removal, while others take it to mean the sense of reason. Both meanings are found in Apte, p. 109, in the entry for अपोहनं, but Apte cites *BG* 15.15 as an example of meaning "reasoning faculty".

329. **apunarāvṛttim** "not returning again; not subject to return (rebirth)". 5.17. Also see *āvṛttim, saṁsāra, punarāvartinaḥ.*

330. **āpūrya** "filling". 11.30.

331. **āpūryamāṇam** "filled up; filled on all sides; ever being filled". 2.70.

332. √ **ārabh** "to begin; to commence; to undertake; to be active or energetic". See *ārabh-, ārambh-.*

333. **ārabhate** "he begins; he commences". 3.7. [√ *ārabh*] Also see *ārambh-.*

334. **ārabhyate** "it is begun; it is undertaken". 18.25. [√ *ārabh*] Also see *ārambh-.*

335. **ārādhanam** "worship; adoration; reverence". 7.22.[92]

336. **arāgadveṣataḥ** "without being motivated by attachment (*rāga*) or hatred (*dveṣa*); free from preferance or resistance". 18.23.

337. **ārambh-**. [√ *ārabh*] Also see *ārabhate, ārabhyate, prārabhate.*

- anārambhāt "by non-initiation (of action); from non-commencement". 3.4.
- ārambhaḥ "a beginning; undertaking; commencement". 14.12.
- samārambhāḥ "actions that are commenced; enterprises; undertakings". 4.19.
- sarvārambhāḥ "all undertakings". 18.48.
- sarvārambhaparityāgī "one renouncing all undertakings; relinquishing all (selfish) enterprises; one who abandons all (selfish) initiatives". 12.16; 14.25.

338. **ārambhaḥ** "a beginning; undertaking; commencement". 14.12. Also see *ārambh-.*

339. **aratiḥ** "dislike; absence of affection". 13.10.

340. **arcitum** "to honor; to praise; to worship". 7.21. [√ *arc. śraddhayārcitum* = to honor with faith]

341. √ **arh** "to deserve; to merit; to be fit for; to have a right to; to be capable of; to be obliged or required to do a thing (often implying duty or obligation); to be able (often translatable by 'can')". Also see *arha, arhasi, arhati.* [This root is the source of the word *arhat,* ("Worthy One"), which is used as a title by Buddhists and Jains.]

---

[92] See footnote on the entry for the word *rādhanam,* which is the reading adopted in the digital text of the Critical Edition.

342. **arha** "respectable; worthy of respect deserving; entitled to; fitting; proper; appropriate; justified; being required; being obliged; being allowed". Also see √ *arh*.

- arhāḥ "(we) should (not kill); (it is not) justified (for us to kill)". 1.37. [*nārhā vayaṁ hantum. nārhā* = *na* + *arhāḥ*).
- arhau "two men who should be honored; both worthy of reverence[93]; two who deserve to be honored". 2.4. [*pūjārhau* = *pūja* + *arhau*).]

343. **arhasi** "would you (please); may you deign to; you should; you ought (to)". [Pres. 2nd. sing. pres. indic. act. of √ *arh*. The 2nd person sing. used with an infinitive is equivalent to a polite imperative and can be translated as "be pleased to", "deign to", or similar polite constructions.[94] The translation may reflect the relationship between the speakers and the context of what they are discussing. When Kṛṣṇa speaks to Arjuna the sense is "you should", but when Arjuna speaks deferentially to Kṛṣṇa the sense is "would you please".]

- arhasi "you should (not grieve)". 2.25. [*nānuśocitum.* Kṛṣṇa speaking to Arjuna.]
- arhasi "you should (not grieve); you have no cause to grieve[95]". 2.26, 27, 30. [*śocitum arhasi.* Kṛṣṇa speaking to Arjuna.]
- arhasi "do not (waver)[96]; you should not tremble". 2.31. [*na vikampitum arhasi.* Kṛṣṇa speaking to Arjuna.]
- arhasi "you should (act); you ought (to act); you must (act)". 3.20. [*kartum arhasi.* Kṛṣṇa speaking to Arjuna.]
- arhasi "please (dispel this doubt of mine completely); pray resolve this doubt of mine completely[97]; may you please; please see fit to". 6.39. [*etan me saṁśayaṁ kṛṣṇa chettum arhasy aśeṣataḥ.* Arjuna speaking to Kṛṣṇa.]
- arhasi "pray tell me[98]; please (tell); please see fit (to describe)". 10.16. [*vaktum arhasi.* Arjuna speaking to Kṛṣṇa.]

---

93 Edgerton, p. 9.

94 Macdonell, p. 28, entry for अर्ह्. Apte, p. 154, entry for अर्ह्, entry 8.

95 Van Buitenen 1981, p. 77.

96 Van Buitenen 1981, p. 77.

97 Van Buitenen 1981, p. 97.

98 Van Buitenen 1981, p. 109.

- arhasi "please put up with me; please see fit (to tolerate); pray bear with me[99]; be pleased to show mercy[100]; please (be merciful)". 11.44 [*arhasi ... soḍhum.* Arjuna speaking to Kṛṣṇa.] Also see *soḍhum.*
- arhasi "pray do your acts in this world[101]; you should (do action in this world); you are obligligated (to perform the duty here)". 16.24. [*karma kartum ihārhasi.* Kṛṣṇa speaking to Arjuna.]

344. **arhati** "(no one) is able (to do); (no one) can (accomplish)" 2.17. [*kartum arhati*]

345. **ari** "enemy".
- arisūdana "O Destroyer of the Enemy". 2.4.
- mitrāripakṣayoḥ "toward friend or enemy sides". 14.25.
- suhṛnmitrāryudāsīnamadhyasthadveṣyabandhuṣu "in friends, enemies, neutrals, mediators, despicable persons, and relatives". 6.9.

346. **arisūdana** "O destroyer of enemies". 2.4.

347. **ārjavam** "straightforwardness; not having ulterior motives; honesty; rectitude". 13.7; 16.1; 17.14; 18.42.

348. **arjuna** "Arjuna". The name of the third Pāṇḍava brother, a leader on the Pāṇḍava side of the great war. His conversation with Kṛṣṇa forms the main content of the *Bhagavadgītā.* A famed hero, he is often referred to by epithets listed in the section "Epithets in the *Bhagavadgītā*" (page 11).
- arjunaḥ "Arjuna". 1.47.
- arjuna uvāca "Arjuna said". 2.4, 54; 3.1, 36; 4.4; 5.1; 6.33, 37; 8.1; 10.12; 11.1, 15, 36, 51; 12.1; 14.21; 17.1; 18.1, 73. [Used to introduce words spoken by Arjuna.]
- arjunam "to Arjuna". 11.50.
- arjuna "O Arjuna". 2.2, 45; 3.7; 4.5, 9, 37; 6.16, 32, 46; 7.16, 26; 8.16, 27; 9.19; 10.32, 39, 42; 11.47, 54; 18.9, 34, 61.
- bhīmārjunasamāḥ "like Bhīma and Arjuna; the peers of Bhīma and Arjuna". 1.4. [Referring to other warriors on the battlefield.]
- keśavārjunayoḥ "Keśava (Kṛṣṇa) and Arjuna". 18.76.

349. **arpaṇa** "an offering; an act of dedication".
- brahmārpaṇam "*Brahman* is the offering". 4.24. Also see *brahman.*

---

[99] Van Buitenen 1981, p. 119.

[100] Edgerton, p. 59.

[101] Van Buitenen 1981, p. 135.

- madarpaṇam "(do it as) an offering to me; surrender it to me". 9.27.

350. **arpitamanobuddhiḥ** "dedicating mind and intellect[102]; with mind and intellect surrendered; with mind and intellect focused". 8.7; 12.14. [*mayyarpitamano-buddhiḥ* ="One who has surrendered his mind and intellect to me"[103]] Also see *buddhi, manas.*

351. **ārtaḥ** "one in miserable condition; one who is afflicted; the distressed; the suffering". 7.16.

352. **arthaḥ** "gain; worldly prosperity; objective; goal; motive; object (of sensory perception)". 2.46; 3.18. Also see *arth-, anukampārtham, atattvārthavat, aty-artham, avahāsārtham, dambhārtham, dharmakāmārthān, dharmasaṁ-sthāpanārthāya, indriyārtha, kāmabhogārtham, madarth-, parasyotsādanārtham, prārthayante, pratyupakārārtham, saṁjñārtham, sarvārthān, satkāramānapūjārtham, tadartham, tadarthīyam, tattvajñānārtha-darśanam, yajñārthāt.*

353. **arthakāmān** "with desire (*kāma*) for gain (*arthaḥ*); who desire worldly prosperity; who seek their ends[104]". 2.5. Also see *kāma.*

354. **arthārthī** "one who aims at a particular object[105]; he who seeks personal ends[106]; the seeker of wealth". 7.16.

355. **arthasaṁcayān** "accumulation of wealth; a collection of objects". 16.12.

356. **arthavyapāśrayaḥ** "subordination to any purpose; needing any outcome; rely upon an end; dependence upon an object[107]". 3.18. Also see *āśrita.*

---

[102] Warrier, p. 278.

[103] Divanji, p. 112, entry #2561.

[104] Minor (p. 31) discusses an ambiguity of how to translate *arthakāmān* in verse 2.5. It is usually taken as modifying *gurūn* ("elders seeking their ends"), but some translators (e.g., Barnett) take it with *bhogān* as applying to Arjuna's goals ("I would enjoy the delights of wealth and pleasure"). Edgerton (pp. 9, 92, note 1 on chapter 2) follows the first approach and adds a note that interfering with a *guru*'s desires was considered a sin. His translation reads: "By having slain my elders who seek their ends, right in this world I should eat food smeared with blood." Warrier (p. 17) is similar: "Killing these people who seek to gain ends of their own, I should be tasting blood-stained enjoyments." Some translators shade the wording as a criticism of the elders, e.g., Zaehner (p. 123) "Were I to slay [my] teachers, ambitious though they be, then should I be eating blood-sullied food."

[105] Divanji, p. 17, entry #375.

[106] Edgerton, p. 39.

[107] Divanji, p. 16, entry #372.

357. **arthe** "for the sake of; in the matter of; in purpose".

- aparihārye 'rthe "in the unavoidable matter of". 2.27.
- indriyasyendriyasyārthe "due to the senses and the objects of the senses; in the senses in relation to their objects". 3.34. Also see *indriya.*
- madarthe "for my sake". 1.9. Also see *madartham.*
- yeṣām arthe "for the sake of whom". 1.33.

358. **āruruksoḥ** "of one who wishes to rise; of (for) someone who wants to climb". 6.3. [*āruruksor muner yogam* = for the sage who wishes to ascend to *yoga*]

359. **aryamā** "Aryaman; the king of a class of the Pitṛs[108]". 10.29. [Aryaman ("comrade") was the first person to enter the realm of departed ancestors (the *manes*), and is now their leader.]

360. √ **aś** "to eat; to partake of". Also see *anna.*

- anaśnataḥ (*an-aśnataḥ*) "one who does not eat (enough)". 6.16. Also see √ *aś.*
- aśnāmi "I partake of; I eat; I accept". 9.26. [Speaking of accepting offerings.]
- aśnan "while eating". 5.8.
- aśnanti "they enjoy (divine pleasures); they partake of (divine pleasures)". 9.20.
- aśnāsi "you eat". 9.27.
- atyaśnataḥ (*ati-aśnataḥ*) "one who overeats; one who eats too much". 6.16.

361. **āśā** "hope; expectation". Also see *āśāpāśaśataiḥ, moghāśā, nirāśīḥ.*

362. **asadgrāhān** "false notions; untrue ideas". 16.10. Also see *asat.*

363. **āsādya** "having gone to; having attained". 9.20.

364. **asakta** "detached; unattached". Also see *asakt-, sakta.*

- asaktaḥ "detached; unattached". 3.7, 19 (twice), 25.
- asaktam "detached; unattached". 9.9; 13.14.

365. **asaktabuddhiḥ** "endowed with an unattached intellect; one who is free from a sense of attachment". 18.49. Also see *asakta, buddhi.*

366. **aśaktaḥ** "incapable; unable". 12.11.

367. **āsaktamanāḥ** "with mind attached to Me; fixing your mind on Me". 7.1. Also see *manas, -manāḥ, sakta.* [*mayy āsaktamanāḥ*]

---

[108] Divanji, p. 17, entry #378.

368. **asaktātmā** "having no attractions; one whose heart is not attached to anything". 5.21. Also see *asakta, ātman.* [*bāhyasparśeṣv asaktātmā* = disinterested in outer sense-impressions]

369. **asaktiḥ** "detachment; absence of attachment". 13.9.

370. **āsam** "I was; I existed". 2.12.

371. **aśamaḥ** "lack of serenity; absence of mental peace; restlessness". 14.12. Also see *śama.*

372. **asamarthaḥ** "unable; incapable of doing a thing". 12.10. Also see *sāmarthyam.* [*a-samarthaḥ*]

373. **asaṁmohaḥ** "lack of confusion; absence of delusion; clarity". 10.4. Also see *moha, saṁmoha.*

374. **asaṁmūḍhaḥ** "undeluded; not confused". 5.20; 10.3; 15.19. Also see *mūḍha,* √ *muh.*

375. **asaṁnyastasaṁkalpaḥ** "without renouncing intention (for results); without detaching from the purpose". 6.2. Also see *saṁkalpa,* √ *saṁnyas, saṁnyasta.*

376. **asaṁśaya** "without doubt". Also see *saṁśaya.*
- asaṁśayam "without doubt; undoubtedly". 6.35; 7.1.
- asaṁśayaḥ "without doubt". 8.7; 18.68.

377. **asaṁyatātmanā** "by one who is not self-controlled". 6.36. Also see *ātman, saṁyam-, yatātman.*

378. **āsana** "sitting; seat".
- ācāryopāsanam "sitting close to the teacher; serving the teacher; showing respect for one's mentor". 13.7.
- āsanam "seat". 6.11.
- kamalāsanastham "seated on a lotus seat". 11.15.
- upaviśyāsane "sitting on a (suitable) seat; having taken a fixed posture[109]". 6.12.
- vihāraśayyāsanabhojaneṣu "while at play (*vihāra*), resting (*śayya*), sitting (*āsana*), or with food (*bhojana*)". 11.42.

379. **asaṅgaśastreṇa** "with the weapon of detachment". 15.3. Also see *saṅga, śastra.*

380. **aśāntasya** "of one who is not peaceful; of one whose mind is not at peace". 2.66. Also see *śāntaḥ.*

381. **āśāpāśaśataiḥ** "with a hundred snares of hopes". 16.12.

382. **asapatnam** "without a rival; unrivaled". 2.8. Also see *sapatnān.*

---

[109] Divanji (p. 28, entry #638) notes that this may be a reference to a body posture (*āsana*).

383. **aśastram** "devoid of weapons; unarmed". 1.46. Also see *śastra*.

384. **aśāstravihitam** "that which is not prescribed by scriptures; not in accordance with guidelines in the scriptures". 17.5. Also see *śāstram, vihita*.

385. **aśāśvatam** "transient, fleeting, impermanent". 8.15. Also see *śāśvata*.

386. **asat** "non-existent; non-being; unreal; untrue; untruthful". 9.19; 11.37; 13.12; 17.28. Also see *asataḥ, gṛhītvāsadgrāhān, sat*.

387. **asataḥ** "the non-existent; the unreal". 2.16. Also see *asat, sataḥ*.

388. **asatkṛtaḥ** "not done well; not treated with due respect; disrespected; insulted; badly treated". 11.42.

389. **asatkṛtam** "without respect; disrespectfully; not done well". 17.22.

390. **asatyam** "unreal; false". 16.8. Also see *satya*.

391. **asau** "that". 11.26; 16.14.

392. **āśaya** "receptacle; abode; seat; source; the heart, mind, or seat of feelings of a being[110]".

- āśayāt "from (their) source (the flowers)". 15.8
- sarvabhūtāśayasthitaḥ "located in the heart of all beings". 10.20. Also see *sthita*.

393. **āścaryāṇi** "wonders; wonderful things". 11.6.

394. **āścaryavat** "wonderous". 2.29 (three times). Also see *sarvāścaryamayam*.

395. **aśeṣataḥ** "completely; entirely; without reservation". 6.24, 39; 7.2; 18.11.

396. **aśeṣeṇa** "completely; entirely; without reservation". 4.35; 10.16; 18.29, 63.

397. **asi** "you are". 4.3, 36; 8.2; 10.17; 11.38, 40, 42, 43, 52, 53; 12.10, 11; 16.5; 18.64, 65. [√ *as*]

398. **asiddhau** "in non-attainment; in failure". 4.22. Also see *siddhau, siddhy-asiddhyoḥ*.

399. **asinā** "with the sword". 4.42. [*jñāna-asinā* = with the sword of knowledge]

400. **āsīnaḥ** "sitting".

- āsīnaḥ "sitting". 14.23.
- āsīnam "sitting". 9.9.

401. **āsīta** "one should sit; he should remain seated". 2.54, 61; 6.14.

402. **asitaḥ** "Asita". 10.13. [Name of a celestial sage.[111]] Also see *Devala*.

---

[110] Apte, p. 235, entry for आशी, subentry आशयः, meaning 8, where *BG* 10.20 is given as a usage example.

[111] Sargeant (p. 423) treats "Asita Devala" as a single name. Divanji (p. 22, entry #497) says Asita was the name of the sage whose family name was Devala. This issue is noted by Minor (p. 314) who summarizes other views on the two names Asita and Devala.

403. **asmābhiḥ** "by us". 1.39.

404. **asmadīyaiḥ** "with ours; by those who are on our side". 11.26.

405. **asmākam** "our; of ours". 1.7, 10.

406. **asmān** "us". 1.36.

407. **asmāt** "from this". 1.39.

408. **asmi** "I am". 7.8, 9 (twice), 10, 11 (twice); 10.21, 22 (four times), 23 (twice), 24, 25 (twice), 28 (three times), 29 (twice), 30, 31 (three times), 33, 36 (three times), 37, 38 (three times); 11.32, 45, 51; 15.18; 16.15; 18.55, 73. [√ *as*]

409. **asmin** "in this". 1.22; 2.13; 3.3; 8.2; 13.22; 14.11; 16.6.

410. **aśnāmi** "I partake of; I accept". 9.26. [Speaking of accepting offerings.] Also see √ *aś.*

411. **aśnan** "eating". 5.8. Also see √ *aś.*

412. **aśnanti** "they enjoy (divine pleasures); they partake of (divine pleasures)". 9.20. Also see √ *aś.*

413. **aśnāsi** "you eat". 9.27. Also see √ *aś.*

414. **aśnute** "one attains". 3.4; 5.21; 6.28; 13.12; 14.20.

415. **aśocyān** "those for whom one need not worry; that which one need not be sorry for". 2.11. Also see √ *śuc.*

416. **aśoṣya** "that which cannot be dried up". 2.24. Also see *śoṣayati.*

417. **aśraddadhāna** "lacking faith". Also see *aśraddhayā, śraddhā.*

- aśraddadhānaḥ "one who has no faith; lacking trust". 4.40.
- aśraddadhānāḥ "those who have no faith; those who do not trust in…". 9.3.

418. **aśraddhayā** "without faith; with lack of faith". 17.28. Also see *aśraddadhāna, śraddhā.*

419. **aśrauṣam** "I have heard". 18.74. [√ *śrū*]

420. **āśrayaḥ** "depending on; one who has taken resort to something". 7.1. [*madāśrayaḥ* = depending on me] Also see *āśrita.*

421. **āśrayet** "it would take hold of; it would cling to; it would light upon (us)[112]". 1.36. Also see *āśrita, madāśrayaḥ, madvyapāśrayaḥ.*

422. **āśrita** "abiding in; resorting to; taking shelter; having the support of". Also see *anāśritaḥ, arthavyapāśrayaḥ, āśrayet, madāśrayaḥ,*

[112] Edgerton, p. 7.

madvyapāśrayaḥ, nirāśrayaḥ, saṁśritāḥ, samupāśritaḥ, śritāḥ, upāśrita, vyapāśritya.

- āśritaḥ "dependent on". 12.11; 15.14.
- āśritāḥ "resorting to; taking recourse in". 7.15; 9.13.
- āśritam "having taken recourse to the support (of a body); embodied [*tanum āśritam*]". 9.11.
- āśritya "taking shelter; taking recourse to; after adopting". 7.29; 16.10; 18.59.

423. **asṛṣṭānnam** (*asṛṣṭa-annam*) "without distributing food; with no food offered". 17.13. Also see *anna, sṛṣṭam,* √ *sṛj.*
424. **aśrupūrṇākulekṣaṇam** "whose troubled (*ākula*) eyes (*īkṣaṇam*) were filled with tears (*aśru-pūrṇa*)". 2.1.
425. **aṣṭadhā** "eightfold; in eight ways". 7.4.
426. **āste** "one sits". 3.6; 5.13.
427. **āsthāya** "having recourse to; having adopted; practicing". 7.20. Also see *āsthita.*
428. **asthiram** "unstable; unsteady". 6.26. Also see *sthira.*
429. **āsthita** "established; attained; adopting; resorting to". Also see *āsthāya, sthita, avasthita.*
    - āsthitaḥ "established; endowed with; adopting". 5.4; 6.31; 7.18; 8.12.
    - āsthitāḥ "attained". 3.20.
430. **asti** "it is; he is; one is". 2.40, 42, 66; 3.22; 4.31, 40; 6.16; 7.7; 8.5; 9.29; 10.18, 19, 39, 40; 11.43; 16.13, 15; 18.40. [√ *as*]
431. **āstikyam** "having faith in scriptures; (religious) faith". 18.42.
432. **astu** "let there be!; may it be!". 2.47; 3.10; 11.31, 39, 40. [√ *as*]
433. **āśu** "quickly; speedily; instantaneously; at once". 2.65.
434. **aśubhān** "inauspicious ones; undesirable ones; unpurified ones". 16.19. Also see *śubh-.*
435. **aśubhāt** "from inauspiciousness". 4.16; 9.1. [Used here to refer to the cycle of births and deaths (*saṁsāra*) from which one seeks to be liberated.] Also see *śubh-.*
436. **aśucau** "unclean; foul". 16.16. Also see *aśuciḥ, śucau.*
437. **aśuciḥ** "one who is of unclean habits; impure". 18.27. Also see *śuciḥ.*
438. **aśucivratāḥ** "those who have taken unclean vows; determined to act with impure intentions". 16.10. Also see *aśuciḥ, śuci, vrata.*
439. **asukham** "unhappy". 9.33. Also see *sukham.*

440. **asura** "demon" [Noun; also see *āsura* "demonic".]
   - gandharvayakṣāsurasiddhasaṁghāḥ "groups of *gandharva*-s, *yakṣa*-s, *asura*-s, and Adepts". 11.22.

441. **āsura** "demonic" [Adj.; Also see *asura* "demon".] Also see *āsuraniścayān*.
   - āsuraḥ "demonic". 16.6.
   - āsurāḥ "demonic ones; demonic men". 16.7.
   - āsuraṁ "demonic". 7.15; 16.6.
   - āsurīm "demonic". 9.12; 16.4, 20.
   - āsurīṣu "into demonic". 16.19.
   - nibandhāyāsurī "the demonic quality (*āsurī*) leads to bondage (*nibandhāya*)". 16.5. [*āsurī* is nom. sing. fem.; agrees with *saṁpad*.]

442. **āsuraniścayān** "one who makes a demonic resolve; having demonic influences". 17.6. Also see *āsura, niścaya*.

443. **aśuśrūṣave** "to one who does not want to listen; to one who is inattentive; to one who has not rendered service; to one who is not obedient". 18.67. Also see *anuśuśruma*.

444. **aśvānām** "of horses; among horses". 10.27.

445. **asvargyam** "unheavenly; not likely to lead to heaven". 2.2. Also see *svargam*.

446. **āśvāsayām āsa** "he caused to take heart; he consoled; he calmed; he helped him recover his breath; he revived his spirits". 11.50. [Literal senses are based on recovering normal breathing (√ *śvas*).[113] This is a causal form of √ *śvas* + √ *ās* with the prefix *ā*. For this construction also see *darśayām āsa* 11.9, 50.]

447. **aśvattha** "the *Aśvattha* tree". [Probably *ficus religiosus*, similar to a banyan tree.][114]
   - aśvatthaḥ "the *aśvattha* tree". 10.26.
   - aśvattham "the *aśvattha* tree". 15.1, 3.

448. **aśvatthāmā** "Aśvatthāmā; Aśvatthāman" 1.8. [The son of Droṇa. Aśvatthāmā is the nom. sing. form of the masc. noun *Aśvatthāman*. Both forms of the name appear in different translations.]

449. **aśvinau** "the two Aśvins". 11.6, 22.

---

[113] Apte, p. 237, entry for आश्वस्, gives "to breathe" as first meaning, with "to breathe freely" as the idea behind "take courage" and other derived senses.

[114] Hill (pp. 236-7, note 1) has a detailed discussion of the nature of this tree, which is common in India. Hill dismisses the idea that it is a banyan, and explains the growth pattern clearly.

450. **asya** "of this; of it; of him". 2.17, 40, 59, 65, 67; 3.18, 34, 40; 6.39; 9.3, 17; 11.18, 38, 43, 52; 13.21; 15.3.

451. **asyām** "in this; in it". 2.72.

452. **ataḥ** "from this; hence; therefore". [Sense depends on context]

- ataḥ param "further on; from this time onward". 2.12.
- ataḥ "from this; therefore". 9.24.
- ata ūrdhvam "from now on; henceforth". 12.8.
- ataḥ "from this; to this". 13.11.
- ataḥ "from this; therefore". 15.18.

453. **atandritaḥ** "free from laziness; without indolence; unwearied". 3.23.

454. **atapaskāya** "to one who does not practice austerities; to one who does not perform penance; an irreligious person". 18.67. Also see *tapas.*

455. **ātatāyinaḥ** "those who have bows drawn to take another's life; aggressors who commit heinous crimes[115]; an enemy who takes an offensive[116]; terrorists". 1.36.

456. **atattvārthavat** "not concerned with truth[117]; far from the truth; that which does not convey the correct notion[118]". 18.22. Also see *tattva, arthaḥ.*

457. **atha** "now; also; then; and". 1.20, 26; 2.26, 33; 3.36; 11.5, 40; 12.9, 11; 18.58. [Often used in literary works to show that a new topic is being taken up.]

458. **athavā** "or; alternatively". 6.42; 10.42; 11.42.

459. **atho** "also; then; and then". 4.35.

460. **atimānaḥ** "excessive egotism; excessive pride". 16.4.[119] Also see *atimānitā.*

461. **atimānitā** "excessive egotism; excessive pride". 16.3. [*nātimānitā = na + atimānitā*] Also see *atimānaḥ, amānitvam.*[120]

462. **atīndriyam** "beyond the senses; transcendental". 6.21. Also see *indriya.*

463. **atinīcam** "too low". 6.11.

464. **atiricyate** "it exceeds; it surpasses". 2.34.

---

[115] Summarizing Apte, p. 208, entry for आततायिन्, meaning 2.

[116] Divanji, p. 24, entry #547.

[117] Gambhīrānanda 1998, p. 937.

[118] Divanji, p. 3, entry #67.

[119] In verse 16.4, the Critical Edition reads *atimānaḥ,* but many vulgate editions read *abhimānaḥ,* with similar meaning.

[120] Divanji (p. 78, entry #1779) has a note that it would be improper to treat *nātimānitā* as two separate words (*na* and *atimānitā*) because what is intended is *anatimānitā* but *na* is substituted for *an.*

465. **ātiṣṭha** "practice; be engaged in". 4.42. [*ātiṣṭhottiṣṭha* = *ātiṣṭha uttiṣṭha*] Also see *uttiṣṭha, tiṣṭh-*.
466. **atisvapnaśīlasya** "one who sleeps too much". 6.16. Also see *svapna*.
467. **atītaḥ** "one who has gone beyond; one who transcends". 14.21; 15.18. Also see *atītya, dvaṁdvātīta, guṇātītaḥ*.
468. **atitaranti** "they cross beyond". 13.25. Also see √ *tṛ*.
469. **atītya** "having gone beyond; going beyond; after transcending". Also see *atītaḥ, dvaṁdvātīta, guṇātītaḥ, samatītya, vyatītāni*.
    - atītya "having gone beyond". 14.20.
    - samatītya "having gone beyond". 14.26.
470. **atīva** "exceedingly; excessively". 12.20.
471. **ativartate** "it transcends; one goes beyond". 6.44; 14.21. [See *śabdabrahmātivartate*]
472. **ātmabhāvasthaḥ** "located in their innermost self; dwelling within their own beings; residing in their hearts; residing in their own very being[121]; remaining in my own true state[122]". 10.11.[123]
473. **ātmabuddhiprasādajam** "arising from clear understanding of the self; that which arises from the purity of one's intellect[124]; which springs from the serenity of one's own spirit[125]; resulting from the favour of one's own intellect[126]; sprung from serenity of soul and of intellect[127]". 18.37. Also see *buddhi, prasāda*.
474. **ātmaiva** [*ātmā eva*] "the self itself; the very self; the very soul". 6.5 (twice), 6 (twice); 7.18. Also see *ātman*.
475. **ātmakāraṇāt** "(doing) for themselves alone; for one's own sake or benefit". 3.13. Also see *ātman*.
476. **ātmamāyayā** "by my *māya*; with my *māya*". 4.6. Also see *māya*.

---

[121] Van Buitenen 1981, p. 109.

[122] Edgerton, p. 51.

[123] Zaehner (pp. 294-5) discusses differing translations of this compound, concluding with the remark that "This revelation of God in the self might be called the 'highest wisdom' corresponding to the 'highest love-and-loyalty' to God mentioned in 18.54."

[124] Gambhīrānanda 1997, p. 699.

[125] Van Buitenen 1981, p. 141.

[126] Divanji, p. 25, entry #556.

[127] Edgerton, p. 87.

477. **ātman** "the self; oneself; the inner self; the soul; the higher self; the lower self; the mind". [The word *ātman* is used with a variety of meanings in the *BG,* but rarely in a purely philosophical sense. Depending on context it may be simply a reflexive pronoun ("oneself"), or it may refer to the inner self with the sense of "the heart", "the mind", or "the physical body". It may also refer to the entire individual empirical self. See page 315 for a Theme Guide that notes examples where different meanings of *ātman* are contrasted within individual verses.] Also see *adhyātma, ahaṁkāravimūḍhātmā, akṛtātmānaḥ, anātmanaḥ, asaktātmā, asaṁyatātmanā, ātma-, avyayātmā, brahmayogayuktātmā, dharmātmā, dhṛtyātmānam, hiṁsātmakaḥ, jitātmā, jitātmanaḥ, jñānāsinātmanaḥ, jñānavijñānatṛptātmā, kāmātmānaḥ, madgatenāntarātmanā, mahātman, māhātmyam, mūḍhagrāheṇātmanaḥ, naṣṭātmānaḥ, niyatātmabhiḥ, paramātmā, paricaryātmakam, praśāntātmā, prasannātmā, pravyathitāntarātmā, prayatātmanaḥ, rāgātmakam, rasātmakaḥ, saṁnyāsayogayuktātmā, saṁnyasyādhyātmacetasā, saṁśayātmanaḥ, sarvabhūtātmabhūtātmā, tulyanindātmasaṁstutiḥ, vaśyātmanā, vidheyātmā, viditātmanām, vijitātmā, vimūḍhātmā, viśuddhātmā, vyavasāyātmikā, yatacittātmā, yatātm-, yogayuktātmā, yuktātmā.*

- ātmā "the self". 6.5 (twice), 6 (three times); 7.18; 9.5; 10.20; 13.32.
- ātmanā "with the self; by the self". 2.55; 3.43; 6.5, 6, 20; 10.15; 13.24, 28.
- ātmanaḥ "of the self". 4.42; 5.16; 6.5 (twice), 6, 11, 19; 8.12; 10.18, 19; 16.21, 22; 17.19; 18.39.
- ātmānām "the self". 3.43; 4.7; 6.5 (twice), 10, 15, 20, 28, 29; 9.34; 10.15; 11.3, 4; 13.24, 28, 29; 18.16, 51.
- ātmani "in the self". 2.55; 3.17; 4.35, 38; 5.21; 6.18, 20, 26, 29; 13.24; 15.11.
- tadātmānaḥ "those who have identified themselves with it; whose self is that; at one with that; with the self directed toward that". 5.17.

478. **ātmaparadeheṣu** "in the bodies of themselves and others; in one's own and another's body". 16.18. Also see *deha, paradharma.*

479. **ātmaratiḥ** "one who delights in the *ātman*; one who takes pleasure in the Self". 3.17.

480. **ātmasaṁbhāvitāḥ** "self-centered; puffed up by their egos[128]". 16.17. Also see *bhāvita, saṁbhava.*

481. **ātmasaṁstham** "well centered in the self; reposing within itself". 6.25. [*ātmasaṁsthaṁ manaḥ kṛtvā* = "having made the mind fixed on the Self" or "merges his mind in the self"[129]]

482. **ātmasaṁyamayogāgnau** "in the fire of the *yoga* of self-control; in the (internal) fire of yogic restraint; in the fire of the discipline of self-control". 4.27. Also see *agni, saṁyama, saṁyamāgniṣu, yoga.*

483. **ātmaśuddhaye** "for self-purification; for the purification of the self". 5.11. Also see *ātman, ātmaviśuddhaye, viśuddhātmā, śuddh-.*

484. **ātmatṛptaḥ** "one who is satisfied within oneself; one who is contented with the self". 3.17. Also see *nityatṛptaḥ, jñānavijñānatṛptātmā, tṛptiḥ.*

485. **ātmaupamyena** "with a sense of likeness to one's own self; the quality of looking upon others as similar to oneself". 6.32.

486. **ātmavaśyaiḥ** "with (senses) under his own control; by the self-disciplined ones". 2.64. Also see *vaśam, vaśyātmanā.*

487. **ātmavāt** "well established in the Self; having realized the Self; possessed of the Self (the *ātman*); self-possessed; one who has acquired control over his heart; the master of yourself; composed".
   - ātmavān "well established in the Self". 2.45.
   - ātmavantam "well established in the Self". 4.41.

488. **ātmavibhūtayaḥ** "special manifestations of the self; self-manifestations; the forms in which one's self has become manifest in a special way". 10.16, 19. Also see *vibhūti.*

489. **ātmavinigrahaḥ** "self-control; complete control over one's lower self". 13.7; 17.16. Also see *nigraha.*

490. **ātmaviśuddhaye** "for the purification of the self; complete purification of oneself". 6.12. Also see *ātmaśuddhaye, viśuddhātmā, śuddh-.*

491. **ātmayogāt** "by my own *yoga*; by my yogic power". 11.47.

492. **atra** "here; in this case; in this matter". 1.4, 23; 4.16; 8.2, 4, 5; 10.7; 18.14.

493. **āttha** "you say". 11.3. [*yathāttha* = just as you say]

494. **atyadbhutam** "extremely wonderful". 18.77. Also see *adbhutam.*

---

[128] Van Buitenen 1981, p. 133.

[129] Van Buitenen 1981, p. 95.

495. **atyāginām** "of non-renouncers; for those who are not men of abandonment; those who have not renounced the world; people unable to relinquish". 18.12. Also see √ *tyaj.*

496. **atyantam** "endless; boundless; everlasting; absolute". 6.28.

497. **ātyantikam** "the final; the highest; the best; the absolute". 6.21.

498. **atyartham** "intensely; exceedingly; very much". 7.17.

499. **atyaśnataḥ** "one who overeats; one who eats excessively". 6.16. Also see *anaśnataḥ,* √ *aś.* [*ati-aśnataḥ*]

500. **atyeti** "one goes beyond; one transcends; one excels". 8.28. [*ati* + √ *i*] Also see *eti.*

501. **atyucchritam** "too high; too elevated". 6.11.

502. **atyuṣṇa** "extremely hot". 17.9. Also see *kaṭvamlalavaṇātyuṣṇatīkṣṇarūkṣa-vidāhinaḥ.* [*ati* + *uṣṇa*]

503. **auṣadham** "herb[130]; edible herb[131]; medicinal herb[132]; medicine[133]". 9.16. Also see *oṣadhīḥ.*

504. **avācyavādān** "abusive words; views that should not be expressed; things that are not to be uttered". 2.36. Also see *vācyam, prajñāvādān.*

505. **avadhyaḥ** "unassailable; inviolable; not liable to be killed". 2.30.

506. **avagaccha** "understand!; know!". 10.41. Also see *gaccha.*

507. **avagamam** "understandable; comprehensible". 9.2. [*pratyakṣāvagamam* = understandable (*avagamam*) by direct perception (*pratyakṣa*)]

508. **avahāsārtham** "for the sake of fun". 11.42. Also see *arthaḥ.*

509. √ **avajñā** "to have a low opinion of; to despise; to treat with contempt; to disregard."[134]

- avajānanti "they look down upon; they disrespect". 9.11.
- avajñātam "as an insult; with contempt". 17.22.

510. **avanipālasaṁghaiḥ** "with groups of kings". 11.26.

511. **avāpnoti** "one gets; one acquires; one attains". 15.8; 16.23; 18.56. Also see *avāp-, āpnoti.*

---

[130] Hill, p. 185.

[131] Warrier, p. 308.

[132] Edgerton, p. 47.

[133] Śaṅkara's commentary says the word *auṣadham* may mean the food eaten by all creatures, such as rice and barley, or it may mean healing herbs which serve as medicine. See Gambhīrānanda 1997, pp. 382-3, and Warrier, p. 308.

[134] Apte, p. 161, entry for अवज्ञा.

512. **avāpsyasi** "you will incur; you will attain". 2.33, 38, 53; 12.10. Also see *avāp-*, *prāpsyasi*.

513. **avāpsyatha** "you (all) will attain". 3.11. [*ava* + √ *āp*.] Also see *avāp-*.

514. **avāptavyam** "is to be attained; is to be gained; fit to be acquired'. 3.22. Also see *anavāptam*, *avāp-*.

515. **avāptum** "to attain; to acquire". 6.36. [*ava* + √ *āp*] Also see *āptum*, *anavāptam*, *avāp-*.

516. **avāpya** "having attained; having acquired; after obtaining". 2.8. Also see *avāp-*.

517. **avāpyate** "it is attained; it is acquired". 12.5. Also see *avāp-*.

518. **avaram** "inferior; lower". 2.49.

519. **āvartate** "one returns". 8.26. Also see *āvṛttim*.

520. **āvartinaḥ** "one who is likely to return; one who is subject to rebirth". 8.16. See *punarāvartinaḥ*, *āvṛttim*.

521. **avaśa** "without control; compelled; involuntarily; against one's will; as if by force". Also see *vaśam*.

- avaśaḥ "without control; compelled". 3.5; 6.44; 8.19; 18.60.
- avaśam "without control; compelled". 9.8.

522. **avasādayet** "one should cause to lower down; one should degrade". 6.5.

523. **avaśiṣyate** "it remains". 7.2.

524. **avaṣṭabhya** "by taking recourse to; relying on; depending on; having adopted (views)". 9.8; 16.9.

525. **avasthātum** "to stand firm; to stay at rest". 1.30. [*na ca śaknomy avasthātum* = "I am not able to stand firmly"[135]; "I am not able to hold my ground"[136]; "I cannot stand still"[137]]

526. **avasthita** "standing; situated; located; posted; assembled". Also see *sthita*, *āsthita*, *samavasthita*, *vyavasthita*, *jñānāvasthitacetasaḥ*.

- avasthitaḥ "located". 9.4; 13.32.
- avasthitāḥ "standing; stationed; assembled". 1.11, 33; 2.6; 11.32.
- avasthitam "located". 15.11.
- avasthitān "standing; staying; arrayed". 1.22, 27.

---

[135] Gambhīrānanda 1997, p. 22.

[136] Van Buitenen 1981, p. 71.

[137] Edgerton, p. 6.

527. **avatiṣṭh-** "stand firm; remain unmoved". Also see *tiṣṭh-*.
- avatiṣṭhate "is well-established". 6.18.
- avatiṣṭhati "one stands firm; one maintains balance". 14.23.
- paryavatiṣṭhate "one becomes steady; one becomes firmly established". 2.65.

528. **āvayoḥ** "of ours; of the two of us". 18.70.
529. **avekṣe** "I see; I look at; I observe; I perceive". 1.23.
530. **avekṣya** "seeing; looking at; observing; perceiving". 2.31.
531. **āveśitacetasām** "of those whose minds are focused on (Me)". 12.7.
532. **āveśya** "located; having focused; having become engrossed in". 8.10; 12.2.
533. **avibhaktam** "undivided; unfragmented". 13.16; 18.20. Also see *vibhakta*.
534. **avidhipūrvakam** "without regard for prescribed procedure; not in the prescribed form; not in the enjoined fashion[138]; not according to the (Vedic) injunctions[139]". 9.23; 16.17. Also see *śāstravidhim, śāstravidhānoktam, vidhānoktāḥ, vidhidṛṣṭaḥ, vidhihīnam*.
535. **avidvāṁsaḥ** "the unwise; unwise people; ignorant people". 3.25. Also see *vidvān*.
536. **avijñeyam** "that which cannot be known; incomprehensible". 13.15. Also see *vijñana, jñeyam*.
537. **avikampena** "with unshakable (*yoga*); with unwavering (*yoga*); with unswerving (discipline)[140]". 10.7. Also see *vikampitum*.
538. **avikāryaḥ** "immutable; incapable of undergoing any change". 2.25. Also see *vikāra*.
539. **avināśi** "indestructible; imperishable; immortal". 2.17. Also see *anāśinaḥ, naśy-, vinaś-, vināś-, nāśitam*.
540. **avināśinam** "indestructible; immortal". 2.21. Also see *anāśinaḥ, naśy-, vinaś-, vināś-*.
541. **avinaśyantam** "not perishing; imperishable; indestructible". 13.27. Also see *naśy-, vinaś-, vināś-*.
542. **avipaścitaḥ** "the unwise ones; the unlearned". 2.42. Also see *vipaścitaḥ*.

---

138 Edgerton, p. 48.
139 Edgerton, p. 77.
140 Edgerton, p. 50.

543. **āviṣṭa** "overpowered; overcome by; filled with; possessed by".
- kṛpayāviṣṭam "disturbed by compassion; overcome by sorrow; filled with pity[141]". 2.1.
- parayāviṣṭaḥ "overwhelmed by supreme (compassion)". 1.28. [*kṛpayā parayāviṣṭaḥ* = "overwhelmed by supreme compassion"[142]]
- sattvasamāviṣṭaḥ "imbued with *sattva*[143]; inspired by *sattva*[144]; one who is possessed all over by the Sattvaguṇa[145]; filled with goodness[146]; man of integrity[147]". 18.10.
- vismayāviṣṭaḥ "awestruck with astonishment; possessed by wonder; filled with amazement". 11.14.

544. **āviśya** "having entered; having penetrated; taking possession of". 15.13, 17.
545. **āvriyate** "it is covered". 3.38. Also see *āvṛta*.
546. **āvṛta** "covered over; enveloped". Also see *samāvṛta, āvṛtya, āvriyate, apāvṛtam*.
- āvṛtā "covered". 18.32.
- āvṛtaḥ "covered". 3.38.
- āvṛtāḥ "covered". 18.48.
- āvṛtam "covered". 3.38, 39; 5.15.

547. **āvṛttim** "return; rebirth". 8.23. Also see *anāvṛttim, apunarāvṛttim, āvartate, nivartate, nivartante, nivartanti, mṛtyusaṁsāravartmani.*
548. **āvṛtya** "having covered over; having enveloped". 3.40; 13.13; 14.9. Also see *āvṛta.*
549. **avyabhicār-** "unswerving".
- avyabhicāriṇī "unswerving; not diverting the mind". 13.10.
- avyabhicāreṇa "with unswerving intention; singularly". 14.26. [Used with adverbial sense.]
- yogenāvyabhicāriṇyā "by unswerving discipline". 18.33. Also see *yogena.*

---

141 Gambhīrānanda 1997, p. 30.
142 Gambhīrānanda 1997, p. 21.
143 Gambhīrānanda 1997, p. 670.
144 Van Buitenen 1981, p. 139.
145 Divanji, p. 148, entry #3404.
146 Edgerton, p. 84.
147 Bolle, p. 296.

550. **avyakta** "unmanifest; the Unmanifest; the Unmanifested". [Used both as an adj. ("unmanifest") and as a noun ("the Unmanifested").] Also see *vyakta.*

- avyaktādīni "unmanifest at the beginning; (their) beginnings are unmanifest". 2.28.
- avyaktaḥ "unmanifest". 2.25; 8.20, 21.
- avyaktā "the Unmanifested (as a goal)". 12.5.
- avyaktam "unmanifest; the Unmanifested". 7.24 ("unmanifest"); 12.1 ("the Unmanifested"); 12.3 ("the Unmanifested"); 13.5 ("the Unmanifested", referring to primordial Nature).
- avyaktamūrtinā "with unmanifested form; by (Me) in unmanifested form; by He who has the Unmanifested as (His) form". 9.4.
- avyaktanidhanāni "unmanifest at the end; (their) ends are unmanifest". 2.28.
- avyaktāsaktacetasām "(those whose) minds are directed toward the Unmanifested". 12.5. Also see *sakta.*
- avyaktasaṁjñake "described as unmanifest; designated as the Unmanifested". 8.18.
- avyaktāt "from the unmanifest". 8.18.
- avyaktāt "(higher) than the unmanifest". 8.20.

551. **avyaktādīni** "unmanifest at the beginning; (their) beginnings are unmanifest". 2.28. Also see *avyakta.*

552. **avyaktamūrtinā** "with unmanifested form; by (Me) in unmanifested form; by He who has the Unmanifested as (His) form". 9.4. Also see *avyakta, mūrtayaḥ, viśvamūrte.*

553. **avyaktanidhanāni** "unmanifest at the end; (their) ends are unmanifest". 2.28. Also see *avyakta, nidhanam.*

554. **avyaktāsaktacetasām** "(those whose) minds are directed toward the Unmanifested". 12.5. Also see *avyakta, sakta.*

555. **avyaktasaṁjñake** "described as unmanifest; designated as the Unmanifested". 8.18. Also see *avyakta.*

556. **avyavasāyinām** [*a-vi-ava-sāyinām*] "of the irresolute ones; of those whose intellect is not steady; of the wavering; of those deprived of practical (wisdom)". 2.41. Also see *vyavasāyaḥ, vyavasāyātmikā.*

557. **avyaya** "imperishable; inexhaustible; immutable; unchangeable; everlasting". Also see *avyayātmā.*

- avyayaḥ "imperishable; inexhaustible; immutable; unchangeable". 11.18; 13.31; 15.17.
- avyayam "imperishable; inexhaustible; immutable; unchangeable". 2.21; 4.1, 13; 7.13, 24, 25; 9.2, 13, 18; 11.2, 4; 14.5; 15.1, 5; 18.20, 56.
- avyayām "imperishable; inexhaustible; immutable; unchangeable". 2.34.
- avyayasya "of the imperishable, of the immutable". 2.17; 14.27.

558. **avyayātmā** "imperishable by nature; immutable essence". 4.6. Also see *ātman, avyaya.*

559. **ayajñasya** "for one who does not perform sacrifices; for one who does not follow the discipline of a *yajña*". 4.31. Also see *yajña.*

560. **ayam** "this". 2.19, 20 (twice), 24 (three times), 25 (three times), 30, 58; 3.9, 36; 4.3, 31, 40; 6.21, 33; 7.25; 8.19; 11.1; 13.31; 15.9; 17.3.

561. **ayaneṣu** "in the divisions of the army".[148] 1.11.

562. **ayaśaḥ** "infamy; disgrace". 10.5; 11.33. Also see *yaśaḥ.*

563. **ayathāvat** "incorrectly; mistakenly; as a thing really is not". 18.31. Also see *anyathā, yathā.*

564. **ayatiḥ** "undisciplined; one who does not make an effort". 6.37.

565. **ayogataḥ** "without adopting the path of *yoga*". 5.6. Also see *yoga.*

566. **āyudhānām** "of weapons; among weapons". 10.28.

567. **āyuḥ**. See *aghāyuḥ, āyuḥsattvabalārogyasukhaprītivivardhanāḥ.*

568. **āyuḥsattvabalārogyasukhaprītivivardhanāḥ** "promoting (*vivardhana*) long life (*āyuḥ*), sāttvic disposition (*sattva*), strength (*bala*), health (*ārogya*), comfort (*sukha*), and cheerfulness (*prīti*)" 17.8. Also see *ārogya, āyuḥ, bala, prīti, sattva, sukha, vivardhana.*

569. **ayukta** "not self-disciplined; with mind not composed; unfocused; not fixed in *yoga*". Also see *yukta.*

- ayuktaḥ "of one not-self disciplined; of one whose mind is not composed; an unfocused person". 5.12; 18.28.
- ayuktasya "of one not-self disciplined; of one whose mind is not composed". 2.66 (twice).

---

[148] Swarupananda, p. 7.

B

ब् = B. भ् = Bh.

570. **babhūva** "he was; he became". 2.9.

571. **baddhāḥ** "bound". 16.12. Also see *bandham.*

572. **badhnāti** "it binds". 14.6. Also see *bandham.*

573. **badhyate** "he is bound". 4.14. Also see *bandham.*

574. **bahiḥ** "outside". 5.27; 13.15. Also see *bāhyān, bāhyasparśeṣu.*

575. **bahu** "many; several, numerous". Also see *bahu-, kriyāviśeṣabahulām.*
   - bahavaḥ "many". 1.9; 4.10; 11.28.
   - bahūn "many". 2.36.
   - bahuna "with more; extensive". 10.42.
   - bahūnām "of many". 7.19.
   - bahūni "many". 4.5; 11.6.

576. **bāhu** "arm". See *anantabāhum, anekabāhūdaravaktranetram, bahubāhūrupādam, caturbhujena, mahābāho, sahasrabāho.*

577. **bahubāhūrupādam** "having many (*bahu*) arms (*bāhu*), thighs (*ūru*), and feet (*pādam*)". 11.23.

578. **bahudaṁṣṭrākarālam** "fearful with many teeth; terrifying with many fangs". 11.23. Also see *daṁṣṭrākarālāni.*

579. **bahūdaram** "having many stomachs". 11.23.

580. **bahudhā** "in many ways". 9.15; 13.4.

581. **bahulāyāsam** "with too much strain; with great effort". 18.24.

582. **bahumataḥ** "well-respected; thought of with respect". 2.35.

583. **bahuśākhāḥ** "many-branched; many-sided". 2.41. Also see *adhaḥśākham, śākhāḥ.*

584. **bahuvaktranetram** "endowed with numerous mouths [or faces] and eyes". 11.23. Also see *vaktra, netra.*

585. **bahuvidhāḥ** "of different types; of many kinds". 4.32. Also see *-vidhā.*

586. **bāhyān** "external". 5.27. [qualifies *sparśān*] Also see *bahiḥ, bāhyasparśeṣu.*

587. **bāhyasparśeṣu** "in external objects of the senses; in the objects of sense perception". 5.21. Also see *bahiḥ, bāhyān, mātrāsparśāḥ, saṁsparśa, sparśān, sparśanam, spṛśan.*

588. **bala** "strength; power; force; the army (as a military force)". Also see *āyuḥsattvabalārogyasukhaprītivivardhanāḥ, hṛdayadaurbalyam, kāmarāgabalānvitāḥ, yogabalena.*

- balam "army; (military) force". 1.10 (twice).
- balam "strength; power; force". 7.11; 16.18.
- balam "(inappropriate use of) force". 18.53.
- balāt "by force". 3.36.
- balavān "strong". 16.14.
- balavat "strong". 6.34.
- balavatā. "of the strong; of the powerful". 7.11.

589. **bālāḥ** "childish people; immature ones". 5.4. [The common meaning is "children" but here it refers to people of immature intellect.]

590. **bandham** ("bondage") Also see *baddhāḥ, badhnāti, badhyate, anubandhaṁ, nibadh-.*

- bandham "bondage". 18.30.
- bandhāt "from bondage". 5.3.
- janmabandhavinirmuktāḥ "completely released from the bondage of birth(s)". 2.51.
- karmabandham "bondage resulting from acts". 2.39.
- karmabandhanaḥ "bound by *karma*; imprisoned by acts". 3.9.
- karmabandhanaiḥ "due to the bondage resulting from acts". 9.28.
- nibandhāyāsurī "demonic (energy leads to) bondage". 16.5.

591. **bandhuḥ** "relative, kinsman".

- bandhuḥ "kinsman; relative". 6.5, 6.
- bandhūn "kinsmen; relatives". 1.27.
- saṁbandhinaḥ "kinsmen; relatives". 1.34.
- suhṛnmitrāryudāsīnamadhyasthadveṣyabandhuṣu "in friends, enemies, neutrals, mediators, despicable persons, and relatives". 6.9.

592. **bata** "alas!". 1.45. [Interjection indicating sorrow, regret, compassion, etc.]

593. **bhagavan** "O Blessed One; O Revered One; O Lord". 10.14, 17. [Voc. sing. of the masc. form of the adj. *bhagavat* used as a form of address.] Also see *śrībhagavān.*

594. **bhāḥ** "light; lustre". 11.12. Also see *bhās-, prabhā.*

595. **bhaikṣam** "mendicancy; living on alms; begging". 2.5.

596. √ **bhaj** "to serve; to be devoted to; to worship". Also see *bhakt-*.

- bhajāmi "I treat; I respond". 4.11. [Context of the passage is reciprocal relations.]
- bhajante "they worship; they adore; they praise; they are devoted". 7.16, 28; 10.8.
- bhajanti "they worship; they adore; they praise; they are devoted". 9.13, 29.
- bhajasva "worship!". 9.33.
- bhajatām "worshipping". 10.10.
- bhajate "is devoted; worships". 6.47; 9.30.
- bhajati "worships; serves; is devoted". 6.31; 15.19.

597. **bhakta** "devotee; devoted; worshipping". Also see *bhakti*. [√ *bhaj*.]

- abhaktāya "to one who is not devoted; to one who neglects worship". 18.67.
- bhaktaḥ "devotee". 4.3; 9.31.
- bhaktaḥ "worshipped; honored; devoted". 7.21.
- bhaktāḥ "devotees; devoted". 9.23, 33; 12.1, 20.
- madbhaktaḥ "my devotee". 9.34; 11.55; 12.14, 16; 13.18; 18.65.
- madbhaktāḥ "my devotees". 7.23.
- madbhakteṣu "in my worshippers; to my devotees". 18.68.

598. **bhakti** "devotion". Also see *bhakta*. [√ *bhaj*.]

- bhaktiḥ "devotion". 13.10.
- bhaktim "devotion". 18.68.
- bhaktimān "full of devotion; pious". 12.17, 19.
- bhaktiyogena "with the *yoga* of devotion". 14.26.
- bhaktyā "with devotion; by devotion". 8.10, 22; 9.14, 26, 29; 11.54; 18.55, 67 (*nābhaktāya* = *na abhaktāya* = not to one who lacks devotion).
- bhaktyupahṛtam "offered with devotion". 9.26.
- ekabhaktiḥ "devoted to one alone; a person of one-pointed devotion; one who is devoted to a single object of devotion". 7.17.
- madbhaktim "devotion to me". 18.54.

599. **bhaktimān** "full of devotion; pious". 12.17, 19. Also see *bhakti*.

600. **bhaktiyogena** "by the practice of devotion". 14.26. [The *yoga* consisting of the practice of spiritual devotion.] Also see *bhakti*, *yoga*.

601. **bhārata** "Descendant of Bharata". Bharata was the founding patriarch for both of the clans that were engaged in the great internecine war that provides the

story line for the *Mahābhārata*. Bhārata is a general patronymic for all his family lines. The epithet is used 22 times in the text, always at the end of a half-verse, a very standardized pattern. Used to refer to Arjuna in 2.14, 18, 28, 30; 3.25; 4.7, 42; 7.27; 11.6; 13.2, 33; 14.3, 8, 9, 10; 15.19, 20; 16.3; 17.3; 18.62. The epithet is also applied to King Dhṛtarāṣṭra in verses 1.24 and 2.10.

602. **bharatarṣabha** "O Bull of the Bharatas". "Bull" (*ṛṣabha*) was a common epithet for a hero, and is used to here to indicate excellence, the "best" of the Bharatas, always at the end of a half-verse, a very standardized pattern. Used as an epithet for Arjuna in 3.41; 7.11, 16; 8.23; 13.26; 14.12; 18.36.

603. **bharatasattama** "O Best (*sattama*) of the Bharatas". Used as an epithet for Arjuna in 18.4.

604. **bharataśreṣṭha** "O Best of the Bharatas". 17.12. Also see *śreṣṭhaḥ*.

605. **bhartā** "nourisher; sustainer; supporter". 9.18; 13.22. [√ *bhṛ*] Also see *bibharti, bhūtabhartṛ*.

606. **bhāṣā** "definition; description; the language (to describe)". 2.54. Also see *bhāṣase*.

607. **bhāsaḥ** "of the light; lustre". 11.12, 30. Also see *bhāḥ, bhās-*.

608. **bhāṣase** "you speak". 2.11. Also see *abhāṣata, bhāṣā, prabhāṣeta*.

609. **bhāsayate** "it illumines; it causes to appear; it makes manifest". 15.6, 12. Also see *bhāḥ, bhās-, sarvendriyaguṇābhāsam* (*-ābhāsam*).

610. **bhasmasāt** "reduced to ashes". 4.37 (twice). [*agnir bhasmasāt kurute* = fire reduces to ashes]

611. **bhāsvatā** "shining; resplendent". 10.11. Also see *bhāḥ, bhās-*.

612. **bhava** "(you) be!; (you) become!". 2.45; 6.46; 8.27; 9.34; 11.33, 46; 12.10; 18.57, 65.

613. **bhāva** "existence; entity; state of being; state of mind; sentiment; thought; contemplation; devotion". Also see *abhāvaḥ, abhāvayataḥ, bhūtabhāvana, bhūtabhāvodbhavakaraḥ, prabhāva, saṁbhava, svabhāv-*. For *bhāva* used as a suffix in compounds see *ātmabhāvasthaḥ, bhūtapṛthagbhāvam, īśvarabhāvaḥ, kārpaṇyadoṣopahatasvabhāvaḥ, madbhāva, mahānubhāvān, nānābhāvān, sadbhāve, sādhubhāve, sarvabhāvena, vimūḍhabhāvaḥ*.

- bhāvaḥ "existence; entity; sense". 2.16; 8.4, 20; 18.17.
- bhāvāḥ "items of creation; states of existence; dispositions". 7.12; 10.5.
- bhāvaiḥ "by these states". 7.13.

- bhāvam "state; existence; mode of being; being; form; concept". 7.15, 24; 8.6; 9.11; 18.20.
- bhāveṣu "in different forms of manifestation". 10.17.

614. **bhavaḥ** "existence; origin; birth". 10.4. Also see *abhāvaḥ, prabhava, prabhaviṣṇu, saṁbhava, udbhavaḥ.*

615. **bhavāmi** "I become". 12.7.

616. **bhāvanā** "feeling of devotion; meditation; contemplation; power of concentration; spiritual faith; firm belief". 2.66. Also see *bhāva.*

617. **bhavanti** "they come forth; they arise; they originate; they exist". 3.14; 10.5; 16.3.

618. **bhavāpyayau** "the origin and dissolution; creation and destruction". 11.2.

619. **bhāvasamanvitāḥ** "endowed with devotion; endowed with faith; filled with fervor[149]; pervaded with (the proper) state (of mind)[150]; endowed with (Kṛṣṇa's) state of being[151]". 10.8. Also see *anvita, bhāva, śraddhayānvitāḥ.*

620. **bhāvasaṁśuddhiḥ** "purity of thoughts". 17.16. Also see *śuddh-.*

621. **bhavat** "you; thou; thy honorable self". [An honorific pronoun used for addressing a highly-respected person in a formal way.]
   - bhavān "you; yourself". 1.8; 10.12; 11.31.
   - bhavantaḥ "you all". 1.11.
   - bhavantam "you; yourself". 11.31.
   - bhavataḥ "of you; your". 4.4.

622. **bhavataḥ**
   - bhavataḥ "of you; your". 4.4 [Gen. sing. masc. of pronoun *bhavat.*]
   - bhavataḥ "(the two) come to be; (both) arise". 14.17 [Pres. 3rd pers.dual of √ *bhū*].

623. **bhavati** "it is; becomes; arises; exists; takes place; is accomplished; is (born)". 1.44; 2.63; 3.14; 4.7, 12; 6.2, 17, 42; 7.23; 9.31; 14.3, 10, 21; 17.2, 3, 7; 18.12. Also see *abhavat, abhibhavati.*

624. **bhāvayantaḥ** "respecting; fostering; causing to live". 3.11.

625. **bhāvayantu** "may they respect; may they foster; may they cause to live". 3.11.

---

[149] Gambhīrānanda 1997, p. 405.

[150] Edgerton, p. 50.

[151] Minor (pp. 309-10) discusses varying interpretations of this compound but feels that the basic meaning of *bhāva* in the *BG* is "mode of being", and that here the context supports "speaking of one's very life in Kṛṣṇa."

626. **bhāvayatānena** "may you respect; may you foster by this; may you cause to live by this". 3.11.
627. **bhavet** "it would be". 1.46; 11.12.
628. **bhaviṣyāmaḥ** "we will exist". 2.12.
629. **bhaviṣyāṇi** "the future". 7.26.
630. **bhaviṣyanti** "they will be; they will live". 11.32.
631. **bhaviṣyatām** "of future happenings; of that which will come into existence in the future". 10.34.
632. **bhaviṣyati** "it will be". 16.13.
633. **bhavitā** "becomes existent; it will come into being". 2.20[152]; 18.69.
634. **bhāvita** "created; produced; inspired by; thought of".
   - ātmasaṁbhāvitāḥ "self-centered; puffed up by their egos[153]". 16.17.
   - saṁbhāvitasya "of one so highly esteemed; of a person of well-established reputation". 2.34.
   - tadbhāvabhāvitaḥ "transformed into that state of being[154]; one who is actuated by the sentiment of identity with it[155]; colored by that image". 8.6. [*smaran bhāvam ... sadā tadbhāvabhāvitaḥ* = "a person always becomes whatever being he thinks of"[156]]
   - yajñabhāvitāḥ "propitiated by the performance of sacrifices". 3.12.
635. **bhaya** "fear". Also see *abhayam, harṣāmarṣabhayodvegaiḥ, kāyakleśa-bhayāt, vigatecchābhayakrodhaḥ, vītarāgabhayakrodhaḥ, vītarāga-bhayakrodhāḥ.*
   - bhayam "fear". 10.4; 18.35.
   - bhayāt "due to fear; out of fear; from fear". 2.35, 40.
   - bhayena "with fear". 11.45.
636. **bhayābhaye** "fear and fearlessness; fear and absence of fear". 18.30.
637. **bhayānakāni** "terrible". 11.27.

---

[152] Śaṅkara (Gambhīrānanda 1997, p. 60) reads *abhavitā* in verse 2.20 rather than *bhavitā*. Divanji notes the alternate reading in his entries #301 (p.13) and #2391 (p. 104). Rāmānuja (Ādidevānanda, p. 74) reads it as *bhavitā* (नायं भूत्वा भविता वा).

[153] Van Buitenen 1981, p. 133.

[154] Sargeant, p. 354.

[155] Divanji, p. 63, entry #1407.

[156] Van Buitenen 1981, p. 101.

638. **bhayāvahaḥ** "that which causes fear (and hence is risky); a sense of dread[157]". 3.35.

639. **bhedam** "difference; variation; distinction (between)". 17.7; 18.29. Also see *buddhibhedam, guṇabhedataḥ.*

640. **bheryaḥ** "large drums; kettledrums[158]". 1.13.

641. **bhīma** "Bhīma; The Terrible One". [Bhīma is also known as Vṛkodara, "Wolf Belly".] See *bhīmābhirakṣitam, bhīmakarmā, bhīmārjunasamāḥ, Vṛkodara, pauṇḍram.*

642. **bhīmābhirakṣitam** "protected by Bhīma on all sides; defended by Bhīma". 1.10. Also see *Bhīma.*

643. **bhīmakarmā** "one who does terrible deeds; one whose actions are formidable". 1.15. [Referring to Bhīma as "Terrible in Action" or "Worker of Terror". Also see *Bhīma, karma.*

644. **bhīmārjunasamāḥ** "like Bhīma and Arjuna; the peers of Bhīma and Arjuna". 1.4. [Referring to other warriors on the battlefield.] Also see Bhīma, Arjuna, *sama.*

645. **bhinnā** "differentiated; divided". 7.4.

646. **bhīṣma** "Bhīṣma". [Bhīṣma is the leader of the Kaurava army on the battlefield. He is referred to as "oldest of the Kurus" (*kuruvṛddhaḥ*) in verse 1.12.]

- bhīṣmābhirakṣitam "protected on all sides by Bhīṣma; defended by Bhīṣma". 1.10.
- bhīṣmadroṇapramukhataḥ "in front of Bhīṣma and Droṇa". 1.25. Also see *Droṇa, pramukhe.*
- bhīṣmaḥ "Bhīṣma". 1.8; 11.26.
- bhīṣmam "Bhīṣma". 1.11; 2.4; 11.34.

647. **bhīṣmābhirakṣitam** "protected on all sides by Bhīṣma; defended by Bhīṣma". 1.10. Also see *Bhīṣma, rakṣ-.*

648. **bhīṣmadroṇapramukhataḥ** "in front of Bhīṣma and Droṇa". 1.25. Also see *Bhīṣma, Droṇa, pramukhe.*

649. **bhīta** "frightened; terrified".

- bhītāḥ "frightened". 11.21.
- bhītam "frightened". 11.50.

---

[157] Van Buitenen 1981, p. 119.

[158] Apte, p. 726, entry for भेरिः, भेरी.

- bhītāni "frightened". 11.36.

650. **bhītabhītaḥ** "taken aback by fear; terror-struck; greatly frightened; with fear and trembling". 11.35.

651. **bhoga** "a pleasure; an enjoyment". Also see *devabhogān, kāmabhogārtham, kāmabhogeṣu, kāmopabhogaparamāḥ*.
    - bhogāḥ "objects of enjoyment". 1.33; 5.22.
    - bhogaiḥ "with objects of enjoyment; with pleasures". 1.32.
    - bhogān "objects of enjoyment; pleasures". 2.5; 3.12.

652. **bhogaiśvarya** "pleasure and power". Also see *aiśvaram*.
    - bhogaiśvaryagatim "attainment of pleasure and overlordship; they aim at pleasure and power". 2.43. Also see *gati*.
    - bhogaiśvaryaprasaktānām "clinging to pleasure and power". 2.44. Also see *prasaktāḥ, sakta*.

653. **bhogī** "one who enjoys; the enjoyer". 16.14.

654. **bhojana** "food". Also see *āhāra*.
    - bhojanam "food". 17.10.
    - vihāraśayyāsanabhojaneṣu "while at play (*vihāra*), resting (*śayya*), sitting (*āsana*), or with food (*bhojana*)". 11.42.

655. **bhokṣyase** "you will enjoy". 2.37. [√ *bhuj*]

656. **bhoktṛ** "the experiencer; the enjoyer". Also see *bhoktṛtve, bhoktum*.
    - bhoktā "experiencer; enjoyer". 9.24; 13.22.
    - bhoktāram "experiencer; enjoyer". 5.29.
    - guṇabhoktṛ "experiencer of the *guṇa*-s; enjoyer of the *guṇa*-s". 13.14. Also see *guṇa*.

657. **bhoktṛtve** "in the experiencing; in the experience; in the quality of being an enjoyer". 13.20.

658. **bhoktum** "to live on (alms)". 2.5. [Inf. of √ *bhuj*]

659. **bhramati** "it wanders; it is whirling". 1.30.

660. **bhrāmayan** "causing to revolve". 18.61.

661. **bhrātṝn** "brothers (and cousins)". 1.26.

662. **bhṛguḥ** "Bhṛgu". 10.25. [A great sage, founder of the Bhārgava lineage of Brahmins.[159]]

663. **bhruvoḥ** "of the two eyebrows". 5.27; 8.10.

---

[159] Smith 2009, p. 797; Apte, p. 725, entry for भृगुः.

664. √ **bhū** "to be". See *ajñānasaṁbhūtam, aparasparasaṁbhūtam, bhūḥ, bhūt-, brahmabhū-, vibhūt-.*

665. **bhūḥ** "(you) be!". 2.47. [Imp. of √ *bhū*]

666. √ **bhuj** "to enjoy". See *bhok-, bhuktvā, bhuñj-, bhuṅkt-.*

667. **bhuktvā** "having enjoyed". 9.21.

668. **bhūmi** "earth; the earth".

- bhūmau "on the earth; over the earth". 2.8.
- bhūmiḥ "earth". 7.4.

669. **bhuñjānam** "enjoying; experiencing (objects of the senses)". 15.10. [√ *bhuj*]

670. **bhuñjate** "they eat; they partake of (sin)". 3.13. [√ *bhuj*]

671. **bhuñjīya** "I would indulge in; I would enjoy". 2.5. [√ *bhuj*]

672. **bhuṅkṣva** "enjoy". 11.33. [√ *bhuj*]

673. **bhuṅkte** "enjoys". 3.12; 13.21. [√ *bhuj*]

674. **bhūta** "a being; a created being; a spirit; a primary element". Also see *adhibutam, bhūta-, bhūtā-, jīvabhūta, mahābhūtāni, sādhibhūtādhidaivam, sarvabhūta-.* [Meaning depends on context.]

- bhūtam "a being; a created being". 10.39.
- bhūtānām "of beings". 4.6; 10.5, 20, 22; 11.2; 13.15; 18.46.
- bhūtāni "beings; spirits (according to context)". 2.28, 30, 34, 69; 3.14, 33; 4.35; 7.6, 26; 8.22; 9.5, 6, 25 (spirits); 15.13, 16.
- 7.11 bhūteṣu "in beings". 7.11; 8.20; 13.16, 27; 16.2; 18.21, 54.

675. **bhūtabhartṛ** "sustainer of beings; supporter of beings". 13.16. Also see *bhūtabhṛt, bibharti, bhartā.*

676. **bhūtabhāvana** "creator of beings; the one who brings beings into being; the originator of beings; the source of objects; source of created beings".

- bhūtabhāvana "O creator of beings". 10.15.
- bhūtabhāvanaḥ "creator of beings". 9.5.

677. **bhūtabhāvodbhavakaraḥ** "what brings all objects into being; the cause of the production of the created beings; the creative act which brings beings into existence; causing (*karaḥ*) origination (*udbhava*) of material beings; relating to the process by which material beings arise and develop". 8.3.

678. **bhūtabhṛt** "sustainer of beings; supporter of beings". 9.5. Also see *bhūtabhartṛ.*

679. **bhūtādim** "that which is the primary cause of created things; the source of (all) beings; the source of things that exist". 9.13. Also see *ādi.*

680. **bhūtagaṇān** "the hosts of spirits[160]; hordes of ghosts[161]; hordes of goblins[162]; the class of spirits or devils[163]; elementals[164]". 17.4. Also see *gaṇa*.

681. **bhūtagrāma** "collectivity of elements; collectivity of beings; the group of beings, elements, or organs". [Meaning depends on context.]

- bhūtagrāmaḥ "collectivity of beings; all categories of beings; the group of the gross elements; multitude of beings; multitude of created beings". 8.19.
- bhūtagrāmam "all groups of beings; multitude of beings; multitude of created beings (that are born of *Prakṛti*)". 9.8.
- bhūtagrāmam "the collected elements; the inner constituents that are brought together; the group of organs; all the organs; the assemblage of elements that constitute the body". 17.6.

682. **bhūtamaheśvaram** "supreme Lord of Beings; highest Lord of the created beings". 9.11. Also see *īśvara*, *maheśvara*.

683. **bhūtaprakṛtimokṣam** "liberation of beings from material nature; release from the nature of created beings". 13.34. Also see *mokṣ-*.

684. **bhūtapṛthagbhāvam** "the state of diversity of living things; the diversity of various beings; the manifoldness of beings; the separate existence of created beings". 13.30. Also see *pṛthak*.

685. **bhūtasargau** "types of creation; types of beings; of created beings;". 16.6. Also see *sarga*.

686. **bhūtasthaḥ** "one who resides in the created beings; abiding in beings; located in beings; contained in the beings". 9.5.

687. **bhūtaviśeṣasaṁghān** "groups of various kinds of beings; hosts of various beings". 11.15.

688. **bhūtejyāḥ** "those who are dedicated to the spirits; those who worship spirits". 9.25. Also see *bhūta* with sense "spirits".

689. **bhūteśa** "O Lord of beings; O Lord of created beings". 10.15. Also see *īśa*.

690. **bhūtiḥ** "well-being; happiness; prosperity". 18.78.

---

[160] Gambhīrānanda 1997, p. 638. The Śaṅkara commentary says that *bhūtagaṇān* includes "the Sapta-mātṛkās (the Seven Mothers) and others" indicating that a broad range of beings may be intended here.

[161] Sargeant, p. 636.

[162] Edgerton, p. 79.

[163] Divanji, p. 106, entry #2436.

[164] Tapasyananda, p. 413.

691. **bhūtvā** "having become; after becoming; having been; after being; having been (born); after being (born)". 2.20, 35, 48; 3.30; 8.19 (twice, *bhūtvā bhūtvā* = after being born again and again); 11.50; 15.13, 14. [Indec. past part. of √ *bhū*] Also see *-tvā*.

692. **bhuvi** "on earth". 18.69.

693. **bhūyaḥ** "again; further; more; much; great". 2.20; 6.43; 7.2; 10.1, 18; 11.35, 39, 50; 13.23; 14.1; 15.4; 18.64.

694. **bibharti** "it sustains; it upholds; it supports". 15.17. [√ *bhṛ*] Also see *bhartā, bhūtabhartṛ*.

695. **bījam** "seed".

- bījam "seed". 7.10; 9.18; 10.39.
- bījapradaḥ "seed-giver". 14.4.

696. **boddhavyam** "that which is required to be known; should be understood; ought to know". 4.17 (three times). Also see *buddhi*.

697. **bodhayantaḥ** "teaching; elightening (one another)". 10.9. Also see *buddhi*.

698. **brahma** "*Brahman*; the Vedas". Also see *brahma-*. Derived from √ *bṛh*, "to increase". The neuter noun *brahman* takes a range of meanings that can be determined only by context within a verse. The grammatical form *brahma* could be either nominative or accusative depending on the structure of the phrase in which it is used. In most verses it refers to *Brahman* as the primordial ground of being, but in some cases it means the Vedas or *Prakṛti* as primordial matter (*mahad brahma*).] Also see *brahma-, brahmaṇā, brahmaṇaḥ, brahmaṇi*.

- brahma "*Brahman*". 4.24; 5.19; 8.1; 8.3; 13.12. [Nom. sing. neut. form of the noun *brahman*.]
- brahma "*Brahman*; (to) *Brahman*". 4.31; 5.6; 7.29; 8.13, 24; 10.12; 13.30; 18.50. [Acc. sing. neut. of the noun *brahman*.]
- brahma "the Vedas". 3.15. [Nom. sing. neut. form of the noun *brahman*. The context of the verse is a description of Vedic ritual action. Here, *brahman* is the Vedas.[165]]

[165] So states Śaṅkara; see Warrier, p. 112.

- brahma "*Prakṛti*; (the great) *Brahman*". 14.3 (*mahad brahma*), 14.4 (*brahma mahad*). [Nom. sing. neut. form of the noun *brahman*.[166]]

699. **brahmā** [The masc. noun *brahman* represents Brahmā, the creator god.] Also see *brahmabhuvanāt, prajāpatiḥ*.

- brahmaṇaḥ "of Brahmā (the creator god)". 8.17. [Gen. sing. masc., *ahar yad brahmaṇo* = the day of Brahmā.[167]]
- brahmaṇaḥ "of Brahmā" or "than Brahmā". 11.37. [Gen. sing. *or* abl. sing.[168]]
- brahmāṇam "Brahmā (the creator god)". 11.15. [Acc. sing. masc.]

700. **brahmabhūta** ("identification with *Brahman*"). Also see *brahmabhūyāya*.

- brahmabhūtaḥ "identification with *Brahman*". 5.24; 18.54.
- brahmabhūtam "identification with *Brahman*". 6.27.

701. **brahmabhuvanāt** "up to the world of Brahmā; from the region of Brahmā downwards[169]; down from the realm of Brahmā[170]". 8.16. [*ā brahmabhuvanāt*] Also see Brahmā, *loka, surendralokam, svargalokam, ā*.

---

[166] The expressions *mahad brahma* (14.3) and *brahma mahad* (14.4) refer to "the Great *Brahman*" or to "the Mahat, *Brahman*", in either case indicating *Prakṛti*. Śaṅkara's commentary on 14.3 (Warrier, p. 471) says that "My womb (*Prakṛti*) is described as *mahat-brahma*, because it is vast in relation to all its effects, and because it is their cause and controller."

[167] Most translators take 8.17 as a reference to Brahmā, but some, including Edgerton (p. 43), take it as the neuter *Brahman*. Bolle (1979, p. 97) translates the idea as "the Eternal's day and the Eternal's night" which also avoids a reference to Brahmā. Śaṅkara's commentary explicitly refers to the creator god.

[168] In 11.37, *brahmaṇaḥ* could be either masculine (Brahmā) or neuter (*Brahman*), but most commentators interpret it as referring to Brahmā. Zaehner (pp. 313-4) argues that it refers to *Brahman*. Grammatically, *brahmaṇaḥ* could be either genitive ("of Brahmā") or ablative ("than Brahmā"), which leads to differences in translation of the passage in 11.37, *garīyase brahmaṇo 'py ādikartre*. For example, Van Buitenen (1981, p. 117) renders this phrase as "Creator more worthy of honor than Brahmā" (with ablative sense). If taken as a genitive the sense may be "the Primal Creator even of the creator (Brahmā)", as in Gambhīrānanda's (1997, p. 455) "who are greater (than all) and who are the first Creator even of Brahmā!" Ādidevānanda (p. 380) is similar.

[169] Divanji, p. 27, entry #603.

[170] Ādidevānanda, p. 281.

702. **brahmabhūyāya** "for identity with *Brahman*". 14.26; 18.53. Also see *brahmabhūta.*

703. **brahmacarya** "celibacy; continence".

- brahmacārivrate "in the vow of a celibate". 6.14. Also see *vrata.*
- brahmacaryam "celibacy". 8.11; 17.14.

704. **brahmāgnau** "in the fire of *Brahman*". 4.24, 25. Also see *agni.*

705. **brahmahaviḥ** "*Brahman* (is) the oblation". 4.24. Also see *hutam.*

706. **brahmakarma** "actions appropriate for a Brāhmaṇa; a Brāhmaṇa's duties; the work of the Brāhmaṇa caste". 18.42. Also see *brāhmaṇa, karma.*

707. **brahmakarmasamādhinā** "by one who is absorbed in work as *Brahman*; by one who has concentration on *Brahman* as the essence of all actions; actions performed with consciousness of *Brahman*; focus on action as consisting of *Brahman*". 4.24. Also see *karma, samādhi.*

708. **brahmākṣarasamudbhavam** "*Brahman* springs from the Imperishable[171]; (the Vedas (*brahman*) originate from the syllable *om* (the imperishable)[172]". 3.15. Also see *akṣara, -udbhava.*

709. **brahman** "*Brahman*". See *brahma, brahma-.*

710. **brāhmaṇa** "Brāhmaṇa; Brahmin". [The name of the first *varṇa* in the Indo-Āryan social order.] Also see *brahmakarma, brahmaṇaḥ, brāhmaṇāḥ, brāhmaṇakṣatriyaviśām, brāhmaṇasya, brāhmaṇe.*

711. **brahmaṇā** "by *Brahman*". 4.24. [Inst. sing. neut. of the noun *brahman.*] Also see *brahma.*

712. **brahmaṇaḥ** "of Brahmā" or "of *Brahman*" or "of the Veda". Also see *brahma.*

- brahmaṇaḥ "of Brahmā". 8.17; 11.37. [Gen. sing. masc. or abl. sing. masc. For discussion of the ambiguity of these references, see their listings under Brahmā.]
- brahmaṇaḥ "of *Brahman*". 6.38 (bewildered on the path of *Brahman*); 14.27 (the foundation of *Brahman*); 17.23 (indicator of *Brahman*). [Gen. sing. neut. of the noun *brahman.*]

---

171 Edgerton, p. 19.

172 The context of the verse is Vedic ritual action. Thus, "this *brahman* itself issues from the Syllable OM" in Van Buitenen 1981, p. 83. Here *brahman* refers to the Vedas.

- brahmaṇaḥ "of the Veda". 4.32 (different types of sacrifices are described in the Vedic tradition). [Gen. sing. neut. of the noun *brahman*.][173]

713. **brāhmaṇāḥ** "the Brāhmaṇas; the Brahmins". 9.33; 17.23. [Nom. pl. of the masc. noun *brāhmaṇa* (a *varṇa*).] Also see *brāhmaṇa*.

714. **brāhmaṇakṣatriyaviśām** "of the Brāhmaṇas, the Kṣatriyas, and the Vaiśyas". 18.41. Also see *Brāhmaṇa, Kṣatriya, Vaiśya*.

715. **brahmāṇam** "Brahmā (the creator god)". 11.15. [Acc. sing. masc.] Also see Brahmā.

716. **brāhmaṇasya** "of a Brāhmaṇa; of a Brahmin". 2.46. [Gen. sing. of the masc. noun *brāhmaṇa* (a *varṇa*).] Also see *brāhmaṇa*.

717. **brāhmaṇe** "(looks upon) a Brāhmaṇa; upon a Brahmin". 5.18. [Loc. sing. of the masc. noun *brāhmaṇa* (a *varṇa*).] Also see *brāhmaṇa*.

718. **brahmaṇi** "in *Brahman*". 5.10, 19, 20. [Loc. sing. neut. of the noun *brahman*.] Also see *brahma*.

719. **brahmanirvāṇam** "the *nirvāṇa* that is *brahman*[174]; the beatitude that is *brahman*[175]; absorption in *Brahman*; identification with *Brahman*; liberation in *Brahman*". 2.72; 5.24, 25, 26. Also see *brahman, nirvāṇaparamām*. [Both words in this compound are difficult to translate.]

720. **brahmārpaṇam** "*Brahman* (is) the offering". 4.24. Also see *arpaṇa*.

721. **brahmasaṁsparśam** "contact with *Brahman*". 6.28. Also see *brahman, bāhyasparśeṣu, mātrāsparśāḥ, saṁsparśa, sparśān, sparśanam, spṛśan*.

722. **brahmasūtrapadaiḥ** "arguments in the *Brahmasūtras*[176]; in aphoristic verses concerning *Brahman*[177]; by statements in the scripture pertaining to *Brahman*". 13.4.

---

[173] The context of the passage seems to call for a reference to the Vedas, and Śaṅkara takes *brahmaṇaḥ* in 4.32 in this sense. Rāmānuja interprets it as the essence of the self (Ādidevānanda, p. 182). Zaehner (p. 195) thinks it refers to *Brahman*.

[174] Van Buitenen 1981, p. 81. Zaehner (p. 159) says, "*Nirvāna* is a Buddhist, not a Hindu term and only becomes acclimatized in Hinduism after its adoption in the Gītā: it does not occur in the classical Upanishads."

[175] Van Buitenen 1981, p. 93.

[176] Van Buitenen 1981, pp. 123, 168 note 3. Van Buitenen thinks this is best taken more broadly as "*sūtras* about Brahman".

[177] Zaehner, p. 335. Zaehner's note explains that while some commentators take this as a reference to the *Brahmasūtras* of Bādarāyana, that work may not have been written at the

723. **brahmavādinām** "of those devoted to *Brahman*; of those who follow the doctrine of *Brahman*; expounders of the Veda[178]; those who study and expound the Vedas[179]". 17.24. Also see *vādinaḥ*.

724. **brahmavid** "knower of *Brahman*; one who knows *Brahman*". Also see *brahman, -vid.*
   - brahmavid "a knower of *Brahman*; one who knows *Brahman*". 5.20.
   - brahmavidaḥ "those who know *Brahman*". 8.24.

725. **brahmayogayuktātmā** "one whose self is well-established in union with *Brahman*; the state of being in union with *Brahman*; his self controlled by contemplating *Brahman*[180]; one whose mind has acquired Brahmayoga[181]; his spirit yoked with the *yoga* of *brahman*[182]". 5.21. Also see *ātman, yoga, yogayukta, yuktātmā.*

726. **brāhmī** "brahmic; of *Brahman*". 2.72 (*eṣā brāhmī sthitiḥ* = this is the state of *Brahman*).

727. **brahmin**. See *brāhmaṇa.*

728. **brahmodbhavam** "that which is born out of *brahman*; that which has arisen from *brahman* (the Veda)". 3.15. [Some commentators take this in the context of ritual action.[183]] Also see *-udbhava.*

729. **bravīmi** "I say; I tell". 1.7. [√ *brū*]

---

time the *BG* was composed, at least in the form we know it today. Zaehner does not "deny that there existed corpora of *sūtras* prior to Bādarāyana, who himself quotes predecessors." Zaehner says it is unlikely this is a reference to the Upaniṣads, thus disagreeing with Edgerton who mentions the Upaniṣads explicitly in the main text of his translation (Edgerton, pp. 65, 99, note 2 on chapter 13).

178 Ādidevānanda, p. 538.

179 Gambhīrānanda 1997, p. 652.

180 Hill, p. 152. Hill thinks that in this verse *yoga* means contemplation.

181 Divanji, p. 102, entry #2340.

182 Van Buitenen 1981, p. 93.

183 Śaṅkara clearly identifies *brahman* here as the Veda, and is followed in that sense by many translators, e.g., Van Buitenen (1981, p. 83) who translates *karma brahmodbhavaṁ viddhi brahmākṣarasamudbhavam* as, "This ritual action, you must know, originates from the *brahman* of the Veda, and this *brahman* itself issues from the Syllable OM." On the other hand, Edgerton (pp. 19, 93 note 3 on chapter 3) translates this line simply as, "Action arises from Brahman, know; And Brahman springs from the Imperishable", adding a note that this may have similarity to 14.3-4 where *Brahman* is equated with *Prakṛti.*

730. **bravīṣi** "you say; you tell". 10.13. [√ *brū*]

731. **bṛhaspatim** "Bṛhaspati". 10.24. [Bṛhaspati, the "Lord of Prayer" or "Lord of Holy Power", the chief priest and preceptor of the gods.[184]]

732. **bṛhatsāma** "Bṛhatsāma; the Great Chant". 10.35. [Madhusūdana Sarasvati identifies this as the particular chant called the *Bṛhatsāma*, based on the *Ṛg* mantra 6.46.1 in praise of Indra as the lord of all.[185]] Also see *Sāma* (*Sāmaveda*).

733. √ **brū** "to speak". See *abravīt, bravīmi, bravīṣi, brūhi.*

734. **brūhi** "(you) tell (me); explain". 2.7; 5.1. [Imp. 2nd pers. sing. of √ *brū.*]

735. **buddhayaḥ** "intellects (designs); the thoughts". 2.41.

736. **buddhi** "intellect; discriminating wisdom; the sense of discrimination; understanding; discernment". Also see *abuddhayaḥ, akṛtabuddhitvāt, alpabuddhayaḥ, arpitamanobuddhiḥ, asaktabuddhiḥ, ātmabuddhi-prasādajam, boddhavyam, bodhayantaḥ, durbuddheḥ, nibodha, sama-buddhayaḥ, samabuddhiḥ, sthirabuddhiḥ, tadbuddhayaḥ, yatendriya-manobuddhiḥ.*

- buddhi "wisdom; discriminating wisdom; understanding; insight; intellect".
- buddhau "in wisdom". 2.49.
- buddheḥ "than wisdom; than intellect". 3.42, 43; 18.29.
- buddhiḥ "wisdom; intellect". 2.39, 41, 44, 52, 53, 65, 66; 3.1, 40, 42; 7.4, 10; 10.4; 13.5; 18.17, 30, 31, 32.
- buddhim "wisdom; intellect". 3.2; 12.8.
- buddhyā "with wisdom; by means of intellect". 2.39; 5.11; 6.25; 18.51.

737. **buddhibhedam** "disturbance in beliefs; bewilderment of the mind; doubt in the mind; sow dissention in the mind". 3.26. Also see *bhedam, guṇabhedataḥ.*

738. **buddhigrāhyam** "that which is capable of being cognized by the intellect; to be attained by means of intellect". 6.21.

739. **buddhimān** "wise one; intelligent person". 4.18; 15.20.

740. **buddhimatām** "of the wise". 7.10. [*buddhir buddhimatām asmi* = I am the wisdom of the wise.]

---

[184] For citation on etymology see Minor, p. 319.

[185] Gambhīrānanda 1998, pp. 634-5.

741. **buddhināśa** "loss of wisdom; the destruction of one's sense of discrimination[186]".

- buddhināśaḥ "loss of wisdom". 2.63.
- buddhināśāt "due to loss of wisdom". 2.63.

742. **buddhisaṁyogam** "reunion with a sense of discrimination". 6.43. Also see *buddhiyoga, saṁyoga.*

743. **buddhiyoga** "the practice of wisdom; the *yoga* of discriminating wisdom". [The *yoga* consisting of use of the mental faculty of *buddhi.*] Also see *buddhisaṁyogam, yoga.*

- buddhiyogam "the practice of wisdom". 10.10; 18.57.
- buddhiyogāt "from the practice of wisdom". 2.49.

744. **buddhiyukta** "endowed with discriminating wisdom". Also see *yukta.*

- buddhiyuktaḥ "one endowed with discriminating wisdom". 2.50.
- buddhiyuktāḥ "those endowed with discriminating wisdom". 2.51.

745. **buddhvā** "after realizing; after ascertaining; after knowing; having understood". 3.43; 15.20.

746. **budhaḥ** "a knower; a wise man; wise one; elightened one". 5.22.

747. **budhāḥ** "knowers; wise men; wise ones; enlightened ones". 4.19; 10.8.

C

च् = C. छ् = Ch.

748. **ca** "and". 1.1, 4 (twice), 5 (three times), 6 (three times), 8 (five times), 9, 11, 13 (twice), 14, 16, 17 (four times), 18 (twice), 19 (twice), 25, 27, 29 (three times), 30 (three times), 31 (twice), 32 (twice), 33 (twice), 34, 38, 42, 43; 2.4, 6, 8, 11 (twice), 12, 19, 23, 24, 26, 27, 29 (three times), 31, 32, 33, 34 (twice), 35, 36, 41, 52, 58, 66 (twice); 3.4, 8, 17 (twice), 18, 22, 24, 38, 39; 4.3, 5, 8, 9, 17 (twice), 18, 22, 27, 28, 40 (twice); 5.1, 2, 5 (twice), 15, 18 (twice), 20, 27; 6.1 (three times), 9, 13, 16 (three times), 20, 21, 22, 29, 30 (twice), 35, 43, 46; 7.4, 9 (three times), 12 (twice), 16, 17, 22, 26 (twice), 29, 30 (twice); 8.1, 2, 4, 5, 7, 10, 12, 23, 28 (twice); 9.4, 5 (twice), 9, 12, 14 (twice), 15, 17, 19 (four times), 24 (twice), 29; 10.2, 3, 4 (twice), 7, 9 (three times), 13, 17, 18, 20 (three times), 22, 23 (twice), 24, 26, 27, 28, 29 (twice), 30 (three times), 31, 32 (twice), 33, 34 (three times), 38, 39; 11.2, 5, 7, 15 (twice), 17,

---

[186] Divanji, p. 101, entry #2304.

20, 22 (four times), 24, 25 (twice), 26, 34 (three times), 36 (twice), 37, 38 (twice), 39 (twice), 42, 43, 45, 48, 49, 50, 53, 54 (twice); 12.1, 3, 13, 15 (twice), 18 (twice); 13.2, 3 (five times), 4, 5 (three times), 8, 9, 10, 14 (twice), 15 (four times), 16 (four times), 18, 19 (three times), 22 (twice), 23, 24, 25, 29, 30, 34; 14.2, 6, 10 (twice), 13 (twice), 17 (twice), 19, 21, 22 (three times), 26, 27 (three times); 15.2 (twice), 3 (twice), 4, 8, 9 (three times), 11, 12, 13 (twice), 15 (four times), 16 (twice), 18 (twice), 20; 16.1 (twice), 4 (three times), 6, 7 (three times), 11, 14, 18; 17.2 (twice), 4, 6, 10 (twice), 12, 14, 15 (twice), 18, 20 (twice), 21, 22, 23 (twice), 25, 26, 27 (three times), 28 (twice); 18.1, 3, 5, 6, 9, 12, 14 (three times), 19 (twice), 22, 25, 28, 29, 30 (three times), 31 (three times), 32, 35, 36, 39 (twice), 41, 42, 43 (twice), 51 (twice), 55, 67 (twice), 69 (twice), 70, 71, 74, 76, 77 (twice).

749. **cailājinakuśottaram** "with a cover (*uttaram*) of cloth (*caila*), processed hide (*ajina*), and *kuśa* grass (*kuśa*)". 6.11.[187]

750. **cakra** "wheel; discus (weapon)".
- cakrahastam "with discus in hand". 11.46. Also see *hastāt.*
- cakram "circle; wheel; cycle (of life)". 3.16. [Figurative use of the word.]
- cakriṇam "with discus". 11.17.

751. **cakṣu** "eye; gaze; seeing".
- cakṣuḥ "the eye". 5.27 ["the gaze"]; 11.8; 15.9.
- jñānacakṣuṣā "with the eye of knowledge". 13.34.
- jñānacakṣuṣaḥ "(one endowed with) the eye of knowledge". 15.10.
- svacakṣuṣā "with your own eye". 11.8.

752. **calam** "moving; unsteady; unstable; restless; fickle; wavering". 6.35; 17.18. Also see *acala, niścalā.*

753. **calati** "one moves; one deviates (from truth)". 6.21.

754. **calitamānasaḥ** "one whose mind has strayed; having a distracted mind". 6.37. Also see *manasācalena, -mānasaḥ.*

755. **camūm** "army". 1.3.

756. **cañcalam** "fickle; unsteady". 6.26, 34.

757. **cañcalatvāt** "due to fickleness; because of unsteadiness". 6.33.

---

[187] Sargeant (p. 282) says the components of the mat are arranged in layers, with fragrant *kuśa* grass at the bottom, antelope skin above that, and cloth on top. Compare Gambhīrānanda's (1997, p. 286) version reading "made of cloth, skin, and *kuśa*-grass, placed successively one below the other". Van Buitenen (1981, p. 95) is less specific, translating the compound as "a cover of cloth, deerskin, or *kuśa* grass." Warrier (p. 227) gives another option, translating it as "covered with a cloth, or hide, and Kuśa grass, one over the other."

758. **cāndramasam** "of the moon; lunar". 8.25.

759. **candramasi** "in the moon". 15.12.

760. **cāpam** "(archer's) bow". 1.47.

761. √ **car**. "to move". Also see *acar-*, *ācar-*.

762. **carācara** "moving and non-moving; the mobile and the immobile; animate and inanimate". [*cara-acara*. Also see *acaram*.]

- carācaram "mobile or immobile; the moving and the non-moving". 10.39.
- carācarasya "of the moving and the non-moving". 11.43.
- sacarācaram "moving and non-moving; the mobile and the immobile; animate and inanimate". 9.10; 11.7. [*sa-cara-acaram*]

763. **caram** "moving; mobile; animate". 13.15. Also see *acaram, carācara*.

764. **caran** "moving; engaging". 2.64. [*viṣayān indriyaiś caran* = experiences the objects with senses]

765. **caranti** "they practice; they follow". 8.11. [*brahmacaryaṁ caranti* = they practice *brahmacarya*]

766. **caratām** "of moving; of roving". 2.67. [*indriyāṇāṁ hi caratām* = "the ranging senses"[188]]

767. **carati** "one moves; one acts; one goes about; one lives; one commits". 2.71; 3.36. Also see *niścarati*.

768. **caturbhujena** "with four arms". 11.46. Also see *bāhu*.

769. **cāturvarṇyam** "the four social classes". 4.13. Also see *varṇa*.

770. **caturvidhā** "four types; of four varieties". Also see *-vidhā*.

- caturvidhāḥ "four types". 7.16.
- caturvidham "of four types". 15.14.

771. **catvāraḥ** "four". 10.6.

772. **cekitānaḥ** "Cekitāna". 1.5. [The name of a Yādava prince allied with the Pāṇḍavas. The name means "Highly Intelligent".]

773. **ceṣṭāḥ** "movements; efforts; functions". 18.14. Also see *yuktaceṣṭasya*.

774. **ceṣṭate** "one behaves; one functions; one acts". 3.33.

775. **cet** "if". 2.33; 3.1, 24; 4.36; 9.30; 18.58.

776. **cetanā** "consciousness; awareness; intelligence". 10.22; 13.6.

777. **cetas** "mind; intelligence". Also see *cetanā, cint-, citta*.

- acetasaḥ "foolish; not mindful; devoid of spiritual vision; deprived of wisdom; witless". 3.32; 15.11; 17.6.

---

[188] Van Buitenen 1981, p. 81.

- ananyacetāḥ "thinking of nothing else; one whose mind has no other object (of devotion)". 8.14.
- anirviṇṇacetasā "with undismayed mind; without losing heart". 6.23.
- apahṛtacetasām "whose thoughts are carried away". 2.44.
- āveśitacetasām "of those whose minds are focused on". 12.7.
- avyaktāsaktacetasām "of those who focus their thinking on the unmanifest". 12.5. Also see *sakta.*
- cetasā "with the mind; mentally". 8.8; 18.57, 72.
- dharmasaṁmūḍhacetāḥ "with minds confused about *dharma;* confused about duty". 2.7.
- jñānāvasthitacetasaḥ "one whose mind is held steady in wisdom; whose mind is well-established in knowledge; one whose mind is stabilized by wisdom". 4.23. Also see *avasthita.*
- lobhopahatacetasaḥ "with minds clouded by greed". 1.38.
- prasannacetasaḥ "with mind calmed; with clear mind". 2.65.
- sacetāḥ "with mind". 11.51. [*asmi saṁvṛttaḥ sacetāḥ* = I have regained my mental composure]
- saṁnyasyādhyātmacetasā "having renounced by means of the mind filled with spiritual wisdom; letting go of things by means of having the mind devoted to the (true) self". 3.30.
- vicetasaḥ "those who have lost their sense of discrimination". 9.12.
- yatacetasām "of those who control their thoughts; of those with disciplined minds". 5.26.
- yuktacetasaḥ "those with well-regulated minds; those who are mentally disciplined". 7.30.

778. **cetasā** "with the mind; mentally". 8.8; 18.57, 72.
779. **chalayatām** "among cheats; of the fraudulent; of the deceivers; of the dishonest". 10.36.
780. **chandāṁsi** "the Vedas; Vedic mantras". 15.1
781. **chandasām** "of Vedic chanting styles; of poetic meters". 10.35.
782. **chandobhiḥ** "with metrical verses". 13.4.
783. **chettā** "dispeller; one who cuts away something or destroys it". 6.39.
784. **chettum** "to cut away; to remove". 6.39.
785. √ **chid** "to cut off". See *chett-, chind-, chinna-, chittvā.*
786. **chindanti** "they cut". 2.23.
787. **chinnābhram** "a dispersed cloud; a cloud that has dissipated". 6.38.

788. **chinnadvaidhāḥ** "those who have cut off the pairs of opposites; with dualistic conflicts uprooted". 5.25. Also see *dvaṁdva, jñānasaṁchinnasaṁśayam.*

789. **chinnasaṁśayaḥ** "one whose doubts are dispelled; free from doubt". 18.10. Also see *saṁśaya.*

790. **chittvā** "having cut off; after cutting; having severed". 4.42; 15.3. [Indec. past part. of √ *chid.*]

791. **cikīrṣuḥ** "intending to make; wishing to do a thing". 3.25. Also see *priyacikīrṣavaḥ.*

792. **cintām** "worry; anxiety". 16.11.

793. **cintayantaḥ** "meditating; contemplating; directing thought to". 9.22. Also see *anucintayan, paricintayan.*

794. **cintayet** "let one think; one should contemplate". 6.25.

795. **cintyaḥ** "conceivable; that can be thought of; suitable for contemplation". 10.17. Also see *acintya.*

796. **cira** "a long time".

- acireṇa "without delay; before long". 4.39. [*a* + *cireṇa*]
- nacirāt "without delay; before long". 12.7. [*na* + *cirāt*]
- nacireṇa "without delay; before long". 5.6. [*na* + *cireṇa*]

797. **citrarathaḥ** "Citraratha". 10.26. [The name of a Gandharva.]

798. **cittam** "the mind; the lower mind; thought". 6.18, 20; 12.9. Also see *anekacitta-vibhrāntāḥ, maccitta, samacittatvam, yatacittasya, yatacittātmā, yata-cittendriyakriyaḥ.*

799. **cūrṇitaiḥ** "broken to pieces; crushed to powder". 11.27.

800. **cyavanti** "they fall; they return (to the mortal world)". 9.24.

D

द् = D. ध् = Dh.

801. **dadāmi** "I give". 10.10; 11.8.

802. **dadāsi** "you give". 9.27.

803. **dadhāmi** "I put; I place; I deposit". 14.3. Also see *vidadhāmi.*

804. **dadhmau** "he blew". 1.12, 15. [√ *dhmā*] Also see *pradadhmatuḥ.*

805. **dadhmuḥ** "they blew". 1.18. [√ *dhmā*] Also see *pradadhmatuḥ.*

806. **dahati** "it burns". 2.23.

807. **daityānāṁ** "of the *Daitya*-s (a type of demon)". 10.30.

808. **daiva** "divine; pertaining to the *deva*-s". Also see *adhidaiva, deva, divya.*
   - daivaḥ "divine". 16.6 (twice).
   - daivam "that which pertains to the gods". 4.25.
   - daivam "the unseen spiritual cause of an effect; divine providence; fate". 18.14.
   - daivī "divine". 7.14; 16.5 (*daivī sampat* "divine energy").
   - daivīm "divine". 9.13; 16.3, 5 (*saṁpadaṁ daivīm* "divine energy").

809. **dakṣaḥ** "astute; skillful in action; capable". 12.16. Also see *dākṣyam.*

810. **dakṣiṇāyanam** "the southern path". 8.25. [*ṣaṇmāsā dakṣiṇāyanam* "six months after the summer solstice; six months when the sun is on the southern path"]

811. **dākṣyam** "competence; skill; astuteness". 18.43. Also see *dakṣaḥ.*

812. **damaḥ** "restraint; self-control". 10.4; 16.1; 18.42.

813. **damayatām** "among disciplinarians". 10.38.

814. **dambha** "hypocrisy; religious hypocrisy; ostentation; pomposity[189]; deceit". Also see *adambhitvam, dambhāhaṁkārasaṁyuktāḥ, dambhamānamadānvitāḥ, dambhārtham.*
   - dambhaḥ "hypocrisy; religious hypocrisy[190]; pomposity". 16.4.
   - dambhena "with hypocrisy; with ostentation[191]; just for show or exhibtion (without honest intent); done out of pride or vanity (instead of out of faith)". 16.17; 17.18 [*tapo dambhena* = contrived austerity].

815. **dambhāhaṁkārasaṁyuktāḥ** "acting out of hypocrisy and egoism; joined with hypocrisy and egoism; accompanied by hypocrisy and egoism". 17.5. Also see *ahaṁkāra, dambha, yukta.*

816. **dambhamānamadānvitāḥ** 1. "filled with (*anvita*) hypocrisy (*dambha*), pride (*māna*), and arrogance/intoxication/lust/frenzy (*mada*)"; *or* 2. "maddened by

---

[189] Ādidevānanda (p. 508) translates it as "pomposity", with Rāmānuja's commentary as "'Dambha or pomposity' is the practice of Dharma for earning a reputation for righteousness".

[190] Apte, p. 492, entry for दंभः, lists the first meanings as "deceit, fraud, trickery", and gives a specific meaning of "religious hypocrisy", citing *BG* 16.4 as an example of this usage. Other meanings include "arrogance, pride, ostentation" as well as other specialized meanings.

[191] Ādidevānanda (p. 517) translates *dambhena* in 16.17 as "with ostentation", with Rāmānuja's commentary as "performed for ostentation with the motive of becoming famous as the performer of sacrifices...."

(*madānvita*) hypocrisy (*dambha*) and pride (*māna*).[192] 16.10. Also see *anvita, dhanamānamadānvitāḥ, dambha, māna, mada.*

817. **dambhārtham** "for the sake of hypocrisy; hypocritical purpose; ulterior motive". 17.12. Also see *dambha, arthaḥ.*

818. **daṁṣṭrākarālāni** "terrible with fangs; with frightening teeth". 11.25, 27. Also see *bahudaṁṣṭrākarālam.*

819. **dāna** "giving; charity; donation; gift; the giving of alms; generosity". Also see *dānakriyāḥ, dambhamānamadānvitāḥ, yajñadānatapaḥ-karma, yajñadānatapaḥkriyāḥ.*
- dānair "by gifts; by donations". 11.48.
- dānam "giving; charity; donation; gift; the giving of alms; generosity". 10.5; 16.1; 17.7, 20 (twice), 21, 22; 18.5, 18.43.
- dāne "in giving; in charity; in donation". 17.27.
- dānena "by charity; by gifts". 11.53.
- dāneṣu "in gifts; in donations". 8.28.

820. **dānakriyāḥ** "acts of giving donations; acts of charity; ceremonies related to the making of gifts[193]". 17.25. Also see *dāna, kriyā.*

821. **dānavāḥ** "the Dānavas; the demons". 10.14.

822. **daṇḍaḥ** "punishment; chastisement". 10.38.

823. **darpa** "vanity; pride; ostentatiousness; arrogance".
- darpaḥ "vanity; arrogance". 16.4.
- darpam "vanity; arrogance". 16.18; 18.53.

---

[192] Zaehner, p. 371 notes that the compound *dambha-māna-mada-anvitāḥ* can be construed as either "maddened by hypocrisy and pride" or "possessed of hypocrisy, pride, and frenzy". His translation uses the first of these options: "maddened are they by hypocrisy and pride", taking *mada-anvitāḥ* as "filled with madness", i.e., "maddened". Miller's (p. 128) "drunk with hypocrisy and pride" is similar, as is Van Buitenen's (1981, p. 133) "the intoxication of vanity and self-pride". On the other hand, Edgerton (p. 77) translates it as "filled with hypocrisy, arrogance, and pride". That is similar to "filled with vanity, pride and arrogance" by Gambhīrānanda (1997, p. 624) and "full of ostentation, pride and arrogance" by Ādidevānanda (p. 513). Divanji (p. 68, entry #1536) has "infested by hypocrisy, pride, and inebriation" which puts a suitably negative spin on *anvita* as "infested".

[193] Divanji, p. 69, entry #1554.

824. **darśanakāṅkṣiṇaḥ** "desirous of seeing; eager to see; longing to behold (it)[194]; yearn for a glimpse[195]; anxious to have a sight[196]". 11.52. Also see √ *kāṅkṣ*.

825. **darśaya** [Imp. 2nd pers. sing. of the causal form of √ *dṛś*.]
- darśaya "show; cause to be seen". 11.45.
- darśayātmānam "show yourself; cause yourself to be seen". 11.4.

826. **darśayām āsa** "he caused to be seen; he revealed" 11.9, 50. [A causal form of √ *dṛś* + √ *ās*; for this construction also see *āśvāsayām āsa*, 11.50]

827. **darśitam** "shown". 11.47.

828. **daśa** "ten". 13.5.

829. **daśanāntareṣu** "in the spaces between the teeth". 11.27.

830. **dāsyāmi** "I will give". 16.15.

831. **dāsyante** "they will give". 3.12.

832. **dātavyam** "that which should be given". 17.20.

833. **datta** "given". Also see *ādatte, devadattam.*
- dattam "given". 17.28.
- dattān "given". 3.12.

834. **dayā** "compassion". 16.2.

835. **deha** "the physical body; the body". Also see *dehin, paurvadehikam, kalevaram, kāya, śarīra.*
- dehāḥ "bodies". 2.18.
- deham "the physical body; the body; in the body (of living beings)". 4.9; 8.13; 15.14.
- dehe "in the body". 2.13, 30; 8.2, 4; 11.7, 15; 13.22, 32; 14.5, 11.
- ātmaparadeheṣu "in the bodies of themselves and others; in one's own and another's body". 16.18.

836. **dehabhṛt** "the bearer of a body; the embodied entity; the embodied being".
- dehabhṛt "the bearer of a body; the embodied entity; the embodied being". 14.14.
- dehabhṛtā "for an embodied person; for the bearer of a body". 18.11.
- dehabhṛtām "of embodied beings". 8.4. [*dehabhṛtāṁ vara* = O Best of Embodied Souls]

---

[194] Sivananda, p. 292.

[195] Van Buitenen 1981, p. 121.

[196] Divanji, p. 68, entry #1544.

837. **dehāntaraprāptiḥ** "obtainment of another body; acquisition of another body". 2.13. Also see *prāptaḥ*.

838. **dehavadbhiḥ** "by the embodied souls". 12.5. [Inst. pl. of *deha* with the suffix -*vat*, having the sense of possession.]

839. **dehasamudbhavān** "the origin of the body[197]; (constituents) which give the body its existence[198]; that spring from the body[199]; which arise in the body[200]; that which arises from the body[201]; that come from bodily existence[202]". 14.20. Also see *-udbhava*.

840. **dehin** "the embodied; the embodied essence; an embodied soul; the *ātman* within a body; the embodied person; the consciousness within a body; the soul". Also see *deha, śarīra, śarīriṇaḥ*.[203]

- dehī "an embodied soul; the *ātman* within a body; the embodied person". 2.22, 30; 5.13; 14.20.
- dehinaḥ "of the embodied soul; of the embodied one; of the person". 2.13, 59.
- dehinam "the embodied soul". 3.40; 14.5, 7.
- dehinām "embodied souls". 17.2.
- sarvadehinām "of all embodied beings; (of consciousness) of all beings". 14.8.

---

[197] Gambhīrānanda 1997, p. 583. The interpretation here is that the *guṇa*-s are "the origin of the body" or "the seed of the birth of the body".

[198] Zaehner, p. 356. Zaehner notes that the "compound more naturally reads, 'which arise from the body', but it is the constituents that give existence to the body not vice versa."

[199] Edgerton, p. 71. Edgerton adds a note on the ambiguity of how this compound can be translated (p. 100, note 1 on chapter 14).

[200] Ādidevānanda, pp. 475-6. The interpretation here is that the *guṇa*-s arise in the body, i.e., spring from Prakṛti transformed into the form of the body.

[201] Divanji, p. 73, entry #1644.

[202] Bolle, p. 273.

[203] The translation of *dehinaḥ* as "soul" is an interpretation of the more literal meaning "the embodied" or "that which has a body". The same terminology is also used in 2.30 (*dehi*), 3.40 (*dehinam*), 12.5 (*dehavadbhiḥ*). Elsewhere in the text, sometimes the word *ātman* is used to refer to the Higher Self, but at other times it is used to mean *one* or *oneself*, e.g., 6.7 (*jitātmanaḥ*), 7.18 (*yuktātmā*), 7.19 (*mahātmā*), 8.15 (*mahātmānaḥ*), 11.12 (*mahātmanaḥ*), 11.20 (*mahātman*), 11.24 (*pravyathitāntarātmā*), 11.37 (*mahātman*), 11.50 (*mahātmā*), 16.9 (*naṣṭātmānaḥ*), 18.74 (*mahātmanaḥ*). In 7.5 and 15.7 the term *jīvabhūta* (individual empirical consciousness) is used.

841. **deśe** "in a place; at a place; in the region". 6.11; 17.20. Also see *adeśakāle, hṛddeśe* (*hṛt-deśe*), *viviktadeśasevitvam.*

842. **deva** "god". Also see *adhidaiva, ādideva, daiva, devabhogān, devadatta, devadeva, devadvijaguruprājñapūjanam, devarṣi, devatā, devavara, devavratāḥ, devayajaḥ, deveśa, deveṣu, divya, sahadeva, vāsudeva.*
   - deva "O God". 11.15, 44, 45.
   - devāḥ "the gods". 3.11, 12; 10.14; 11.52.
   - devam "God; divinity". 11.11, 14.
   - devān "the gods". 3.11; 7.23; 9.25; 11.15; 17.4.
   - devānām "of the gods". 10.2, 22.

843. **devabhogān** "godly pleasures; the enjoyments of the gods". 9.20. Also see *deva, bhoga.*

844. **devadattam** "Devadatta". 1.15. [The name of Arjuna's conch, (lit.) Given by god.]

845. **devadeva** "God of gods". Also see *deva.*
   - devadeva "O God of gods". 10.15.
   - devadevasya "of the God of gods". 11.13.

846. **devadvijaguruprājñapūjanam** "worship (*puja*) of the gods (*deva*), the twice-born (*dvija*), the teachers (*guru*), and the wise (*prājña*)". 17.14.

847. **devalaḥ** "Devala". 10.13. [Name of a celestial sage.[204]] Also see *Asita.*

848. **devarṣi** "divine sage". Also see *ṛṣi.*
   - devarṣiḥ "divine sage". 10.13.
   - devarṣīṇām "of the divine sages; among the divine sages". 10.26.

849. **devatā** "deity; divinity". Also see *deva.*
   - devatāḥ "the gods". 4.12.
   - anyadevatāḥ "other gods". 7.20.
   - anyadevatā "other gods". 9.23. [Shown in many editions as part of a compound: *anyadevatābhaktāḥ,* ("devotees of other gods"), but shown divided as *anyadevatā bhaktāḥ* in the Critical Edition.]

850. **devavara** "O most excellent of the gods". 11.31. Also see *deva.*

---

[204] Sargeant (p. 423) treats "Asita Devala" as a single name. Divanji (p. 72, entry #1630) says Devala was the name of the father or the family of the celestial sage named Asita. This issue is noted by Minor (p. 314) who summarizes other views on the two names Asita and Devala.

851. **devavratāḥ** "those who are dedicated to the gods; those who observe vows to the gods". 9.25. Also see *deva, vrata.*

852. **devayajaḥ** "those who worship the gods; those who sacrifice to the gods". 7.23. Also see *deva.*

853. **deveśa** "O Lord of the gods". 11.25, 37, 45. Also see *deva, īśa.*

854. **deveṣu** "among the gods". 18.40. Also see *deva.*

855. **dhāma** "abode; light[205]". 8.21; 10.12; 11.38; 15.6.

856. **dhana** "wealth; riches; prosperity". Also see *dhanamānamadānvitāḥ.*

- dhanam "wealth". 16.13.
- dhanāni "riches". 1.33.

857. **dhanamānamadānvitāḥ** 1. "filled with (*anvita*) wealth (*dhana*), pride (*māna*), and arrogance/intoxication/lust/frenzy (*mada*)"; *or* 2. "maddened by (*madānvita*) their pride in wealth (*dhanamāna*)"; *or* 3. "Filled with (*anvita*) the madness and pride (*mānamada*) of wealth (*dhana*)"[206] [The 3rd alternative could be stated as "One who has contracted pride and self-importance due to (the acquisition of) wealth".[207]] 16.17. Also see *anvita, dambhamāna-madānvitāḥ, dhana, māna, mada.*

---

[205] Śaṅkara interprets *dhāma* as *tejas* in 10.12, translated by Warrier (p. 329) as "effulgence" in the commentary but using the more common "abode" in the translation. Also see Apte, p. 525, entry for धामन्, meanings 5, 6, and 7 for light, glory, power, etc.

[206] Zaehner, p. 372, notes that the compound *dhana-māna-mada-anvitāḥ* can be construed as either "maddened by their pride in wealth" or "filled with the madness and pride of wealth". Zaehner's translation uses the first of these options, "maddened by their pride in wealth", taking *mada-anvitāḥ* as "filled with the madness". Minor (p. 442) notes the issue of divergent translations and cites "possessed of pride and arrogance of wealth", as following Śaṅkara, saying that is the interpretation by most modern commentators. Minor cites Rāmānuja's interpretation as "possessed of the arrogance of wealth and pride". Thus Van Buitenen (1981, p. 133) translates it as "drunk with wealth and pride", which is similar to "possessed of the intoxication of wealth and pride" in Ādidevānanda (p. 517). Edgerton (p. 77) translates it as "full of pride and arrogance of wealth" and adds a note (p. 101, note 3 on chapter 16) that Śaṅkara interprets the compound in that way, and rejecting Rāmānuja's "of the arrogance of wealth and pride" as implausible. Compare "filled with (*anvita*) pride (*māna*) and intoxication (*mada*) of wealth (*dhana*)" in Gambhīrānanda 1997, p. 628.

[207] Divanji, p. 74, entry #1690.

858. **dhanaṁjaya** "Winner of Wealth; Conqueror of Wealth; Master of Wealth". [Epithet of Arjuna, always used at the end of a half-verse, a very standardized pattern.]

- dhanaṁjaya "O Winner of Wealth; O Arjuna". 2.48, 49; 4.41; 7.7; 9.9; 12.9; 18.29, 72.
- dhanaṁjayaḥ "the Winner of Wealth; Arjuna". 1.15; 10.37; 11.14.

859. **dhanuḥ** "bow". 1.20.

860. **dhanurdharaḥ** "the archer; the bowman; the bow-bearer". 18.78. [Referring to Arjuna.]

861. **dhāraṇām** See *yogadhāraṇām.*

862. **dhārayāmi** "I support; I maintain; I sustain". 15.13. [√ *dhṛ*]

863. **dhārayan** "holding; maintaining; believing; thinking". 5.9; 6.13. Also see *upadhāraya.*

864. **dhārayate** "it holds; it holds to; one maintains". 18.33, 34.

865. **dharma** "law; established order; tradition; custom; rule; duty; religious duty; virtue; right; justice; nature; character; essential quality". Also see *adharma, dharma-, dharmya, dharmyāmṛtam, jātidharmāḥ, kula-dharmāḥ, paradharma, sādharmyam, sarvadharmān, śāśvatadharma-goptā, svadharma, trayīdharmam, utsannakuladharmāṇām.*

- dharmasya "of righteousness; of duty; of *dharma*". 2.40; 4.7; 9.3; 14.27.
- dharmam "righteousness; duty; *dharma*". 18.31, 32.
- dharme "in *dharma*". 1.40. [*dharme naṣṭe* = when tradition perishes]

866. **dharmakāmārthān** "duty (*dharma*), pleasure (*kāma*), and material prosperity (*artha*); righteous conduct (*dharma*), objects of desire (*kāma*), and riches (*artha*)[208]; Law, Profit, and Pleasure[209]". 18.34. Also see *arthaḥ, dharma, kāma.*

867. **dharmakṣetre** "in the field (*kṣetra*) of righteousness (*dharma*); at Dharmakṣetra". 1.1. Also see *dharma.*

868. **dharmasaṁmūḍhacetāḥ** "with minds confused about *dharma*; confused about duty". 2.7. Also see *dharma.*

869. **dharmasaṁsthāpanārthāya** "for the reinstatement of righteousnesss; for the re-establishing of *dharma*". 4.8. Also see *arthaḥ, dharma.*

870. **dharmātmā** "righteous; virtuous; one who has become identical with *dharma*". 9.31. Also see *ātman.*

---

[208] Divanji, p. 75, entry #1694.

[209] Van Buitenen 1981, p. 141.

871. **dharmāviruddhaḥ** "that which is not opposed to *dharma*; not contrary to ethical principles". 7.11. Also see *dharma*.

872. **dharmya** "in accordance with *dharma*; in agreement with moral law; righteous; as prescribed by the laws of duty; conducive to what is right; sacred". Also see *dharma, dharmyāmṛtam*.

- dharmyam "righteous; sacred". 2.33; 9.2; 18.70.
- dharmyāt "than a just (war)". 2.31.

873. **dharmyāmṛtam** "the nectar of righteousness; ambrosial virtue; true immortality; 'this elixir of Law'[210]". 12.20. Also see *amṛta, dharma*.

874. **dhārtarāṣṭrāḥ** "the Dhārtarāṣṭras; the sons of Dhṛtarāṣṭra; Dhṛtarāṣṭra's men; Dhṛtarāṣṭra's warriors; Dhṛtarāṣṭra's party". [The Kaurava army supporting King Dhṛtarāṣṭra.]

- dhārtarāṣṭrāḥ "the Dhārtarāṣṭras; the sons of Dhṛtarāṣṭra; Dhṛtarāṣṭra's men". 1.46; 2.6.
- dhārtarāṣṭrān "the Dhārtarāṣṭras; the sons of Dhṛtarāṣṭra; Dhṛtarāṣṭra's men". 1.20, 36, 37.
- dhārtarāṣṭrāṇām "of the Dhārtarāṣṭras; of the sons of Dhṛtarāṣṭra; of Dhṛtarāṣṭra's men". 1.19.

875. **dhārtarāṣṭrasya** "of Dhṛtarāṣṭra's son; for Duryodhana". 1.23.

876. **dhāryate** "it is maintained". 7.5.

877. **dhātṛ** "sustainer; one who supports".

- dhātā 9.17; 10.33.
- dhātāram 8.9.

878. **dhenūnām** "of cows; among cows". 10.28.

879. **dhīmat** "intelligent; wise; endowed with wisdom". Also see *sthitadhīḥ*.

- dhīmatā "by the wise". 1.3.
- dhīmatām "of the wise". 6.42.

880. **dhīra** "wise; intelligent; composed; self-possessed; steadfast".

- dhīraḥ "firm; steady; composed; steadfast; self-possessed; wise; the wise man; a man of wisdom; an intelligent man". 2.13; 14.24.
- dhīram "the wise man; a self-possessed man; the steadfast man". 2.15.

881. **dhṛṣṭadyumnaḥ** "Dhṛṣṭadyumna". 1.17. [The Commander-in-chief of the Pāṇḍava army. Dhṛṣṭadyumna was the son of Drupada. He is mentioned by name in verse 1.17 and by his epithet "Son of Drupada" in verse 1.3.]

---

[210] Van Buitenen 1981, p. 123.

882. **dhṛṣṭaketuḥ** "Dhṛṣṭaketu". 1.5. [The king of Cedi, allied with the Pāṇḍavas. The name means "Bold Leader".]

883. **dhṛtarāṣṭra** "Dhṛtarāṣṭra". [The blind king of the Kauravas.]

- dhṛtarāṣṭra "Dhṛtarāṣṭra". 1.1.
- dhṛtarāṣṭrasya "of Dhṛtarāṣṭra". 11.26.

884. **dhṛti** "steadiness; steadfastness; firmness; fortitude; perseverance; constancy; persistence; tenacity; determination".[211]

- dhṛteḥ "of fortitude; of persistence; of steadfastness". 18.29.
- dhṛtigṛhītayā "held with firmness; held in check with firmness; regulated with fortitude". 6.25. Also see *gṛhyate*.
- dhṛtiḥ "steadfastness; fortitude; firmness; steadiness; persistence". 10.34; 13.6; 16.3; 18.33, 34, 35 (stubbornness), 43.
- dhṛtim "steadiness; firmness; courage". 11.24.
- dhṛtyā "by fortitude; with firmness; with persistence". 18.33, 34.
- dhṛtyātmānam "controlling oneself with fortitude; restraining oneself with firmness". 18.51. Also see *ātman*.
- dhṛtyutsāhasamanvitaḥ "endowed with fortitude and enthusiasm; full of steadiness and energy". 18.26. Also see *anvita*.

885. **dhruva** "sure; certain; sound; steady; fixed; definite; immutable; eternal". Also see *adhruvam, acala, niścalā*.

- dhruvā "sure; sound (policy)". 18.78.
- dhruvaḥ "definite; certain; fixed". 2.27.
- dhruvam "definite; certain; fixed; the eternal". 2.27; 12.3.

886. **dhūmaḥ** "smoke". 8.25.

887. **dhūmenāgnir** "fire (covered) by smoke". 18.48. Also see *agni*.

888. **dhūmenāvriyate** "it is covered by smoke". 3.38. Also see *āvṛta*.

---

[211] Śaṅkara's commentary defines *dhṛti* in verse 16.3 as "a particular function of the mind which removes the tedium of the body and organs when they become exhausted, and being rejuvenated by which the body and organs do not feel any fatigue." His commentary on this word in verse 18.43 gives the example of "one who is not depressed under all circumstances, being sustained by doggedness." Gambhīrānanda 1997, pp. 618, 705. Professor Anthony Biduck points out that the idea of *dhṛti* as an innate impulse of an organism to persist in its own being is similar to the concept of *conatus* in classical and later philosophy (personal communication, 23 August 2014). See, for example, Spinoza's *Ethics*, part 3, propositions 6 through 9, which briefly define *conatus* as a striving by any living organism to persevere in its being. This may be the sense of *dhṛti* in *BG* verse 13.6 in particular.

889. **dhyāna** "meditation; contemplation" Also see *dhyānayogaparaḥ, dhyāyanta, dhyāyataḥ.*

- dhyānam "meditation; contemplation". 12.12.
- dhyānāt "than meditation; than contemplation". 12.12.
- dhyānena "through meditation; by contemplation". 13.24.

890. **dhyānayogaparaḥ** "one who is devoted to the spiritual discipline of meditation; one for whom the spiritual practice of meditation is the highest duty; one who is solely devoted to the practice of *yoga* consisting of contemplation". 18.52. Also see *dhyāna, yoga, -para.*

891. **dhyāyantaḥ** "meditating on; thinking on; contemplating". 12.6. Also see *dhyāna.*

892. **dhyāyataḥ** "dwells on [objects of the senses]; ponders upon; thinks on; contemplates". 2.62. Also see *dhyāna.*

893. **dīpaḥ** "a lamp". 6.19. Also see *jñānadīpena, jñānadīpite.*

894. **dīptahutāśavaktram** "with face shining like a blazing fire; with mouth like a blazing fire consuming oblations". 11.19. Also see *hutāśa, vaktra.*

895. **dīptam** "illuminated; bright". 11.24. Also see *pradīptam.*

896. **dīptānalārkadyutim** "blazing like the fiery radiance of the sun; having the splendor of a blazing fire and the sun; lustre like that of glowing fire or the sun". 11.17.

897. **dīptaviśālanetram** "endowed with glowing wide eyes". 11.24. Also see *viśāla, netra.*

898. **dīptimantam** "emitting light; having lustre". 11.17.

899. **dīrghasūtrī** "a procrastinator; of procrastinating nature; dilatory". 18.28. [*dīrghasūtrin*]

900. **diśaḥ** "directions". 6.13; 11.20, 25, 36.

901. **divi** "in heaven; in the sky". 9.20; 11.12; 18.40.

902. **divya** "divine". Also see *daiva, deva.*

- anekadivyābharaṇam "(adorned) with numerous divine ornaments". 11.10.
- divyagandhānulepanam "annointed with divine fragrant ointments; annointed with celestial aromatic unguents; annointed with divine perfumes". 11.11.
- divyāḥ "divine". 10.16, 19.
- divyam "divine". 4.9; 8.8, 10; 10.12; 11.8.
- divyamālyāmbaradharam "wearing divine garlands and clothing". 11.11.

- divyān "divine". 9.20; 11.15.
- divyānām "of divine". 10.40.
- divyānekodyatāyudham "with numerous divine weapons raised (for battle)". 11.10. Also see *udya.*
- divyāni "divine". 11.5.
- divyau "divine". 1.14.

903. **divyagandhānulepanam** "annointed with divine fragrant ointments; annointed with celestial aromatic unguents; annointed with divine perfumes". 11.11. Also see *gandha, √ lip.*

904. **divyamālyāmbaradharam** "wearing divine garlands and clothing". 11.11.

905. **divyānekodyatāyudham** "with numerous divine weapons raised (for battle)". 11.10. Also see *aneka, udya.*

906. **dīyate** "it is given". 17.20, 21, 22. [√ *dā*]

907. **doṣa** "defect; fault; sin; wrong". Also see *janmamṛtyujarāvyādhi-duḥkhadoṣānudarśanam, jitasaṅgadoṣāḥ, kārpaṇyadoṣopahatasva-bhāvaḥ, sadoṣam, nirdoṣam.*

- doṣaiḥ "by sinful acts; by evil deeds". 1.43.
- doṣam "fault; sin; wrong". 1.38, 39.
- doṣavat "full of fault; sinful". 18.3.
- doṣeṇa "faulty; with defects; with deficiency; with imperfection". 18.48.

908. **drakṣyasi** "you will see". 4.35. [2nd. pers. sing. fut. act √ *dṛś.*]

909. **draṣṭā** "witness; one who sees; a person of insight". 14.19. Also see *upadraṣṭā.*

910. **draṣṭum** "to see". 11.3, 4, 7, 8, 46, 48, 53, 54.

911. **draupadeyāḥ** "Sons of Draupadī". 1.6, 18. [Draupadī was the co-wife of the Pāṇḍava brothers.]

912. **dravanti** "they flow; they run; they run away; they flee". 11.28, 36. [√ *dru*]

913. **dravya** "that which is material".

- dravyamayāt "from the material; that in which material objects are made use of". 4.33.
- dravyayajñāḥ "those who perform material sacrifices". 4.28. Also see *yajña.*

914. **dṛḍha** "fixed; firm; strong; difficult to bend; unyielding".

- dṛḍham "difficult to bend; resistant to change; unyielding; stubborn". 6.34. [describing the mind]

- dṛḍhena "firm; unyielding; strong; sharp". 15.3. [describing a cutting tool: *śastreṇa dṛḍhena* = "with the hardened axe".[212]]

915. **dṛḍham** "firmly; very much; throughly". 18.64. [Indec. adv.]

916. **dṛḍhaniścayaḥ** "one who has made a firm resolve; with unyielding determination; resolute in decisions[213]". 12.14. Also see *niścaya*.

917. **dṛḍhavratāḥ** "with firm resolve; those who are unyielding in the observance of vows (*vrata*); steady; persevering". 7.28; 9.14.

918. **droṇa** "Droṇa". [The teacher of both the Kauravas and the Pāṇḍavas. Duryodhana addresses Droṇa as "teacher" (*ācārya*) in 1.2 and 1.3.] See "Who's Who", page 5.
    - bhīṣmadroṇapramukhataḥ "in front of Bhīṣma and Droṇa". 1.25. Also see *Bhīṣma, pramukhe.*
    - droṇaḥ "Droṇa". 11.26.
    - droṇam "Droṇa". 2.4; 11.34.

919. **dṛṣṭaḥ** "seen". 2.16.

920. **dṛṣṭapūrvam** "seen before; previously seen". 11.47. Also see *adṛṣṭapūrva, dṛṣṭvā.*

921. **dṛṣṭavān** "seen". 11.52, 53. [*dṛṣṭavān asi* = you have seen]

922. **dṛṣṭim** "view; viewpoint; way of looking at things; attitude". 16.9. Also see *vidhidṛṣṭaḥ.*

923. **dṛṣṭvā** "having seen; after seeing". 1.2, 20, 28; 2.59; 11.20, 23, 24, 25, 45, 49, 51. [Indec. past participle of √ *dṛś-paśy.*[214]] Also see *dṛṣṭapūrvam, adṛṣṭapūrvam.*

924. **drupadaḥ** "Drupada". 1.4, 18. [See "Who's Who", page 5.]

925. **drupadaputreṇa** "by the son (*putra*) of Drupada; by Dhṛṣṭadyumna". 1.3. [Dhṛṣṭadyumna, the son of Drupada, is chief of the Pāṇḍava army.]

926. **duḥkha** "affliction; misery; difficulty; pain". Also see *duḥkha-, sukhaduḥkh-, janmamṛtyujarāduḥkhaiḥ, janmamṛtyujarāvyādhi-duḥkhadoṣānudarśanam, samaduḥkhasukha, sarvaduḥkhānām, śītoṣṇasukhaduḥkha,*
    - duḥkham "misery; pain; painful; difficulty; difficult; unhappiness; unpleasantness;". 6.32; 10.4; 13.6; 14.16; 18.8.

---

[212] Van Buitenen 1981, p. 131.

[213] Van Buitenen 1981, p. 123.

[214] Translators show considerable variation in handling the time sense of the word, sometimes giving it a present sense ("seeing") rather than the more correct past sense ("having seen"). See grammatical note on entry for suffix *–tvā*.

- duḥkham "difficult; not easy". 5.6; 12.5. [Used adverbially]
- duḥkhena "by affliction; by misfortune; by sorrow". 6.22.
- duḥkheṣu "in miseries". 2.56.

927. **duḥkhahā** "that which puts an end to misery". 6.17.
928. **duḥkhālayam** "the abode of misery". 8.15.
929. **duḥkhāntam** "the end of misery". 18.36.
930. **duḥkhasaṁyogaviyogam** "disconnection (*viyoga*) from the connection (*saṁyoga*) with miseries (*duḥkha*); severance of contact with sorrow".[215] 6.23. Also see *saṁyoga*.
931. **duḥkhaśokāmayapradāḥ** "promoters of misery (*duḥkha*), worries (*śoka*), and diseases (*āmaya*); those which result in discomfort, melancholy, and sickness". 17.9. Also see *śoka, āmaya*.[216]
932. **duḥkhataram** "greater misery; more difficulty". 2.36.
933. **duḥkhayonayaḥ** "origins of misery; sources of sorrow". 5.22. Also see *yoni*.
934. **durāsadam** "difficult to overcome; difficult to conquer[217]; indomitable[218]; that which can be reached or caught hold of with difficulty[219]; difficult to apprehend[220]; hard to get at[221]". 3.43.
935. **dūrastham** "distant; located far off; remotely situated". 13.15. Also see *dūreṇa*.
936. **duratyayā** "hard to go beyond; difficult to master; hard to overcome". 7.14.
937. **durbuddheḥ** "of the evil-minded; of the malicious-minded; of one whose intelligence is swayed by evil propensities[222]". 1.23. Also see *durmatiḥ, buddhi*.
938. **dūreṇa** "by far; by a long way; exceedingly". 2.49. Also see *dūrastham*.
939. **durgatim** "a wretched condition; a bad state". 6.40. Also see *sarvadurgāṇi, gati*.

---

[215] Bolle's (p. 275) "loosening of sorrowful ties" captures the idea well. Divanji (p. 71, entry #1602) interprets *duḥkhasaṁyogaviyogam* differently, translating it as "That, union with and separation from which, are difficult to secure."

[216] Verse 17.9 deals with types of food, so Bolle (1979, pp. 189, 275) translates *duḥkha* as "nausea" here.

[217] Sargeant, p. 200.

[218] Van Buitenen 1981, p. 85.

[219] Divanji, p. 70, entry #1583.

[220] Gambhīrānanda 1998, p. 264.

[221] Edgerton, p. 22.

[222] Divanji, p. 70, entry #1587.

940. **durlabhataram** "difficult to obtain". 6.42. Also see √ *labh, sudurlabhaḥ, sulabhaḥ.*

941. **durmatiḥ** "one who has a vicious way of thinking[223]; incorrect perspective". 18.16. Also see *durbuddheḥ, sthiramatiḥ, matiḥ.*

942. **durmedhā** "a stupid person; an unwise person; dull-witted; a fool[224]". 18.35. Also see *medhā.*

943. **durnigraham** "difficult to control". 6.35. Also see *nigraha.*

944. **durnirīkṣyam** "difficult to look at". 11.17. Also see √ *īkṣ.*

945. **duryodhana** "Duryodhana". 1.2. A leading general of the Kauravas. He is the eldest son of King Dhṛtarāṣṭra. His name literally means "Tough Fighter" or "Wicked Warrior". He is called Dhārtarāṣṭra, "Dhṛtarāṣṭra's son", in verse 1.23. See "Who's Who", page 5.

946. **duṣkṛtām** "of the doers of wicked acts; of the evil-doers; the unrighteous". 4.8. Also see *duṣkṛtinaḥ, kṛta.*

947. **duṣkṛtinaḥ** "doers of harm; those who act badly; wrong-doers". 7.15. Also see *duṣkṛtām, kṛtin.*

948. **duṣprāpaḥ** "difficult to acquire". 6.36.

949. **duṣpūra** "difficult to fill; difficult to satisfy; hard to satiate".

- duṣpūram "difficult to satisfy". 16.10.
- duṣpūreṇānalena "by insatiable fire; fire that is difficult to quench". 3.39.

950. **duṣṭāsu** "corrupted; spoiled". 1.41. Also see *praduṣyanti.*

951. **dvaṁdva** "duality; a pair of opposites". [Such as attraction and aversion, pleasure and pain, etc.] Also see *chinnadvaidhāḥ.*

- dvaṁdvaḥ "the pair; the copulative compound". 10.33. [In grammar, a compound consisting of two nouns which, if not compounded, would be joined by the copulative particle *ca.* In this type of compound the two nouns are equally-balanced.]
- dvaṁdvaiḥ "from duality; from inner conflicts". 15.5.
- dvaṁdvamohanirmuktā "completely released from the delusion of duality; freed from the delusion of pairs of opposites". 7.28. Also see *moha, nirmukta.*
- dvaṁdvamohena "by the delusion of duality; by the delusion of pairs of opposites". 7.27. Also see *moha.*

---

[223] Divanji, p. 70, entry #1588.

[224] Zaehner, p. 392.

- dvaṁdvātītaḥ "one who has transcended the pairs of opposites; beyond opposites; one who is beyond inner conflicts". 4.22.
- nirdvaṁdvaḥ "free from the pairs of opposites; free from inner conflicts". 2.45; 5.3.

952. **dvaṁdvamohanirmuktā** "free from the delusion of duality; freed from the delusion of pairs of opposites". 7.28. Also see *chinnadvaidhāḥ, dvaṁdva, moha, mukta.*

953. **dvaṁdvamohena** "by the delusion of duality; by the delusion of pairs of opposites". 7.27. Also see *chinnadvaidhāḥ, dvaṁdva, moha.*

954. **dvāram** "door; gateway". 16.21. [*trividhaṁ narakasyedaṁ dvāram* = this threefold gateway to hell] Also see *navadvāre, sarvadvāra, svargadvāram, tamodvāraih.*

955. **dvau** "two (types)". 15.16; 16.6.

552. **dveṣa** "hatred; aversion; ill-will; antagonism". Also see *adveṣṭā, arāga-dveṣataḥ, dveṣ-, dviṣataḥ, icchādveṣasamutthena, rāgadveṣ-.*

- dveṣaḥ "hatred". 13.6.
- dveṣṭi "one hates". 2.57; 5.3; 12.17; 14.22; 18.10.

956. **dveṣya** "despicable persons; contemptible people".

- dveṣyaḥ "despicable person, contemptible person". 9.29.
- suhṛnmitrāryudāsīnamadhyasthadveṣyabandhuṣu "in friends, enemies, neutrals, mediators, despicable persons, and relatives". 6.9.

957. **dvija** "twice-born".

- devadvijaguruprājñapūjanam "worship (*puja*) of the gods (*deva*), the twice-born (*dvija*), the teachers (*guru*), and the wise (*prājña*)". 17.14.
- dvijottama "O best among the twice-born". 1.7. [Referring to Droṇa.]

958. **dviṣataḥ** "the hating; those who hate". 16.19. Also see *dveṣa, pradviṣantaḥ.*

959. **dvividhā** "of two types". 3.3. Also see *-vidhā.*

960. **dyāvāpṛthivyoḥ** "(between) heaven and earth; of the sky and the earth". 11.20. Also see *pṛthivī.*

961. **dyūtam** "gambling; playing with dice[225]". 10.36.

---

[225] Some commentators take this as a reference to the game of dice in which Yudhiṣṭhira lost his kingdom. Without that event the entire war might never have taken place. See Zaehner, p. 301.

E

ए = E.

962. **ebhiḥ** "by these; from these". 7.13; 18.40.

963. **ebhyaḥ** "to them; by these". 3.12; 7.13.

964. **edhāṁsi** "pieces of sacrificial firewood". 4.37. [Pl. of *indhana,* fuel used for sacrificial fires.]

965. **eka** "one; single; only; alone".
- ekā "one (and only one); single (minded); integrated; unified". 2.41.
- ekaḥ "alone". 11.42.
- ekaḥ "one; only one". 13.33.
- ekam "one". 3.2; 5.1, 4, 5; 10.25; 18.20, 66.
- ekam "the one". 13.5. [Referring to the inner organ, *manas.*]
- ekasmin "in one". 18.22.
- ekayā "with one; by one". 8.26.
- ekena "(by you) alone; only by (you)". 11.20.

966. **ekabhaktiḥ** "devoted to one alone; a person of one-pointed devotion; one who is devoted to a single object of devotion". 7.17. Also see *bhakti.*

967. **ekāgra** "one-pointed; concentrated on a single object".
- ekāgram "one-pointed". 6.12.
- ekāgreṇa "with one-pointed concentration". 18.72.

968. **ekākī** "alone; by oneself". 6.10.

969. **ekākṣaraṁ** "the single-syllable (om, ॐ)". 8.13. Also see *akṣara* ("syllable").

970. **ekāṁśena** "by one (*eka*) portion (*aṁśa*)". 10.42. Also see *aṁśa.*

971. **ekāntam** "always; invariably; solely; exclusively". 6.16.

972. **ekāntikasya**. See *aikāntikasya.*

973. **ekastham** "assembled in one place; standing in one place; standing as one; concentrated at one place; centered in one; converged; united in one; abiding in one; abiding as a unity[226]". 11.7, 13; 13.30.

974. **ekatvam** "oneness; unity". 6.31.

975. **ekatvena** "as one; as unity; as unified". 9.15.

976. **eke** "some (people); one group". 18.3.

---

[226] Tapasyananda, p. 288; also translated as "abiding unified" in verse 11.13, p. 290.

977. **enam** "this". 2.19 (twice), 21, 23 (three times), 25, 26 (twice), 29 (three times); 3.37, 41; 4.42; 6.27; 11.50; 15.3, 11 (twice).
978. **enām** "this". 2.72.
979. **eṣā** "this". 2.39, 72; 7.14.
980. **eṣaḥ** "this". 3.10, 37 (twice), 40; 10.40; 18.59.
981. **eṣām** "of these; their". 1.42.
982. **eṣyasi** "you will go to; you will attain". 8.7; 9.34; 18.65. [√ *i*]
983. **eṣyati** "one will go". 18.68. [√ *i*]
984. **etadyonīni** "originating from that (these two types of Nature); having this as their source". 7.6. [The two sources are the higher and lower Natures.] Also see *yoni*.
985. **etaiḥ** "by these; with these; from these". 1.43; 3.40; 16.22.
986. **etām** "this". 1.3; 7.14; 10.7; 16.9.
987. **etān** "these". 1.22, 25, 35, 36; 14.20. 21 (twice), 26.
988. **etāni** "these". 14.12, 13; 15.8; 18.6, 13.
989. **etasya** "of this". 6.33.
990. **etat** "this". 2.3, 6; 3.32; 4.3, 4; 6.26, 39, 42; 10.14; 11.3, 35; 12.11; 13.1, 6, 11, 18; 15.20; 16.21; 17.16, 26; 18.63, 72, 75.
991. **etāvat** "this much; so much; so far". 16.11.
992. **etayoḥ** "of these two". 5.1.
993. **ete** "these". 1.23, 38; 2.15; 4.30; 7.18; 8.26, 27; 11.33; 18.15.
994. **etena** "by this". 3.39; 10.42.
995. **eteṣām** "of these". 1.10.
996. **eti** "one goes to; one comes to; one attains". 4.9 (twice); 8.6; 11.55. [√ *i*] Also see *atyeti*.
997. **eva** "indeed; verily; truly; even; also; only, alone; just by; itself; exactly". 1.1, 6, 8, 11 (twice), 13, 14, 19, 27, 30, 34, 36, 42; 2.5, 6, 12 (twice), 24, 28, 29 (twice), 47, 55; 3.2,[227] 4, 12, 17 (twice), 18, 20 (twice), 21, 22; 4.3, 11, 15, 20, 24, 25 (twice), 36; 5.8, 13, 15, 18, 19, 22, 23, 24, 27, 28; 6.3, 5 (twice), 6 (twice), 16, 18, 20, 21, 24, 26, 40, 42, 44; 7.4, 12 (twice), 14, 18 (three times), 21, 22; 8.4, 5, 6, 7, 10, 18, 19, 23, 28; 9.12, 16, 17, 19, 23, 24, 30, 34; 10.1, 4, 5, 11, 13, 15, 20, 32, 33, 38, 41 (twice); 11.8, 22, 25, 26, 28, 29, 33 (twice), 35, 40, 45, 46 (twice), 49; 12.4, 6, 8 (twice), 13; 13.4, 5, 8, 14, 15, 19 (twice), 25, 29, 30; 14.10, 13, 17 (twice), 22, 23; 15.4, 7, 9, 15 (twice),

[227] In verse 3.2, the Critical Edition reads *vyāmiśreṇaiva* (*vyāmiśreṇa eva*). Most Vulgate editions read *vyāmiśreṇeva* (*vyāmiśreṇa iva*).

16; 16.4, 6, 19, 20; 17.2, 3, 6, 11, 12, 15, 18, 27 (twice); 18.5 (twice), 8 (twice), 9 (twice), 14, 19, 29, 31, 35, 42, 50, 62, 65, 68. [A particle generally used to emphasize the word it follows. Best translation depends on sense of the passage.]

998. **evākṣayaḥ** (*eva akṣayaḥ*) "alone imperishable". 10.33. Also see *akṣaya.*

999. **evam** "thus; in this way". 1.24, 47; 2.9, 25, 38; 3.16, 43; 4.2, 9, 15, 32 (twice), 35; 6.15, 28; 9.21, 28, 34; 11.3, 9; 12.1; 13.23, 25, 34; 15.19; 18.16.

1000. **evaṁrūpaḥ** "in this form". 11.48. Also see *rūpa.*

1001. **evaṁvidhaḥ** "in this way; in this form; in this aspect". 11.53, 54. Also see *-vidhā.*

G

ग्= G. घ्= Gh.

1002. **gaccha** "go". 18.62. Also see *avagaccha.*

1003. **gacchan** "going; while moving". 5.8.

1004. **gacchanti** "they go; they attain". 2.51; 5.17; 8.24; 14.18 (twice); 15.5. Also see *gacchati.*

1005. **gacchati** "one goes". 6.37, 40. Also see *adhigacchati, āgacchet, gacchanti, nigacchati.*

1006. **gadinam** "bearing a mace; armed with a club". 11.17, 46.

1007. **gahanā** "inscrutable; difficult to understand". 4.17.

1008. **gajendrāṇām** "of lordly elephants; among elephants of the best type". 10.27. Also see *hastini.*

1009. **gām** "the earth". 15.13.

1010. **gamaḥ** "go (the way of)". 2.3. [*klaibyaṁ mā sma gamaḥ* = definitely do not go the way of impotency]

1011. **gamyate** "it is reached; it is attained". 5.5.

1012. **gaṇa** "group; host; category".

- maṇigaṇāḥ "group of gems; strands of pearls". 7.7. Also see *maṇi.*
- suragaṇāḥ "the groups of gods; the hosts of gods; the throngs of gods". 10.2. Also see *sura.*

- bhūtagaṇān "the hosts of spirits[228]; hordes of ghosts[229]; hordes of goblins[230]; the class of spirits or devils[231]; elementals[232]". 17.4. Also see *bhūta*.

1013. **gandha** "smell; aroma; scent". Also see *divyagandhānulepanam*.
- gandhaḥ "smell; aroma". 7.9.
- gandhān "smells; aromas". 15.8.

1014. **gandharva** "Gandharva". [A class of semidivine entity, said to be the divine musicians of the gods.]
- gandharvāṇāṁ "among the *gandharva*-s". 10.26.
- gandharvayakṣāsurasiddhasaṁghāḥ "groups of *gandharva*-s, *yakṣa*-s, *asura*-s, and *siddha*-s". 11.22.

1015. **gandharvayakṣāsurasiddhasaṁghāḥ** "groups of *gandharva*-s, *yakṣa*-s, *asura*-s, and Adepts". 11.22.

1016. **gāṇḍīvam** "Gāṇḍīva". 1.30. [The name of Arjuna's bow, given to him by the god Agni.]

1017. **gantāsi** "you will go to; you will reach". 2.52.

1018. **gantavyam** "reached; to be attained". 4.24.

1019. **garbha** "embryo; seed".
- garbhaḥ "embryo". 3.38.
- garbham "seed; embryo". 14.3

1020. **garīya** "weightier; more venerable". [Comp. degree of the adj. *guru*.]
- garīyaḥ "more advisable; preferable; greater; (lit.) weightier ". 2.6. [Used to describe which of two choices is better, with sense "which of the alternatives carries more weight".]
- garīyān "greater; more venerable; (lit.) weightier". 11.43.
- garīyase "greater; more venerable; (lit.) weightier ". 11.37.

1021. **gatāgatam** "the (repetitive) state of going and returning; the cycle of birth and death". 9.21.

1022. **gataḥ** "restored (to my own nature); returned (to a normal state)". 11.51.

---

[228] Gambhīrānanda 1997, p. 638. The Śaṅkara commentary says that *bhūtagaṇān* includes "the Sapta-mātṛkās (the Seven Mothers) and others" indicating that a broad range of beings may be intended here.

[229] Sargeant, p. 636.

[230] Edgerton, p. 79.

[231] Divanji, p. 106, entry #2436.

[232] Tapasyananda, p. 413.

1023. **gatāḥ** "gone to; attained". 8.15; 14.1; 15.4.

1024. **gatarasam** "tasteless; juices gone; flavor gone". 17.10. Also see *rasaḥ*.

1025. **gatasaṁdehaḥ** "free from doubts; one whose doubts have been dissolved". 18.73.

1026. **gatasaṅgasya** "of one free from attachment". 4.23. Also see *saṅga*.

1027. **gatāsūn** "the dead; those whose vital breath has left the body". 2.11. Also see *agatāsūn*.

1028. **gatavyathaḥ** "free from worries; free from pain; who has overcome a feeling of distress". 12.16. Also see *pravyathita, vyapetabhīḥ*.

1029. **gati** "state; goal; movement; way; path; position". Also see *bhogaiśvaryagatim, durgatim, svargatim*.

- gatī "(two) movements; (two) paths; (two) goals". 8.26.
- gatiḥ "state; goal; way". 4.17; 9.18; 12.5.
- gatim "state; goal; way". 6.37, 45; 7.18; 8.13, 21; 9.32; 13.28; 16.20, 22, 23.

1030. **gātrāṇi** "limbs". 1.29.

1031. **gatvā** "having reached; having attained". 14.15; 15.6.

1032. **gavi** "in a cow; upon a cow". 5.18.

1033. **gāyatrī** "Gāyatrī". 10.35. [The name of a Vedic meter consisting of 24 syllables arranged into three groups of eight syllables. Also the name of a specific verse in Gāyatrī meter (the "Gāyatrī *mantra*").]

1034. **gehe** "in the home; in the family". 6.41.

1035. **ghātayati** "it causes to kill". 2.21. [√ *han*]

1036. **ghnataḥ**"killed; slain". 1.35. Also see *kulaghnānām*.

1037. **ghora** "terrible; terrifying".

- ghoram "terrible; terrifying". 11.49.
- ghoram "terrible; extreme (austerities)". 17.5.
- ghore "terrible". 3.1.

1038. **ghoṣaḥ** "sound; noise; resonance". 1.19. Also see *sughoṣamaṇipuṣpakau*.

1039. **ghrāṇam** "the sense of smell; the nose". 15.9.

1040. **girām** "among utterances; of words". 10.25.

1041. **gītam** "sung; chanted; recited". 13.4.

1042. **glāniḥ** "decay; exhaustion; suppression". 4.7.

1043. **govinda** "Govinda". [A name of Kṛṣṇa. For discussion of meaning see page 13.]

- govinda "O Govinda". 1.32.
- govindam "Govinda". 2.9.

1044. **grasamānaḥ** "swallowing". 11.30. Also see *grasiṣṇu.*

1045. **grasiṣṇu** "one who is in the habit of swallowing; devourer; destroyer (of the universe)". 13.16. Also see *grasamānaḥ.*

1046. **gṛhītvā** "having grasped; after grasping; having taken hold of; after taking". 15.8; 16.10 ("holding conceptions"). [Indec. past part. of √ *grah.*] Also see *-tvā.*

1047. **gṛhītvāsadgrāhān** "having held evil ideas; holding untruthful conceptions". 16.10. [*gṛhītva-asad-grāhān*] Also see *asat.*

1048. **gṛhṇan** "while accepting; grasping; taking". 5.9.

1049. **gṛhṇāti** "it wears (clothing); it puts on". 2.22.

1050. **gṛhyate** "it can be controlled; it is restrained". 6.35. Also see *dhṛtigṛhītayā, nigraha, nigṛh-.*

1051. **gṛṇanti** "they praise" . 11.21.

1052. **guḍākeśa** "Guḍākeśa". [An epithet of Arjuna. For discussion of meaning see page 17.]

- guḍākeśa "O Guḍākeśa". 10.20; 11.7.
- guḍākeśaḥ "Guḍākeśa". 2.9.
- guḍākeśena "by Guḍākeśa". 1.24.

1053. **guhy-** ("secret") Also see *rahasyam.*

- guhyād guhyataraṁ "more secret than all secrets". 18.63.
- guhyam "secret". 11.1; 18.68, 75.
- guhyatamaṁ "most secret". 9.1; 15.20.
- maunaṁ caivāsmi guhyānāṁ "among secrets I am silence". 10.38.
- rājaguhyaṁ "king of secrets". 9.2. [Divanji notes that this could be translated either as, "That which is to be protected or concealed by the members of the princely order or that which is a king amonst the things to be protected or concealed, i.e., the highest secret." Of these two, Divanji considers the first to be the preferable meaning.[233]]
- sarvaguhyatamam "most secret of all". 18.64. Also see *sarva.*

1054. **guṇa** Also see compounds with *guṇa-, jaghanyaguṇavṛttasthāḥ, nirguṇam, nirguṇatvāt, nistraiguṇyaḥ, rajoguṇasamudbhavaḥ, sarvendriyaguṇābhāsam, traiguṇyaviṣayāḥ, viguṇaḥ.* Also see *sattva, raja, tamas.*

- guṇāḥ "the *guṇa*-s". 3.28; 14.5, 23.

---

[233] Divanji, p. 126, entry #2894.

- guṇaiḥ "by the *guṇa*-s; from the attributes; according to the qualities". 3.5, 27; 13.23; 14.23; 18.40, 41.
- guṇān "the *guṇa*-s; the attributes; the qualities". 13.19, 21; 14.20, 21 (twice), 26.
- guṇebhyaḥ "than the *guṇa*-s; from the *guṇa*-s". 14.19 (twice).
- guṇeṣu "in the *guṇa*-s". 3.28.

1055. **guṇabhedataḥ** "depending on the distribution of the *guṇa*-s; according to the prevailing *guṇa*[234]; distinguished according to the qualities[235]; on account of the distinction between the inherent attributes[236]". 18.19. Also see *bhedam, buddhibhedam.*

1056. **guṇabhoktṛ** "enjoyer of the *guṇa*-s; experiencer of the qualities". 13.14.

1057. **guṇakarma** "*guṇa*-s and *karma*-s (if treated as a *dvandva* compound); action of the *guṇa*-s". Also see *karma.*

- guṇakarmasu "(attached) to the activities of the *guṇa*-s; in the actions (*karma*) of the qualities (*guṇa*); (attached) to the constituents' works[237]; in inherent attributes and acts[238]". 3.29.
- guṇakarmavibhāgayoḥ "distribution (*vibhāga*) of the qualities (*guṇa*) and actions (*karma*); division made on the basis of one's inherent attributes and acts[239]; how constituents and works are parcelled out in categories[240]". 3.28.
- guṇakarmavibhāgaśaḥ "in accordance with the distribution of qualities (*guṇa*-s) and actions (*karma*); on the basis of a division made according to the inherent attributes and acts[241]; with categories of 'constituents' and works[242]". 4.13.

1058. **guṇamayaiḥ** "by (these states) composed of the *guṇa*-s". 7.13.

---

234 Van Buitenen 1981, p. 139.
235 Sargeant, p. 680.
236 Divanji, p. 52, entry #1175.
237 Zaehner, p. 172.
238 Divanji, p. 52, entry #1172.
239 Divanji, p. 52, entry #1170.
240 Zaehner, p. 172.
241 Divanji, p. 52, entry #1171.
242 Zaehner, p. 186.

1059. **guṇamayī** "composed of the *guṇa*-s; consisting solely of the inherent attributes[243]". 7.14.

1060. **guṇānvitam** "accompanied by the *guṇa*-s; invested with *guṇa*-s". 15.10. Also see *anvita.*

1061. **guṇapravṛddhāḥ** "nourished by the *guṇa*-s; which grow due to the inherent attributes (of Nature)". 15.2. Also see √ *pravṛddh.*

1062. **guṇasaṁkhyāne** "in the theory of the Strands[244]; in the philosophical analysis of qualities[245]; in the reckoning of the *guṇa*-s; the in the theory of constituents; in the context of the *guṇa*-s; in the distribution of the *guṇa*-s; in the differences of the *guṇa*-s". 18.19. Also see *guṇa, sāṁkhya.*

1063. **guṇasaṁmūḍhāḥ** "those who are deluded by the *guṇa*-s". 3.29.

1064. **guṇasaṅgaḥ** "contact with the *guṇa*-s; attachment to the *guṇa*-s". 13.21. Also see *saṅga.*

1065. **guṇataḥ** "according to the *guṇa*-s; on the basis of the inherent attributes". 18.29. [*guṇa* + *tas,* having the sense of the abl. case termination.]

1066. **guṇātītaḥ** "one who has transcended the *guṇa*-s". 14.25. Also see *atītya, dvaṁdvātīta.*

1067. **guru** "a (revered) teacher; a preceptor; one who is fit to be respected (such as an elder or a preceptor, used in the sense of a person who has *gravitas*); heavy".

- devadvijaguruprājñapūjanam "worship (*puja*) of the gods (*deva*), the twice-born (*dvija*), the teachers (*guru*), and the wise (*prājña*)". 17.14.
- guruḥ "(revered) teacher". 11.43.
- gurūn "respected elders; preceptors". 2.5 (twice).
- guruṇā "by great; by heavy". 6.22. [Inst. sing. of the masc. form of the adj. *guru; na duḥkhena guruṇāpi vicālyate,* "not affected even by great affliction".]

---

243 Divanji, p. 52, entry #1177.

244 Edgerton, p. 85.

245 Miller, p. 138.

H

ह् = H. Visarga = Ḥ (not used as the initial sound of a word).

1068. **ha** "Hah!". 2.9. [Indec. interjection. A particle expressive of grief or regret.]

1069. √ **hā** "to leave; to give up; to forsake; to abandon; to neglect (duty)". See *hāniḥ, hitvā, jahāti, prajahāti.*

1070. √ **han** "to kill; to hurt; to strike". See *abhyahanyanta, ahatvā, ghātayati, haniṣye, hantāram, hanti, hantum, hata, hatvā, hinasti, jahi, prajahi, upahanyām.*

1071. **hāniḥ** "cessation; removal". 2.65. [√ *hā*]

1072. **haniṣye** "I will kill". 16.14. [√ *han*]

1073. **hanta** "well then; come then; very well". 10.19. [Indec. particle indicating enthusiasm, compassion, or benediction.]

1074. **hantāram** "a killer; a slayer". 2.19.

1075. **hanti** "it kills; one kills". 2.19, 21; 18.17.

1076. **hantum** "to kill". 1.35, 37, 45.

1077. **hanyamāne** "even though in being killed". 2.20.

1078. **hanyate** "it is killed". 2.19, 20.

1079. **hanyuḥ** "if they were to kill; they should kill". 1.46. Also see *upahanyām.*

1080. **haranti** "they carry away; they disturb (the mind)". 2.60. [√ *hṛ*]

1081. **harati** "it carries away; it deprives one of (wisdom)". 2.67. [√ *hṛ*]

1082. **hari** "Hari". [Used to refer to Kṛṣṇa.]

- hareḥ "of Hari". 18.77.
- hariḥ "Hari". 11.9.

1083. **harṣa** "delight; joy; jubilation; exhultation; exhilaration".[246] Also see *romaharṣa.*

- harṣam "delight; joy". 1.12.
- harṣāmarṣabhayodvegaiḥ "(free) from agitation (*udvega*) caused by delight (*harṣa*), intolerance (*āmarṣa*), and fear (*bhaya*)" *or* "(free) from delight (*harṣa*), intolerance (*āmarṣa*), fear (*bhaya*), and agitation (*udvega*)". 12.15. Also see *āmarṣa, bhaya, vegam.*

---

[246] Śaṅkara defines *harṣa* as "elation of the mind on acquiring a thing dear to oneself, and is manifested by horripilation, shedding of tears, etc." Gambhīrānanda 1997, p. 488.

- harṣaśokānvitaḥ "filled with (*anvita*) delight (*harṣa*) and grief (*śoka*); overpowered by joy or sorrow". 18.27. Also see *anvita, śoka*.

1084. **hastāt** "from (my) hand". 1.30. Also see *cakrahastam*.

1085. **hastini** "on an elephant". 5.18. Also see *gajendrāṇām*.

1086. **hata** "killed". [√ *han*] Also see *kārpaṇyadoṣopahatasvabhāvaḥ, lobhopahatacetasaḥ*.

- hatam "killed". 2.19.
- hataḥ "killed". 2.37; 16.14.
- hatān "killed". 11.34.

1087. **hatvā** "having killed; after killing; having slain; after slaying; by killing". 1.31, 36, 37; 2.5, 6; 18.17. [Indec. past part. of √ *han,* sometimes used with sense "by slaying".] Also see *ahatvā, -tvā*.

1088. **haviḥ** "an oblation or a burnt offering". 4.24. Also see *hutam*.

1089. **hayaiḥ** "by horses". 1.14.

1090. **he** "oh!; ho! hey!". 11.41 (three times). [Indec. particle.]

1091. **hetu** "cause; reason; motive". Also see *ahaitukam, kāmahaitukam, karmaphalahetuḥ, phalahetavaḥ*.

- hetavaḥ "causes; causative factors". 18.15.
- hetoḥ "for the sake of". 1.35.
- hetuḥ "cause". 13.20 (twice).
- hetunā "for (this) reason". 9.10. [*hetunā anena*]

1092. **hetumadbhiḥ** "with logical arguments". 13.4.

1093. **hi** "indeed; surely; because". 1.11, 37, 42; 2.5, 8, 15, 27, 31, 41, 49, 51, 60, 61, 65, 67; 3.5 (twice), 8, 12, 19, 20, 23, 34, 41; 4.3, 7, 12, 17, 38; 5.3, 19, 22; 6.2, 4, 5, 27, 34, 39, 40, 42, 44; 7.14, 17, 18, 22; 8.26; 9.24, 30, 32; 10.2, 14, 16, 18, 19; 11.2, 20, 21, 24, 31; 12.5, 12; 13.21, 28; 14.27; 18.4, 11, 48. [Depending on context, the particle *hi* may have an emphatic sense (*indeed* or *surely*) or a causal sense (*because* or *for*). Some Vulgate editions have an alternate reading including *hi* in verse 9.21.]

1094. **himālayaḥ** "the Himālaya mountains". 10.25.

1095. **hiṁsā** "injury; harm". Also see *ahiṁsā*.

- hiṁsām "violence; injury; harm". 18.25.
- hiṁsātmakaḥ "violent-natured; bent on injury; injurious by nature". 18.27. Also see *ātman*.

1096. **hinasti** "one harms". 13.28. [√ *han*]

1097. **hitakāmyayā** "with (your) well-being in view; with desire for (your) welfare; a desire to do good". 10.1. Also see *hita, kāma, kāmyānām, sarvabhūtahite, ahitāḥ.*

1098. **hitam** "welfare". 18.64. Also see *hitakāmyayā, sarvabhūtahite, ahitāḥ.*

1099. **hitvā** "having abandoned (your duty); after forsaking (your duty); having disregarded (your duty)". 2.33. [Indec. past part. of √ *hā.*] Also see *–tvā.*

1100. √ **hṛ** "to carry away; to deprive one of". see *haranti, harati, hriyate, saṁharate.*

1101. **hṛdayadaurbalyam** "weakness of the heart; faint-heartedness". 2.3. Also see *hṛt, bala.*

1102. **hrīḥ** "modesty". 16.2.

1103. **hṛṣīkeśa** "Lord of the senses; Bristling Haired One". For discussion of alternate meanings of this epithet of Kṛṣṇa see page 13.

- hṛṣīkeśa "O Lord of the senses". 11.36; 18.1.
- hṛṣīkeśaḥ "Lord of the senses". 1.15, 24; 2.10.
- hṛṣīkeśam "Lord of the senses". 1.21; 2.9.

1104. **hṛṣitaḥ** "delighted; thrilled". 11.45. [√ *hṛṣ*]

1105. **hriyate** "one is carried away". 6.44. [√ *hṛ*]

1106. **hṛṣṭaromā** "one who has the hair on their body standing on end". 11.14.

1107. **hṛṣyāmi** "I am thrilled; I am delighted". 18.76, 77. [√ *hṛṣ*]

1108. **hṛṣyati** "is exhilarated; is delighted". 12.17. [√ *hṛṣ*]

1109. **hṛt** "the heart". Also see *hṛdayadaurbalyam, suhṛ-.*

- hṛdayāni "the hearts". 1.19.
- hṛddeśe "in the heart region". 18.61. Also see *deśe.*
- hṛdi "in the heart". 8.12; 13.17; 15.15.
- hṛdyāḥ "hearty; nourishing; pleasing". 17.8.
- hṛtstham "residing in the heart". 4.42.

1110. **hṛtajñānāḥ** "robbed of knowledge". 7.20. Also see *jñāna.*

1111. **hutam** "an oblation offered into fire; an offering; something offered". 4.24; 9.16; 17.28. Also see *haviḥ.*

1112. **hutāśa** "fire; (lit.) oblation-eater". See *dīptahutāśavaktram* (11.19).[247]

[247] Apte, p. 1029, entry for हुत–आशः, 1. fire.

I

इ = I. ई = Ī.

1113. √i "to go". See *eti, atyeti, eṣyasi, eṣyati, upaiti, upeta, upetya, upaiṣyasi, parayopetāḥ, vyapetabhīḥ.*

1114. **iccha** "wish for". 12.9. [*icchāptum* = seek to attain]

1115. **icchā** "a wish; a desire". 13.6. Also see *vigatecchābhayakrodhaḥ.*

1116. **icchādveṣasamutthena** "by that which has arisen out of desire (*icchā*) and aversion (*dveṣa*)". 7.27. Also see *rāgadveṣa-.*

1117. **icchāmi** "I wish; I want". 1.35; 11.3, 31, 46; 18.1. [√ *iṣ*]

1118. **icchantaḥ** "wanting; wishing for; desiring". 8.11.

1119. **icchasi** "you wish; you want". 11.7; 18.60, 63. [√ *iṣ*]

1120. **icchati** "one wishes". 7.21. [√ *iṣ*]

1121. **idam** "this". 1.10, 21, 28; 2.1, 2, 10, 17; 3.31, 38; 7.2, 5, 7, 13; 8.22, 28; 9.1, 2, 4; 10.42; 11.19, 20 (twice), 41, 47, 49 (twice), 51, 52; 12.20; 13.1; 14.2; 15.20; 16.13 (four times[248]), 21; 18.46, 67, 68.

1122. **idānīm** "now; at this moment". 11.51; 18.36.

1123. **īdṛśam** "like this; of such aspect". 2.32; 6.42.

1124. **īdṛk** "like this; of such aspect". 11.49.

1125. **īḍyam** "adorable". 11.44. [*īśam īḍyam* = adorable Lord; the Lord who is worthy of being worshipped]

1126. **iha** "here (referring to time, place, or direction); in this world; in this case".

- apīha [*api iha*] "even here (in this world)" 2.5.
- asyeha [*asya iha*] "of it here (in this world)". 15.3.
- ekeha [*ekā iha*] "one in this matter; here in this world [there is only] one". 2.41.
- iha "here; in this place; in this world; in this matter". 3.37; 4.12, 38; 11.32; 17.18, 28.
- ihaikastham [*iha ekastham*] "located here in one place; assembled here". 11.7.
- ihaiva [*iha eva*] "indeed here on earth". 2.5; 5.19.

---

[248] The Critical Edition has *idam* four times in verse 16.13. Some Vulgate editions read *imam* for one of these, reducing the count to three.

- ihārhasi [*iha arhasi*] "here you should; in this world you are obliged". 16.24.
- jahātīha [*jahāti iha*] "he casts off here (in this world); he leaves aside here (in this world)". 2.50.
- kāleneha [*kālena iha*] "with time here (in this world); in the course of a long time here (in this world)". 4.2.
- naiveha [*na eva iha*] "not truly here (in this world)". 6.40.
- nākṛteneha [*na akṛtena iha*] "not with non-action in this case; nor with inaction in this world". 3.18.
- nānuvartayatīha [*na anuvartayati iha*] "one does not cause (the wheel) to revolve here (in this world); he does not make (the cycle) revolve here (in this world)". 3.16.
- neha [*na iha*] "not here (in this world)". 7.2.
- nehābhikramanāśaḥ [*na iha abhikramanāśo 'sti*] "in this world no effort is lost". 2.40.
- śaknotīhaiva [*śaknoti iha eva*] "he can even here in this world; he is able in this very world". 5.23.

1127. **īhante** "they are eager for; they desire (for themselves)". 16.12. [√ *īh*]

1128. **īhate** "he is eager for; he desires (for himself)". 7.22. [√ *īh*]

1129. **ijyate** "it is offered; it is performed; it is sacrificed". 17.11, 12. Also see √ *yaj, ijyayā, yaṣṭavyam.*

1130. **ijyayā** "through performance of a sacrifice". 11.53. Also see √ *yaj, ijyate, yajña, yaṣṭavyam.*

1131. √ **īkṣ** "to see".

- durnirīkṣyam "difficult to look at". 11.17. [*dus + nis +* √ *īkṣ*]
- īkṣate "he sees; he views; he looks at". 6.29; 18.20.
- nirīkṣe "I see; I behold; I look at". 1.22. [*nir +* √ *īkṣ*]
- samīkṣya "having seen; having looked at; contemplating; observing". 1.27. [*sam +* √ *īkṣ*]
- vīkṣante "they see; they view; they gaze at; they observe". 11.22. [*vi +* √ *īkṣ*]

1132. **īkṣate** "he sees; he views; he looks at". 6.29; 18.20. Also see √ *īkṣ.*

1133. **ikṣvākave** "to Ikṣvāku". 4.1. [Ikṣvāku was the first king of the Solar dynasty.]

1134. **imāḥ** "these". 3.24; 10.6.

1135. **imam** "this". 1.28; 2.33; 4.1, 2; 9.8, 33; 13.33; 16.13 [Vulgate][249]; 17.7; 18.68, 70, 74, 76.
1136. **imām** "this". 2.39, 42.
1137. **imān** "these". 10.16; 18.17.
1138. **imau** "these two". 15.16.
1139. **ime** "these". 1.33; 2.12, 18; 3.24.
1140. **indriya** "organ (of sense or action); a motor or sensory organ".[250] Also see *atīndriyam, indriy-, jitendriyaḥ, karmendriy-, saṁyatendriyaḥ, sarvāṇīndriyakarmāṇi, sarvendriy-, śrotrādīnīndriyāṇi, vijitendriyaḥ, yatacittendriyakriyaḥ, yatendriyamanobuddhiḥ*. [
    - indriyaiḥ "by the senses; with the senses and motor organs". 2.64; 5.11.
    - indriyāṇām "of the senses". 2.8, 67; 10.22.
    - indriyāṇi "the senses; the sense organs". 2.58, 60, 61, 68; 3.7, 40, 41, 42; 4.26; 5.9; 13.5; 15.7 [*indriyāṇi daśaikam* = the ten organs].
    - indriyasya "of a sense". 3.34 (twice).
    - indriyebhyaḥ "than the senses; (superior) to the sense organs". 3.42.

    Examples of compound constructions:
    - indriyāṇīndriyārthebhyaḥ "(withdrawing) the senses from (their) objects; (withdrawing) the sense organs from the objects of the senses". 2.58, 68.
    - indriyāṇīndriyārtheṣu "the senses (are interacting with) their sense objects; the senses (are operating on) their objects; the organs function (in regard to) the objects of the organs". 5.9. [*indriyāṇīndriyārtheṣu vartanta*]
    - indriyasyendriyasyārthe "due to the senses and the objects of the senses; in the senses in relation to their objects". 3.34. Also see *arthe*.
    - manaḥprāṇendriyakriyāḥ "the functions of the mind (*manaḥ*), the life force (*prāṇa*), and the senses (*indriya*); the operation of the mind, the vital breath, and the organs (of sense and action)". 18.33.

---

[249] The Critical Edition has *idam* four times in verse 16.13. Some Vulgate editions read *imam* for one of these, reducing the count to three.

[250] The ten *indriyas* include five sense organs (eye, ear, skin, tongue, and nose) and five motor organs (hands, feet, mouth, and the two excretory and reproductive organs). The five sense organs are the *jñānendriyas*, the organs of knowledge. The five motor organs are the *karmendriyas*, the organs of action. In some passages, the *indriyas* refer primarily to the five sense organs. Verse 13.5 refers explicitly to the "ten organs" (*indriyāṇi daśaikam*) including both the *jñānendriyas* and the *karmendriyas*.

- manaḥṣaṣṭhānīndriyāṇi "the senses with the mind as the sixth unit; those to which the mind is added as the sixth". 15.7. Also see *manas.*
- viṣayendriyasaṁyogāt "from contact between the senses and the objects (of the senses)". 18.38. Also see *viṣaya, saṁyoga.*

1141. **indriyāgniṣu** "in the fire of he senses; in the fire of the organs of sense and action". 4.26. Also see *agni.*

1142. **indriyagocarāḥ** "the objects of the senses". 13.5. Also see *indriyārtha.*

1143. **indriyagrāmam** "all the senses; the group of the organs of sense and action". 6.24; 12.4.

1144. **indriyakarmāṇi** "functions and actions of the senses and motor organs". 4.27.

1145. **indriyārāmaḥ** "one who takes delight (*ārāma*) in the senses; indulging in the objects of the senses;". 3.16. Also see *antarārāmaḥ,* √ *ram-.*

1146. **indriyārtha** "sense objects; objects of the sense organs". Also see *arthaḥ, indriya, indriyagocarāḥ.*

- indriyāṇīndriyārthebhyaḥ "(withdrawing) the senses from (their) objects; (withdrawing) the sense organs from the objects of the senses". 2.58, 68.
- indriyāṇīndriyārtheṣu "the senses (are interacting with) their sense objects; the senses (are operating on) their objects; the organs function (in regard to) the objects of the organs". 5.9. [*indriyāṇīndriyārtheṣu vartanta*]
- indriyārthān "the objects of the senses". 3.6.
- indriyārtheṣu "in sense objects; (attached) to the objects of the senses". 6.4.
- indriyārtheṣu "(detachment) toward objects of the senses; (dispassion) with regard to sense objects". [*indriyārtheṣu vairāgyam*] 13.8.
- indriyasyendriyasyārthe "due to the senses and the objects of the senses; in the senses in relation to their objects". 3.34. Also see *arthe.*

1147. **iṅgate** "wavers; flickers; is agitated". [√ *iṅg* = to shake or be agitated]

- iṅgate "it flickers". 6.19. [*yathā dīpo nivātastho neṅgate*]
- iṅgate "one does not waver; one is not agitated; one does not react[251]". 14.23. [*yo 'vatiṣṭhati neṅgate* = "he stirs not but remains steadfast"[252]]

1148. √ **iṣ** "to wish for; to want". See *icch-, anicchan, anviccha.*

1149. **īśa** "the Lord". Also see *bhūteśa, deveśa, īśvara, vitteśa.*

- īśam "the Lord". 11.15, 44.

---

[251] Van Buitenen 1981, p. 129.

[252] Warrier, p. 485.

1150. **iṣṭa** "desired; wished for". Also see *iṣṭa-, iṣṭā-, aniṣṭam.*

- iṣṭaḥ "dear; desired". 18.64, 70.
- iṣṭāḥ "desired". 17.9.
- iṣṭam "wished for; that which is desirable". 18.12.
- iṣṭān "desired". 3.12.

1151. **iṣṭakāmadhuk** "the longed-for (*iṣṭa*) cow that fulfills all desires (*kāmadhuk*); yielder of the coveted objects of desire[253]; the yielder of the desired fruits[254]". 3.10. Also see *iṣṭa, kāmadhuk.*

1152. **iṣṭāniṣṭopapattiṣu** "in desirable and undesirable events; the accrual of fruits which are desired and those which are not desired". 13.9. Also see *aniṣṭam, iṣṭa.*

1153. **iṣṭvā** "worshipping; having worshipped". 9.20. [Indec. past. part. of √ *yaj.*] Also see √ *yaj, yajña, -tvā.*

1154. **iṣubhiḥ** "with arrows". 2.4.

1155. **īśvara** "master; sovereign; lord; the Lord; god". Also see *aiśvaram, anīśvaram, bhogaiśvarya, bhūtamaheśvara, īśa, īśvarabhāvaḥ, loka-maheśvara, mahāyogeśvara, maheśvara, parameśvara, viśveśvara, yogeśvara.*

- īśvaraḥ "the Lord; god". 4.6; 15.8 [Here taking the form of an individual soul as the individul sovereign self[255]], 15.17; 16.14 "omnipotent; sovereign" [Here indicating the way an ignorant person thinks of themselves as being in control or autonomous]; 18.61.
- īśvaram "the Lord; god". 13.28.

1156. **īśvarabhāvaḥ** "royal state; monarchy; leadership; authority; mastery". 18.43. Also see *īśvara.*

1157. **itaḥ** "from here; from this". 7.5; 14.1.

1158. **itaraḥ** "another; other". 3.21.

1159. **iti** "thus; in this way; as well; so; truly". 1.25, 44; 2.9, 42; 3.27, 28; 4.3, 4, 14, 16; 5.8, 9; 6.2, 8, 18, 36; 7.4, 6, 12, 19; 8.13, 21; 9.6; 10.8; 11.4, 21, 41 (twice), 50; 13.1 (twice), 11, 18, 22; 14.5, 11, 23; 15.17, 20; 16.11, 15; 17.2, 11, 16, 20, 23, 24, 25, 26,

---

[253] Gambhīrānanda 1998, pp. 221-2. This interpretation associates "coveted" (*iṣṭa*) with "objects of desire" (*kāma*).

[254] Divanji, p. 31, entry #701.

[255] Verses 15.7-8 explain a relationship between individual souls and Īśvara. See Van Buitenen (1981, p. 169, notes 2 and 3) for a possible interpretation of these verses.

27 (twice), 28; 18.3 (twice), 6, 8, 9, 11, 18, 32, 59, 63, 64, 70, 74. [In some cases, the word *iti* is used to indicate the end of a quotation.]

1160. **iva** "like; as if". 1.30; 2.10, 58, 67; 3.2 (twice[256]), 36; 5.10; 6.34, 38; 7.7; 11.44 (twice); 13.16; 15.8; 18.37, 38, 48. [Indec. particle used for making comparisons, similes, or to express the idea of "as if".]

1161. **iyam** "this". 7.4, 5.

J

ज् = J. झ् = Jh.

1162. **jagannivāsa** "Abode of the Universe; Receptacle of the Universe". 11.25, 37, 45. Also see *nivāsaḥ*.

1163. **jāgarti** "it is awake; he is wakeful". 2.69. Also see *jāgrati*.

1164. **jagat** "world; universe". Also see *loka, viśva*.
   - jagannivāsa "Abode of the Universe; Receptacle of the Universe". 11.25, 37, 45.
   - jagat "the world". 7.5, 13; 9.4, 10; 10.42; 11.7, 13, 30, 36; 15.12; 16.8.
   - jagataḥ "of the world". 7.6; 8.26; 9.17; 16.9.
   - jagatpate "O Lord of the Universe". 10.15.

1165. **jaghanyaguṇavṛttasthāḥ** "those whose conduct is characterized by the lowest (*jaghanya*) quality (*guṇa*); those whose behavior is under the influence of the lowest *guṇa*". 14.18. Also see *guṇa*. [The Vulgate reads *jaghanyaguṇavṛttisthā*.[257]]

1166. **jāgrataḥ** "of keeping awake". 6.16.

1167. **jāgrati** "(all beings are) awake; they are wakeful". 2.69. Also see *jāgarti*.

1168. **jahāti** "one leaves aside". 2.50. [√ *hā*] Also see *prajahāti*.

1169. **jahi** "destroy; kill". 3.43; 11.34. [Imp. 2nd pers. sing. of √ *han*.] Also see *prajahi*.

---

[256] In verse 3.2, the Critical Edition reads *vyāmiśreṇaiva* (*vyāmiśreṇa eva*) but Śaṅkara, Rāmānuja, and Madhusūdana Sarasvati all read *vyāmiśreṇeva* (*vyāmiśreṇa iva*) giving the sense of "seemingly conflicting" and a second use of *iva* in the verse.

[257] For a comment on how the Vulgate reading is followed by many commentators, see Divanji, p. 5, entry #1275. Śaṅkara adopts the reading *jaghanyaguṇavṛttasthā* which is used in the Critical Edition, and explains *vṛtta* as meaning *nidrālasyādi* ("sleep, idleness, etc."). It therefore appears to refer to conduct or behavior.

1170. **jāla** "net; snare". See *mohajālasamāvṛtāḥ* (16.16).

1171. **jāhnavī** "Jāhnavī; Gaṅgā; the river Ganges". 10.31. [A name of the river Ganges derived from the sage Jahnu.[258]]

1172. **jana**

- janaḥ "people". 3.21.
- janāḥ "people; persons". 7.16; 8.17, 24; 9.22; 16.7; 17.4, 5.
- janānām "of people; of persons". 7.28.

1173. **janādhipāḥ** "kings; rulers of men". 2.12.

1174. **janakādayaḥ** "Janaka and others". 3.20. [There was more than one king named Janaka, but the reference seems to be to a great philosopher-king, a member of the Kṣatriya class. In the *Rāmāyaṇa,* Janaka was the father of Sītā, the wife of the hero Rāma.]

1175. **jānan** "knowing". 8.27. Also see *jānāti, jāne.* [√ *jñā*]

1176. **janārdana** "O Motivator of Men, O Rouser of Men". 1.36, 39, 44; 3.1; 10.18; 11.51. [Epithet of Kṛṣṇa. The verb *ard* has a range of meanings, including "to rouse" or "to agitate".[259]]

1177. **janasaṁsadi** "in a crowd of people; in the society of men". 13.10.

1178. **jānāti** "one knows". 15.19. Also see *jānān, jāne.* [√ *jñā*]

1179. **janayet** "one should produce; one should create". 3.26.

1180. **jāne** "I know". 11.25. Also see *jānan, jānāti.* [√ *jñā*]

1181. **janma** "birth". Also see *janma-, anekajanmasaṁsiddhaḥ.*

- janma "birth". 2.27; 4.4 (twice), 4.9 (twice); 6.42; 8.15, 16.
- janmanām "of births". 7.19.
- janmani "in birth". 16.20 (twice). [*janmani janmani* = while taking birth after birth]
- janmāni "births". 4.5.
- punarjanma "birth again; rebirth". 4.9; 8.15, 16.

1182. **janmabandhavinirmuktāḥ** "completely released from the bondage of birth(s)". 2.51. Also see *bandham,* √ *muc, mukta, nirmukta.*

1183. **janmakarmaphalapradām** "giving rise to rebirth and the fruits of action; resulting in acts leading to births". 2.43. Also see *karmaphala.*

1184. **janmamṛtyujarāduḥkhaiḥ** "from the miseries (*duḥkha*) of birth (*janma*), death (*mṛtyu*), and old age (*jarā*)". 14.20. Also see *janma, mṛtyu, jarā, duḥkha.*

---

[258] Bhattacharyya, p. 125.

[259] Apte, p. 152, entry for अर्द्.

1185. **janmamṛtyujarāvyādhiduḥkhadoṣānudarśanam** "contemplation (*darśana*) of the fault (*doṣa*) consisting of the miseries (*duḥkha*) of birth (*janma*), death (*mṛtyu*), old age (*jarā*), and disease (*vyādhi*)". 13.8. Also see *janma, mṛtyu, jarā, vyādhi, duḥkha.*

1186. **jantavaḥ** "living beings; creatures; people". 5.15.[260]

1187. **japayajñaḥ** "a sacrifice in the form of *japa*; sacrifice consisting of repetition of a *mantra*; sacrifice consisting of repetitive prayer". 10.25. Also see *yajña.*

1188. **jarā** "old age".

- jarā "old age". 2.13.
- jarāmaraṇamokṣāya "liberation (*mokṣa*) from old age (*jarā*) and dying (*maraṇa*)". 7.29. Also see *maraṇa, mokṣ-.*
- janmamṛtyujarāduḥkhaiḥ "from the miseries (*duḥkha*) of birth (*janma*), death (*mṛtyu*), and old age (*jarā*)". 14.20.
- janmamṛtyujarāvyādhiduḥkhadoṣānudarśanam "contemplation (*anu-darśana*) of the fault (*doṣa*) consisting of the miseries (*duḥkha*) of birth (*janma*), death (*mṛtyu*), old age (*jarā*), and disease (*vyādhi*)". 13.8.

1189. **jarāmaraṇamokṣāya** "toward release from old age and dying; for becoming free of old age and death". 7.29. Also see *jarā, mokṣ-. maraṇa.*

1190. **jātāḥ** "the born". 10.6. Also see *jātasya, abhijāta.*

1191. **jātasya** "of the born". 2.27. Also see *jātāḥ.*

1192. **jātidharmāḥ** "traditions of the community; duties appropriate to one's community; societal traditions; class Laws[261]". 1.43. Also see *dharma, kuladharmāḥ.*

1193. **jātu** "ever; at any time; at all; verily". 2.12; 3.5, 23.

1194. **jayaḥ** "victory". 10.36. Also see *vijayaḥ.*

1195. **jayadratham** "Jayadratha". 11.34. [The king of Sindhudeśa. See "Who's Who", page 5.]

1196. **jayājayau** "in victory and defeat". 2.38.

1197. **jāyante** "the arise; they are born". 14.12, 13. Also see *upajāyante*

1198. **jāyate** "it arises; it is born". 1.29, 41; 2.20; 14.15 (twice). Also see *abhijāyate, saṁjāyate, upajāyate.*

---

[260] Divanji (p. 57, entry #1284) interprets this as, "A creature or a human being devoid of the sense of discrimination". This is based on the meaning of a *jantuḥ* as an animal of the lower order. See Apte, p. 446, entry for जन्तुः, meaning 3. Most commentators do not make this distinction, translating using the primary meaning of "creatures" or "beings".

[261] Van Buitenen 1981, p. 73.

1199. **jayema** "we should conquer". 2.6.

1200. **jayeyuḥ** "they should conquer". 2.6.

1201. **jetāsi** "you will win; you will conquer". 11.34.

1202. **jhaṣāṇām** "among fish; among aquatic animals". 10.31.

1203. **jighran** "smelling". 5.8.

1204. **jigīṣatām** "of those who desire victory". 10.38.

1205. **jijīviṣāmaḥ** "we shall (not) wish to live[262]; we would (not) want to survive". 2.6. Also see √ *jīv*.

1206. **jijñāsuḥ** "one who desires to know; seeker of knowledge". 6.44; 7.16. [√ *jña*]

1207. **jīrṇāni** "old; worn out". 2.22 (twice).

1208. **jitaḥ** "conquered; overcome; subdued". 5.19; 6.6.

1209. **jitasaṅgadoṣāḥ** "those who have conquered the impurity of attachment". 15.5. Also see *doṣa, saṅga*.

1210. **jitātman** "one who has acquired control over the self; self-controlled one". Also see *ātman*.

- jitātmā "self-controlled one". 18.49.
- jitātmanaḥ "of the self-controlled one". 6.7.
- vijitātmā "one who has self-control". 5.7.

1211. **jitendriyaḥ** "one who has self-control; one who has control of the senses". 5.7. Also see *indriya, vijitendriyaḥ*.

1212. **jitvā** "having overcome; after having conquered". 2.37; 11.33.

1213. √ **jīv** "to live". Also see *jijīviṣāmaḥ, tyaktajīvitāḥ*.

- jīvabhūtaḥ "a being; the individual living soul; becoming (an individual) soul; that which has acquired the form of a sentient being[263]". 15.7.

---

[262] Hill, p. 112.

[263] Divanji, p. 59, entry #1330.

- jīvabhūtām "it is the Life (soul)[264]; Very Life[265]; the life-force[266]; consisting of the *jīvas*; consisting of souls; which comprises the order of souls[267]; individual empirical consciousness[268]". 7.5.
- jīvaloke "in the world of life[269]; in the world of the living; the region in which sentient beings reside[270]". 15.7. Also see *loka*.
- jīvanam "life; the life force". 7.9.
- jīvati "he lives". 3.16.
- jīvitena "with life; by life". 1.32.

1214. √ **jñā** "to know". See *jñā-, jān-, abhijān-, ajān-, ajñā-, avajñā, jijñāsuḥ, parijñātā, prajān-, pratijān-, vijān-, vijñā-*.

1215. **jñāna** "wisdom; knowledge". 3.39, 40; 4.34, 39 (twice); 5.15, 16; 7.2; 9.1; 10.4, 38; 12.12; 13.2 (twice), 11, 17, 18; 14.1, 2, 9, 11, 17; 15.15; 18.18, 19, 20, 21 (twice), 42, 63. Also see *jñān-, ajñān-, vijñān-, adhyātmajñānanityatvam* (13.11); *hṛtajñānāḥ* (7.20); *māyayāpahṛtajñānāḥ* (7.15); *moghajñānāḥ* (9.12); *parijñātā* (18.18); *sarvajñānavimūḍhān* (3.32); *tattvajñānārthadarśanam* (13.11).

1216. **jñānacakṣuṣa** Also see *cakṣu*.

- jñānacakṣuṣā "with the eye of knowledge". 13.34.
- jñānacakṣuṣaḥ "(one endowed with) the eye of knowledge". 15.10.

1217. **jñānadīpena** "by the lamp of knowledge". 10.11. Also see *dīpaḥ*.

1218. **jñānadīpite** "illuminated by wisdom; kindled by knowledge". 4.27. Also see *dīpaḥ*.

1219. **jñānagamyam** "approachable by knowledge; that which can be realized through knowledge".13.17.

1220. **jñānāgnidagdhakarmāṇam** "one who has burnt off his actions with the fire of wisdom; whose *karma* is burned away in the fire of knowledge". 4.19.

1221. **jñānāgniḥ** "the fire of knowledge".4.37. Also see *agni*.

---

[264] Edgerton, p. 38. Edgerton's concept is clear in context of his translation: "It is the Life (soul), great-armed one, / By which this world is maintained."

[265] Hill, p. 166. Hill's note discusses different understandings of *jīvabhūta*, saying that Ś. calls it *kṣetrajña*, which he identifies with *puruṣa*.

[266] Miller, p. 73.

[267] Van Buitenen 1981, p. 99.

[268] Sharma, Morgan and Pitts, pp. 138-9.

[269] Hill, p. 238.

[270] Divanji, p. 59, entry #1332.

1222. **jñānānām** "of (all types of) wisdom; of (all) knowledge". 14.1.

1223. **jñānanirdhūtakalmaṣāḥ** "whose sins are shaken off by knowledge". 5.17.

1224. **jñānaplavena** "with the boat of knowledge".4.36.

1225. **jñānasaṁchinnasaṁśayam** "doubt has been removed by knowledge". 4.41. Also see *chinnadvaidhāḥ, saṁśaya.*

1226. **jñānasaṅgena** "by attachment to knowledge".14.6. Also see *saṅga.*

1227. **jñānāsinā** "with the sword of knowledge". 4.42. [*jñāna-asinā-ātmanaḥ*[271]]

1228. **jñānasya** "of knowledge".18.50.

1229. **jñānāt** "than knowledge". 12.12.

1230. **jñānatapasā** "by the ascetic practice of knowledge; by austerities consisting of the effort to acquire knowledge". 4.10. Also see *tapas.*

1231. **jñānāvasthitacetasaḥ** "one whose mind is held steady in wisdom; whose mind is well-established in knowledge; one whose mind is stabilized by wisdom". 4.23. Also see *avasthita.*

1232. **jñānavat "possessed of wisdom".**

- jñānavān "a wise man". 3.33; 7.19.
- jñānavatām "of wise men; among the wise". 10.38.

1233. **jñānavijñānanāśanam** "destroyer of material and spiritual wisdom; destroyer of knowledge and discrimination". 3.41. Also see *vijñāna, nāśanam.*

1234. **jñānavijñānatṛptātmā** "contented with practical and spiritual knowledge; one whose soul is satisfied by knowledge and spiritual insight". 6.8. Also see *ātman, vijñāna, ātmatṛptaḥ, nityatṛptaḥ, tṛptiḥ.*

1235. **jñānayajña** "the sacrifice of knowledge". Also see *yajña.*

- jñānayajñaḥ "the sacrifice of knowledge" 4.33.
- svādhyāyajñānayajñāḥ "those whose sacrifice consist of Vedic study and the pursuit of knowledge" 4.28.
- jñānayajñena "by the sacrifice of knowledge" 9.15; 18.70.

---

[271] Translators vary in handling *ātmanaḥ* in *jñāna-asinā-ātmanaḥ*. Madhusūdana (Gambhīrānanda 1998, p. 329) explains the construction as "with the sword of Self-Knowledge, with the sword in the form of conviction about the Self". Rāmānuja's comment is "by the sword of the knowledge of the self" (Ādidevānanda, p. 188). Śaṅkara applies *ātmanaḥ* to *saṁśayam* as "doubt of your own" (Gambhīrānanda 1997, p. 230-1).

1236. **jñānayoga** "the discipline of knowledge". [The *yoga* consisting of knowledge.] Also see *yoga.*

- jñānayogavyavasthitiḥ "steadfast in the discipline of knowledge". 16.1. [Divanji interprets this as "Determination of the separate functions of *Jñāna* and *Yoga*".[272]] Also see *vyavasthita.*
- jñānayogena "the *yoga* of knowledge; the discipline of knowledge". 3.3.

1237. **jñāne** "in knowledge". 4.33.

1238. **jñānena** "like knowledge; by knowledge". 4.38; 5.16.

1239. **jñānin** "man of wisdom".

- jñānī "the man of wisdom; the learned man; the wise man". 7.16, 17, 18.
- jñānibhyaḥ "(superior to) the wise men". 6.46.
- jñāninaḥ "wise men; of a wise man". 3.39; 4.34; 7.17.

1240. **jñāsyasi** "you will know". 7.1.

1241. **jñātavyam** "knowable". 7.2.

1242. **jñātena** "known". 10.42.

1243. **jñātum** "to know". 11.54. Also see *vijñātum.*

1244. **jñātvā** "having understood", "after knowing". 4.15, 16, 32, 35; 5.29; 7.2; 9.1, 13; 13.12; 14.1; 16.24; 18.55. [Indec. past. part. of √ *jña.*]

1245. **jñeya.** Also see *avijñeyam.*

- jñeyaḥ "known; considered". 5.3; 8.2.
- jñeyam "to be known; the object of knowledge; the knowable". 1.39; 13.12, 16, 17, 18; 18.18.

1246. **joṣayet** "you would inspire (others to act); you would cause (them) to enjoy; you would make them interested in". 3.26. [√ *juṣ*]

1247. **juhoṣi** "you offer as an oblation". 9.27. Also see *yajña, juhvati.* [√ *hu*]

1248. **juhvati** "one offers as an oblation". Also see *yajña, juhoṣi.* [√ *hu*]

- juhvati "offer as an oblation; sacrifice; (those who) sacrifice; offers oblation; one offers". 4.26 (twice), 27, 29, 30.
- upajuhvati "one offers as an oblation". 4.25.

1249. √ **jval** "to burn brightly; to blaze".

- abhivijvalanti "flaming forth; burning all over intensely; emitting flames on all sides". 11.28. [*abhi* + *vi* + √ *jval*]
- jvaladbhiḥ "with flaming, with fiery". 11.30.
- jvalanam "flame, bright fire". 11.29.

---

[272] Divanji, p. 60, entry #1352.

1250. **jyāyaḥ** "better; superior". 3.8.

1251. **jyāyasī** "better; superior". 3.1.

1252. **jyoti** "light; heavenly light".

- antarjyotiḥ "inner light". 5.24.
- jyotiḥ "light". 8.24, 25; 13.17.
- jyotiṣāṁ "among lights". 10.21; 13.17.

K

क् = K. **ख्** = Kh.

1253. **kā** "what?". 1.36; 2.28, 54; 17.1.

1254. **kaccit** "whether?; is it that?; has it?". 6.38; 18.72 (twice).

1255. **kadācana** "ever; at any time". 2.47; 18.67. [*kadā cana*]

1256. **kadācit** "ever; at any time". 2.20 [*kadā cit*]

1257. **kaḥ** "who?; what?". 8.2; 11.31; 16.15.

1258. **kaiḥ** "with whom?; by what?". 1.22; 14.21.

1259. **kāla** "time".

- adeśakāle "at the wrong place and time; without regard to the appropriate place and time". 17.22. Also see *deśe.*
- antakāle "at the final time; at the time of death". 2.72; 8.5.
- prayāṇakāle "at the time of death; at the time of departure; at the time of the last journey". 7.30; 8.2, 10.
- kālaḥ "time". 10.30, 33; 11.32.
- kālam "time". 8.23.
- kālānalasaṁnibhāni "similar to the fire of time; like the fire of destruction". 11.25.
- kāle "in time; at the time". 8.23; 17.20.
- kālena "with time; in the course of time". 4.2, 38.
- kāleṣu "at times". 8.7, 27.

1260. **kalayatām** "among calculators". 10.30.

1261. **kalevaram** "the body". 8.5, 6. Also see *deha, kāya, śarīra.*

1262. **kalmaṣa** "sin, evil".

- yajñakṣapitakalmaṣāḥ "whose sins have been destroyed through sacrifice". 4.30.

- jñānanirdhūtakalmaṣāḥ "whose sins have been shaken off by knowledge". 5.17.
- kṣīṇakalmaṣāḥ "whose sins have been destroyed". 5.25.
- akalmaṣam "free from sin; free of blemish". 6.27.
- vigatakalmaṣaḥ "freed from sin". 6.28.

1263. **kalpa** "an age". [A cosmic division of time.]
   - kalpādau "at the beginning (*ādi*) of a *kalpa*". 9.7.
   - kalpakṣaye "at the end of the *kalpa*; at the dissolution of the *kalpa*". 9.7.
1264. **kalpakṣaye** "at the end of the *kalpa*; at the dissolution of the *kalpa*". 9.7.
1265. **kalpate** "he is fit for; he is qualified for". 2.15; 14.26; 18.53. [3rd pers. sing. √ *kḷp*]
1266. **kalyāṇakṛt** "one who does good actions; one who acts virtuously". 6.40.
1267. **kam** "whom?; what?". 2.21 (twice).
1268. **kām** "what?; which?". 6.37.
1269. **kāma** "desire; longing for objects of enjoyment". Also see *arthakāmān, dharmakāmārthān, hitakāmyayā, kāma-, kāmātmānaḥ, kāmepsunā, kāmopabhogaparamāḥ, kāmyānām, kandarpaḥ, sarvakāmebhyaḥ, vinivṛttakāmāḥ, yoddhukāmān.*
   - kāmaḥ "desire ". 2.62; 3.37; 7.11; 16.21.
   - kāmāḥ "desires". 2.70.
   - kāmaiḥ "by desires". 7.20.
   - kāmam "desire". 16.10, 18; 18.53.
   - kāmān "desires". 2.55, 71; 6.24; 7.22.
   - kāmāt "from desire". 2.62.
1270. **kāmabhogārtham** "in order to indulge their desire[273]; for the sake of enjoyment of desired objects; for gratification of desires; having desire and pleasure as their aim". 16.12. Also see *arthaḥ, bhoga, kāma, kāmabhogeṣu, kāmopabhogaparamāḥ.*
1271. **kāmabhogeṣu** "the pleasures of desire[274]; in the enjoyment of desires; in gratification of desires; enjoyment of the desired objects". 16.16. Also see *bhoga, kāma-, kāmabhogārtham, kāmopabhogaparamāḥ.*

---

[273] Van Buitenen 1981, p. 133.

[274] Van Buitenen 1981, p. 133.

1272. **kāmadhuk** "Kāmadhuk; Kāmadhenu; a cow with the power to fulfill all desires; the wish-fulfilling cow; Cow-of-Wishes[275]; the Cow of Plenty[276]".

- iṣṭakāmadhuk "the longed-for (*iṣṭa*) cow that fulfills all desires (*kāmadhuk*); yielder of the coveted objects of desire[277]; the yielder of the desired fruits[278]". 3.10.
- kāmadhuk "the cow that fulfills all desires". 10.28.

1273. **kāmahaitukam** "having lust as the cause; that which has desire as its motive". 16.8. Also see *hetu*.

1274. **kāmakāmāḥ** "desirous of desires; desiring objects of desire; craving desires". 9.21. Also see *kāmakāmī*.

1275. **kāmakāmī** "one who desires objects of desire; one who runs after desires; the man who lusts after desires[279]". 2.70. Also see *kāmakāmāḥ*.

1276. **kāmakārataḥ** "according to one's own will; as one desires; prompted by desire". 16.23.

1277. **kāmakāreṇa** "due to action motivated by desire; by action resulting from desire". 5.12. Also see *karaṇam*.

1278. **kāmakrodhaparāyaṇāḥ** "given over to desire and anger; devoted to desire and anger". 16.12. Also see *krodha, parāyaṇa*.

1279. **kāmakrodhaviyuktānām** "of those who are released from desire and anger". 5.26. Also see *krodha, yukta, viyoga, rāgadveṣaviyuktaiḥ*.

1280. **kāmakrodhodbhavam** "arising from desire and anger". 5.23. Also see *krodha, -udbhava*.

1281. **kamalapatrākṣa** "O Lotus-petal-eyed One". 11.2. Also see *patram*.

1282. **kamalāsanastham** "seated on a lotus seat". 11.15. Also see *āsana*.

1283. **kāmarāgabalānvitāḥ** "driven with the force of desires and attachments; desires and passions fortify them[280]; full of force of lust and greed[281]; full of the

---

[275] Edgerton, pp. 19, 53.

[276] Bolle, p. 279; Van Buitenen 1981, p. 111.

[277] Gambhīrānanda 1998, pp. 221-2. This interpretation associates "coveted" (*iṣṭa*) with "objects of desire" (*kāma*).

[278] Divanji, p. 31, entry #701.

[279] Edgerton, p. 16.

[280] Bolle, p. 279.

[281] Warrier, p. 532.

strength of passion and desire[282]; filled with desire, passion, and violence[283]". 17.5. Also see *anvita, bala, kāma, rāga*.

1284. **kāmarāgavivarjitam** "free from desire and attachment; free from lust and passion; devoid of appetite and attachment[284]". 7.11. Also see *kāma, rāga, vivarjita*.

1285. **kāmarūpa** "in the form of desire; having the nature of desire; appearing as desire". Also see *kāma, rūpa*.

- kāmarūpam "in the form of desire; having the form of desire". 3.43.
- kāmarūpeṇa "by this in the form of desire; by (the eternal enemy) in the form of desire". 3.39.

1286. **kāmasaṁkalpavarjitāḥ** "free from intentions motivated by desire; free from ulterior motives". 4.19. Also see *kāma, saṁkalpa, varjita*.

1287. **kāmātmānaḥ** "concerned with fulfillment of desires; who has identified oneself with desires[285]". 2.43. Also see *ātman, mahātman, yatātman*.

1288. **kāmepsunā** "by one who is desirous of the results; by someone longing for fulfillment of desires; with a wish to obtain desires". 18.24. [*kāma* + *īpsunā*]

1289. **kāmopabhogaparamāḥ** "totally immersed in the indulgence of desires[286]; engrossed in fulfillment of desire and pleasures". 16.11. Also see *bhoga, kāmabhogārtham, kāmabhogeṣu, -parama*.

1290. **kāmyānām** "full of desire; done with a view to acquire a desired object; undertaken to achieve desires". 18.2. Also see *hitakāmyayā*.

1291. **kandarpaḥ** "Kāma, the god of love; the creative principle". 10.28.

1292. √ **kāṅkṣ** "to wish, to desire; to long for; to look forward to".

- aphalākāṅkṣibhiḥ "by those who do not long for fruits; by those who do not desire rewards; by those who do not covet fruits". 17.11, 17. Also see *phala*.

---

[282] Hill, p. 250.

[283] Edgerton, p. 79. Edgerton takes it as a compound of three traits, but adds a note mentioning the alternate interpretation of "with the power of desire and passion" followed by Hill and others.

[284] Warrier, p. 259.

[285] Divanji, p. 43, entry #981.

[286] Van Buitenen 1981, p. 133.

- darśanakāṅkṣiṇaḥ "desirous of seeing; eager to see; longing to behold (it)[287]; yearn for a glimpse[288]; anxious to have a sight[289]". 11.52.
- kāṅkṣantaḥ "those aspiring for; those desiring; people wanting; those who long for; those who look forward to". 4.12.
- kāṅkṣati "he desires; he hankers; he longs for; he aspires to; he craves". 5.3; 12.17; 14.22; 18.54.
- kāṅkṣe "I desire; I aspire; I wish". 1.32.
- kāṅkṣitam "wished for; desired; looked forward to". 1.33.
- mokṣakāṅkṣibhiḥ "by those who wish for release; by those seeking to attain liberation; by the seekers of liberation[290]". 17.25.
- phalākāṅkṣī "one desiring rewards; one expecting a reward; one wanting fruits". 18.34.

1293. **kapidhvaja** "Monkey-bannered". 1.20. This term refers to the figure of a monkey appearing on the flag of Arjuna's chariot. Many commentators assume the monkey is Hanumān.[291]

1294. **kapilaḥ** "Kapila".10.26. [The sage Kapila, considered to be the founder of Sāṅkhya philosophy.]

1295. **-kara** "causing". [ifc.] See *akīrtikaram, anudvegakaram, bhūtabhāvodbhavakaraḥ, saṁkara, suduṣkaram.*

1296. **karaṇam** "instrument; means; organ of action". 18.14, 18. Also see *kāraṇam.*

1297. **kāraṇam** "cause; means; an instrument".6.3 (twice); 13.21. Also see *ātmakāraṇāt, kāmakāreṇa, karaṇam, kāryakāraṇakartṛtve.*

1298. **kāraṇāni** "causes; causative factors". 18.13.

1299. **kārayan** "causing action; causing a thing to be done; getting something done". 5.13.

1300. **kariṣyasi** "you will do". 2.33; 18.60.

1301. **kariṣyati** "it will do; it will accomplish". 3.33.

1302. **kariṣye** "I will do". 18.73.

1303. **karma** "action; work; religious rite; duty (e.g., *kṣatrakarma*)". Also see *akarma, akarmakṛt, akurvata, guṇakarma, jñānāgnidagdhakarmāṇam,*

---

287 Sivananda, p. 292.

288 Van Buitenen 1981, p. 121.

289 Divanji, p. 68, entry #1544.

290 Sivananda, p. 455.

291 In *MBh.* 3.150.15, Hanumān granted a boon to Bhīma, saying he would take the place of a flag on Arjuna's chariot (*vijayasya dhvajasthaḥ*). See Van Buitenen 1975, p. 509.

karm-, kṛtsnakarmakṛt, karmin, kriya, kurv-, kury-, naiṣkarmya, puṇyakarmaṇām, sarvakarma, svakarma, sarvāṇīndriyakarmāṇi, vikarmaṇaḥ, yajñadānatapaḥkarma, yajñadānatapaḥkriyāḥ.

- karma "action" 2.49; 3.5, 8 (twice), 9, 15, 19 (twice), 24; 4.9, 15 (twice), 16 (twice), 18, 21, 23; 5.11; 6.1, 3; 7.29; 8.1; 16.24; 17.27; 18.3, 8, 9, 10, 15, 18, 19, 23, 24, 25, 44 "duty (of the Śūdra class); work (of the Śūdra class)", 47 "(one's own) duty; (one's own) work"; 48 "(natural) duty; work (to which one is born)".
- karmabhiḥ "from (the bondage of) actions". 3.31; "(is not bound) by actions" 4.14.
- karmaṇā "by action; with action". 3.20; 18.60.
- karmaṇaḥ "(superior) to action; (better) than action; (more important) than action". 3.1.
- karmaṇaḥ "(aside) from action; (other than that) action; (except) action" 3.9.
- karmaṇaḥ "of action". 4.17 (twice); 14.16; 18.7, 12.
- karmaṇām "of acts; of actions". 3.4; 4.12 (possibly with sense "ritual acts"[292]); 5.1; 14.12. 18.2 (possibly with sense "ritual acts"[293]). Also see *puṇyakarmaṇām* (7.28; 18.71); *sarvakarmaṇām* (18.13).
- karmaṇi "in action; with action". 2.47; 3.1, 22, 23, 25; 4.18, 20; 14.9; 17.26; 18.45 (with sense "in one's duty", *sve sve karmaṇi*).
- karmāṇi "actions". 2.48; 3.27, 30; 4.14, 41; 5.10, 14; 9.9; 12.6, 10; 13.29; 18.6, 11, 41 (with sense "duties" of the social classes).
- karmasu "in (or to) actions; in (or to) works". 2.50; 6.4, 17; 9.9. Also see *guṇakarmasu* (3.29).

Examples of noteworthy compounds involving karma:

- bhīmakarmā "one who does terrible deeds; one whose actions are terrible". 1.15. [Referring to Bhīma as "Terrible in Action" or "Worker of

---

[292] Sargeant, p. 212.

[293] *kāmyānāṁ karmaṇāṁ nyāsaṁ saṁnyāsaṁ kavayo viduḥ.* Śaṅkara (Gambhīrānanda 1997, p. 658) gives examples of Vedic sacrifices done with a desire for reward and refers to the *nitya-karma* (daily obligatory duties). Madhusūdana Sarasvati's commentary also gives examples of Vedic rites in explaining this verse; see Gambhīrānanda 1998, pp. 862-3. Sargeant, p. 663, takes it in the ritual sense, translating *kāmyānāṁ karmaṇāṁ* as "rites undertaken to achieve desires".

Terror". Bhīma is also known as Vṛkodara, "Wolf Belly".] Also see Bhīma, Vṛkodara.

- brahmakarma "actions appropriate for a Brāhmaṇa; a Brāhmaṇa's duties". 18.42.
- brahmakarmasamādhinā "by one who is absorbed in work as *Brahman*; by one who has concentration on *Brahman* as the essence of all actions; actions performed with consciousness of *Brahman*; focus on action as consisting of *Brahman*". 4.24. Also see *samādhi.*
- kṣatrakarma "the natural duties of the Kṣatriyas". 18.43.
- matkarmakṛn "performing actions for me". 11.55.
- matkarmaparamaḥ "performer of actions for me only; solely devoted to acts done for my sake". 12.10. Also see *matparama, -parama*
- prāṇakarmāṇi "activities of the vital breath". 4.27.
- indriyakarmāṇi "functions and actions of the senses and motor organs". 4.27.
- moghakarmāṇaḥ "(those whose) actions are futile". 9.12.
- ugrakarmāṇaḥ "(doers of) terrible deeds". 16.9.
- vaiśyakarma "the natural duties of the Vaiśyas". 18.44. Also see *vaiśya.*
- yogasaṁnyastakarmāṇam "one who has abandoned (the bondage of) actions by *yoga*; one who has renounced action through *yoga*; one who has given up the performance of religious rites by *yoga*, i.e., according to the theory of *karmayoga*[294]; one who has dedicated (his) actions (to God) through *yoga*[295]; renouncing (all) works in *yoga*[296]". 4.41. Also see √ *saṁnyas, saṁnyasta, yoga.*

1304. **karmabandha** "bondage of acts". Also see *karma, bandham.*

- karmabandham "bondage resulting from acts". 2.39.
- karmabandhanaḥ "bound by *karma*; imprisoned by acts". 3.9.
- karmabandhanaiḥ "due to the bondage resulting from acts". 9.28.

1305. **karmacodanā** "the (threefold) inducement to action; the instigator(s) of action; the inspiration(s) to action". 18.18. [Nom. sing. fem. but with plural sense due to being "threefold" (*trividhā*). *codanā* = that which impels, from √ *cud*, "to impel, to incite".[297]] Also see *karma.*

---

[294] Divanji, p. 124, entry #2833.

[295] Gambhīrānanda 1998, p. 328.

[296] Zaehner, p. 198.

[297] See Minor, p. 471; Gambhīrānanda 1998, pp. 904-5.

1306. **karmaja** "born from action; arising out of action".

- karmajam "born out of action; arising from action". 2.51.
- karmajā "born out of action; arising from action; born from ritual acts". 4.12. [Used in the context of Vedic ritual action.]
- karmajān "born out of action; arising from action". 4.32.

1307. **karmākhilam** "all action; action in its entirety; actions in their totality". 4.33. Also see *akhilam*.

1308. **karmānubandhīni** "linked with works[298]; followed by actions[299]; resulting in acts[300]; apt to produce actions later[301]; that which has *karma* as its result; having *karma* as a consequence; promoting *karma*; [the roots are] the sequences of actions[302]". 15.2. Also see *anubandha*.

1309. **karmaphala** "fruit of action; result of action". Also see *karma, phala*.

- janmakarmaphalapradām "giving rise to rebirth and the fruits of action; resulting in acts leading to births". 2.43.
- karmaphalahetuḥ "one who is motivated by the fruit of action; one who has acquisition of the result of (one's) actions as the cause of doing the actions". 2.47. Also see *hetu, phalahetavaḥ*.
- karmaphalam "fruit of action". 5.12; 6.1.

---

[298] Zaehner (p. 360) translates *adhaś ca mūlāny anusaṁtatāni karmānubandhīni manuṣyaloke* as, "Below its roots proliferate inseparably linked with works in the world of men." This wording emphasizes linkage without attributing causality in one direction or another (either the roots causing the *karma* or the *karma* causing the roots.

[299] Gambhīrānanda (1997, pp. 594-6) translates *karmānubandhīni* as "followed by actions" as the sense of the Śaṅkara commentary, saying that, "(these roots) are said to be *karma-anubandhīni* since actions (*karma*) that are characterized as righteous and unrighteous follow as their product (*anubandha*), (i.e.) succeed the rise of those (attraction, repulsion, etc.)."

[300] Ādidevānanda, p. 485, translates the Rāmānuja commentary as reading "The meaning is that the effects of acts causing bondage become roots in the world of men. For, the effect of actions done in the human state brings about the further condition of men, beasts, etc., down below, and of divinities etc., up above."

[301] Gambhīrānanda (1998, pp. 780-1) translates the idea as "The secondary roots, which are apt to produce actions later in the human body, spread downwards also." The note on *karmānubandhīni* is that "they are those that are apt to produce later (*anubandhīni*) the actions (*karma*) characterized as righteous or unrighteous;—where?—*manuṣya-loke*, in the human body...".

[302] Bolle, p. 241.

- karmaphalaprepsuḥ "desiring to obtain the fruit of action; one who longs for the fruit of one's acts; eager for results of action". 18.27.
- karmaphalasaṁyogam "connection with the result of action; a connection between an act and its fruit". 5.14. Also see *saṁyoga.*
- karmaphalāsaṅgam "attachment to the fruit of an act". 4.20. Also see *saṅga.*
- karmaphalatyāgaḥ "renunciation of the fruit of action". 12.12. Also see *tyāga.*
- karmaphalatyāgī "one who renounces the fruit of action". 18.11. Also see *tyāgī.*
- karmaphale "in fruit of action". 4.14.
- sarvakarmaphalatyāgam "renunciation of the fruit of all action". 12.11; 18.2.

1310. **karmasaṁgrahaḥ** "the composition of action; the component parts of an act; the summary of action[303]". 18.18. Also see *saṁgraheṇa, lokasaṁgraham.*

1311. **karmasaṁjñitaḥ** "is called action; that which is designated as *karma*". 8.3.

1312. **karmasaṁnyāsāt** "(compared to) the renunciation of action". 5.2. [*karmasaṁnyāsāt karmayogo viśiṣyate* = the practice of *karmayoga* is superior to giving up acts] Also see *saṁnyāsa.*

1313. **karmasamudbhavaḥ** "arises out of action; is born from *karma*". 3.14. Also see *-udbhava.*

1314. **karmasaṅga** "attachment to action". Also see *karmabandha, karma, saṅga.*

- karmasaṅgena "by attachment to action; by (egoistic) contact with action". 14.7.
- karmasaṅginām "among those who are attached to action". 3.26.
- karmasaṅgiṣu "with those who are attached to action". 14.15.

1315. **karmayoga** "the practice of action; communion through detached and dedicated work[304]". [The *yoga* consisting of performing action in a spiritually-detached way. Performing action in the spirit of making a religious sacrifice.] Also see *yoga.*

- karmayogaḥ "the practice of action". 5.2 (twice).
- karmayogam "the practice of action". 3.7.

---

[303] Edgerton, p. 85; Minor, p. 471.

[304] Tapasyananda, p. 149.

- karmayogena "by the practice of action". 3.3; 13.24.

1316. **karmendriyaiḥ** "with the organs of motor action; with the motor organs (through which he acts); with the powers of action". 3.7. Also see *indriya.*

1317. **karmendriyāṇi** "the organs of motor action; the motor organs (through which he acts); the powers of action". 3.6. Also see *indriya.*

1318. **karmibhyaḥ** "(higher) than men of action; (superior) to performers of action; (greater) than those who perform ritual works[305]". 6.46. [Abl. pl. masc. of the noun *karmin,* "a doer; one devoted to a life of action" or "a doer (of rituals); one who is active (in ritual)".] Also see *karma.*

1319. **karṇa** "Karṇa". Also see *sūtaputra* ("son of a charioteer").

- karṇaḥ "Karṇa". 1.8.
- karṇam "Karṇa". 11.34.

1320. **karomi** "I do". 5.8.

1321. **karoṣi** "you do". 9.27.

1322. **karoti** "one does; one performs; he acts; he does work". 4.20; 5.10; 6.1; 13.31.

1323. **kārpaṇyadoṣopahatasvabhāvaḥ** "my very being is stricken by the defect (*doṣa*) of limited understanding (*kārpaṇya*); with my nature overpowered by the defect due to unenlightenment (*kārpaṇya*)[306]; my natural disposition has been vitiated by a sense of pity[307]; with my heart stricken by the fault of weak compassion[308]; one whose nature is obscured by the blemish of helplessness[309]". 2.7. [The noun *kārpaṇyam* can take a range of meanings, including two different senses that could fit the passage. It can mean compassion in the sense of pity. It can also mean "imbecility" and *BG* 2.7 is specifically listed as an

---

[305] In the context of Vedic ritual, *karmin* refers to: "ritualists", Ādidevānanda, p. 238; "those who perform ritual work", Sargeant, p. 317;"man of ritual work", Bolle, p.-281. For Śaṅkara's interpretation of *karma* here as referring to the *Agnihotra* ritual, etc., see Gambhīrānanda 1997, p. 313.

[306] Gambhīrānanda 1998, p. 72. The commentary interprets the word *kārpaṇyam* as an abstract form of *kṛpaṇa,* meaning "miser", one who cannot bear the loss of possessions. Everyone who has not realized the Self is of that kind, i.e., unwilling to part with worldly enjoyments. The defect arising from that is characterized by a sense of ownership due to superimposition of the non-Self.

[307] Tapasyananda, p. 43.

[308] Ādidevānanda, p. 58.

[309] Divanji, p. 44, entry #996.

example of that meaning by Apte.[310] In 2.7 Arjuna suffers from a lack of right understanding of the situation, suggesting a "defect of limited understanding". Similarly, the word *kṛpaṇa* can mean "void of judgement".[311]] The "defect of pity" (*kārpaṇyadoṣa*) is close to Nietzsche's criticism of pity on the basis of it having a weakening effect.[312]] Also see *doṣa, kṛpaṇāḥ, svabhāva, hata, lobhopahatacetasaḥ.*

1324. **karṣati** "it pulls; it draws to itself". 15.7.

1325. **karśayantaḥ** "wracking; causing to injure; tormenting". 17.6.

1326. **kartā** "the doer; the agent of action; the performer; the creator". 3.24, 27; 18.14, 18, 19, 26, 27, 28. Also see *ādikartre, kartāram.*

1327. **kartāram** "the doer; the agent of action; the performer; the creator". 4.13; 14.19; 18.16. Also see *ādikartre, akartāram, kartā.*

1328. **kartavyam** "assigned duty; that which ought to be done; action that should be performed". 3.22. Also see *kartavyāni.*

1329. **kartavyāni** "assigned duties; things which ought to be done; actions that should be performed". 18.6. Also see *kartavyam.*

1330. **kartṛtvam** "acting; the quality of being an actor; doership". 5.14. Also see *akarm-, akartāram.*

1331. **kartum** "to do; to act". 1.45; 2.17; 3.20; 9.2; 12.11; 16.24; 18.60. [Inf. of √ *kṛ*]

1332. **karuṇaḥ** "compassionate; merciful". 12.13.

1333. **kāryam** "that which should be done; required". 3.17, 19; 6.1; 18.5, 9, 31. Also see *kāry-, akārya.*

1334. **kāryakāraṇakartṛtve** "regarding the creatorship of action and its agent". 13.20. Also see *kāraṇa.*

1335. **kāryākārye** "in regard to what ought to be done and what ought not to be done". 18.30.

1336. **kāryākāryavyavasthitau** "in determining what to do and what not to do; distinguishing what should and should not be done". 16.24. Also see *vyavasthita.*

---

310 Apte, p. 352, entry for कार्पण्यं.

311 Apte, p. 371, entry for कृपण.

312 "Pity stands opposed to the tonic emotions which heighten our vitality: it has a depressing effect. We are deprived of strength when we feel pity. That loss of strength which suffering as such inflicts on life is still further increased and multiplied by pity. Pity makes suffering contagious." Friedrich Nietzsche, *The Antichrist.* Reprinted in *The Portable Nietzsche* (Penguin: 1954), pp. 572-573.

1337. **kāryate** "made to act". 3.5. [√ *kṛ*]

1338. **kārye** "in a form; in an aspect; in the to-be-done". 18.22.

1339. **kaścana** "anyone whoever; anything whatever; in any way". 3.18; 6.2; 7.26; 8.27. [*kaś cana*]

1340. **kaścit** "anyone; someone; any whatever". 2.17, 29 (twice); 3.5, 18; 6.40; 7.3 (twice); 18.69. [*kaś cit*]

1341. **kāśirājaḥ** "The "King of Kāśī". 1.5. Kāśī refers to a region (modern Vārāṇasī) and its people. Also see *kāśyaḥ*.

1342. **kaśmalam** "dejection of mind; depression of spirits; despair; timidity; a sinful act; a prohibited act". 2.2.

1343. **kasmāt** "from what?; why?". 11.37.

1344. **kasyacit** "of anyone; of whosoever". 5.15. [*kasya cit*]

1345. **kāśyaḥ** "The "King of Kāśī". 1.17. Also see *kāśirājaḥ*.

1346. **katarat** "which (of the two)". 2.6.

1347. **katham** "how; in which manner". 1.37, 39; 2.4, 21; 4.4; 8.2 (twice); 10.17; 14.21.

1348. **kathaya** "tell!; say!; describe!". 10.18.

1349. **kathayantaḥ** "speaking of; talking about; extolling". 10.9.

1350. **kathayataḥ** "speaking; narrating; relating; declaring". 18.75.

1351. **kathayiṣyāmi** "I will speak about; I will describe; I will declare". 10.19.

1352. **kathayiṣyanti** "they will speak about; they will relate". 2.34.

1353. **kaṭu** "bitter, sharp, pungent, acrid". 17.9. See *kaṭvamlalavaṇātyuṣṇatīkṣṇa-rūkṣavidāhinaḥ*.

1354. **kaṭvamlalavaṇātyuṣṇatīkṣṇarūkṣavidāhinaḥ** "Bitter (*kaṭu*), sour (*amla*), salty (*lavaṇa*), very hot (*atyuṣṇa*), sharp (*tīkṣṇa*), dry (*rūkṣa*), or causing a burning sensation (*vidāhina*)". 17.9. [Describing foods.[313] Some of the terms have a range of possible meanings. *kaṭu* = bitter, sharp, pungent, acrid. *amla* = sour. *lavaṇa* = salty. *atyuṣṇa* (*ati* + *uṣṇa*) = extremely hot. *tīkṣṇa* = sharp, pungent.[314]

---

[313] Śaṅkara's commentary says that the word *ati*, meaning "excessively", should be connected to all seven terms in the compound beginning with *kaṭu* (Warrier, p. 535). This interpretation is repeated by Madhusūdana (Gambhīrānanda 1998, p. 842). If this interpretation were followed, the translation of the compound would begin with "excessively", e.g., "excessively bitter, sour, salty, hot, pungent, harsh, or burning."

[314] Rāmānuja's commentary (Ādidevānanda, p. 530) notes that foods may be *tīkṣṇa* (sharp) due to extremes of temperature, either very hot or very cold.

rūkṣa = astringent[315], dry, harsh, coarse. *vidāhina* = causing a burning sensation, causing great heat, causing inflammation[316].

1355. **kaumāram** "childhood". 2.13.

1356. **kaunteya** "Kaunteya; Son of Kuntī".

- kaunteya "O Son of Kuntī; O Arjuna". 2.14, 37, 60; 3.9, 39; 5.22; 6.35; 7.8; 8.6, 16; 9.7, 10, 23, 27, 31; 13.1, 31; 14.4, 7; 16.20, 22; 18.48, 50, 60. See entry for this epithet on page 17. The epithet Kaunteya ("Son of Kuntī") means the same thing as Pārtha ("Son of Pṛthā"). Yudhiṣṭhira is called *kuntīputra* ("son of Kuntī") in 1.16.
- kaunteyaḥ "the son of Kuntī; Arjuna". 1.27.

1357. **kauśalam** "capacity; skill; skillfulness; good fortune". 2.50. Also see *kuśale*.

1358. **kavi** "poet; a sage; a seer; learned person; wise person".

- kavayaḥ "sages; wise people". 4.16; 18.2.
- kaviḥ "sage; poet". 10.37.
- kavim "seer; sage". 8.9. [*kaviṁ purāṇam* = "the ancient seer"[317]]
- kavīnām "of sages; among poets". 10.37.

1359. **kāya** "the physical body". Also see *yatavākkāyamānasaḥ, deha, kalevaram, śarīra.*

- kāyam "the physical body". 11.44.
- kāyena "with the physical body". 5.11.

1360. **kāyakleśabhayāt** "due to fear of bodily pain". 18.8. Also see *bhaya, kāya, kleśa.*

1361. **kāyaśirogrīvam** "the trunk of the body (*kāya*), the head (*śiraḥ*), and the neck (*grīva*)". 6.13.

1362. **ke** "which ones?". 12.1.

1363. **kecit** "some of them; some". 11.21, 27; 13.24. [*ke cit*]

---

[315] Apte (p. 805, entry for रूक्ष) defines *rūkṣa* as "astringent" when applied to taste. Meanings such as "rough" or "harsh" apply to other senses such as touch or sound. Other concepts include "dry" or "parched" in the sense of being without liquid. Madhusūdana (Gambhīrānanda 1998, p. 842) gives examples of foods that are devoid of oil.

[316] Apte, p. 856, entry for विदाहः.

[317] Verse 8.9 includes epithets drawn from the Upaniṣads. The phrase *kaviṁ purāṇam* ("the ancient seer") suggests *Īśa Upaniṣad* 8, where *kavim* is interpreted as "omniscient", seeing all in the past, present, and future (Gambhīrānanda 1989, vol. 1, p. 16). "The ancient seer" is Edgerton's translation (p. 43).

1364. **kena** "by what?". 3.36.

1365. **kenacit** "by whatever; with anything". 12.19.

1366. **keśava** "Keśava". See entry for this epithet on page 14.[318]

- keśava "O Keśava". 1.31; 2.54; 3.1; 10.14. [Always at the end of a half-verse, a very standardized pattern.]
- keśavasya "of Keśava". 11.35.

1367. **keśavārjunayoḥ** "Keśava (Kṛṣṇa) and Arjuna". 18.76. Also see Arjuna.

1368. **keśiniṣūdana** "O Keśiniṣūdana; O Slayer of Keśin (a demon)". 18.1. See entry for this epithet on page 14.

1369. **keṣu keṣu** "in what various; in whatever; in what and what". 10.17. [Loc. pl. of the masc. form of the interrog. pronoun *kiṁ*. Repetition indicates distribution.]

1370. **kevala** "alone; only; solely; merely; exclusively".

- kevalam "alone; mere; only". 4.21; 18.16.
- kevalair "alone; merely (with); only (with)". 5.11

1371. **kha** "the sky; the sky-element; the ether; space".

- kham "space; the sky". 7.4.
- khe "in space; in the ether". 7.8. [Referring to sound (*śabdaḥ*).]

1372. **kilbiṣam** "sin; blemish". 4.21; 18.47. Also see *saṁśuddhakilbiṣaḥ, sarvakilbiṣaiḥ.*

1373. **kim** "what? how? why?". 1.1, 32 (twice), 35; 2.36, 54 (three times); 3.1, 33; 4.16 (twice); 8.1 (five times); 9.33; 10.42; 16.8.

1374. **kimācāraḥ** "of what conduct?; of what kind of behavior?". 14.21. Also see *ācāra.*

1375. **kiṁcana** "anything whatever". 3.22. [*kiṁ cana*]

1376. **kiṁcit** "anything whatever". 4.20; 5.8; 6.25; 7.7; 13.26. [*kiṁ cit*]

1377. **kirīṭī** "the crowned one". 11.35. [Referring to Arjuna.]

1378. **kirīṭinam** "crowned; wearing a crown". 11.17, 46.

1379. **kīrtayantaḥ** "praising; extolling; glorifying". 9.14. Also see *kīrti.*

1380. **kīrti** "fame". Also see *akīrti, kīrtayantaḥ, parikīrtitaḥ, prakīrtyā, saṁprakīrtitaḥ.*

- kīrtiḥ "fame". 10.34.
- kīrtim "fame". 2.33.

---

[318] Also used in an unnumbered prefatory verse to chapter thirteen that does not appear in the Critical Edition.

1381. **klaibyam** "impotence; unmanliness; passivity; cowardice". 2.3.

1382. **kledayanti** "they become wet". 2.23. Also see *akledyaḥ*.

1383. **kleśaḥ** "difficulty; toil; trouble; anguish". 12.5. Also see *kāyakleśabhayāt*.

1384. √ **kṛ** "to make". See *kara-, kāra-, kariṣ-, karm-, karo-, kart-, kāry-, kriy-, kṛta-, kṛtā-, kṛte-, kṛti-, kṛtv-, kuru, kuruṣva, kurute, kurv-, kury-*.

1385. **kratuḥ** "the act of sacrifice; the ritual; the ceremony; a type of Vedic ritual[319]". 9.16.

1386. **kriyā** "activity; performance; a religious rite or ceremony". Also see *dānakriyāḥ, luptapiṇḍodakakriyāḥ, manaḥprāṇendriyakriyāḥ, yajña-dānatapaḥkriyāḥ, yajñatapaḥkriyāḥ, karma*.

- kriyābhiḥ "by [other] practices; by [other] ceremonies". 11.48.
- kriyāviśeṣabahulām "abounding in (many) specific rites; replete with various ritual acts". 2.43. Also see *bahu*.

1387. **kriyaḥ**. See *akriyaḥ, yatacittendriyakriyaḥ*.

1388. **kriyamāṇāni** "done; performed". 3.27; 13.29.

1389. **kriyante** "are done; are performed". 17.25.

1390. **kriyate** "is done; is performed". 17.18, 19; 18.9, 24.

1391. **krodha** "anger".

- akrodhaḥ "absence of anger". 16.2.
- kāmakrodhaparāyaṇāḥ "given over to desire and anger; devoted to desire and anger". 16.12. Also see *kāma, parāyaṇa*.
- kāmakrodhaviyuktānām "of those who are released from desire and anger". 5.26. Also see *kāma, yukta*.
- kāmakrodhodbhavam "arising from desire and anger". 5.23. Also see *kāma*.
- krodhaḥ "anger". 2.62; 3.37; 16.4, 21.
- krodham "anger" 16.18; 18.53.
- krodhāt "from anger". 2.63.
- vigatecchābhayakrodhaḥ "one who is free of desire, fear, and anger". 5.28.

---

[319] *Kratu* and *yajña* are both mentioned in verse 9.16. Śaṅkara and some others take *kratu* to refer to a class of Vedic sacrifices, but other disagree on specifics (Hill, p. 184, note 5). Śaṅkara says (Warrier, p. 308): "अहं क्रतुः, श्रौतकर्मभेदः अहमेव । अहं यज्ञः स्मार्तः ।". This distinguishes *kratu* as a type of Vedic (*śrauta*) rite, as opposed to a *yajña* as a rite enjoined by *smṛti*. Rāmānuja (Sampatkumaran, p. 234) takes *kratu* to be a type of Vedic sacrifice, giving Jyotiṣṭoma as an example. Apte, p. 379, entry for क्रतुः, gives the first meaning as "a sacrifice" but lists meaning 14 as having the Vedic sense of a sacrifice such as Aśvamedha.

- vītarāgabhayakrodhaḥ "one who is free of attachment, fear, and anger". 2.56.
- vītarāgabhayakrodhāḥ "those who are free of attachment, fear, and anger". 4.10.

1392. **kṛpaḥ** "Kṛpa". 1.8. [Name of a warrior, the brother-in-law of Droṇa, the maternal uncle of Aśvatthāmā. The name (in feminine form, *kṛpā*) means "pity" or "compassion", referring to the fact that Krpa was found in a clump of grass as an infant and was adopted in an act of compassion.[320]]

1393. **kṛpaṇāḥ** "pitiful; pitiable; wretched; void of judgement[321]". 2.49. Also see *kārpaṇyadoṣopahatasvabhāvaḥ*.

1394. **kṛpayā** "by compassion; by pity; with pity; by sorrow; with tenderness". 1.28. [*kṛpayā parayāviṣṭaḥ* = "overwhelmed by supreme compassion"[322]] Also see *āviṣṭa*.

1395. **kṛpayāviṣṭam** "disturbed by compassion; overcome by sorrow; filled with pity[323]". 2.1. [*kṛpayā āviṣṭam*] Also see *āviṣṭa*.

1396. **kṛṣigorakṣyavāṇijyam** "plowing, cow-herding (*gorakṣya*), and trade". 18.44. Also see *rakṣ-*.

1397. **Kṛṣṇa** "Kṛṣṇa". See "Who's Who", page 6.

- kṛṣṇa "O Kṛṣṇa". 1.28, 32, 41; 5.1; 6.34, 37, 39; 11.41; 17.1.
- kṛṣṇaḥ "Kṛṣṇa". 18.78.
- kṛṣṇam "Kṛṣṇa". 11.35.
- kṛṣṇāt "from Kṛṣṇa". 18.75.

1398. **kṛṣṇaḥ** "dark; black". 8.25. Also see *śuklakṛṣṇe*.

1399. **kṛta** "done; performed". Also see *akṛta, nānāvarṇākṛtīni*. [As a component within other words.]

- ahaṁkṛtaḥ "egoistic". 18.17. Also see *ahaṁkāra*.
- asatkṛtaḥ "not done well; done with disrespect; insulting". 11.42.
- asatkṛtam "not well-done; done with disrespect". 17.22.
- duṣkṛtām "of the doers of wicked acts; of the evil-doers; the unrighteous". 4.8. Also see *duṣkṛtinaḥ*.
- kulakṣayakṛtam "caused by the destruction of families". 1.38, 39.
- mahīkṛte "for the sake of the land". 1.35.

---

[320] Sargeant, p. 46.

[321] Apte 1965, p. 371, entry for कृपण.

[322] Gambhīrānanda 1997, p. 21.

[323] Gambhīrānanda 1997, p. 30.

- puṇyakṛtān "of those who do meritorious acts; of the righteous people". 6.41.
- sukṛtaduṣkṛte "good and bad deeds; virtues and vices". 2.50.
- sukṛtam "a good deed; virtue;". 5.15. Also see *sukṛt-*.
- sukṛtasya "well-done; vituous; noble". 14.16.

1400. **kṛtakṛtyaḥ** "perfectly successful; one who has discharged one's duty and therefore feels oneself relieved of a heavy burden[324]". 15.20.

1401. **kṛtam** "done; performed".4.15 (twice); 17.28; 18.23.

1402. **kṛtaniścayaḥ** "one who has made a firm resolve; well-determined". 2.37. Also see *niścaya.*

1403. **kṛtāñjaliḥ** "with folded hands; one who has hands folded together in supplication". 11.14; 11.35.

1404. **kṛtānte** "doctrine; school; system; in making a conclusion". 18.13.

1405. **kṛtena** "by performance of action; by an act which has been done". 3.18. Also see *akṛtena.*

1406. **kṛtin** "a doer".
- duṣkṛtinaḥ "doers of harm; those who act badly; wrong-doers". 7.15. Also see *duṣkṛtām.*
- sukṛtinaḥ "doers of good deeds; those who act well; righteous people". 7.16. Also see *sukṛt-*.

1407. **kṛtsna** "all; whole; entire". Also see *akṛtsnavidaḥ, kṛtsnakarmakṛt, kṛtsnavid.*
- kṛtsnam "the whole, the entire". 1.40; 7.29; 9.8; 10.42; 11.7, 13; 13.33 (twice).
- kṛtsnasya "of the whole, of the entire". 7.6.
- kṛtsnavat "as if it were the whole; as though it were all". 18.22.

1408. **kṛtsnakarmakṛt** "a doer of all actions; a performer of all actions; doing all work; one who has discharged all his duties[325]; doing all the right acts[326]". 4.18. Also see *kṛtsna, karma.*

1409. **kṛtsnavid** "one who knows completely; the man of complete knowledge; the knower of the All; one who knows all that is to be known; one who understand

---

[324] Divanji, p. 45, entry #1052.

[325] Divanji, p. 47, entry #1059.

[326] Bolle, p. 282.

the universal aspect". 3.29. [Śaṅkara interprets this as one who knows the Self.[327]] Also see *kṛtsna, -vid.*

1410. **kṛtvā** "having done; after doing; having performed; after making; after rendering". 2.38; 4.22; 5.27 (twice); 6.12, 25; 11.35; 18.8, 68. Also see *sahasrakṛtvaḥ.*

1411. **krūrān** "cruel, ruthless". 16.19.

1412. **kṣamā** "forgiveness; patience". 10.4, 34; 16.3.

1413. **kṣāmaye** "I beg forgiveness; I ask pardon". 11.42.

1414. **kṣamī** "one who has the quality of forgiveness; a forgiving person". 12.13.

1415. **kṣaṇam** "a moment". 3.5.

1416. **kṣāntiḥ** "forgiveness". 13.7; 18.42.

1417. **kṣara** "perishable". Also see *akṣara* ("imperishable").

- kṣaraḥ "the perishable". 8.4; 15.16 (twice).
- kṣaram "the perishable". 15.18.

1418. **kṣatrakarma** "the natural duties of the Kṣatriyas". 18.43. Also see *kṣatriya, karma.*

1419. **kṣatriya** "Kṣatriya". [The name of the second *varṇa* in the Indo-Āryan social order.]

- brāhmaṇakṣatriyaviśām "of the Brāhmaṇas, the Kṣatriyas, and the Vaiśyas". 18.41. Also see *Brāhmaṇa, Vaiśya.*
- kṣatrakarma "the natural duties of the Kṣatriyas". 18.43.
- kṣatriyāḥ "Kṣatriyas". 2.32.
- kṣatriyasya "for a Kṣatriya". 2.31.

1420. **kṣaya** "destruction". Also see *kṣīṇa.*

- akṣayam "indestructible". 5.21.
- evākṣayaḥ "alone indestructible" (*eva akṣayaḥ*). 10.33.
- kalpakṣaye "at the end of the *kalpa*; at the dissolution of the *kalpa*". 9.7.
- kṣayam "loss, harm". 18.25
- kṣayāya "leading to the destruction". 16.9.
- kulakṣayakṛtam "caused by destruction of family; arising from the destruction of one's family". 1.38, 39.
- kulakṣaye "in the destruction of the family". 1.40.
- lokakṣayakṛt "destroyer of the world; maker of the dissolution of the world". 11.32.

---

[327] Gambhīrānanda 1997, p. 161.

1421. **kṣema** "happiness; well-being; security; keeping what is acquired".

- kṣemataram "more beneficial; greater happiness; more ease; healthier; better". 1.46. [Comp. degree of adj. *kṣema.*]
- niryogakṣemaḥ "without concern for getting and keeping; beyond acquisition and conservation[328]". 2.45.
- yogakṣemam "fulfillment and maintenance of well-being; acquisition of that which is not in one's possession and the preservation of that which is[329]". 9.22.

1422. **kṣetrajña** "knower of the field; knower of the *kṣetra*". Also see *kṣetram, kṣetrī, kṣetrakṣetrajña-.*

- kṣetrajñaḥ "knower of the *kṣetra*". 13.1.
- kṣetrajñam "knower of the *kṣetra*". 13.2.

1423. **kṣetrakṣetrajñasaṁyogāt** "from the association of the field and the Knower of the field[330]; due to the union of Kṣetra (body) and Kṣetrajña (Spirit)[331]; the coming into contact of the Kṣetra and its knower[332]; due to the union of the body and consciousness". 13.26. Also see *saṁyoga.*

1424. **kṣetrakṣetrajñayoḥ** "of the *kṣetra* and the knower of the *kṣetra*; of the field and the knower of the field". 13.2, 34.

1425. **kṣetram** "field; *kṣetra*". 13.1, 3, 6, 18, 33. Also see *kṣetrajña, kṣetrakṣetrajña-, dharmakṣetre, kurukṣetre, sarvakṣetreṣu.*

1426. **kṣetrī** "the owner of the field; the knower of the *kṣetra*; the Lord". 13.33. Also see *kṣetrajña.*

1427. **kṣīṇa** "destroyed, exhausted". Also see *kṣaya.*

- kṣīṇakalmaṣāḥ "those whose evils have been eliminated; those whose sins have been destroyed". 5.25.
- kṣīṇe "on exhaustion". 9.21.

1428. **kṣīṇakalmaṣāḥ** "whose sins have been destroyed". 5.25.

1429. **kṣipāmi** "I throw; I hurl; I cast". 16.19.

1430. **kṣipram** "quickly; immediately". 4.12; 9.31.

1431. **kṣudram** "small; base; low; mean". 2.3.

---

[328] Van Buitenen 1981, p. 79.

[329] Divanji, p. 123, entry #2823.

[330] Gambhīrānanda 1997, p. 555.

[331] Sivananda, p. 348.

[332] Divanji, pp. 49-50, entry #1120.

1432. **kula** "family".
- kulam "family". 1.40.
- kulasya "of the family". 1.42.
- kule "in a family". 6.42.

1433. **kuladharmāḥ** "family traditions; the traditional rules of conduct observed in one's family[333]; family Laws[334]; family religious rites[335]". 1.40, 43. Also see *dharma, jātidharmāḥ, utsannakuladharmāṇām.*

1434. **kulaghnānām** "of the destroyers of the family". 1.42, 43. Also see *ghnataḥ.*

1435. **kulakṣayakṛtam** "caused by destruction of family; arising from the destruction of one's family". 1.38, 39.

1436. **kulakṣaye** "in the destruction of the family". 1.40.

1437. **kulastriyaḥ** "women of the family". 1.41. Also see *strī.*

1438. **kuntibhojaḥ** "Kuntibhoja". 1.5. [An ally of the Pāṇḍavas. The childless Kuntibhoja adopted Kuntī, who became Pāṇḍu's wife, the mother of Arjuna.]

1439. **kuntīputraḥ** "son of Kuntī (referring to Yudhiṣṭhira)". 1.16. Also see *putra.*

1440. **kūrmaḥ** "a tortoise". 2.58.

1441. **kuru** "perform; do; act". 2.48; 3.8; 4.15; 12.11; 18.63. Also see *namaskuru.* [Imp. 2nd pers. sing. √ *kṛ*]

1442. **kurukṣetre** "on the field (*kṣetra*) of the Kurus; in the land of the Kurus; on Kuru ground; on the field of the Kurus; in the battlefield called Kurukṣetra". 1.1. [Kurukṣetra was a region in the north of India, located near modern Delhi.]

1443. **kurūn** "the Kurus; the Kauravas". 1.25. [Acc. pl. masc. of the noun *kuru.* Both sides of the war belonged to the Kuru lineage, but the term is used here to refer to the Kaurava army of Duryodhana.]

1444. **kurunandana** "O Descendant of the Kurus; O delight of the Kurus". 2.41; 6.43; 14.13. [Used to refer to Arjuna.]

1445. **kurupravīra** "O great hero of the Kurus; O extraordinary hero of the Kurus". 11.48. [Used to refer to Arjuna.]

1446. **kurusattama** "O best of the Kurus". 4.31. Also see *śreṣṭhaḥ.* [Used to refer to Arjuna.]

1447. **kuruśreṣṭha** "O best of the Kurus". 10.19. [Used to refer to Arjuna.]

1448. **kuruṣva** "do; perform". 9.27. [Ātma. imp. 2nd pers. sing. √ *kṛ*]

---

333 Divanji, p. 46, entry #1042.

334 Van Buitenen 1981, p. 73.

335 Sivananda, p. 15.

1449. **kurute** "does". 3.21; 4.37 (twice, *bhasmasāt kurute* = it burns to ashes). [3rd pers. sing. √ *kṛ*]

1450. **kuruvṛddhaḥ** "oldest of the Kurus". 1.12. [An epithet of Bhīṣma.]

1451. **kurvan** "doing; performing action". 4.21; 5.7, 13; 12.10; 18.47. [√ *kṛ*]

1452. **kurvāṇaḥ** "doing; performing action". 18.56. [√ *kṛ*]

1453. **kurvanti** "they perform action". 3.25; 5.11. [√ *kṛ*]

1454. **kuryām** "I should perform action". 3.24. [√ *kṛ*]

1455. **kuryāt** "one should perform action". 3.25. [√ *kṛ*]

1456. **kuśale** "in agreeable (action); in favorable (action)". 18.10. Also see *akuśalam, kauśalam.*

1457. **kusumākaraḥ** "the flower-bearer[336]; abounding with flowers; the Spring season; the vernal season". 10.35.

1458. **kutaḥ** "from where; whence". 2.2, 66; 4.31; 11.43.

1459. **kūṭastha** "(lit.) standing on a peak[337]; unchangeable[338]; perpetually the same; unperturbed[339]; immovable[340]; immutable[341]; stable-minded; unshakable".

- kūṭasthaḥ 6.8; 15.16.

---

[336] Edgerton, p. 53.

[337] Van Buitenen (1981, pp. 95, 121, 131) uses the literal translations "firm on his peak", "standing on the peak", and "the One-on-the-Peak" in the three verses where *kūṭastha* appears. He says (p. 168, note 2) that the first use of *kūṭastha* in a technical sense as a qualification of the pure *ātman* appears to be in the *BG*. Minor (pp. 211-2, 364-5, 428-9) notes the literal meaning of *kūṭastha* as "standing at the top" and reviews the complexities of various interpretations of the word.

[338] Apte, p. 368, entry for कूट-स्थः, says it means "the Supreme Soul (immoveable, unchangeable, and perpetually the same)", listing *BG* 6.8 and 12.3 as uses with those senses.

[339] Gambhīrānanda (1998, p. 390) translates *kūṭasthaḥ* as "unperturbed" when it is used in 6.8 and renders Madhusūdana Sarasvati's commentary as "*kūṭasthaḥ* means one who remains unperturbed even in the proximity of objects...". But in 12.3 (pp. 687-8) he translates it as "seated in Māyā", accepting an alternative line of thinking first put forth by Śaṅkara. He repeats this view when translating it as "existing in Māyā" in 15.15 (p. 797).

[340] Edgerton (pp. 32, 62, 74) consistently translates *kūṭastha* as "immovable" but his two notes on the word (pp. 95, 98-9) say that the precise meaning is unclear, and that the commentators have no consistent tradition regarding it. He says that the same word is found in Pāli where it means something like "not subject to change", or perhaps literally "abiding on a mountaintop" as if "above the battle", i.e., not subject to external influences.

[341] Macdonell (pp. 71-2, entry for कूट-स्थः) gives a range of meanings including the literal "being in the highest place" as well as "immovable, immutable".

- kūṭastham 12.3.

1460. **kvacit** "anywhere; at any time; whatsoever". 18.12.

L

ऌ = L. ॡ = Ḹ.

1461. √ **labh** "to obtain". See *labh-, lobh-, lubh-, durlabhataram, sudurlabhaḥ, sulabhaḥ, upalabhyate.*
    - labdhā"is gained". 18.73. [*smṛtir labdhā* = memory regained]
    - labdham "has been gained; acquired". 16.13.
    - labdhvā "after obtaining; after attaining; after getting". 4.39; 6.22.
    - labhante "they obtain; they attain". 2.32; 5.25; 9.21.
    - labhasva "earn; obtain". 11.33.
    - labhate "one attains; one gets". 4.39; 6.43; 7.22; 18.45, 54.
    - labhe "I attain; I get". 11.25.
    - labhet "one would attain; one would get". 18.8.
1462. **lābhālābhau** "gain and loss". 2.38. [*lābha* and *alābha*]
1463. **lābham** "gain; an attainment". 6.22. Also see *yadṛcchālābhasaṁtuṣṭaḥ.*
1464. **labhyaḥ** "is attainable". 8.22. Also see *lobha.*
1465. **lāghavam** "disrespect; treating one lightly". 2.35.
1466. **laghvāśī** "one who eats little; one who takes light meals". 18.52.
1467. **lavaṇa** "salty". 17.9. See *kaṭvamlalavaṇātyuṣṇatīkṣṇarūkṣavidāhinaḥ.*
1468. **lelihyase** "you lick again and again, you lick voraciously". 11.30. [√ *lih*]
1469. **limpanti** "they taint; they bind; they cover". 4.14. Also see √ *lip.*
1470. **liṅgaiḥ** "by marks; by signs, by characteristics". 14.21.
1471. √ **lip** "to smear; to stain; to annoint".
    - divyagandhānulepanam "annointed with divine fragrant ointments; annointed with celestial aromatic unguents; annointed with divine perfumes". 11.11.
    - limpanti "they taint; they have effect upon (as bonds); they cover". 4.14.
    - lipyate "one is tainted; one becomes polluted". 5.7, 10; 13.31; 18.17. [Sometimes with the sense of "be affected by".]
    - upalipyate "it is tainted; it is smeared; it is polluted". 13.32 (twice).
1472. **lobhaḥ** "greed; avarice; acquisitiveness". 14.12, 17; 16.21. Also see *labhyaḥ, lobhopahatacetasaḥ, lubdhaḥ, rājyasukhalobhena.*

1473. **lobhopahatacetasaḥ** "with minds clouded by greed". 1.38. Also see *kārpaṇya-doṣopahatasvabhāvaḥ, hata, cetas.*

1474. **loka** "the world; the mundane world; the universe; units of the universe; a region; a realm; creation; creatures; living beings; beings of the world; people; society". [Meaning depends on context.] Also see *ābrahmabhuvanāt, jagat, jīvaloke* (√ *jīv*), *surendralokam, svargalokam, trailokyarājyasya.*

- lokaḥ "man[342]; (this) man; the world[343]; this world[344]". 3.9.
- lokaḥ "an ordinary person[345]; people[346]; the world[347]". 3.21.
- lokaḥ "the world; (this) world; the mundane world". 4.31, 40; 7.25.
- lokaḥ "the world; society". 12.15.
- lokāḥ "worlds; the heavenly worlds; people[348]; men[349]". 3.24.
- lokāḥ "worlds[350]". 8.16.
- lokāḥ "the creatures in the world[351]; beings of the world; the worlds[352]". 11.23.
- lokāḥ "creatures[353]; beings of the world; men[354]; the worlds[355]". 11.29.
- lokam "world; the human world". 9.33.
- lokam "world; the human world". 13.33.
- lokān "the worlds; the heavenly worlds". 6.41.
- lokān "the worlds". 10.16.

---

[342] Gambhīrānanda 1997, p. 143.

[343] Van Buitenen 1981, p. 83.

[344] Ādidevānanda, p. 125.

[345] Gambhīrānanda 1997, p. 155.

[346] Van Buitenen 1981, p. 83.

[347] Sargeant, p. 178; Ādidevānanda, p. 135.

[348] Van Buitenen 1981, p. 83.

[349] Ādidevānanda, p. 137.

[350] Van Buitenen 1981, p. 103; Ādidevānanda, p. 281.

[351] Gambhīrānanda 1997, pp. 443.

[352] Van Buitenen 1981, p. 115; Sargeant, p. 475; Ādidevānanda, p. 370.

[353] Gambhīrānanda 1997, p. 448.

[354] Van Buitenen 1981, p. 115; Ādidevānanda, p. 374.

[355] Sargeant (p. 481) gives "worlds" in word-by-word vocabulary but translates as "creatures".

- lokān "the worlds[356]; the creatures[357]". 11.30.
- lokān "the worlds[358]; the creatures[359]". 11.32.
- lokān "the worlds[360]". 14.14.
- lokān "people[361]; men[362]; creatures[363]; worlds[364]". 18.17.
- lokān "worlds; realms[365]". 18.71.
- lokasya "of the world; to the world[366]; of people; into people[367]; for anyone[368]". 5.14.
- lokasya "of the world[369]; of the universe; of all beings[370]". 11.43.
- lokāt "by the world; due to society". 12.15.
- loke "in the world; on earth[371]; in this land[372]". 2.5.
- loke "in the world". 3.3.
- loke "in the world". 4.12. [*mānuṣe loke* = in the human world; in the world of men[373]]
- loke "in the world". 6.42.
- loke "in the world; in the universe". 10.6.

---

356 Sargeant, p. 482. Ādidevānanda (p. 370) translates *lokān* as "worlds" but the commentary interprets it as referring to the kings who are being consumed.

357 Gambhīrānanda 1997, p. 449.

358 Sargeant, p. 484; Ādidevānanda, p. 376.

359 Gambhīrānanda 1997, p. 450.

360 Translated as "worlds" by Van Buitenen (1981, p. 129) with a note saying the sense may be "domestic environment and social position" (note 1 for section 36[14] on p. 169).

361 Sargeant, p. 678.

362 Ādidevānanda, p. 560.

363 Gambhīrānanda 1997, pp. 679-680.

364 Van Buitenen 1981, p. 139, with sense "the three worlds".

365 Ādidevānanda, p. 602.

366 Ādidevānanda, p. 198.

367 Van Buitenen 1981, p. 91.

368 Gambhīrānanda 1997, p. 254.

369 Sargeant, p. 495.

370 Gambhīrānanda 1997, p. 462.

371 Sargeant, p. 90.

372 Van Buitenen 1981, p. 73.

373 Van Buitenen 1981, p. 87.

- loke "in the world[374]; in the universe[375]; in creatures[376]; in the multitude of creatures[377]". 13.13.
- loke "in the world". 15.16.
- loke "in the world". 15.18.
- loke "in the world". 16.6.
- lokeṣu "in the worlds". 3.22. [*triṣu lokeṣu* = in the three worlds] Also see *lokatraya.*

Compounds meaning the human world:

- manuṣyaloke "in the human world; in the region where humans reside". 15.2.
- martyalokam "the mortal world; the region of the mortals". 9.21.
- naralokavīrāḥ "heroes of the human world; heroes of the region where humans reside". 11.28.
- nṛloke "in the human world; the region where humans reside". 11.48.

1475. **lokakṣayakṛt** "destroyer of the world; maker of the dissolution of the world". 11.32.

1476. **lokamaheśvara** Great Lord of the Worlds; the Great Lord of the Universe". Also see *īśvara, maheśvara.*

- lokamaheśvaram "Great Lord of the Worlds; the Great Lord of the Universe". 10.3.
- sarvalokamaheśvaram "Great Lord of All the Worlds; Great Sovereign of the Entire Universe". 5.29.

1477. **lokasaṁgraham** "holding together the world; the preservation of the world; setting an example for the world; (wishing to inspire) cooperation and order among people; maintaining the social order; the order of the world; the control of the world[378]; making people undertake their duties and preventing them

---

[374] Sargeant, p. 541.

[375] Van Buitenen 1981, p. 125.

[376] Gambhīrānanda 1997, p. 532.

[377] Gambhīrānanda 1997, p. 533.

[378] Edgerton, p. 20.

from going astray[379]". 3.20, 25. Also see *karmasaṁgrahaḥ, saṁgraheṇa*. [From *saṁ* + √ *grah*, to hold, and thus, support, protect.[380]]

1478. **lokatraya** "the three worlds". [Earth, the atmosphere (the middle region), and heaven.] Also see *trailokyarājyasya*. Phrase *triṣu lokeṣu* ("in the three worlds") in verse 3.22 is listed under *loka*.

- lokatrayam "the three worlds; the threefold world". 11.20; 15.17.
- lokatraye "in the three worlds; in the threefold world". 11.43.

1479. **lubdhaḥ** "greedy; avaricious". 18.27. Also see *lobhaḥ*.

1480. **luptapiṇḍodakakriyāḥ** "those for whom the ceremonies of offering rice-balls and libations of water are discontinued; deprived of offerings of food and water". 1.42. Also see *kriyā*.

M

म् = M. Anusvāra = Ṁ (not used as the initial sound of a word).

Candrabindu = M̐ (not used as the initial sound of a word).

1481. **mā** "do not". 2.3, 47 (three times); 11.34, 49 (twice); 16.5; 18.66. [A prohibitive particle indicating something should not be done. In 2.3 it is intensified by the following particle *sma* to indicate a particularly strong injunction.]

1482. **maccitta** "having the mind directed toward Me; with mind focused on Me". Also see *citta*.

- maccittaḥ "mind directed toward Me". 6.14; 18.57, 58.
- maccittāḥ "(their) minds directed toward Me". 10.9.

1483. **madam** "vanity; pride; arrogance". 18.35. Also see *dambhamānamadānvitāḥ, dhanamānamadānvitāḥ*.

1484. **madanugrahāya** "for the stake of bestowing grace (*anugraha*) on me; as a favor to me; in order to bless me". 11.1.

1485. **madarpaṇam** "(do it as) an offering to me; dedication to me; surrender it to me". 9.27. Also see *arpaṇa*.

1486. **madartham** "for my sake". 12.10. Also see *arthaḥ, madarthe*.

1487. **madarthe** "for my sake". 1.9. Also see *arthe, madartham*.

---

[379] Gambhīrānanda 1998, p. 237.

[380] Translators have various interpretations of this compound. For a summary see Minor, pp. 125-6.

1488. **madāśrayaḥ** "depending on me; one who has taken resort to me". 7.1. Also see *āśrayaḥ, āśrita, madvyapāśrayaḥ.*

1489. **madbhakta** "my devotee". Also see *bhakta.*

- madbhaktaḥ "my devotee". 9.34; 11.55; 12.14, 16; 13.18; 18.65.
- madbhaktāḥ "my devotees". 7.23.
- madbhakteṣu "in my worshippers; to my devotees". 18.68.

1490. **madbhaktim** "devotion to me". 18.54. Also see *bhakti.*

1491. **madbhāva** "my nature; my state of being; my essential state; identification with me; being in me".

- madbhāvāḥ "having their being in me; partaking of my nature; co-existing with me". 10.6.
- madbhāvam "my nature; my state of being; my essential state; identification with me". 4.10; 8.5; 14.19.
- madbhāvāya "to my state of being; for identification with me". 13.18.

1492. **madgataprāṇāḥ** "with their life force taking shelter in Me; those whose vitality is absorbed in Me; those whose life goes toward Me". 10.9. Also see *madgatenāntarātmanā, prāṇa.*

1493. **madgatenāntarātmanā** "with his innermost self fused to Me[381]; inwardly absorbed in me; with his mind fixed on me". 6.47. Also see *ātman, madgataprāṇāḥ.*

1494. **mādhava.** [See comment on this epithet of Kṛṣṇa on page 15.]

- mādhavaḥ " Mādhava". 1.14.
- mādhava "O Mādhava". 1.37.

1495. **madhusūdana** "Madhusūdana; Slayer of Madhu (a demon)". [See comment on this epithet on page 15.]

- madhusūdana "O Madhusūdana; O Slayer of Madhu". 1.35; 2.4; 6.33; 8.2.
- madhusūdanaḥ "Madhusūdana; Slayer of Madhu". 2.1.

1496. **madhya** ""the middle. Also see *anādimadhyāntam, vyaktamadhyāni.*

- madhyam "the middle". 10.20, 32; 11.16.
- madhye "in the middle". 1.21, 24; 2.10; 8.10; 14.18.

1497. **madhyastha** "neutral, mediator; (lit.) standing in the middle". Also see *udāsīna.*

- suhṛnmitrāryudāsīnamadhyasthadveṣyabandhuṣu "in friends, enemies, neutrals, mediators, despicable persons, and relatives". 6.9.

---

381 Tapasyananda, p. 187.

1498. **madvyapāśrayaḥ** "on who has thrown himself on my support; one who is dedicated to me". 18.56. Also see *āśrayaḥ, āśrita, madāśrayaḥ*.

1499. **madyājin** "my worshipper; one who sacrifices to me; sacrificing for me; one who is dedicated to me". Also see *yajña*.

- madyājī "my worshipper; those who sacrifice to me; sacrificing for me". 9.34; 18.65.
- madyājinaḥ "those dedicated to me; those who sacrifice to me; my worshippers". 9.25.

1500. **madyogam** "my *yoga*; the *yoga* in which I am the goal". 12.11. Also see *yoga*.

1501. **mahābāho** "O Long-armed One". Used to refer to Arjuna in 2.26, 68; 3.28, 43; 5.3, 6; 6.35; 7.5; 10.1; 14.5; 18.13. Used to refer to Kṛṣṇa in 6.38; 11.23; 18.1. Used to refer to Abhimanyu in 1.18 (*mahābāhuḥ*). [For discussion of the meaning of this epithet see page 11.] Also see *bāhu*.

1502. **mahābhūtāni** "the great elements". 13.5. [The five gross primary elements: earth, water, fire, air, and space.] Also see *bhūta*.

1503. **mahad brahma** "the great *Brahman*". [Here used as a technical term meaning *Prakṛti*.] Also see *brahma*.

- mahad brahma "the great *Brahman*". 14.3.
- brahma mahad "the great *Brahman*". 14.4.

1504. **mahad yoniḥ** "the great womb; the great source". 14.4. Also see *yoni*.

1505. **mahān** "great". See *mahat*.

1506. **mahānubhāvān** "greatly (*mahā*) dignified (*anubhāvan*); very noble-minded; great souls". 2.5.

1507. **mahāpāpmā** "enormous sinful intent; a great sinner[382]; very sinful[383]; the great evil[384]". 3.37. Also see *pāpa*.

1508. **mahāratha** "great charioteer; great warrior".[385] Also see *ratham*.

- mahārathaḥ "great charioteer". 1.4, 17.
- mahārathāḥ "great charioteers". 1.6; 2.35.

---

[382] Gambhīrānanda 1997, p. 168.

[383] Edgerton, p. 22.

[384] Van Buitenen 1981, p. 85.

[385] Literally "great chariot", used in the *BG* to refer to various prominent warriors. It may have been a formal military term as discussed in Gambhīrānanda 1997 (p. 13), but Minor (p. 5) notes it is used in 1.6 for all of the Pāṇḍava heroes and that its sense is probably non-technical. Van Buitenen (p. 69) translates it as "great warrior" in 1.4 where it is applied to Drupada, and "good warriors" in 1.6 where it refers to others.

1509. **maharṣi** "great sage". Also see *ṛṣi.*

- maharṣayaḥ "a great sage". 10.2, 6.
- maharṣīṇāṁ "of the great sages". 10.2, 25.
- maharṣisiddhasaṁghāḥ "groups of great Sages and Adepts". 11.21.

1510. **maharṣisiddhasaṁghāḥ** "groups of great Sages and Adepts". 11.21.

1511. **mahāśanaḥ** "enormous appetite; great craving". 3.37.

1512. **mahāśaṅkham** "a great conch". 1.15. Also see *śaṅkha.*

1513. **mahat** "great". Also see *mahad-, mahā-.*

- mahān "great". 9.6; 18.77
- mahat "great". 1.45; 11.23.
- mahatā "in the course of a long (time)". 4.2.
- mahataḥ "from great (fear)". 2.40.
- mahati "in the great (chariot)". 1.14.
- mahatīm "the great (army)". 1.3.

1514. **mahātman** "great soul; One who has a highly-developed soul". [Comp. adj. *mahātman* used as a noun.] Also see *ātman, kāmātmānaḥ, māhātmyam, yatātman.*

- mahātmā "great soul". 7.19; 11.50.
- mahātman "O Great Soul". 11.20, 37.
- mahātmanaḥ "of the great soul". 11.12 (applied to Kṛṣṇa); 18.74 (applied to Arjuna).
- mahātmānaḥ "great souls". 8.15; 9.13.

1515. **māhātmyam** "greatness; magnanimity; exalted nature; majesty; nobility of soul". 11.2. Also see *ātman, mahātman.*

1516. **mahāyogeśvaraḥ** "the great Lord of *yoga*". 11.9. Also see *īśvara, maheśvara, yogeśvara.*

1517. **maheśvara** "Great Lord; Great Master". Also see *īśvara, mahāyogeśvara, parameśvara.*

- bhūtamaheśvaram "supreme Lord of Beings; highest lord of the created beings". 9.11.
- lokamaheśvaram "Great Lord of the Worlds; the Great Lord of the Universe". 10.3.
- maheśvaraḥ "Great Lord; Great Sovereign". 13.22.
- sarvalokamaheśvaram "Great Lord of All the Worlds; Great Sovereign of the Entire Universe". 5.29.

1518. **maheṣvāsāḥ** "great archers". 1.4.

1519. **mahī** "the earth".

- mahīkṛte "(doing it) for the sake of this land; for the sake of (winning) the world". 1.35.
- mahīkṣitām "rulers of the earth; kings; ruling princes". 1.25. [*mahī* (earth) + *kṣitām* (rulers)]
- mahīm "the earth; earthly (empire)". 2.37.
- mahīpate "O Ruler of the Earth; O King of the Earth". 1.21 [An epithet applied to Dhṛtarāṣṭra by Saṁjaya.]

1520. **mahimānam** "greatness; power; majesty". 11.41.

1521. **maitraḥ** "friendly". 12.13.

1522. **makaraḥ** "the Makara". 10.31. [Name of an aquatic creature that is either regarded as a mythical "sea monster" or identified as various specific creatures such as the crocodile, shark, or dolphin. In all cases the sense is of an aquatic creature that is large and remarkable.]

1523. **malena** "with dirt; with impurity". 3.38. Also see *amalān, nirmalam, nirmalatvāt.*

1524. **mām** "me". 1.46; 2.7; 3.1; 4.9, 10, 11, 13, 14 (twice); 5.29; 6.30, 31, 47; 7.1, 3, 10, 13, 14, 15, 16, 18, 19, 23, 24, 25, 26, 28, 29, 30 (twice); 8.5, 7 (twice), 13, 14, 15, 16; 9.3, 9, 11, 13, 14 (twice), 15, 20, 22, 23, 24, 25, 28, 29, 30, 32, 33, 34 (twice); 10.3, 8, 9, 10, 14, 24, 27; 11.8, 53, 55; 12.2, 4, 6, 9; 13.2; 14.26; 15.19 (twice); 16.18, 20; 17.6; 18.55 (twice), 65 (twice), 66, 67, 68.

1525. **mama** "of me; my; of my; mine". 1.7, 29; 2.8; 3.23; 4.11; 7.14, 17, 24; 8.21; 9.5, 11; 10.7, 40, 41; 11.1, 7, 49, 52; 13.2; 14.2, 3; 15.6, 7; 18.78.

1526. **māmaka** "my; mine; belonging to me; my own".

- māmakāḥ "mine; my own; my people". 1.1.
- māmakam "mine; my own". 15.12.
- māmikām "mine; my own". 9.7.

1527. **mamātmā** "My Self". 9.5. [*mama-ātmā*] Also see *ātman.*

1528. **maṁsyante** "they will think; they will believe". 2.35. [√ *man*]

1529. √ **man** "to think". See *manaḥ-, manas, mano-, many-, matvā, maṁsyante, mantavyaḥ.*

1530. **-manāḥ** "minded (ifc.)". Also see *manas.*

- anudvignamanāḥ "one whose mind is not troubled; not perturbed mentally; not distressed". 2.56. Also see *vigna.*
- mayy āsaktamanāḥ "with mind attached to Me; fixing your mind on Me". 7.1.

- prītamanāḥ "one whose mind is pleased; with a happy mind". 11.49. Also see *prīti.*

1531. **manaḥprāṇendriyakriyāḥ** "the activities (*kriyāḥ*) of the mind (*manaḥ*), the life force (*prāṇa*), and the senses (*indriya*); the operation of the mind, the vital breath, and the organs (of sense and action)". 18.33.

1532. **manaḥprasādaḥ** "tranquillity of mind". 17.16. Also see *prasāda.*

1533. **manaḥṣaṣṭhānīndriyāṇi** "the senses with the mind as the sixth unit; those to which the mind is added as the sixth". 15.7. Also see *indriya.*

1534. **mānāpamānayoḥ**. See *mānāvamānayoḥ.*

1535. **manas** "mind". Also see *manaḥ-, -manāḥ, manas-, mānas-, mano-, ananyamanasaḥ, arpitamanobuddhiḥ, manmanāḥ, praśāntamanasam, śarīravāṅmanobhiḥ, yatendriyamanobuddhiḥ.*

- manaḥ "the mind". 1.30; 2.60, 67; 3.40, 42; 5.19; 6.12, 14, 25, 26, 34, 35; 7.4; 8.12; 10.22; 11.45; 12.2, 8; 15.9; 17.11.
- manasā "with the mind; mentally". 3.6, 7; 5.11, 13; 6.24; 8.10.
- manasaḥ "than the mind". 3.42.

1536. **manasācalena** "with unmoving mind". 8.10. Also see *calitamānasaḥ.*

1537. **mānasa** "pertaining to the mind; mental; mentally". Also see *manas.*

- calitamānasaḥ "one whose mind has strayed; having a distracted mind". 6.37. Also see *manasācalena.*
- mānasāḥ jātāḥ "mind-born creatures". 10.6.
- mānasam "mental". 17.16.
- niyatamānasaḥ "one whose mind is under control; one with well-regulated mind". 6.15.
- śokasaṁvignamānasaḥ "with mind disturbed by melancholy; one whose mind is perturbed by grief". 1.47. Also see *śoka, vigna.*
- yatavākkāyamānasaḥ "controlling speech (*vāk*), body (*kāya*), and mind (*manas*)". 18.52.

1538. **mānava** "a human being; person". Also see *mānuṣa.*

- mānavaḥ "human being; person". 3.17; 18.46.
- mānavāḥ "human beings; persons; people". 3.31.

1539. **manavaḥ** "the (four) Manus". 10.6. [Each cosmic age (*yuga*) in the Indian cyclic system has its own primal man, similar to the concept of Adam.] Also see *manave, manuḥ.*

1540. **mānāvamānayoḥ** "in honor and dishonor". 6.7; 12.18; 14.25.[386]

1541. **manave** "to Vaivasvata Manu". 4.1. Also see *manavaḥ, manuḥ*.

1542. **mandān** "foolish ones; the slow-witted; the dull-minded". 3.29.

1543. **maṇi** "gem; jewel; pearl".

- maṇigaṇāḥ "group of gems; strands of pearls". 7.7.
- sughoṣamaṇipuṣpakau "Sughoṣa and Maṇipuṣpaka". 1.16. Also see *maṇi*. [Nakula's conch was named Sughoṣa. Sahadeva's conch was named Maṇipuṣpaka.]

1544. **maṇigaṇāḥ** "group of gems; strands of pearls". 7.7. Also see *gaṇa, maṇi*.

1545. **maṇipuṣpaka** "having gems as flowers; Jewel-Flowered[387]". 1.16. See *sughoṣamaṇipuṣpakau*. [Sahadeva's conch was named Maṇipuṣpaka.] Also see *maṇi, puṣpa*.

1546. **manīṣiṇaḥ** "wise ones; enlightened sages". 2.51; 18.3.

1547. **manīṣiṇām** "of wise persons". 18.5.

1548. **manmanāḥ** "thinking of Me; keeping the mind on Me". 9.34; 18.65. Also see *manas, ananyacetāḥ, ananyamanasaḥ, manmayāḥ*.

1549. **manmayāḥ** "identified with Me; absorbed in Me; thinking solely of Me". 4.10. Also see *manmanāḥ*.

1550. **manogatān** "(objects) that enter the mind; (desires) emerging from the mind; mental". 2.55. Also see *manas*.

1551. **manoratham** "a desire; desired object that is pleasing to the mind; a craving; a wish; an ambition". 16.13. [(lit.) "the car (*ratha*) of the mind".] Also see *manas*.

1552. **mantavyaḥ** "to be thought; to be considered; should be regarded as". 9.30.

1553. **mantra** "*mantra*; sacred prayer; sacred chanting; an incantation; sacred text".

- mantraḥ "*mantra*; sacred chanting; prayer; an incantation". 9.16.
- mantrahīnam "without *mantras*; bereft of *mantras*; in which *mantras* are not used; (performed) without (chanting of relevant) prayers; lacking the sacred formula". 17.13. [Śaṅkara's commentary says this includes *mantras* without correct intonation and accurate pronunciation.[388]]

---

[386] The Critical Edition reads *mānāvamānayoḥ* in 6.7; 12.18; 14.25. Some Vulgate editions read *mānāpamānayoḥ* in some verses with same meaning.

[387] Flood and Martin, p. 4.

[388] तं असृष्टान्नं मन्त्रहीनं स्वरतः वर्णतः वा वियुक्तं मन्त्रहीनम् । Translated by Warrier (p. 537) as "'Without sacred chants' refers to chants defective as regards accents and consonantal sounds."

1554. **manuḥ** "Manu". 4.1. [Vaivasvata Manu, the name of the first man in the Vaivasvata Manvantara. Each cosmic age (*yuga*) in the Indian cyclic system has its own primal man, similar to the concept of Adam.] Also see *manavaḥ, manave, mānuṣa.*

1555. **mānuṣa** "human". Also see *mānava, manuṣya, manuṣyaloke, manuḥ.*
- mānuṣam "human (form)". 11.51. [*mānuṣaṁ rūpam*]
- mānuṣe "in the human (world)". 4.12. [*mānuṣe loke*]
- mānuṣīm "human (form)". 9.11. [*mānuṣīṁ tanum*]

1556. **manuṣya** "a human being; a person". Also see *mānuṣa.*
- manuṣyāḥ "persons; people; human beings". 3.23; 4.11.
- manuṣyāṇām "of persons; of people; of human beings". 1.44; 7.3.
- manuṣyeṣu "among people; among humans". 4.18; 18.69.

1557. **manuṣyaloke** "in the human world; in the region where humans reside". 15.2. Also see *loka, mānuṣa.*

1558. **manyante** "they think". 7.24. [√ *man*]

1559. **manyase** "you think; you believe; you consider". 2.26; 11.4; 18.59. [√ *man*]

1560. **manyate** "one thinks; one believes one considers". 2.19; 3.27; 6.22; 18.32. [√ *man*]

1561. **manye** "I think; I believe; I consider". 6.34; 10.14. [√ *man*]

1562. **manyeta** "one should think". 5.8. [√ *man*]

1563. **maraṇa** "dying". Also see √ *mṛ, mṛtyu, mart-.*
- maraṇāt "than death; than dying". 2.34.
- jarāmaraṇamokṣāya "toward release from old age and dying; for becoming free of old age and death". 7.29. Also see *mokṣ-.*

1564. **mārdavam** "gentleness; kindness; softness of heart". 16.2.

1565. **mārgaśīrṣaḥ** "Mārgaśīrṣa". 10.35. [The name of a lunar month in the Indian calendar, roughly corresponding to November-December. The name derives from the constellation Orion, which is called Mṛgaśīrṣa (deer's head) in Sanskrit.]

1566. **marīciḥ** "Marīci". 10.21. [The name of the chief of the Maruts.]

Translated by Gambhīrānanda (1997, p. 643) as "*mantra-hīnam,* in which *mantras* are not used, which is bereft of *mantras,* intonation and distinct pronunciation". Sāṅkara's use of technical terms such as *svarataḥ* (स्वरतः) and *varṇataḥ* (वर्णतः) shows awareness of chanting theory. Madhusūdana's commentary essentially repeats Sāṅkara's view, and Gambhīrānanda (1998, p. 847) adds a note of his own that the defect arises "when the proper cadences are not observed, and the letters are pronounced wrongly."

1567. **martyalokam** "the mortal world; the region of the mortals". 9.21. Also see *loka, mṛtyu.*

1568. **martyeṣu** "among mortals". 10.3. Also see *mṛtyu.*

1569. **marut** [the Maruts, a group of Vedic gods]
- marutaḥ "the Maruts". 11.6.
- marutaḥ "the Maruts". 11.22.
- marutām "of the Maruts". 10.21.

1570. **mārutaḥ** "the wind". 2.23.

1571. **māsānām** "among months; of months". 10.35. Also see *ṣaṇmāsā.*

1572. **matā** "is thought; is considered; is deemed". 3.1; 16.5.

1573. **mātā** "mother". 9.17.

1574. **mataḥ** "is thought; is considered to be". 6.32, 46, 47; 11.18; 18.9.

1575. **matāḥ** "are thought; are considered to be". 12.2.

1576. **matam** "view; opinion; believed".
- matam "a view; an opinion". 3.31, 32; 7.18; 18.6. [noun *mata*]
- matam "considered to be; believed". 13.2. [participial adj. *mata*]

1577. **mate** "(the two) are considered to be". 8.26. [dual]

1578. **matiḥ** "view; belief; considered opinion". 6.36; 18.70, 78. Also see *durmatiḥ, sthiramatiḥ.*

1579. **matkarmakṛn** "performing actions for me". 11.55.

1580. **matkarmaparamaḥ** "performer of actions for me only; solely devoted to acts done for my sake". 12.10. Also see *matpara, matparama, -parama.*

1581. **matpara** "devoted to me; intent on me as the highest goal". Also see *matparama, matparāyaṇaḥ, -para.*
- matparaḥ "devoted to me". 2.61; 6.14; 18.57.
- matparāḥ "devoted to me". 12.6.

1582. **matparama** "devoted to me; intent on me as the highest goal". Also see *matpara, matparāyaṇaḥ, matkarmaparamaḥ, -parama.*
- matparamāḥ "devoted to me". 12.20.
- matparamaḥ "devoted to me". 11.55.

1583. **matparāyaṇaḥ** "solely devoted to me". 9.34. Also see *matpara, matparama, parāyaṇa.*

1584. **matprasādāt** "through my grace". 18.56, 58. Also see *prasad.*

1585. **mātrāsparśāḥ** "objects of the senses". 2.14. Also see *bāhyasparśeṣu, nabhaḥ-spṛśam, saṁsparśa, sparśān, sparśanam, spṛśan.*

1586. **matsaṁsthām** "firmly located in me; firmly abiding in me". 6.15. Also see *matsthāni, sthānam.*

1587. **matsthāni** "located in me; abiding in me". 9.4, 5, 6. Also see *matsaṁsthām, antaḥsthāni, prakṛtisthāni, sthānam.*

1588. **mattaḥ** "from me; than me". 7.7, 12; 10.5, 8; 15.15.

1589. **mātula** "a maternal uncle".

- mātulāḥ "maternal uncles". 1.34.
- mātulān "maternal uncles". 1.26.

1590. **matvā** "having come to think; thinking; believing". 3.28; 10.8; 11.41. Also see √ *man.*

1591. **maunam** "silence; reticence; taciturnity; ability to hold one's tongue". 10.38; 17.16.

1592. **maunī** "one who observes silence; one whose speech is like a *munī* (a type of sage); a taciturn person". 12.19.

1593. **mayā** "by me". 1.22; 3.3; 4.3, 13; 7.22; 9.4, 10; 10.17, 39, 40; 11.2, 4, 33, 34, 41, 47; 15.20; 16.13, 14, 15; 18.63, 73.

1594. **māyā** "magic power of illusion; the illusory aspect of creation; illusory power of manifestation; wizardry". Also see *māyayā.*

- ātmamāyayā "by my *māyā*; with my *māyā*". 4.6.
- māyā "illusion". 7.14.
- māyām "illusion". 7.14.
- māyayā "by *māyā*". 18.61.
- māyayāpahṛtajñānāḥ "those whose knowledge is destroyed by *māyā*". 7.15. Also see *jñāna.*
- yogamāyāsamāvṛtaḥ "veiled by *yogamāyā*; enveloped by the power of illusion; covered by the magic of (my) *yoga*". 7.25. Also see *samāvṛta, yoga.*

1595. **mayi** "in me; on me". 3.30; 4.35; 6.30, 31; 7.7, 12; 8.7; 9.29; 12.2, 6, 7, 8 (three times), 9, 14; 13.10; 18.57, 68.

1596. **mayyāsaktamanāḥ** "with mind attached to Me; fixing your mind on Me". 7.1. Also see *ananyacetāḥ, ananyamanasaḥ, manas, -manāḥ.* [*mayy āsaktamanāḥ*]

1597. **me** "me; my; mine; to me; of me; from me".

- me "me; to me; of me; mine; my". 1.21, 29, 30, 46; 2.7; 3.2, 22, 31, 32; 4.3, 5, 9, 14; 5.1; 6.30, 36, 39, 47; 7.4, 5, 18; 9.5, 26, 29, 31; 10.1, 2, 13, 18, 19; 11.4, 5, 8, 18, 31, 45 (twice), 47, 49; 12.2, 14, 15, 16, 17, 19, 20; 13.3; 16.6, 13; 18.4, 6, 64 (twice), 65, 69 (twice), 70, 77. [Dat. or gen. sing.]

- me "from me". 18.13, 36, 50. [Irregular use as abl. sing.]

1598. **medhā** "intelligence; wisdom; mental vigor". 10.34. Also see *alpamedhasām, durmedhā, medhāvī.*

1599. **medhāvī** "an intelligent person; a wise person". 18.10. Also see *medhā.*

1600. **meruḥ** "Meru". 10.23. [Mt. Meru, a fabled golden mountain located in the Himālyaya range, regarded as the axis of the universe and abode of the gods.]

1601. **miśram** "mixed". 18.12. Also see *vyāmiśreṇa.*

1602. **mithyā** "in vain; falsely". 18.59.

1603. **mithyācāraḥ** "a person with false behavior; a hypocrite". 3.6. Also see *ācāra.*

1604. **mitra** ("friend").
- mitradrohe "in hatred of friends; in hostility to friends". 1.38. Also see *adrohaḥ.*
- mitrāripakṣayoḥ "toward friend or enemy sides". 14.25.
- mitre "toward friend". 12.18.
- suhṛnmitrāryudāsīnamadhyasthadveṣyabandhuṣu "in friends, enemies, neutrals, mediators, despicable persons, and relatives". 6.9.

1605. **modiṣya** "I will rejoice; I will enjoy myself". 16.15.

1606. **mogha** ("in vain; futile; useless; fruitless; unsuccessful") [√ *muh*]
- moghajñānāḥ "(those whose) knowledge is futile". 9.12.
- moghakarmāṇaḥ "(those whose) actions are futile". 9.12. [In this context the meaning is "engaging in useless rites".[389]]
- mogham "in vain; to no purpose". 3.16.
- moghāśāḥ "(those having) futile hopes". [*mogha + āśāḥ*] 9.12.

1607. **moha** "delusion". Also see √ *muh, mogha, mohayasi, mohena, mohinīm, mohita, mūḍh-, saṁmoha, vimūḍh-, vimuh-.*
- dvaṁdvamohanirmuktā "completely released from the delusion of duality; freed from the delusion of pairs of opposites". 7.28. Also see *dvaṁdva, mukta, nirmukta.*
- dvaṁdvamohena "by the delusion of duality; by the delusion of pairs of opposites". 7.27. Also see *dvaṁdva.*
- mohaḥ "delusion". 11.1; 14.13; 18.73.
- mohajālasamāvṛtāḥ "caught with snares of delusion; enveloped by the snare of delusion; the net of delusion envelops them". 16.16. Also see *samāvṛta.*

---

[389] Apte, p. 774, entry for मोघ, compounded with -कर्मन् "engaging in useless rites".

- mohakalilam "the mire of delusion; mud of delusion; the turbidity of delusion; the murky waters of delusion; the thicket of delusion; the confusion of delusion". 2.52.
- moham "delusion". 4.35; 14.22.
- mohanam "a delusion; something that deludes; the cause of delusion; deluding factor; deluding". 14.8; 18.39.
- mohāt "out of delusion; due to delusion; through delusion". 16.10; 18.7, 25, 60.
- nirmānamohāḥ "those who are devoid of pride (*nirmāna*) and delusion (*moha*); those who are free of arrogance and infatuation". 15.5.
- pramādamohau "negligence (*pramāda*) and delusion (*moha*)". 14.17. Also see *pramāda.*

1608. **mohajālasamāvṛtāḥ** "caught with snares of delusion; entangled in the snare of delusion; ; the net of delusion envelops them". 16.16. Also see *moha, samāvṛta.*

1609. **mohakalilam** "the mire of delusion; mud of delusion; the turbidity of delusion; the murky waters of delusion; the thicket of delusion; the confusion of delusion". 2.52. Also see *moha.*

1610. **mohanam** "a delusion; something that deludes; the cause of delusion; deluding factor; deluding". 14.8; 18.39. Also see *moha.*

1611. **mohayasi** "you delude (me); you confuse (me)". 3.2. Also see *moha, √ muh.*

1612. **mohinīm** "deluding; confusing". 9.12. Also see *moha, √ muh.*

1613. **mohita** "deluded; confused". Also see *moha, √ muh.*
   - ajñānavimohitāḥ "those who are deluded by ignorance". 16.15.
   - mohitāḥ "deluded; confused". 4.16.
   - mohitam "deluded; confused". 7.13.

1614. **mokṣ-** "to release". Also see *√ muc, mucyante, mukta, pramucyate, vimokṣ-, vimucya, vimuk-, nirmukta.*
   - bhūtaprakṛtimokṣam "liberation of beings from material nature; release from the nature of created beings". 13.34.
   - jarāmaraṇamokṣāya "toward release from old age and dying; for becoming free of old age and death". 7.29. Also see *jarā, maraṇa.*
   - mokṣakāṅkṣibhiḥ "by those seeking to attain release; by those who desire liberation; by the seekers of liberation[390]". 17.25. Also see *√ kāṅkṣ.*

---

[390] Sivananda, p. 455.

- mokṣam "release; liberation". 18.30.
- mokṣaparāyaṇaḥ "one having liberation as the highest goal; one who is solely devoted to achieving release". 5.28. Also see *parāyaṇa.*
- mokṣayiṣyāmi "I will release; I will liberate". 18.66.
- mokṣyase "you will be released; you will be liberated". 4.16; 9.1, 28.
- śarīravimokṣaṇāt "complete liberation from the body". 5.23.
- vimokṣāya "to complete release; to final liberation". 16.5.
- vimokṣyase "you will be completely released; you will have final liberation". 4.32.

1615. **mṛgāṇām** "of animals; of wild animals; of beasts". 10.30. [*Mṛga* often means "deer" or "antelope" but is used here as a general term for a type of animal.[391]] Also see *mṛgendraḥ.*

1616. **mṛgendraḥ** "King of Beasts; the lord of animals; the lion (?); the tiger (?)". 10.30. Also see *mṛgāṇām.* [Śaṅkara's commentary says this is the lion or the tiger.[392] Madhusūdana Sarasvati identifies it as the lion.[393]]

1617. **mriyate** "it dies". 2.20.

1618. **mṛtam** "dead". 2.26.

1619. **mṛtasya** "of the dead". 2.27.

1620. **mṛtyu** "death". Also see *amṛta, maraṇa, marty-.*
- janmamṛtyujarāduḥkhaiḥ "from the miseries (*duḥkha*) of birth (*janma*), death (*mṛtyu*), and old age (*jarā*)". 14.20.
- janmamṛtyujarāvyādhiduḥkhadoṣānudarśanam "contemplation (*anudarśana*) of the fault (*doṣa*) consisting of the miseries (*duḥkha*) of birth (*janma*), death (*mṛtyu*), old age (*jarā*), and disease (*vyādhi*)". 13.8.
- mṛtam "dead". 2.26.
- mṛtasya "of the dead". 2.27.
- mṛtyuḥ "death". 2.27; 9.19; 10.34.
- mṛtyum "death". 13.25.
- mṛtyusaṁsārasāgarāt "from the ocean of the world of mortality; from the ocean of death and rebirth; from the ocean of worldly existence characterized by death[394]". 12.7. Also see *saṁsāra.*

---

[391] Apte, p. 769, entry for मृगः, includes meanings for *mṛga* as an animal in general, a quadruped, a wild beast, and game in general.

[392] Gambhīrānanda 1997, p. 419.

[393] Gambhīrānanda 1998, p. 629.

[394] Tapasyananda, p. 320.

- mṛtyusaṁsāravartmani "in the path of death and rebirth; in the cycle of death (and rebirth); the path of mortality". 9.3. Also see *saṁsāra, vartmānuvartante, āvṛttim.*

1621. √ **muc** "to release; to be free of". See *mokṣ-, mukt-, mumukṣubhiḥ, nirmukta, pramucyate, vimucya.*

1622. **mucyante** "they are freed; they are liberated". 3.13, 31. Also see *vimucya.*

1623. **mūḍh-** "confused, muddled, bewildered". Also see √ *muh, vimūḍh-, vimuhyati.*

- ahaṁkāravimūḍhātmā "he whose self is deluded by egoism (*ahaṁkāra*)". 3.27.
- amūḍhāḥ "undeluded ones; unconfused people". 15.5
- asaṁmūḍhaḥ "undeluded; not confused". 5.20; 10.3; 15.19.
- dharmasaṁmūḍhacetāḥ "those whose minds are confused about what is right; confused about correct conduct". 2.7.
- guṇasaṁmūḍhāḥ "those who are deluded by the *guṇa*-s". 3.29.
- mūḍhaḥ "deluded; confused". 7.25.
- mūḍhāḥ "deluded ones; confused people". 7.15; 9.11; 16.20.
- mūḍhagrāheṇātmanaḥ "with deluded notion of the self; with confused grasp of the self". 17.19. [Divanji translates *mūḍhagrāheṇa* as (with) "the firmness of an idiot".[395]]
- mūḍhayoniṣu "in wombs of the deluded; among the stupid species[396]" 14.15. [Divanji interprets *mūḍhayoni* as "an idiotic class of beings, very probably quadrupeds".[397]] Also see *yoni.*
- sarvajñānavimūḍhāṁs "deluded about all knowledge; bereft of all knowledge; confusing all knowledge". 3.32
- vimūḍhaḥ "deluded; confused". 6.38.
- vimūḍhāḥ "the deluded; those who are confused". 15.10.
- vimūḍhabhāvaḥ "state of delusion; confused state; deluded state of being". 11.49.
- vimūḍhātmā "deluded self; confused self; one whose self is overcome with delusion". 3.6.

---

[395] Divanji, p. 116, entry #2656.

[396] Gambhīrānanda 1997, p. 579.

[397] Divanji, p. 116, entry #2657.

1624. **mūḍhagrāheṇātmanaḥ** "with deluded notion of the self; with confused grasp of the self". 17.19. [Divanji translates mūḍhagrāheṇa as (with) "the firmness of an idiot".[398]]

1625. **mūḍhaḥ** "deluded; confused". 7.25.

1626. **mūḍhāḥ** "deluded ones; confused people". 7.15; 9.11; 16.20.

1627. **mūḍhayoniṣu** "in wombs of the deluded" 14.15. [Divanji interprets *mūḍhayoni* as "an idiotic class of beings, very probably quadrupeds".[399]]

1628. √ **muh** "to be deluded; to be crazed". See *moh-, mūḍh-, muhy-, saṁmoh-, vimohayati, vimūḍh-, vimuhyati.*

1629. **muhur muhuḥ** "again and again; at every moment". 18.76.

1630. **muhyati** "he is deluded; he is confused". 2.13; 8.27. Also see *moha,* √ *muh.*

1631. **muhyanti** "they are deluded; they are confused". 5.15. Also see *moha,* √ *muh.*

1632. **mukha** "mouth; face". Also see *viśvatomukha, sarvatokṣiśiromukham, pramukhe, abhimukhāḥ.*

- mukham "mouth". 1.29.
- mukhāni "faces". 11.25.
- mukhe "in the face (tradition)". 4.32. [*brahmaṇo mukhe* = "in the Vedic tradition"[400]; "in the storehouse of the Veda"[401]; "as paths to *Brahman*"[402]]

1633. **mukhyam** "the chief; the principal". 10.24. Also see *yodhamukhyaiḥ.*

1634. **mukta** "free; freed from; liberated". Also see *dvaṁdvamohanirmuktāḥ, janmabandhavinirmuktāḥ, vimukta,* √ *muc.*

- muktaḥ "free; liberated; a liberated person". 5.28; 12.15; 18.71.
- muktam "free from". 18.40.
- muktasya "of one who is liberated". 4.23.

1635. **muktasaṅgaḥ** "free from attachment". 3.9; 18.26. Also see *saṅga.*

1636. **muktvā** "freed from (the body); leaving aside (the body)". 8.5. [*muktvā kalevaram* = leaving aside (the body)]

1637. **mūla** "root".

- mūlāni "roots". 15.2

---

398 Divanji, p. 116, entry #2656.

399 Divanji, p. 116, entry #2657.

400 Sharma, Morgan and Pitts. p. 94.

401 Swarupananda, p. 114.

402 Tapasyananda, p. 130. Van Buitenen (1981, p. 164, note 15 on section 26[4]) interprets "the mouth of Brahman" as "the sacrificial fire, both figurative and literal." Edgerton (p. 94, note 9 on Chapter 4) discusses various possible interpretations of *brahmaṇo mukhe.*

- suvirūḍhamūlam "well-grown (*su-virūḍha*) root (*mūla*); well rooted; with its root firmly grounded". 15.3.
- ūrdhvamūlam "with roots above (*ūrdhva*); having its root upwards". 15.1. Also see *ūrdhvam.*

1638. **mumukṣubhiḥ** "by seekers of release; by those who desire to be liberated". 4.15. [Inst. pl. masc. of a desiderative noun from √ *muc.*]

1639. **muniḥ** "sage; anchorite; recluse; one leading a detached life of spiritual aspiration".

- munayaḥ "sages". 14.1.
- muneḥ "of a sage". 2.69; 6.3.
- muniḥ "a sage". 2.56; 5.6, 28; 10.26.
- munīnām "of sages; among sages". 10.37.

1640. **mūrdhni** "in the head; in the forehead". 8.12.

1641. **mūrtayaḥ** "forms; manifestations". 14.4. Also see *avyaktamūrtinā, viśva-mūrte.*

N

ङ्= Ṅ. **ञ्**= Ñ. **ण्** = Ṇ. **न्**= N.

1642. **na** "no; not". 1.30, 31, 32 (twice), 35, 37, 38, 39; 2.3, 6 (twice), 8, 9, 11, 12 (six times), 13, 15, 16 (twice), 17, 19 (three times), 20 (four times), 23 (four times), 25, 26, 27, 29, 30, 31 (twice), 33, 38, 40 (twice), 42, 44, 57 (twice), 66 (three times), 70, 72; 3.4 (twice), 5, 8, 16, 17, 18 (three times), 22 (twice), 23, 24, 26, 28, 29, 32, 34; 4.5, 9, 14 (three times), 20, 21, 22, 31, 35, 38, 40 (three times), 41; 5.3 (twice), 4, 6, 7, 8, 10, 13 (twice), 14 (three times), 15 (twice), 20 (twice), 22; 6.1 (twice), 2, 4 (twice), 5, 11 (twice), 16 (four times), 19, 21, 22 (twice), 25, 30 (twice), 33, 38, 39, 40 (three times); 7.2, 7, 12, 13, 15, 25 (twice), 26; 8.5, 15, 16, 20, 21, 27; 9.4, 5 (twice), 9, 24, 29 (twice), 31; 10.2 (twice), 7, 14 (twice), 18, 19, 39, 40; 11.8, 16 (three times), 24, 25 (twice), 31, 32, 37, 43, 47, 48 (four times), 53 (four times); 12.7, 8, 9, 15 (twice), 17 (four times); 13.12 (twice); 23, 28, 31 (twice), 32 (twice); 14.2 (twice), 19, 22 (twice), 23 (twice); 15.3 (four times), 4, 6 (four times), 10, 11; 16.3, 7 (four times), 23 (three times); 17.28; 18.3, 5, 7, 8, 10 (twice), 11, 12, 16, 17 (four times), 35, 40, 47, 48, 54 (twice), 58, 59, 60, 67 (four times), 69 (twice).

1643. **nabhaḥ** "sky". 1.19.

1644. **nabhaḥspṛśam** "touching the sky". 11.24. Also see *bāhyasparśeṣu, mātrāsparśāḥ, saṁsparśa, sparśān, sparśanam, spṛśan.*

1645. **nābhaktāya** "not to one who lacks devotion". [*na abhaktāya*]. 18.67. Also see *bhakti.*

1646. **nacirāt** "without delay; before long". 12.7. [*na* + *cira*] Also see *cira.*

1647. **nacireṇa** "without delay; before long". 5.6. [*na* + *cira*] Also see *cira.*

1648. **nadīnām** "of rivers". 11.28.

1649. **nāgānām** "among Nāgas[403]; of cobras'. 10.29.

1650. **naḥ** "to us; of us; for us". 1.32, 33, 36; 2.6 (twice).

1651. **naikṛtikaḥ** "one who cuts off the interests of others; undermining others; malicious; wicked; deceitful; dishonest". 18.28. [The Critical Edition reads *naikṛtikaḥ*. Most Vulgate editions read *naiṣkṛtikaḥ.*]

1652. **naiṣkarmya** "freedom from action; exemption from acts or their consequences[404]". Also see *karma.*

- naiṣkarmyam "freedom from (the bondage of) action; transcendence from action; actionlessness; the state beyond *karma*". 3.4.
- naiṣkarmyasiddhim "attainment of freedom from (the bondage of) action; success in transcending action; success in actionlessness; attaiment of the state beyond *karma*". 18.49. Also see *siddhi.*

1653. **naiṣṭhikīm** "final; concluding; fixed; constant; perfect; absolute; complete; abiding". 5.12.

1654. **nakṣatrāṇām** "among the luminaries of the night sky; among the stars; among the lunar mansions; among the constellations". 10.21.

1655. **nakulaḥ** "Nakula". 1.16. The fourth of the Pāṇḍava brothers, one of twin sons born to Mādrī, the wife of Pāṇḍu, in fact fathered by the two Aśvins.

1656. **namaḥ** "a bow; a salutation; obeisance". Also see *namas-, nameran.*

- namaḥ "a bow; a salutation; obeisance". 11.31, 40 (twice).
- namo namaḥ "a bow; obeisance". 11.39 (twice). [Repeated to indicate frequency of the act.]

1657. **namaskṛtvā** "after bowing; after paying obeisance". 11.35. Also see *kṛtvā.*

1658. **namaskuru** "(you) make obeisance; (you) make a salutation". 9.34; 18.65. Also see *kuru.* [*namas* + Imp. 2nd pers. sing. √ *kṛ*]

1659. **namasyantaḥ** "bowing; saluting me". 9.14.

---

[403] *Nāga*-s are a class of semi-divine beings having serpentine characteristics.

[404] Apte, p. 572, entry for नैष्कर्म्य.

1660. **namasyanti** "they bow; they pay obeisance". 11.36.

1661. **nameran** "they may pay obeisance". 11.37.

1662. **nāmayajñaiḥ** "with sacrifices in name only". 16.17. Also see *yajña*.

1663. **nānābhāvān** "various entities[405]; the existence of separate entities[406]; different (*nānā*) beings". 18.21.

1664. **nānāśastrapraharaṇāḥ** "endowed with many (*nānā*) assault (*praharanāḥ*) weapons (*śastra*)[407]; armed with various weapons and missiles[408]; endowed with many types of (hand-to-hand) weapons (including) weapons that are thrown (such as spears); assailing with various weapons". 1.9.

1665. **nānāvarṇākṛtīni** "of various (*nānā*) colors (*varṇa*) and shapes (*ākṛtīni*)". 11.5. Also see *varṇa*.

1666. **nānāvidhāni** "of several varieties; of different categories; various; multiple". 11.5. Also see *-vidhā*.

1667. **nānyagāminā** "by going toward no other; by that which does not become diverted to any other object". 8.8. [*na anya gāminā*]

1668. **nara** "a man; a person; a human being".

- naraḥ "a man; a person". 2.22; 5.23; 12.19; 16.22; 18.15, 45, 71.
- naraiḥ "by men; by people". 17.17.
- narāṇām "of men; among people". 10.27.

1669. **nāradaḥ** "Nārada". 10.13, 26. [A divine sage.]

1670. **narādhamāḥ** "the lowest of men; the worst type of people". Also see *adhamām*.

- narādhamāḥ "". 7.15.
- narādhamān "". 16.19.

1671. **narādhipam** "king of men". 10.27.

1672. **naraka** "hell".

- narakasya "of hell". 16.21.
- narakāya "to hell; for hell; into hell". 1.42.
- narake "in hell; into hell". 1.44; 16.16.

1673. **naralokavīrāḥ** "heroes of the human world; heroes of the region where humans reside". 11.28. Also see *loka*.

1674. **narapuṁgavaḥ** "the best of men; bull among men". 1.5.

---

[405] Sivananda, p. 482.

[406] Divanji, p. 78, entry #1780.

[407] Sharma, Morgan and Pitts, p. 7, vocabulary entry.

[408] Sivananda, p. 6.

1675. **nārīṇām** "of the feminine". 10.34.

1676. **nāsābhyantaracāriṇau** "(the two) moving inside the nose". 5.27.

1677. **nāśanam** "destroyer; cause of destruction". 16.21. Also see *jñānavijñāna-nāśanam.*

1678. **nāśāya** "for destruction". 11.29 (twice). Also see *vināśāya.*

1679. **nāśayāmi** "I destroy". 10.11.

1680. **nāsikāgram** "the tip of the nose". 6.13. [*nāsikā + agram*]

1681. **nāśitam** "destroyed". 5.16. Also see *avināśi.*

1682. **naṣṭaḥ** "destroyed; lost". Also see *pranaṣṭaḥ.*

- naṣṭaḥ "destroyed; lost". 4.2; 18.73.
- naṣṭān "destroyed; lost". 3.32.
- naṣṭe "destroyed". 1.40.

1683. **naṣṭātmānaḥ** "lost souls[409]; ruined souls[410]; soul-less[411]; lost to themselves[412]; of depraved character[413]; those whose conscience is dead[414]; "having lost the reality of their lives[415]"; self-destructive people[416]". 16.9.

---

[409] Hill, p. 245; Van Buitenen 1981, p. 133; Zaehner, p. 371; Tapasyananda, p. 400. Edgerton (p. 77) translates as "men of lost souls". Warrier (p. 518) translates as "having lost their souls" with Śaṅkara's commentary, "Relying on this philosophy, having lost their proper nature, falling away from practices leading to the next world...". एतां दृष्टिं अवष्टभ्य आश्रित्य नष्टात्मानः नष्टस्वभावाः विभ्रष्टपरलोकसाधनाः). Sampatkumaran (p. 401) translates as "men of lost souls" with Rāmānuja's commentary "by whom the self is not perceived as distinct from the body." Ādidevānanda (p. 512) translates as "men of lost souls" with Rāmānuja's commentary "do not realize that the self is different from the body" (अदृष्टदेहातिरिक्तात्मानः). Madhusūdana's commentary (Gambhīrānanda 1998, p. 816) says that the "depraved view" is that of the materialist Lokāyatikas, whose philosophy was just attacked in verse 16.8.

[410] Sivananda, p. 420; Swarupananda, p. 341.

[411] Tilak, vol. 2, p. 1154.

[412] Miller, p. 128.

[413] Gambhīrānanda 1997, p. 623.

[414] Divanji, p. 78, entry #1774.

[415] Bolle, p. 181.

[416] The eternal *ātman* is perfect, but we can chose to either lift our embodied personalities up, or tear ourselves down. The point of the verse is not that these people do not have souls at all, but that they have chosen to turn away from the indwelling reality that is within them as it is within all beings (see verses 6.30-31 and verse 16.18, *mām ātma-para-deheṣu*). Such people are their own worst enemies (see verses 6.5-6). One who sees Divinity equally present in all creatures, sees indeed (verse 13.27, *samaṁ sarveṣu bhūteṣu tiṣṭhantaṁ parameśvaram*).

1684. **nātimānitā** "excessive egotism; excessive pride". 16.3. [*nātimānitā* = *na* + *atimānitā*] Also see *amānitvam.*[417]

1685. **naśyati** "is destroyed; perishes". 6.38. Also see *praṇaś-, vinaṅkṣyasi, vinaś-, vināś-, avinaś-, avināś-.*

1686. **naśyatsu** "while being destroyed; perishing". 8.20. Also see *vinaṅkṣyasi, vinaś-, vināś-, avinaś-, avināś-.*

1687. **navadvāre** "in the nine gates". 5.13. Also see *dvāram, sarvadvāra.* [*navadvāre pure* = in the city of nine gates, i.e., the body]

1688. **nāvam** "a boat". 2.67.

1689. **navāni** "new". 2.22 (twice).

1690. **nāyakāḥ** "leaders". 1.7.

1691. **nayana** "eye". See *anekavaktranayanam.* Also see *netra.*

1692. **nayet** "it should lead; it should direct; it should bring". 6.26.

1693. **netra** "eye". Also see *anekavaktranayanam, nayana.*

- anekabāhūdaravaktranetram "endowed with many arms, bellies, mouths [or faces], and eyes". 11.16. Also see *aneka, bahu, udara, vaktra.*
- bahuvaktranetram "endowed with numerous mouths [or faces] and eyes". 11.23. Also see *bahu, vaktra.*
- dīptaviśālanetram "endowed with glowing wide eyes". 11.24. Also see *dīpta, viśāla.*
- śaśisūryanetram "having the moon and sun as eyes". 11.19. Also see *śaśi, sūrya.*

1694. **nibadh-** "bound". Also see *bandham; nibandhāyāsurī.*

- nibaddhaḥ "bound". 18.60.
- nibadhnanti "they bind". 4.41; 9.9; 14.5.
- nibadhnāti "it binds". 14.7, 8.
- nibadhyate "he is bound". 4.22; 5.12; 18.17.

1695. **nibandhāyāsurī** "demonic (energy leads to) bondage". 16.5. Also see *bandham.*

1696. **nibodha** "know; understand". 1.7; 18.13, 50. Also see *buddhi.*

There is no being that can exist without the divine reality that Kṛṣṇa represents (verse 10.39). God views all beings as inherently equal (verse 9.29). That said, we cannot escape the karmic consequences of our actions (see verses 3.32, 4.9).

[417] Divanji (p. 78, entry #1779) has a note that it would be improper to treat *nātimānitā* as two separate words (*na* and *atimānitā*) because what is intended is *anatimānitā* but *na* is substituted for *an.*

1697. **nidhanam** "death".

- avyaktanidhanāni "with the unmanifest at the end". 2.28.
- nidhanam "death". 3.35.

1698. **nidhānam** "treasure-house; treasury; receptacle; abode; that which is preserved". 9.18; 11.18, 38.

1699. **nidrā** "sleep". Also see *svapna*.

- nidrālasyapramādottham "arising out of sleep, indolence, and delusion". 18.39. Also see *alasaḥ, pramāda*.
- pramādālasyanidrābhiḥ "by negligence, indolence, and sleep". 14.8. Also see *alasaḥ, pramāda*.

1700. **nigacchati** "one attains; one reaches". 9.31; 18.36. Also see *gacchati*.

1701. **nigraha** "restraint; control". Also see *ātmavinigrahaḥ, durnigraham, gṛhyate*.

- nigrahaḥ "restraint; control". 3.33.
- nigraham "restraint; control". 6.34.

1702. **nigṛhītāni** "controlled; held back". 2.68. Also see *gṛhyate, nigraha*.

1703. **nigṛhṇāmi** "I withhold; I hold back". 9.19. Also see *gṛhyate, nigraha*.

1704. **nihatya** "having killed; having struck down". 1.36.

1705. **nihatāḥ** "been killed; been struck down". 11.33.

1706. **niḥspṛhaḥ** "one who is free from desires; one who is devoid of longing". 2.71; 6.18. Also see *spṛhā, vigataspṛhaḥ*.

1707. **niḥśreyasakarau** "generating (*karau*) the highest bliss (*niḥ-śreyasa*); that which leads to final beatitude; bestowing liberation". 5.2. Also see *śreyaḥ*.

1708. **nimiṣan** "while closing the eyes". 5.9. Also see *unmiṣan*.

1709. **nimittāni** "signs; portents; evil omens". 1.31.

1710. **nimittamātram** "only an instrument; merely an instrumental cause". 11.33.

1711. √**nind** "to blame; to censure; to find fault with; to condemn". See *tulyanindāstutiḥ, tulyanindātmasaṁstutiḥ*.

1712. **nindantaḥ** "condemning; censuring; despising". 2.36. Also see √ *nind*.

1713. **niragniḥ** "without fire; one who does not maintain a sacrificial fire". 6.1. Also see *agni*.

1714. **nirahaṁkāraḥ** "free from ego; free from egoism; free from vanity; free from I-faculty[418]; without self-pride[419]; without self-centeredness[420]". 2.71; 12.13. Also see *ahaṁkāra, anahaṁkāraḥ, anahaṁvādī.*

1715. **nirāhārasya** "of one who is abstaining from food". 2.59. Also see *āhāra.*

1716. **nirāśīḥ** "without wish; free of wishes; free from expectations; free from attachment to outcomes; without longing". 3.30; 4.21; 6.10.

1717. **nirāśrayaḥ** "free from dependence on anything; in need of nothing; dependent on nothing; one who does not tie his mind to a particular object or person". 4.20. Also see *āśrita.*

1718. **nirdeśaḥ** "designation; indicator; apellation". 17.23. Also see *anirdeśyam.*

1719. **nirdoṣam** "without fault; without flaws; unblemished; innocent". 5.19. Also see *doṣa.*

1720. **nirdvaṁdvaḥ** "free from the pairs of opposites; free from inner conflicts". 2.45; 5.3. Also see *dvaṁdva.*

1721. **nirguṇam** "free from the *guṇa*-s; without (the influence of) the *guṇa*-s; that which is without attributes". 13.14. Also see *guṇa.*

1722. **nirguṇatvāt** "because it transcends the *guṇa*-s; due to being without any attributes; due to having no qualities". 13.31. Also see *guṇa.*

1723. **nirīkṣe** "I see; I behold; I look at". 1.22. Also see √ *īkṣ.*

1724. **nirmalam** "pure; spotless; without impurity". 14.16. Also see *malena, amalān, nirmalatvāt.*

1725. **nirmalatvāt** "due to purity; free from impurity". 14.6. Also see *malena, amalān, nirmalam.*

1726. **nirmamaḥ** "without egoism; free from pride; free from sense of ownership; free from possessiveness; detached". 2.71; 3.30; 12.13; 18.53.

1727. **nirmānamohāḥ** "those who are devoid of pride (*nirmāna*) and delusion (*moha*); those who are free of arrogance and infatuation". 15.5. Also see *moha.*

1728. **nirmukta** "free from". Also see √ *muc, mokṣ-.*

- dvaṁdvamohanirmuktā "completely released from the delusion of duality; freed from the delusion of pairs of opposites". 7.28. Also see *dvaṁdva, moha;* √ *muh.*

---

[418] Edgerton, p. 63

[419] Van Buitenen 1981, p. 123.

[420] Van Buitenen 1981, p. 81.

- janmabandhavinirmuktāḥ "completely released from the bondage of birth(s)". 2.51.

1729. **niruddham** "restrained; controlled; kept in check; held back". 6.20.

1730. **nirudhya** "having restrained; having controlled; confining". 8.12. Also see *ruddhvā.*

1731. **nirvairaḥ** "devoid of enmity; devoid of ill-will". 11.55. Also see *vairiṇa.*

1732. **nirvāṇa** See *brahmanirvāṇam, nirvāṇaparamām.*

1733. **nirvāṇaparamām** "perfect liberation; supreme *nirvāṇa*; beyond *nirvāṇa*[421]". 6.15. Also see *brahmanirvāṇam, -parama.*

1734. **nirvedam** "indifference[422]; detachment[423]; dispassion[424]; aversion[425]; disgust[426]; disenchanted[427]". 2.52.

1735. **nirvikāraḥ** "free from the tendency to undergo change; not changed [by something]". 18.26. Also see *vikāra.*

1736. **niryogakṣemaḥ** "without concern for getting and keeping; beyond acquisition and conservation[428]". 2.45. Also see *kṣema, yogakṣemam.*

1737. **niśā** "night". 2.69 (twice).

1738. **niścalā** "unmoving; unmoved; motionless; fixed; firm; stable". 2.53. Also see *acala, calam.*

1739. **niścarati** "it moves away; it wanders away; it slips off; it strays". 6.26. Also see *carati.*

1740. **niścaya** "a settled view; a definite decision; conclusion; determination". Also see *āsuraniścayān, dṛḍhaniścayaḥ, kṛtaniścayaḥ.*

    - niścayam "a settled view; a definite decision; conclusion; determination". 18.4.

---

[421] Van Buitenen (1981, pp. 95, 165, note 6 in § 28[6]) translates *śāntiṁ nirvāṇaparamāṁ matsaṁsthām adhigacchati* as "attains to the peace that lies in me, beyond *nirvāṇa*", with a note that *nirvāṇaparamām* is "beyond *nirvāṇa*" because it is not pure extinction but a postive union of the persisting *ātman* with the personal God."

[422] Divanji, p. 82, entry #1860.

[423] Warrier, p. 73.

[424] Gambhīrānanda 1997, p. 98.

[425] Edgerton, p. 14.

[426] Sampatkumaran, p. 53.

[427] Van Buitenen 1981, p. 79.

[428] Van Buitenen 1981, p. 79.

- niścayena "with a settled view; with a definite decision; definitely; wholeheartedly". 6.23.

1741. **niścitāḥ** "certain; fully convinced; having come to a definite conclusion; feeling sure". 16.11.

1742. **niścitam** "certainly; definitely; well-determined; considered". 2.7; 18.6. Also see *suniścitam, viniścitaiḥ*.

1743. **niścitya** "for certain; after considering all aspects; after determining the facts". 3.2. [*ni* + √ *cit*]

1744. **niṣṭhā** "confident belief; faith; foundation; state". Also see *tanniṣṭhāḥ*.
    - niṣṭhā "a confident belief; discipline; steadfastness; style (of living) = lifestyle". 3.3. [*dvividhā niṣṭhā* = a two-fold discipline; "two-fold spiritual path"[429]; "the twofold path of devotion"[430]; "a twofold position"[431]]
    - niṣṭhā "faith[432]; foundation[433]; status; state; condition[434]; standing". 17.1.
    - niṣṭhā "condition; state; consummation". 18.50. [*niṣṭhā jñānasya yā parā* = "which is the supreme consummation of Knowledge"[435]; "which is the pinnacle of knowledge"[436]]

1745. **nistraiguṇyaḥ** "one who is free from the three *guṇa*-s; one who transcends the three *guṇa*-s". 2.45. Also see *guṇa, traiguṇa*.

1746. **nītiḥ** "wise political policy; statesmanship; statecraft; right conduct; prudent guidance". 10.38; 18.78.

1747. **nitya** "continual; constant; always; eternal; everlasting". Also see *nityayukta, anitya, adhyātmajñānanityatvam, adhyātmanityāḥ*.
    - nityābhiyuktānām "having eternal communion (with Me); ever attached (to Me)". 9.22.
    - nityaḥ "eternal". 2.20, 24.
    - nityajātam "eternally born; ever being born". 2.26.
    - nityam "forever; constantly; always; eternally, ever". 2.21, 26, 30; 3.15, 31; 9.6; 10.9; 11.52; 13.9; 18.52.

---

[429] Tapasyananda, p. 87.

[430] Swarupananda, p. 73.

[431] Van Buitenen 1981, p. 81.

[432] Tapasyananda, p. 412.

[433] Van Buitenen 1981, p. 135.

[434] Swarupananda, p. 349.

[435] Gambhīrānanda 1998, p. 971.

[436] Van Buitenen 1981, p. 143.

- nityaśaḥ "always, constantly, uninterruptedly". 8.14.
- nityasaṁnyāsī "a perpetual renouncer; forever a recluse". 5.3. Also see *saṁnyāsī*.
- nityasattvasthaḥ "always abiding in *sattva*". 2.45. Also see *nitya, sattva.*
- nityasya "of the eternal; of the everlasting". 2.18.
- nityatṛptaḥ "always satisfied; ever contented". 4.20. Also see *ātmatṛptaḥ, jñānavijñānatṛptātmā, tṛptiḥ.*
- nityavairiṇā "by the perpetual enemy". 3.39. Also see *vairiṇa.*

1748. **nityayukta** "always joined; ever dedicated; always disciplined; ever-steadfast" Also see *nitya, śāśvata, yukta.*

- nityābhiyuktānām "having eternal communion (with Me); ever self-possessed". 9.22.
- nityayuktaḥ "always joined; ever dedicated; always disciplined; ever-steadfast". 7.17.
- nityayuktāḥ "always joined; always dedicated; always disciplined; ever-steadfast". 9.14; 12.2.
- nityayuktasya "of the ever-disciplined". 8.14.

1749. **nivartante** "they return; they revert (to the cycle of rebirth and death)". 8.21; 9.3; 15.6. Also see *āvṛttim.*

1750. **nivartanti** "they return (to the cycle of rebirth and death)". 15.4. Also see *āvṛttim.*

1751. **nivartate** "it recedes; it reverts".

- nivartate "(the inner urge) ceases to operate; it recedes". 2.59. Also see *vinivartante.*
- nivartate "one reverts; one returns; one is re-born". 8.25. Also see *āvṛttim.*

1752. **nivartitum** "to turn away (from sin); to get away; to desist from". 1.39.

1753. **nivāsaḥ** "abode; place of residence". 9.18. Also see *jagannivāsa.*

1754. **nivasiṣyasi** "you will dwell; you will find rest in". 12.8.

1755. **nivātasthaḥ** "standing in a place without wind". 6.19.

1756. **niveśaya** "cause to enter; cause to rest in; place; focus (your intellect)". 12.8.

1757. √ **nivṛt** "to cease; to stop; to recede". Also see √ *pravṛt.*

- nivṛttāni "(their) cessations; (their) non-occurrings; (their) absences". 14.22. [Contrasted with *saṁpravṛttāni.*]
- nivṛttiṁ "inactivity; cessation; action to be avoided; what ought not to be done". 16.7; 18.30. [Contrasted with *pravṛttim.*]

1788. **pañcamam** "the fifth". 18.14.

1789. **pāñcajanyam** "Pāñcajanya". 1.15. [The name of Kṛṣṇa's conch.]

1790. **pāṇḍava** "related to Pāṇḍu". For Pāṇḍu, see page 7.

- pāṇḍava "O son of Pāṇḍu; O Arjuna". 4.35; 6.2; 11.55; 14.22; 16.5.
- pāṇḍavaḥ "the son of Pāṇḍu; Arjuna". 1.14, 20; 11.13.
- pāṇḍavāḥ " the sons of Pāṇḍu". 1.1.
- pāṇḍavānām "of the Pāṇḍavas; among the family of Pāṇḍu". 10.37.
- pāṇḍavānīkam "the army of the Pāṇḍavas". 1.2.

1791. **paṇḍit** "learned person; wise person".

- paṇḍitāḥ "learned people; the wise; the wise ones". 2.11; 5.4, 18.
- paṇḍitam "learned person; wise person". 4.19.

1792. **pāṇḍuputrāṇām** "of the sons of Pāṇḍu". 1.3. Also see *putra*.

1793. **pāpa** "sin; evil". Also see *agham, mahāpāpmā, pāpa-, pūtapāpāḥ, sarvapāpaiḥ, sarvapāpebhyaḥ*.

- pāpāḥ "sinners". 3.13.
- pāpam "sin". 1.36, 45; 2.33, 38; 3.36; 5.15; 7.28.
- pāpāt "from sin". 1.39.
- pāpebhyaḥ "among sinners". 4.36.
- pāpena "with sin; by sin". 5.10.
- pāpeṣu "in sinners; in the unrighteous". 6.9. [The English translation of *sādhuṣv api ca pāpeṣu* calls for something like "saints and sinners".]

1794. **pāpakṛttamaḥ** "the greatest sinner; the worst among sinners". 4.36. Also see *pāpa*.

1795. **pāpayonayaḥ** "of inferior origin; of inauspicious birth; born of sin; one whose low birth is the result of one's sins[441]". 9.32. Also see *yoni*.

1796. **pāpmānam** "that evil[442]; this sin; sin personified or incarnate[443]; sinful thing[444]; evil demon[445]". 3.41.

1797. **-para** "holding as highest; devoted to". Also see *-parama, tatpara*. [Used as a suffix.]

- dhyānayogaparaḥ "engaged in meditation". 18.52.
- matparaḥ "devoted to me". 2.61; 6.14; 18.57.

---

441 Divanji, p. 87, entry #1980.

442 Van Buitenen 1981, p. 85.

443 Divanji, p. 87, entry #1987.

444 Sivananda, p. 77.

445 Sargeant, p. 198.

- matparāḥ "devoted to me". 12.6.
- svargaparāḥ "intent on attainment of heaven". 2.43.

1798. **parā** "higer; superior; highest; supreme".

- parā "higher; superior to". 3.42.
- parā "highest; supreme". 18.50.

1799. **paradharma** "another's duty; a duty appropriate to someone else; another's assignment". Also see *dharma, svadharma, ātmaparadeheṣu.*

- paradharmaḥ "another's duty". 3.35.
- paradharmāt "than another's duty". 3.35; 18.47.

1800. **paraḥ** "higher; greater; the other; another".

- paraḥ "other; another". 4.40. Also see *apara, ātmaparadeheṣu.*
- paraḥ "beyond". 8.20.
- paraḥ "supreme". 8.22.
- paraḥ "supreme". 13.22.

1801. **param** "higher; greater; later; beyond".

- param "the Higher One; the Supreme". 2.59; 3.19; 13.34.
- param "supreme; ultimate". 3.11; 7.24; 8.10, 28; 10.12 (twice); 11.18, 38 (twice), 47; 13.12; 14.1; 18.75.
- param "superior to". 3.42, 43.
- param "beyond". 7.13; 13.17; 14.19.
- param "real". 9.11.
- param "later; subsequent". 2.12 [*ataḥ param* = hereafter]; 4.4.

1802. **parām** "supreme; higher; other; subtle (nature)"

- parām "supreme". 4.39; 6.45; 9.32; 13.28; 14.1; 16.22, 23; 18.54, 62, 68.
- parām "higher; other; subtle (nature)". 7.5.

1803. **-parama** "holding as highest; devoted to". Also see *-para.* [Used as a suffix.]

- kāmopabhogaparamāḥ "totally immersed in the indulgence of desires[446]". 16.11.
- matkarmaparamaḥ "solely devoted to acts done for my sake". 12.10.
- matparamāḥ "devoted to me". 12.20
- matparamaḥ "devoted to me". 11.55.

---

[446] Van Buitenen 1981, p. 133.

- nirvāṇaparamām "perfect liberation; supreme *nirvāṇa*; beyond *nirvāṇa*[447]". 6.15.

1804. **paramaḥ** "excellent". 6.32.

1805. **paramam** "supreme; highest".
    - paramam "supreme; highest; absolute". 8.3, 8, 21; 10.12; 11.1, 9, 18; 15.6; 18.64, 68.
    - paramam "most important (instruction)".10.1

1806. **paramām** "supreme; highest; absolute". 8.13, 15, 21; 18.49.

1807. **paramātmā** "the Supreme Self; the highest self; the Supreme Soul; Supreme Consciousness". 6.7; 13.22, 31; 15.17. Also see *ātman*.

1808. **parameśvara** "Supreme Lord; Highest Lord". Also see *īśvara*.
    - parameśvara "O Supreme Lord". 11.3.
    - parameśvaram "the Supreme Lord". 13.27.

1809. **parameṣvāsaḥ** "the best (*parama*) archer (*iṣu* + *āsaḥ*)". 1.17. [*iṣu* (arrow) + *āsaḥ* (thrower, bowman)]

1810. **paraṁparāprāptam** "through instruction from teacher to disciple; that which has been acquired traditionally from generation to generation[448]". 4.2. Also see *prāptaḥ*.

1811. **paraṁtapa** "(lit.) Enemy-Burner; Scorcher of the Foe; Destroyer of Enemies; One who inflicts pain on the enemy". Also see *tapas*.
    - paraṁtapa. "O Destroyer of Enemies". Used as an epithet of Arjuna in 2.3; 4.2, 5, 33; 7.27; 9.3; 10.40; 11.54; 18.41.
    - paraṁtapa. "O Destroyer of Enemies". Used as an epithet of Dhṛtarāṣṭra in 2.9.[449]

1812. **parāṇi** "superior to". 3.42.

---

[447] Van Buitenen (1981, pp. 95, 165, note 6 in § 28[6]) translates *śāntiṁ nirvāṇaparamāṁ matsaṁsthām adhigacchati* as "attains to the peace that lies in me, beyond *nirvāṇa*", with a note that the state is *nirvāṇaparamām* (beyond *nirvāṇa*) "because it is not pure extinction but a postive union of the persisting *ātman* with the personal God."

[448] Divanji, p. 85, entry #1926.

[449] The Critical Edition reads *evam uktvā hṛṣīkeśaṁ guḍākeśaḥ paraṁtapa*, ending the line with a vocative *paraṁtapa*, addressing Dhṛtarāṣṭra. Vulgate editions read *evam uktvā hṛṣīkeśaṁ guḍākeśaḥ paraṁtapaḥ*, ending the line with a nominative *paraṁtapaḥ*, agreeing with *guḍākeśaḥ* (Arjuna).

1813. **parasparam** "mutual; each other; one another". 3.11; 10.9. Also see *aparasparasaṁbhūtam*.

1814. **parastāt** "beyond". 8.9.

1815. **parasyotsādanārtham** "that aims at injuring others[450]; to effect another's downfall[451]". 17.19. Also see *arthaḥ*. [*parasya utsādana-artham*]

1816. **parataḥ** "superior; beyond; higher than".

- parataḥ "superior". 3.42.
- parataram "superior". 7.7.

1817. **parayā** "with intense; with profound; with supreme". 1.28; 12.2; 17.17.

1818. **parāyaṇa** "holding as highest; devoted to; focused on".

- kāmakrodhaparāyaṇāḥ "devoted to desire (*kāma*) and anger (*krodha*)". 16.12.
- matparāyaṇaḥ "devoted to me". 9.34.
- mokṣaparāyaṇaḥ "devoted to achieving liberation". 5.28.
- prāṇāyāmaparāyaṇāḥ "devoted to the practice of regulating the flow of vital energy". 4.29.
- śrutiparāyaṇāḥ "devoted to Vedic injunctions; devoted to what has been heard". 13.25.
- tatparāyaṇāḥ "devoted to that". 5.17.

1819. **parayāviṣṭaḥ** "overwhelmed by supreme (compassion)". 1.28. [*kṛpayā parayāviṣṭaḥ* = "overwhelmed by supreme compassion"[452]] Also see *āviṣṭa*.

1820. **paricakṣate** "is called; is designated; (people) call it". 17.13, 17.

1821. **paricintayan** "thinking about; meditating on; reflecting on". 10.17. Also see *anucintayan, cintayantaḥ*.

1822. **paridevanā** "affliction; lamentation; complaint". 2.28.

1823. **paricaryātmakam** "rendering service". 18.44.

1824. **paridahyate** "it burns all over". 1.30.

1825. **parigraham** "greed; acceptance of gifts" 18.53. Also see *aparigraha*.

1826. **parijñātā** "the knower". 18.18.

1827. **parikīrtitaḥ** "proclaimed; made known; is considered to be". 18.7, 27. Also see *kīrti, prakīrtyā, saṁprakīrtitaḥ*.

1828. **parikliṣṭam** "reluctantly; half-heartedly; vexatiously". 17.21.

---

[450] Warrier, p. 541.

[451] Van Buitenen 1981, p. 137.

[452] Gambhīrānanda 1997, p. 21.

1829. **parimārgitavyam** "should be sought for; must be sought". 15.4.

1830. **pariṇāme** "in maturity; as it matures; at the culmination; in effect; in the result; in development; when transformed; ultimately". 18.37, 38.

1831. **paripanthinau** "the (two) enemies; the (two) adversaries". 3.34.

1832. **paripraśnena** "by raising questions; with repeated questions; by comprehensive questioning". 4.34.

1833. **parisamāpyate** "it is brought to an end; it culminates; it comes to fulfillment". 4.33. Also see *samāpnoṣi.* [√ *āp* + prefixes *sam* and *pari.*]

1834. **pariśuṣyati** "it dries up; it is parching". 1.29.

1835. **paritrāṇāya** "to deliverance; for protection". 4.8. [*pari* + √ *trā*]

1836. **parityāgaḥ** "complete renunciation". 18.7. Also see *parityāgī, parityajya, tyāga.*

1837. **parityāgī** "a complete renouncer". Also see *parityajya, tyāga, tyāgī.*

- sarvārambhaparityāgī "one renouncing all undertakings; relinquishing all (selfish) enterprises; one who abandons all (selfish) initiatives". 12.16; 14.25.
- śubhāśubhaparityāgī "one who relinquishes (judgements between) the auspicious and the inauspicious; renouncing good and evil (objects)[453]". 12.17.

1838. **parityajya** "after renouncing; having renounced; renouncing completely". 18.66. Also see *parityāgaḥ, tyāga.*

1839. **parjanya** "rain".

- parjanyāt "due to rain; from rain". 3.14.
- parjanyaḥ "rain". 3.14.

1840. **parṇāni** "leaves". 15.1.

1841. **pārtha** "son of Pṛthā". This is a very common epithet for Arjuna, used 42 times throughout the text. Pṛthā is another name for Kuntī, Arjuna's mother. Kuntī was the wife of Pāṇḍu. 1.25-26; 2.3, 21, 32, 39, 42, 55, 72; 3.16, 22-23; 4.11, 33; 6.40; 7.1, 10; 8.8, 14, 19, 22, 27; 9.13, 32; 10.24; 11.5, 9; 12.7; 16.4, 6; 17.26, 28; 18.6, 30-35, 72, 74, 78.

1842. **pāruṣyam** "rudeness; harshness; unkind speech; abusive language". 16.4.

1843. **paryāptam** "limited; just barely sufficient; sufficient". 1.10. See *aparyāptam* for discussion of this word.

---

[453] Edgerton, p. 63.

1844. **paryavatiṣṭhate** "one becomes steady; one becomes firmly established". 2.65. Also see *tiṣṭh-, avatiṣṭh-*.

1845. **paryupāsate** "they worship; they serve; they honor; they revere; they venerate". 4.25; 9.22; 12.1, 3, 20. Also see *upāsate*.

1846. **paryuṣitam** "left-over; stale; spoiled; that which has stayed over-night". 17.10.

1847. **paśya** "see!; behold! perceive! look at!". 1.3, 25; 9.5; 11.5, 6 (twice), 7, 8. Also see *prapaśya, prapaśyadbhiḥ*.

1848. **paśyāmi** "I see; I perceive". 1.31; 6.33; 11.15, 16 (twice), 17, 19. Also see *anupaśyāmi, prapaśyāmi*.

1849. **paśyan** "seeing; perceiving; beholding". 5.8; 6.20; 13.28. Also see *saṁpaśyan*.

1850. **paśyanti** "they see; they perceive". 1.38; 13.24; 15.10, 11 (twice). Also see *anupaśyanti*.

1851. **paśyataḥ** "of the seeing (sage); for (a person who is) perceiving (correctly)". 2.69.

1852. **paśyati** " one sees; one perceives". 2.29; 5.5 (twice); 6.30 (twice), 32; 13.27 (twice), 29 (twice); 18.16 (twice). Also see *apaśyat, anupaśyati*.

1853. **paśyet** "one should see; one may perceive". 4.18.

1854. **pātakam** "sin". 1.38.

1855. **pataṁgāḥ** "moths; insects". 11.29.

1856. **patanti** "they fall". 1.42; 16.16.

1857. **pathi** "on the path; on the way; in the approach". 6.38.

1858. **patram** "leaf".

- kamalapatrākṣa "O Lotus-petal-eyed One". 11.2.
- padmapatram "a lotus leaf; the leaf of a lotus plant". 5.10.
- patram "a leaf". 9.26.

1859. **pātre** "a worthy recipient; a fit person for a gift". 17.20. Also see *apātrebhyaḥ*.

1860. **pauṇḍram** "Pauṇḍra". 1.15. [The name of Bhīma's conch. The name may be related to the region of Puṇḍra.[454]] Also see *Bhīma*.

1861. **pauruṣam** "manhood (in men, *nṛṣu*), manliness, potency, virility, might, strength" 7.8; "strength, ability" 18.25. Also see *puruṣa*.

1862. **paurvadehikam** "of the previous embodiment; that relating to the previous birth". 6.43. Also see *deha*.

---

[454] Minor, p. 11; Apte, p. 635, entry for पौंड्रः; Sargeant, p. 53.

1863. **pautra** "grandson". Also see *putra.*

- pautrāḥ "grandsons". 1.34.
- pautrān "grandsons". 1.26.

1864. **pāvakaḥ** "fire". 2.23; 10.23; 15.6.

1865. **pavanaḥ** "the wind; The Purifier". 10.31.

1866. **pāvanāni** "purifiers". 18.5.

1867. **pavatām** "among purifiers". 10.31.

1868. **pavitram** "purifier; sanctifier; pure; holy". 4.38; 9.2, 17; 10.12.

1869. **phala** "fruit; result; consequence; reward". Also see *aphalākāṅkṣibhiḥ, aphalaprepsunā, janmakarmaphalapradām, karmaphala, puṇyaphalam, śubhāśubhaphalaiḥ, tyāgaphalam.*

- phalam "fruit; reward; result". 2.51; 5.4; 7.23; 9.26 (lit.); 14.16 (three times); 17.12, 21, 25; 18.9, 12.
- phalāni "fruits; results". 18.6.
- phale "in the fruit". 5.12.
- phaleṣu "in the fruits". 2.47.

1870. **phalahetavaḥ** "those motivated by fruits". 2.49. Also see *hetu, karmaphalahetuḥ.*

1871. **phalākāṅkṣī** "one desiring rewards; one expecting a reward; one wanting fruits". 18.34. Also see *aphalākāṅkṣibhiḥ, √ kāṅkṣ.*

1872. **pīḍayā** "with difficulty; causing pain; by tormenting". 17.19.

1873. **pitāmaha** "grandfather". Also see *prapitāmahaḥ.*

- pitāmahaḥ "grandfather". 1.12. [Referring to Bhīṣma, the granduncle of the Kauravas and the Pāṇḍavas.]
- pitāmahaḥ "grandfather". 9.17. [Referring to Brahmā (Hiraṇyagarbha), who is known as the grandfather of the universe.[455]]
- pitāmahāḥ "grandfathers". 1.34.
- pitāmahān "grandfathers". 1.26.

1874. **pitṛ** "father; forefather; an elderly relations on one's side; a deceased ancestor".

- pitā "father". 9.17; 11.43, 44; 14.4.
- pitaraḥ "fathers; forefathers". 1.34.
- pitaraḥ "forefathers; (deceased) ancestors". 1.42.
- pitṝn "fathers". 1.26.

---

[455] Sivananda (p. 215) says Absolute *Brahman* is the grandfather.

- pitṝn "(deceased) ancestors". 9.25.
- pitṝṇām "of the (deceased) ancestors". 10.29.

1875. **pitṛvratāḥ** "those dedicated to the forefathers; those who observe vows with a view to propitiate the manes[456]". 9.25. Also see *vrata*.

1876. **prabhā** "light; lustre; radiance; splendor". 7.8. Also see *bhāḥ*.

1877. **prabhāṣeta** "should speak". 2.54. Also see *bhāṣā, bhāṣase*.

1878. **prabhava** "birth; origin; source". Also see *bhavaḥ, apratimaprabhāva, prabhaviṣṇu*.
- prabhavaḥ "the origin; the source". 7.6; 9.18; 10.8.
- prabhavam "the origin; the source". 10.2.
- prabhavanti "they come into existence; they come forth; they appear". 8.18; 16.9.
- prabhavati "it comes into existence; it comes forth; it makes its appearance". 8.19.
- saṁkalpaprabhavān "owing their origin to intention; whose origins lie in one's intention". 6.24. Also see *saṁkalpa*.
- svabhāvaprabhavaiḥ "arising out of their innate nature; born of their own nature". 18.41.

1879. **prabhāva** "splendor; glory; efficacy; power; miraculous power".
- apratimaprabhāva "O Incomparable Glory; O One of Infinite Influence; O One Whose Prowess is Unparalleled". 11.43.
- yatprabhāvaḥ "the powers he is endowed with; of what kind of prowess". 13.3.

1880. **prabhaviṣṇu** "creator; originator". 13.16. Also see *viṣṇu*.

1881. **prabhuḥ** "the Lord; the Master; the Supreme Authority".
- prabhuḥ "the Lord; the Supreme". 5.14; 9.18, 24.
- prabho "O Lord". 11.4; 14.21.

1882. **pradadhmatuḥ** "(the two) blew forcefully". 1.14. [√ *dhmā*] Also see *dadhm-*.

1883. **prādhānyataḥ** "principally; the most prominent". 10.19.

1884. **pradīptam** "blazing; fully ignited". 11.29. Also see *dīptam*.

1885. **pradiṣṭam** "is announced; is spelled out; laid down; prescribed; assigned". 8.28.

1886. **praduṣyanti** "they are corrupted; they become spoiled". 1.41. Also see *duṣṭāsu*.

---

[456] Divanji, p. 88, entry # 2000.

1887. **pradviṣantaḥ** "hating intensely; loathing". 16.18. Also see *dveṣa, dviṣataḥ*.

1888. **prāha** "he spoke; he told; he communicated". 4.1. Also see *āha, prāhuḥ*.

1889. **prahasan** "laughing; smiling; mocking". 2.10.

1890. **prahāsyasi** "you will eliminate; you will completely destroy". 2.39.

1891. **prahlādaḥ** "Prahlāda". 10.30. [Prahlāda ("Full of joy") was a famous demon with an ardent devotion to Viṣṇu. His father was the demon, who did not like the fact that his son worshipped an enemy of the demons. Hiraṇyakaśipu rejected his son and attempted to kill him several times, but Prahlāda was protected by the grace of Viṣṇu. According to the *Viṣṇu Pūrāṇa,* Viṣṇu took on the *avatara* of Narasiṁha, the Man-Lion, to slay Hiraṇyakaśipu.]

1892. **prahṛṣyati** "it rejoices; it is delighted; it is exhilarated". 11.36.

1893. **prahṛṣyet** "on should rejoice; one should be delighted; one should feel exhilarated". 5.20.

1894. **prāhuḥ** "they say; they describe; they call". 6.2; 13.1; 15.1; 18.2, 3. Also see *prāha, āhuḥ*.

1895. **prajāḥ** "progeny; beings; creatures; people; mankind". 3.10, 24; 10.6.

1896. **prajahāti** "one leaves aside; one abandons; one relinquishes". 2.55. [*pra* + √ *hā*] Also see *jahāti*.

1897. **prajahi** "destroy; slay; kill; strike down". 3.41. [*pra* + √ *han*] Also see *jahi*.

1898. **prajanaḥ** "procreating; begetting; cause of generation". 10.28. Also see *svajana, saṁjanayan*.

1899. **prajānāmi** "I understand; I know". 11.31. [*pra* + √ *jñā*]

1900. **prajānāti** "one understands; one knows; one distinguishes". 18.31. [*pra* + √ *jñā*]

1901. **prajāpatiḥ** "Prajāpati". 3.10; 11.39. [The Lord (*pati*) of Creatures (*prajā*); the primordial creator god.] Also see Brahmā.

1902. **prajñā** "wisdom". Also see *devadvijaguruprājñapūjanam, prajānāmi, prajānāti*.

- prajñā "wisdom". 2.57, 58, 61, 68.
- prajñām "wisdom". 2.67.
- prajñāvādān "wise words". 2.11. [*prajñāvādāṁś ca bhāṣase* = "and you pay lip service to wisdom; and (yet) you speak words of wisdom; you

speak words that are fit to be spoken by the wise (yet you do not understand properly)."][457] Also see *avācyavādān*.

- sthitaprajñaḥ "a man of steady wisdom; a man (is) of firm judgement (who...); one well-grounded in wisdom". 2.55.
- sthitaprajñasya "a person of steady wisdom; a man of firm judgement; of one well-grounded in wisdom". 2.54.

1903. **prāk** "before; prior to". 5.23.

1904. √ **prakāś** "to shine; to become visible or manifest; come to light". [*pra* + √ *kāś*]

- aprakāśaḥ "absence of light; absence of illumination; unenlightenment". 14.13.
- prakāśakam "an illuminator; that which enlightens; illuminating". 14.6.
- prakāśaḥ "light; shine; manifested; apparent; visible; shining". 7.25; 14.11.
- prakāśam "light; illumination". 14.22.
- prakāśayati "it illuminates; it enlightens; it causes to appear". 5.16; 13.33 (twice).

1905. **prakīrtyā** "having widespread reputation; much spoken of; renown". 11.36. Also see *kīrti, parikīrtitaḥ, saṁprakīrtitaḥ.*

1906. **prākṛtaḥ** "vulgar; unwise; discourteous". 18.28.

1907. **prakṛteḥ** "of nature". 3.27, 29, 33; 9.8.

1908. **prakṛtiḥ** "nature". 7.4; 9.10; 13.20; 18.59. Also see *bhūtaprakṛtimokṣam* "liberation of beings from nature" (13.34).

1909. **prakṛtijaiḥ** "arising from nature". 3.5; 18.40.

1910. **prakṛtijān** "arising out of nature". 13.21.

1911. **prakṛtim** "nature; (one's own) nature; natural". 3.33; 4.6; 7.5; 9.7, 8, 12, 13; 11.51; 13.19, 23.

1912. **prakṛtisaṁbhavāḥ** "arising out of Nature; born from *Prakṛti*; constituting Nature". 14.5. [*sattvaṁ rajas tama iti guṇāḥ prakṛtisaṁbhavāḥ "sattva, rajas,* and *tamas*, these are the three *guṇa*-s constituting *Prakṛti*".] Also see *saṁbhava.*

1913. **prakṛtisaṁbhavān** "arising out of Nature; born from *Prakṛti*". 13.19. Also see *saṁbhava.*

1914. **prakṛtisthaḥ** "located in Nature". 13.21.

---

[457] Commentators and translators vary in their understanding of the phrase *prajñāvādāṁś ca bhāṣase* ("You speak wise words"). In context the statement is ironic. Arjuna is speaking *as if* he were wise, but he does not understand the situation properly.

1915. **prakṛtisthāni** "evolving from Nature; that are part of *Prakṛti*". 15.7. Also see *antaḥsthāni, matsthāni, sthānam.*

1916. **prakṛtyā** "by nature". 7.20; 13.29.

1917. **pralapan** "while speaking; talking". 5.9.

1918. **pralaya** "dissolution; death".

- pralayaḥ "dissolution". 7.6; 9.18.
- pralayam "death". 14.14, 15.
- pralaye "at the time of dissolution". 14.2.

1919. **pralayāntām** "up to the time of dissolution; up to the time of death". 16.11.

1920. **pralīnaḥ** "dying; dissolving". 14.15.

1921. **pralīyante** "they dissolve; they merge". 8.18.

1922. **pralīyate** "it dissolves; it melts away; it merges". 8.19. Also see *pravilīyate.*

1923. **pramāda** "negligence; inattentiveness; carelessness".

- nidrālasyapramādottham "arising out of sleep, indolence, and delusion". 18.39. Also see *alasaḥ, nidrā.*
- pramādaḥ "negligence". 14.13.
- pramādālasyanidrābhiḥ "by negligence, indolence, and sleep". 14.8. Also see *alasaḥ, nidrā.*
- pramādamohau "negligence and delusion". 14.17. Also see *moha.*
- pramādāt "due to negligence; inadvertently". 11.41.
- pramāde "in negligence". 14.9.

1924. **pramāṇam** "a model; a standard; an authoritative guide". Also see *aprameya.*

- pramāṇam "model, standard". 3.21.
- pramāṇam "authoritative guide; authority". 16.24.

1925. **pramāthi** "turbulent; whirling; agitating; deluding". 6.34.

1926. **pramāthīni** "turbulent; whirling; agitating; over-powering". 2.60.

1927. **pramucyate** "one is released; one is liberated". 5.3; 10.3. Also see *mokṣ-, √ muc.*

1928. **pramukhataḥ** "in front of". 1.25. See *bhīṣmadroṇapramukhataḥ.*

1929. **pramukhe**"in front of". 2.6. Also see *bhīṣmadroṇapramukhataḥ, mukha.*

1930. **prāṇa** "life force; vital energy; vital breath; the breath of life". Also see *apāna, prāṇin.*

- apāne juhvati prāṇaṁ prāṇe 'pānaṁ tathāpare । prāṇāpānagatī ruddhvā prāṇāyāmaparāyaṇāḥ ॥ "Still others, after being absorbed in the practice of restraining the flow of *apāna* and *prāṇa*, offer as a sacrifice the joining of *prāṇa* into *apāna* and *apāna* into *prāṇa*". 4.29. Also see *parāyaṇa.*

- madgataprāṇāḥ "with their life force taking shelter in Me; those whose vitality is absorbed in Me; those whose life goes toward Me". 10.9.
- manaḥprāṇendriyakriyāḥ "the functions of the mind (*manaḥ*), the life force (*prāṇa*), and the senses (*indriya*); the operation of the mind, the vital breath, and the organs (of sense and action)". 18.33.
- prāṇakarmāṇi "activities of the vital breath". 4.27.
- prāṇam "the life force". 4.29; 8.10, 12.
- prāṇān (prāṇāṁs) "life". 1.33; 4.30. [4.30: *prāṇān prāṇeṣu juhvati* = they offer their life force (breath of life) as sacrifice into their breath]
- prāṇāpānagatī "the movement of the upward and downward breaths". 4.29.
- prāṇāpānasamāyuktaḥ "accompanied by the life force (*prāṇa*) and eliminative wind (*apāna*); united with the upward and downward breaths". 15.14. Also see *yukta.*
- prāṇāpānau "the inhaling and exhaling breaths; the upward and downward breaths". 5.27.
- prāṇāyāmaparāyaṇāḥ "being absorbed in the practice of regulating the flow of vital energy; one who is devoted to restraining the flow of *prāṇa* (and *apāna*)". 4.29. Also see *parāyaṇa.*
- prāṇe "in the breath; in the *prāṇa*". 4.29.
- prāṇeṣu "in the breaths; in the vital breaths". 4.30.

1931. **praṇamya** "having bowed; after bowing". 11.14, 35, 44. Also see *praṇidhāya, praṇipātena.*

1932. √ **praṇaś** "to be destroyed; to perish; to disappear; to be lost". Also see *vinaś-*.

- pranaṣṭaḥ "has been destroyed; has been dispelled". 18.72. Also see *naṣṭa.*
- na praṇaśyāmi "I am not lost". 6.30. ["I am not lost to him, and he is not lost to Me" or "He does not lose sight of me, nor I of him." *tasyāhaṁ na praṇaśyāmi sa ca me na praṇaśyati.*]
- praṇaśyanti "they are destroyed; they vanish; they are lost". 1.40.
- praṇaśyati "one perishes; one is destroyed; one is lost". 2.63; 6.30; 9.31.

1933. **praṇavaḥ** "the syllable *om* (ॐ)". 7.8. Also see *om*; *oṁkāra* (9.17).

1934. **prāṇāyāmaparāyaṇāḥ** "being absorbed in the practice of regulating the flow of vital energy; one who is devoted to restraining the flow of *prāṇa* (and *apāna*)". 4.29. Also see *prāṇa, parāyaṇa.*

1935. **praṇayena** "with love; with affection". 11.41.

1936. **prāṇe** "in the breath; in the *prāṇa*". 4.29. Also see *prāṇa.*

1937. **prāṇeṣu** "in the breaths; in the vital breaths". 4.30. Also see *prāṇa.*

1938. **praṇidhāya** "having prostrated oneself; having bowing down the body". 11.44. [*praṇidhāya kāyam*] Also see *praṇipātena, praṇamya.*

1939. **prāṇin** "a living being". Also see *prāṇa.*

- prāṇināṁ deham "in the body of living beings". 15.14.

1940. **praṇipātena** "with prostration". 4.34. [An obeisance made by prostrating oneself on the ground.] Also see *praṇidhāya, praṇamya.* [Van Buitenen's translation "submit to them" captures the meaning of the gesture.[458]]

1941. **prāñjalayaḥ** "with hands folded in supplication or prayer". 11.21. Also see *kṛtāñjaliḥ.*

1942. **prapadyante** "they approach; they take refuge in; have access to". 4.11; 7.14, 15, 20.

1943. **prapadyate** "one resorts to; one takes refuge". 7.19.

1944. **prapadye** "I seek shelter; I seek refuge". 15.4.

1945. **prapannam** "sought shelter; taken refuge". 2.7. Also see *anuprapannā.*

1946. **prapaśya** "visualize!; see!". 11.49. Also see *paśya.*

1947. **prapaśyadbhiḥ** "by discerning; by those who are visualizing". 1.39. Also see *paśya.*

1948. **prapaśyāmi** "I visualize; I perceive; I see". 2.8. Also see *paśyāmi.*

1949. **prapitāmahaḥ** "the primordial ancestor[459]; the Great-grandfather[460]; the Progenitor of all[461]". 11.39. Also see *pitāmahaḥ.*

1950. **prāpnuvanti** "they attain; they reach". 12.4. [*pra* + √ *āp*] Also see *āpnuvanti.*

1951. **prāpnuyāt** "one should attain; one may reach". 18.71. [*pra* + √ *āp*] Also see *āpnuyām.*

---

[458] Van Buitenen 1981, p. 89.

[459] Zaehner, p. 315.

[460] Śaṅkara (Gambhīrānanda 1997, p. 458), Rāmānuja (Ādidevānanda, p. 383), and Madhusūdana Sarasvati (Gambhīrānanda 1998, p. 671) interpret this as the father even of Brahmā (Hiraṇyagarbha, the grandfather). Divanji's note (p. 93, entry #2133) says it means the source of the Hiraṇyagarbha, i.e., the *Avyakta* (the Unmanifest).

[461] Tapasyananda, p. 303.

1952. **prāpsyasi** "you will attain". 2.37; 18.62. [*pra* + √ *āp*] Also see *avāpsyasi.*

1953. **prāpsye** "I will attain". 16.13. [*pra* + √ *āp*]

1954. **prāptaḥ** "attained; having acquired". 18.50. [*pra* + √ *āp*] Also see *dehāntara-prāptiḥ, paraṁparāprāptam.*

1955. **prāpya** "attaining; having attained; getting; incurring; having reached". 2.57, 72; 5.20 (twice); 6.41; 8.21, 25; 9.33. [*pra* + √ *āp*] Also see *aprāpya.*

1956. **prāpyate** "is attained; is reached". 5.5. [*pra* + √ *āp*]

1957. **prārabhate** "one initiates; he undertakes". 18.15 [*pra* + √ *rabh*] Also see *ārambh-.*

1958. **prārthayante** "they seek the objective; they pray for; they long for". 9.20. Also see *arthaḥ.*

1959. **prasabham** "forcibly; impetuously; presumptuosly". 2.60; 11.41.

1960. √ **prasad** "to be pleased, be gracious or propitious; be appeased or soothed; be satisfied". Also see *prasāda, prasanna.*

- prasādaye (tvam) "I beg your grace". 11.44.
- prasīda "be gracious; be merciful". 11.25, 31, 45.

1961. **prasāda** "clarity; tranquillity; grace". Also see *prasad, prasanna.*

- ātmabuddhiprasādajam "arising from clear understanding of the self". 18.37.
- manaḥprasādaḥ "tranquillity of mind". 17.16.
- matprasādāt "through my grace". 18.56, 58.
- prasādam "tranquillity". 2.64.
- prasāde "in tranquillity". 2.65.
- tatprasādāt "through his grace". 18.62.
- tvatprasādāt "through your grace; due to your favor; from your kindness". 18.73.
- vyāsaprasādāt "through the grace of Vyāsa". 18.75.

1962. **prasaktāḥ** "firmly attached; addicted". 16.16. Also see *bhogaiśvarya-prasaktānām, sakta.*

1963. **prasaṅgena** "with attachment; by clinging". 18.34. Also see *saṅga.*

1964. **prasanna** "pacified; cleared". Also see *prasad, prasāda.*

- prasannacetasaḥ "one whose mind is pacified; clear-minded". 2.65.
- prasannena "with grace; graciously". 11.47.
- prasannātmā "one who is pacified; serene-souled; one of tranquil mind". 18.54. Also see *ātman, praśāntātmā.*

1965. **praśānta** "at peace; calm; serene; still". Also see *śāntaḥ*.
   - praśāntamanasam "one whose mind is calm". 6.27. Also see *manas*.
   - praśāntasya "of one with a serene disposition; of a peaceful soul". 6.7.
   - praśāntātmā "keeping tranquil; with the mind tranquil; with tranquil soul; self all stilled; with self serene; one whose mind is at peace within oneself". 6.14. Also see *ātman, prasannātmā*.
1966. **praśaste** "for a praiseworthy [action]; for a laudable [act]; for an auspicious [rite]". 17.26.
1967. **prasaviṣyadhvam** "you will beget; you multiply". 3.10.
1968. **prasīda** "be gracious; be merciful". 11.25, 31, 45. Also see √ *prasad*.
1969. **prasidhyet** "it can be accomplished; it can be obtained; it can succeed". 3.8. [*pra* + √ *sidh*. The Critical Edition reads *prasidhyet*; most Vulgate editions read *prasiddhyet*.]
1970. **prasṛta** "spread out; extended; unfolded; emanated".
   - prasṛtā "spread out; emanated". 15.4.
   - prasṛtāḥ "spread out". 15.2.
1971. **pratapanti** "they burn". 11.30. [*pra* + √ *tap*]
1972. **pratāpavān** "mighty; powerful". 1.12. [*pra* + √ *tap*]
1973. **prathitaḥ** "known as; declared; famous; celebrated". 15.18.
1974. **prati** "directed towards; in regard to". 2.43.
1975. **pratijāne** "I promise". 18.65. [*prati* + √ *jñā*]
1976. **pratijānīhi** "know for certain". 9.31. [*prati* + √ *jñā*]
1977. **pratipadyate** "one reaches; one attains". 14.14.
1978. **pratiṣṭh-** "established". Also see *tiṣṭh-*.
   - acalapratiṣṭham "remains unchanged[462]; stays unmoved; that which has been immovably fixed[463]; well-established with stability; unmoving and stable". 2.70.
   - apratiṣṭhaḥ "without a foundation; without support; unstable". 6.38.
   - apratiṣṭham "without a foundation; without support; unstable". 16.8.
   - pratiṣṭhā "the basis; foundation; substratum". 14.27.
   - pratiṣṭhāpya "having firmly established; after arranging". 6.11.

---

[462] Gambhīrānanda 1998, p. 204.

[463] Divanji, p. 2, entry #38.

- pratiṣṭhitā "established; well-grounded; stable; standing firm". 2.57, 58, 61, 68.
- pratiṣṭhitam "is based on; is established in[464]; is present in". 3.15.
- saṁpratiṣṭhā "continuance; continued existence; stability; foundation". 15.3.

1979. **pratiyotsyāmi** "I will fight against; I will fight back; I will counterattack". 2.4. [*prati* + √ *yudh*] Also see *yotsye*.

1980. **pratyakṣāvagamam** "understandable (*avagamam*) by direct perception (*pratyakṣa*); demonstrable before the eyes". 9.2.

1981. **pratyanīkeṣu** "in the opposing force; in the enemy army". 11.32.

1982. **pratyavāyaḥ** "obstacle; impediment". 2.40.

1983. **pratyupakārārtham** "for the sake of receiving a reward or something in return; expecting reciprocation". 17.21. Also see *arthaḥ*.

1984. **pravadanti** "they speak; they expound; they debate". 2.42; 5.4. Also see *vadanti, vadati*.

1985. **pravadatām** "among debaters; among lecturers". 10.32. Also see *vādaḥ*.

1986. √ **pravakṣ** "explain, declare". [*pra* + √ *vac*] Also see *vakṣyāmi*.
   - pravakṣyāmi "I will explain". 4.16; 9.1; 13.12; 14.1.
   - pravakṣye "I will explain". 8.11.

1987. **pravālāḥ** "sprouts; shoots; new leaves". 15.2. [*viṣaya-pravālāḥ* = objects of senses (*viṣaya*) as its sprouts (*pravālāḥ*)].[465]

1988. **pravartante** "they proceed; they work; they begin". 16.10; 17.24. Also see √ *pravṛt*.

1989. **pravartate** "it proceeds; it works; it turns; it is set in motion". 5.14; 10.8. Also see √ *pravṛt*.

1990. **pravartitam** "set in motion; initiated; set turning; generated". 3.16. Also see √ *pravṛt*.

1991. **praveṣṭum** "to enter". 11.54.

1992. **pravibhakta** "divided; distributed; apportioned". Also see *vibhakta*.
   - pravibhaktam "divided; distributed". 11.13.
   - pravibhaktāni "divided; distributed". 18.41.

1993. **pravilīyate** "it dissolves; it melts away; it merges". 4.23. Also see *pralīyate*.

---

[464] Tapasyananda, p. 92, adds a gloss to his translation of *tasmāt sarvagataṁ brahma nityaṁ yajñe pratiṣṭhitam*: "Therefore, the all-comprehending Veda is established in sacrifice (that is, has performance of sacrifice as its fundamental teaching)." Here, *brahma* is the Vedas.

[465] Apte, p. 662, प्रबा(वा)ल, –लं = var. of प्रवाल (*pravāla*).

1994. **praviśanti** "they enter". 2.70 (twice). Also see *viśanti.*

1995. √ **pravṛddh** "to grow; to increase; to be augmented".

- guṇapravṛddhāḥ "nourished by the *guṇa*-s; which grow due to the inherent attributes (of Nature)". 15.2.
- pravṛddhaḥ "grown (in power); grown (in stature); enlarged; matured; full-grown[466]; grown old[467]; manifesting fully[468]". 11.32.
- pravṛddhe "when well-grown; when predominant; with preponderance". 14.14. [*yadā sattve pravṛddhe* = when *sattva* is fully-developed.]

1996. √ **pravṛt** "to proceed; to happen; to begin; to begin to operate; to strive; to engage in; to make progress". Also see √ *nivṛt, pravart-.*

- abhipravṛttaḥ "engaged in (action); proceeding with (action)". 4.20.
- apravṛttiḥ "inactivity; indolence; lack of striving". 14.13.
- pravṛttaḥ "engaged; come forth; arisen; have proceeded; have become active" 11.32.
- pravṛtte "about to begin; at the commencement (of battle); ready for action". 1.20.
- pravṛttiḥ "undertaking action; activity; striving". 14.12.
- pravṛttiḥ "creation; coming forth; origin; (original) activity; manifestation". 15.4; 18.46.
- pravṛttim "activity; endeavor" 11.31. [*na hi prajānāmi tava pravṛttim* = I do not understand what you are doing]
- pravṛttim "activity; endeavor; progress". 14.22.
- pravṛttim "action; (desirable) action; what is to be done". 16.7; 18.30. [Contrasted with *nivṛttim.*]
- saṁpravṛttāni "(their) coming into existence; (their) appearance; (when they) happen". 14.22. [Contrasted with *nivṛttāni.*]

1997. **pravyathita** "tremble; shudder; be struck with fear; be distressed". Also see *gatavyathaḥ.*

- pravyathitāḥ "quaking; have become awestruck; [the worlds] are in panic[469]". 11.23.
- pravyathitam "quaking; trembling; tremble; shaking; shaken; shuddering; perturbed; awestruck; distressed; unsettled". 11.20, 45.

---

[466] Sivananda, p. 278.

[467] Van Buitenen 1981, p. 117.

[468] Ādidevānanda, p. 376.

[469] Van Buitenen 1981, p. 115.

- pravyathitāntarātmā "quaking in my inner being; with my inner soul agitated; one whose heart is perturbed; trembling of the inner self; terrified at heart". 11.24. Also see *ātman, antarātmanā.*

1998. **prayacchati** "he offers". 9.26.

1999. **prayāṇakāle** "at the time of death; at the time of departure; at the time of the last journey". 7.30; 8.2, 10. Also see *kāla.*

2000. **prayātāḥ** "(after) passing away; having departed; the dead". 8.23, 24. Also see *prayāti.*

2001. **prayatātmanaḥ** "one whose self is pure; a pure-hearted person; a pious soul; one who practices self-restraint". 9.26. Also see *yatātman.*

2002. **prayāti** "one passes away; one departs; one dies". 8.5, 13. Also see *prayātāḥ.*

2003. **prayatnāt** "with effort; from exertion". 6.45.

2004. **prayujyate** "it is used; it is employed". 17.26. [Pass. 3rd pers. sing. of √ *yuj,* with the prefix *pra-,* used in the sense of to be used for something.] Also see *yujyate.*

2005. **prayuktaḥ** "impelled; propelled". 3.36. Also see *yukta.*

2006. **pṛcchāmi** "I ask". 2.7.

2007. **pretān** "ghosts; spirits of the dead; dead persons". 17.4.

2008. **pretya** "hereafter; on departure (from this world)". 17.28; 18.12. [*pra* + √ *ī*]

2009. **prītamanāḥ** "one whose mind is pleased; with a happy mind; with heart at ease". 11.49. Also see *manas.*

2010. **prīti**

- prītiḥ "happiness; joy; satisfaction".1.36.
- prītipūrvakam "with love; with affection". 10.10.
- prīti (āyuḥsattvabalārogyasukhaprītivivardhanāḥ) "cheerfulness; happiness; delight". 17.8.

2011. **priya** "dear; liked". Also see *priya-, apriyam, sāttvikapriyāḥ, tāmasa-priyam, tulyapriyāpriyaḥ.*

- priyaḥ "dear".7.17 (twice); 9.29; 11.44; 12.14, 15, 16, 17, 19; 17.7 ("favored" food); 18.65.
- priyāḥ "(they are) dear". 12.20.
- priyam "favorable". 5.20. Also see *apriyam.*

2012. **priyacikīrṣavaḥ** "eager to please[470]; wishing to please[471]; who have come to do a favor; who want to do things that will be liked". 1.23. Also see *cikīrṣuḥ*.

2013. **priyahitam** "pleasant and wholesome". 17.15.

2014. **priyakṛttamaḥ** "dearest; the best friend; the best of those who do pleasant things". 18.69.

2015. **prīyamāṇāya** "(to you who are) beloved; (to you who are) dear (to me)". 10.1.

2016. **priyataraḥ** "dearer". 18.69.

2017. **priyāya**[472] "to a beloved". 11.44. [*priyaḥ priyāyārhasi* = as a lover with the beloved]

2018. **procy-** "said; stated; declared; proclaimed; taught". [*pra* + √ *vac*] Also see *prokt-*.

- procyamānam "being said; being stated; being spoken of; being described". 18.29.
- procyate "it is said (to be); it is declared; it is described". 18.19. Also see *ucyate*.

2019. **prokt-** "said; stated; declared; proclaimed; taught". [*pra* + √ *vac*. Also see *procy-*.]

- proktā "was said; was stated; declared; proclaimed; taught". 3.3. [√ *vac*]
- proktaḥ "taught; imparted; declared; proclaimed; described; has been described; explained; has been stated; has been expounded; propounded". 4.3; 6.33; 10.40; 16.6.
- proktam "is stated; declared; is declared (to be); is said (to be); called". 8.1; 13.11; 17.18; 18.37.
- proktāni "declared; expounded; proclaimed; stated". 18.13.
- proktavān "said; spoke; taught; having spoken; having declared; having imparted". 4.1, 4.

2020. **protam** "strung; fastened; woven; interspersed". 7.7.

2021. **pṛṣṭhataḥ** "from the rear; behind". 11.40.

---

[470] Warrier, p. 10.

[471] Sivananda, p. 10.

[472] Commentators disagree on handling of *sandhi* in the expression *priyaḥ priyāyārhasi*. Rāmānuja takes it as *priyaḥ priyāya arhasi* and Śaṅkara takes it as *priyaḥ priyāyāḥ arhasi* (Sampatkumaran, p. 299, note 574). Tilak (vol. 2, pp. 1089-90) reviews the question in detail and prefers the simpler grammatical solution of *priyāya arhasi*. Divanji (p. 98, entry #2245) lists the word as *priyāyāḥ* with discussion of the alternatives.

2022. **pṛthagvidhā** "various types". Also see *-vidhā*.

- pṛthagvidhaḥ "the various types". 10.5.
- pṛthagvidham "in a separate manner; each separately". 18.14.
- pṛthagvidhān "of various types". 18.21.

2023. **pṛthak** "separately; distinct; separate". 1.18 (twice); 5.4; 13.4; 18.1, 14. Also see *bhūtapṛthagbhāvam*.

2024. **pṛthaktvena** "separately; treated as separate entities; mutually distinct; as manifold; as diversified". 9.15; 18.21, 29.

2025. **pṛthivī** "the earth". Also see *dyāvāpṛthivyoḥ*.

- pṛthivīm "the earth". 1.19.
- pṛthivyām "on the earth; in the earth". 7.9; 18.40.

2026. **pṛthivīpate** "O lord of the earth; O king". 1.18. [Referring to Dhṛtarāṣṭra.]

2027. **pūjā** "honor; respect; homage; worshipping"

- devadvijaguruprājñapūjanam "worship (*pūjā*) of the gods (*deva*), the twice-born (*dvija*), the teachers (*guru*), and the wise (*prājña*)". 17.14.
- pūjārhāu "worthy of reverence; fit to be worshipped". 2.4.
- pūjyaḥ "worthy of reverence; fit to be worshipped". 11.43.
- satkāramānapūjārtham "for eliciting respect, honor, and reverence". 17.18. [*satkāra* + *māna* + *pūjā* + *artham*]

2028. **pumān** "a man; a person; a human being". 2.71. Also see *puṁsaḥ*.

2029. **puṁsaḥ** "of a man; for a person". 2.62. Also see *pumān*.

2030. **punaḥ** "again". 4.35; 5.1; 8.26; 9.7, 8 (twice), 33; 11.16, 39, 49, 50; 16.13; 17.21; 18.24, 40, 77 (twice).

2031. **punarāvartinaḥ** "return again; are subject to return (rebirth)". 8.16. Also see *saṁsāra, apunarāvṛttim*.

2032. **punarjanma** "birth again; rebirth". 4.9; 8.15, 16. Also see *janma, anekajanma-saṁsiddhaḥ*.

2033. **puṇya** "religious merit". Also see *puṇyakarmaṇām, puṇyakṛtān, puṇyaphalam*.

- puṇyaḥ "sacred; pure; auspicious". 7.9. [*puṇyo gandhaḥ pṛthivyām* = the pure scent in the earth]
- puṇyāḥ "holy; pure". 9.33.
- puṇyam "holy; pure; sacred; meritorious". 9.20; 18.76.
- puṇye "merit". 9.21. [*kṣīṇe puṇye* = upon the exhaustion of merit]

2034. **puṇyakarmaṇām** "of those who have acted with merit; of (persons) of meritorious conduct; of people who do holy acts; of doers of good works; of those whose acts are pure". 7.28; 18.71. Also see *karma, puṇya.*

2035. **puṇyakṛtān** "of those who have done meritorious acts; of doers of good works". 6.41. [*puṇyakṛtāṁl lokān*[473] = "worlds which are gained by merit"[474] or "worlds of the doers of right"[475]] Also see *puṇya.*

2036. **puṇyaphalam** "the fruit of a meritorious act". 8.28. Also see *phala, puṇya.*

2037. **purā** "in ancient times; in the days of yore; previously". 3.3, 10; 17.23.

2038. **purāṇa** "ancient".

- purāṇaḥ "ancient". 2.20; 11.38.
- purāṇam "ancient". 8.9.
- purāṇī "ancient". 15.4.

2039. **purātanaḥ** "ancient". 4.3.

2040. **purastāt** "from the front; before" 11.40.

2041. **pure** "in the city (of nine gates)". 5.13. [Referring to the body.]

2042. **purodhasām** "of priests; among the priests". 10.24.

2043. **purujit** "Purujit" . 1.5. A Kunti prince, an ally of the Pāṇḍavas, sometimes identified with Kuntibhoja.[476]

2044. **puruṣa** "person; consciousness; spirit". [Interpretation of this word depends on context. The ordinary meaning is "a male person", or when plural, "Mankind" in general or "people". Also used to refer to the individual soul and to God in the sense of the "Supreme Person". As a technical term in Sāṁkhya philosophy, *Puruṣa* is absolute Consciousness, standing apart from Nature (*Prakṛti*). In this sense sometimes translated as "Spirit" as opposed to "Matter".] Also see *pūruṣa, pauruṣam.*

- puruṣaḥ "a man; a person". 2.21; 3.4; 17.3.
- puruṣaḥ "a person's spirit; the individual self; the soul". 8.4. [Used in a philosophical context within the individual body (*dehe*).]
- puruṣaḥ "(the Supreme) Person; (the Supreme) Self; (the Supreme) Spirit". 8.22. [*puruṣaḥ sa paraḥ*]

---

473 For discussion of reading *puṇyakṛtāṁl lokān* as *puṇyakṛtām* (gen. pl.) rather than *puṇyakṛtān* (acc. pl.) see Divanji, p. 88, entries #2005 and #2006.

474 Van Buitenen 1981, p. 97.

475 Edgerton, p. 36.

476 For variations in handling of Purujit see "Who's Who", p. 7.

- puruṣaḥ "(the Primeval) Person; (the Primeval) Being". 11.18 [*sanātanas tvaṁ puruṣo mato me*]
- puruṣaḥ "(the Ancient) Person; (the Ancient) Spirit". 11.38. [*puruṣaḥ purāṇas*]
- puruṣaḥ "Consciousness; the Spirit". 13.20, 21, 22. [Contrasted with *prakṛti* as a Sāṁkhya technical term.]
- puruṣaḥ "(the Highest) Person; (The Highest) Spirit; (the Supreme) Puruṣa". 15.17. [*uttamaḥ puruṣaḥ,* contrasted with ordinary *puruṣa*-s.]
- puruṣāḥ "men; people". 9.3.
- pūruṣaḥ (= *puruṣa*) "a man; a person". 3.19, 36. This alternative spelling of *puruṣa* is used by poetic license to satisfy metrical requirements in two places.
- puruṣam "a man; a person". 2.15.
- puruṣam "(to the Supreme Divine) Person; (to the Supreme Divine) Self; (to the Supreme Divine) Spirit". 8.8. (*paramaṁ puruṣam divyam*)
- puruṣam "(to the Supreme) Person; (to the Supreme) Self; (to the Supreme) Spirit". 8.10. (*paraṁ puruṣam upaiti divyam*)
- puruṣam "(the Eternal Divine) Person; (the Eternal Divine) Spirit". 10.12. (*puruṣaṁ śāśvatam divyam*)
- puruṣam "Consciousness; Spirit". 13.0 [Supernumerary verse], 19, 23. [Contrasted with *Prakṛti* as a Sāṁkhya technical term.]
- puruṣam "(the Primordial) Person; (the Primal) Spirit". 15.4. (*ādyaṁ puruṣam*)
- puruṣasya "of a man; of a person". 2.60.
- puruṣau "*puruṣa*-s". 15.16. (*dvāv imau puruṣau loke* = There are two types of *puruṣa*-s in the world)
- puruṣarṣabha "O bull among men". 2.15. [Epithet of Arjuna, indicating excellence.]
- puruṣavyāghra "O tiger among men". 18.4. [Epithet of Arjuna, indicating excellence.]
- puruṣottama "O best among men; O Highest *Puruṣa*". 8.1. [Voc. sing., used as an epithet of Kṛṣṇa, possibly with wordplay on the ordinary meaning ("O best among men") as opposed to the spiritual meaning ("O Highest *Puruṣa*") as used more clearly in 10.15 and 11.3.]

- puruṣottama "O Highest *Puruṣa*; O Supreme Person; O Supreme Being; O Supreme Spirit". 10.15; 11.3. [Voc. sing., used as an epithet of Kṛṣṇa, possibly with wordplay on the ordinary meaning as used in 8.1.]
- puruṣottamaḥ "the Highest *Puruṣa*; the Supreme Person; the Supreme Being; the Supreme Spirit". 15.18.
- puruṣottamam "the Highest *Puruṣa*; the Supreme Person; the Supreme Being; the Supreme Spirit". 15.19.

2045. **pūruṣaḥ** (= *puruṣa*) "a man; a person". 3.19, 36. This alternative spelling of *puruṣa* is used by poetic license in two places to satisfy metrical requirements.

2046. **puruṣarṣabha** "O bull among men". 2.15. [Epithet of Arjuna, indicating excellence.] Also see *puruṣa*.

2047. **puruṣavyāghra** "O tiger among men". 18.4. [Epithet of Arjuna, indicating excellence.] Also see *puruṣa*.

2048. **puruṣottama** "best among men; Supreme *Puruṣa*". Also see *puruṣa*.
    - puruṣottama "O best among men; O Highest *Puruṣa*". 8.1. [Voc. sing., used as an epithet of Kṛṣṇa, possibly with wordplay on the ordinary meaning ("O best among men") as opposed to the spiritual meaning ("O Highest *Puruṣa*") as used more clearly in 10.15 and 11.3.]
    - puruṣottama "O Highest *Puruṣa*; O Supreme Person; O Supreme Being; O Supreme Spirit". 10.15; 11.3. [Voc. sing., used as an epithet of Kṛṣṇa, possibly with wordplay on the ordinary meaning as used in 8.1.]
    - puruṣottamaḥ "the Highest *Puruṣa*; the Supreme Person; the Supreme Being; the Supreme Spirit". 15.18.
    - puruṣottamam "the Highest *Puruṣa*; the Supreme Person; the Supreme Being; the Supreme Spirit". 15.19.

2049. **pūrvābhyāsena** "by previous practice". 6.44. Also see *abhyāsa*.

2050. **pūrvaiḥ** "by the ancients; by the prior ones". 4.15 (twice).

2051. **pūrvam** "previously; beforehand". 11.33.

2052. **pūrvataram** "long ago; from time immemorial; in days of yore". 4.15.

2053. **pūrve** "in the past; in previous times; in a prior age". 10.6.

2054. **puṣkalābhiḥ** "with numerous; with abundant; copious[477]; long[478]; abounding[479]; rich in contents[480]; elaborate[481]; splendid[482]; complete[483]". 11.21.

2055. **puṣṇāmi** "I nourish". 15.13.

2056. **puṣpa** "flower". Also see *maṇipuṣpaka.*

- puṣpam "a flower". 9.26.
- puṣpitāṁ "flowery; elaborate". 2.42. [*puṣpitāṁ vācam* = flowery words]

2057. **pūtāḥ** "purified". 4.10.

2058. **pūtapāpāḥ** "those purified of all sin; those cleansed of their sins". 9.20. Also see *pāpa.*

2059. **pūti** "putrid; stinking". 17.10.

2060. **putra** "son". Also see *pautra, drupadaputreṇa, kuntīputraḥ, pāṇḍu-putrāṇām, sūtaputraḥ.*

- putrāḥ "sons". 1.34; 11.26.
- putrān "sons". 1.26.
- putrasya "of a son". 11.44.

2061. **putradāragṛhādiṣu** "(attachment to) sons (*putra*), wives (*dāra*), homes (*gṛha*), etc. (*ādi*)". 13.9.

R

र् = R. ऋ = Ṛ. ॠ = Ṝ.

2062. **rādhanam** "worship; adoration; reverence". 7.22.[484]

---

[477] Zaehner, p. 308.

[478] Van Buitenen 1981, p. 115.

[479] Tapasyananda, p. 294. Hill (p. 206, note 4) says that his translation as "abounding" is based on Śaṅkara's comment *saṁpūrṇa,* but that John Davies "sublime" is also possible.

[480] Warrier (pp. 358-9) translates Śaṅkara's comment (स्तुतिभिः पुष्कलाभिः संपूरणाभिः) as "rich in content" meaning that the hymns are "complete in all respects."

[481] Gambhīrānanda (1997, p. 442) translates Śaṅkara's sense as "elaborate, full".

[482] Swarupananda, p. 252.

[483] Sivananda (p. 272) says that the word means "complete or well-worded praises or praises full of deep meanings."

[484] In 7.22a, many Vulgate editions read *tasyārādhanam,* which is often parsed as *tasya ārādhanam.* The Critical Edition digital text reads *tasyā rādhanam,* which without *sandhi* is

2063. **rāga** "attachment; passion (for something); desire". See *arāgadveṣataḥ, kāma-rāga-, vairāgya, vītarāg-*.

2064. **rāgadveṣau** "attachment (*rāga*) and hatred (*dveṣa*)". 3.34; 18.51. Also see *arāgadveṣataḥ, icchādveṣasamutthena, rāgadveṣaviyuktaiḥ*.

2065. **rāgadveṣaviyuktaiḥ** "by persons free from attachment (*rāga*) and hatred (*dveṣa*)". 2.64. Also see *rāgadveṣau, arāgadveṣataḥ, icchādveṣasamutthena, yukta, kāmakrodhaviyuktānām, viyoga*.

2066. **rāgātmakam** "characterized by passionate attachment; having the nature of attachment". 14.7.

2067. **rāgī** "one who is swayed by feeling of attachment (*rāga*); strongly partial; passionate". 18.27.

2068. **rahasi** "solitary, secluded, private". 6.10.

2069. **rahasyam** "secret". 4.3. Also see *guhy-*.

2070. **rāja** "king; royal". Also see *kāśirājaḥ, rāja-, rājya*.

- rājā "the Royal; the king". 1.2. [Referring to Duryodhana.]
- rājā "the Royal; the king". 1.16. [Referring to Yudhiṣṭhira.]
- rājan "O king". 11.9; 18.76, 77. [Referring to Dhṛtarāṣṭra.]

2071. **rājaguhyam** "the royal secret; king of secrets; the most important secret". 9.2. [Divanji notes that this could be translated either as, "That which is to be protected or concealed by the members of the princely order or that which is a king amonst the things to be protected or concealed, i.e., the highest secret." Of these two, Divanji considers the first to be the preferable meaning.[485]] Also see *guh-, rājavidyā*.

2072. **rājarṣayaḥ** "saintly kings; royal sages". 4.2; 9.33. Also see *rāja, ṛṣi*.

2073. **rajas** "*rajas*". Also see *rājasa, rajoguṇasamudbhavaḥ, śāntarajasam*. [*Rajas* is one of the three fundamental qualities (*guṇa*) of Nature (*Prakṛti*). It is associated with passion and activity.]

- rajaḥ "*rajas; rajoguṇa*". 14.5, 7, 9, 10 (3 times); 17.1.
- rajasaḥ "of *rajas*; of *rajoguṇa*". 14.16, 17.
- rajasi "in *rajas*; in the *rajoguṇa* state; when *rajas* predominates". 14.12, 15.

---

tasyāḥ rādhanam, corresponding to Divanji's entries for these words as *tasyāḥ* (p. 64, entry #1440) and *rādhanam* (p. 127, entry #2910). Divanji's entries follow the commentary of Śaṅkara, where *tasyāḥ* is interpreted as "that form of the deity" (Gambhīrānanda 1997, p. 332). Madhusūdana's commentary follows Śaṅkara (Gambhīrānanda 1998, p. 521).

[485] Divanji, p. 126, entry #2894.

2074. **rājasa** "endowed with *rajas*; having a predominance of *rajoguṇa*". Also see *rajas*.

- rājasaḥ 18.27.
- rājasāḥ 7.12; 14.18; 17.4.
- rājasam 17.12, 18, 21; 18.8, 21, 24, 38.
- rājasasya "of one who has a predominance of *rajoguṇa*". 17.9.
- rājasī 17.2; 18.31, 34.

2075. **rājavidyā** "royal knowledge; the king of sciences; a science fit to be known by the members of the princely order[486]". 9.2. Also see *rājaguhyam, vidyā*.

2076. **rajoguṇasamudbhavaḥ** "arising from *rajoguṇa*; having the *guṇa rajas* as the source". 3.37. Also see *guṇa, rajas, -udbhava*.

2077. **rājya** "a kingdom; dominion". Also see *rāja, rājyasukhalobhena, trailokyarājyasya*.

- rājyam "kingdom; empire". 1.32, 33; 2.8; 11.33.
- rājyena "with a kingdom; with an empire". 1.32.

2078. **rājyasukhalobhena** "out of greediness for the joys of an empire; thru greed for the joys of kingship[487]; out of greed for kingship and pleasures[488]; for greed of sovereignty and pleasure[489]". 1.45. Also see *lobha*.

2079. √ **rakṣ** "to protect; to guard".

- abhirakṣantu "protect on all sides". 1.11.
- bhīṣmābhirakṣitam "defended on all sides by Bhīṣma". 1.10.
- kṛṣigorakṣyavāṇij "plowing, cow-herding (*gorakṣya*), and trade". 18.44.

2080. **rakṣa** "Rakṣa; a type of demon". [A type of demonic semidivine entity. In popular usage the noun is also sometimes spelled *Rākṣa*.[490]]

- rakṣāṁsi "the *Rakṣa*-s". 11.36.
- yakṣarakṣāṁsi " *Yakṣa*-s and *Rakṣa*-s". 17.4.
- yakṣarakṣasām "among the *Yakṣa*-s and *Rakṣa*-s". 10.23.

2081. **rākṣasīm** 9.12 "fiendish".

2082. √ **ram** "to be pleased; to be delighted". See *ramanti, ramate, uparamate, antarārāmaḥ, indriyārāmaḥ*.

2083. **rāmaḥ** "Rāma". 10.31.

---

486 Divanji (p. 126, entry #2897) considers this to be the preferable meaning.

487 Edgerton, p. 8.

488 Van Buitenen 1981, p. 73.

489 Hill, p. 109.

490 Feuerstein and Feuerstein, p. 211, note 23, is an example of the spelling *rākṣa*.

2084. **ramanti** "they are full of delight; they rejoice; they are joyful; they are pleased". 10.9. Also see *ramate, uparamate*. [√ *ram*]

2085. **ramate** "one delights; one takes delight (in); one rejoices; one is joyful". 5.22; 18.36. Also see *ramanti, uparamate*. [√ *ram*]

2086. **raṇasamudyame** "in raising (this) battle; in undertaking (this) battle; in preparation on the battlefield". 1.22. Also see *udya*.

2087. **raṇāt** "from battle; from the battlefield". 2.35.

2088. **raṇe** "in battle; on the battlefield". 1.46; 11.34.

2089. **rasaḥ** "liking; taste; inclination; interest". 2.59; 7.8. Also see *gatarasam*.

2090. **rasanam** "the tongue; the organ of taste". 15.9.

2091. **rasātmakaḥ** "full of sap; the essence of sap; sapful; juicy[491]; endowed with moisture". 15.13. Also see *ātman, rasyāḥ*.

2092. **rasavarjam** "except flavor[492]; with the exception of the taste (for them)[493]; except for inner urge; to the exclusion of liking, interest, or inclination[494]". 2.59.

2093. **rasyāḥ** "succulent; juicy; tasty; delectable". 17.8. Also see *rasātmakaḥ*.

2094. **ratāḥ** "devoted to; engaged in; delighting in". 5.25; 12.4. Also see *vedavādaratāḥ*.

2095. **ratham** "the chariot". 1.21. Also see *mahāratha*.

2096. **rathopasthe** "in the seat (*upastha*) of the chariot (*ratha*)". 1.47.

2097. **rathottamam** "the excellent chariot (*ratha*); the best of chariots". 1.24.

2098. **rātri** "night". Also see *ahorātravidaḥ*.

- rātriḥ "". 8.25.
- rātrim "". 8.17.

2099. **rātryāgame** "at the advent of night". 8.18, 19.

2100. **raviḥ** "the sun". 10.21; 13.33.

2101. **ṛcchati** "he attains". 2.72; 5.29.

2102. **ṛddham** "prosperous; rich". 2.8.

2103. **ripuḥ** "an enemy". 6.5.

2104. **ṛk** "*Ṛgveda*; *ṛc*, a mantra of the *Ṛgveda*". 9.17. Also see Veda.

---

[491] Edgerton, p. 74; Ādidevānanda, p. 494.

[492] Edgerton, p. 15. Edgerton adds a note that the simple meaning of *rasa* is "flavor" but some commentators give less literal interpretations of the word here.

[493] Gambhīrānanda 1997, pp. 105-6. The Śaṅkara commentary notes that "taste" means subtle attachment.

[494] Divanji, p. 126, entry #2883.

2105. **romaharṣa** "bristling (*harṣa*) of the hair (*roma*); hair standing on end". Also see *harṣa.*

- romaharṣaḥ "hair standing on end". 1.29.
- romaharṣaṇam "causing the hair to stand on end" 18.74.

2106. **ṛṣayaḥ** "sages". 5.25; 10.13. Also see *ṛṣi.*

2107. **ṛṣi** "sage; seer".

- devarṣiḥ "divine sage". 10.13.
- devarṣīṇām "of the divine sages". 10.26.
- maharṣayaḥ "the great sages". 10.2, 6.
- maharṣīṇām "of the great sages". 10.2, 25.
- maharṣisiddhasaṁghāḥ "groups of great sages and perfected ones" 11.21.
- rājarṣayaḥ "royal sages" 4.2; 9.33.
- ṛṣayaḥ "sages". 5.25; 10.13.
- ṛṣibhiḥ "by the sages". 13.4.
- ṛṣīn "sages". 11.15.

2108. **ṛtam** "true; right". 10.14.

2109. **ṛte** "without". 11.32.

2110. **ṛtūnām** "of seasons; among seasons". 10.35.

2111. **ruddhvā** "restraining; controlling". 4.29. Also see *nirudhya.*

2112. **rudhirapradigdhān** "stained with blood". 2.5.

2113. **Rudras**, the. [A group of Vedic demigods.]

- rudrādityāḥ "the Rudras and the Ādityas".11.22. Also see *āditya.*
- rudrān "the Rudras". 11.6.
- rudrāṇām "among the Rudras". 10.23.

2114. **rūkṣa** "astringent[495], dry, harsh, coarse". 17.9. See *kaṭvamlalavaṇātyuṣṇa-tīkṣṇarūkṣavidāhinaḥ.*

2115. **rūpa** "form". Also see *acintyarūpam, anantarūpa, kāmarūpa, sattvānurūpā, ugrarūpaḥ, viśvarūpa.*

- rūpam "form". 11.3, 9, 20, 23, 45, 47, 49 (twice), 50, 51, 52; 15.3; 18.77.
- rūpāṇi "forms". 11.5.
- rūpasya "of the form".11.52.
- rūpeṇa "of form". 11.46.

---

[495] Apte (p. 805, entry for रूक्ष) defines *rūkṣa* as "astringent" when applied to taste. Meanings such as "rough" or "harsh" apply to other senses such as touch or sound. Other concepts include "dry" or "parched" in the sense of without liquid. Madhusūdana (Gambhīrānanda 1998, p. 842) gives examples of foods that are devoid of oil.

S

श् = ś. ष् = ṣ. स् = s.

2116. **sā** "she; that". 2.69; 6.19; 11.12; 17.2; 18.30, 31, 32, 33, 34, 35.

2117. **sabāndhavān** "along with (*sa*) kinsmen (*bāndhavān*)". 1.37.[496] Also see *svajana*.

2118. **śabda** "sound".

- śabdaḥ "sound". 1.13; 7.8.
- śabdādīn "sound, etc.". 4.26; 18.51. [*śabdādīn viṣayān* = sound and other objects of the senses]

2119. **śabdabrahmātivartate** "he goes beyond the words of the Vedas; goes above the stage requiring the aid of Vedic ritualism[497]; goes beyond the Brahmic word[498]; the word-*Brahman* (the Vedic religion)[499]; he proceeds beyond the *brahman* that is the Veda[500]; the sphere of Vedic injunctions[501]; rises superior to the performer of Vedic actions[502]; transcends the result of the performance of Vedic rituals[503]; transcends the Veda[504]; beyond theology[505]; beyond the externals of religion[506]". 6.44. Also see *ativartate*.

2120. **sacarācaram** "moving and non-moving; the mobile and the immobile; animate and inanimate". 9.10; 11.7. Also see *carācara*.

2121. **sacchabdaḥ** [*sat śabdaḥ*] "the word *sat*". 17.26. Also see *sat*.

2122. **sacetāḥ** "with mind, in thinking". 11.51. [*asmi saṁvṛttaḥ sacetāḥ* = I have regained my mental composure]

---

[496] The Critical Edition reads *sabāndhavān*, as followed by Van Buitenen (1981, p. 72). Some other sources have *svabāndhavān*, as followed by Sargeant (p. 75). For discussion of variants see Minor, p. 14.

[497] Tapasyananda, p. 186.

[498] Sivananda, p. 152.

[499] Edgerton, p. 36.

[500] Van Buitenen 1981, p. 97.

[501] Warrier, p. 249.

[502] Swarupananda, p. 160.

[503] Gambhīrānanda 1997, p. 311.

[504] Gambhīrānanda 1998, p. 485.

[505] Ryder, p. 54.

[506] Bolle, p. 81.

2123. **sadā** "always; forever". 5.28; 6.15, 28; 8.6; 10.17; 18.56.

2124. **sadasadyonijanmasu** "in births taking place in good and bad species of beings; births in good and evil wombs". 13.21. Also see *sat, asat, janma, yoni.*

2125. **sadasat** [*sat* + *asat*] "existence and non-existence". 11.37. Also see *sat, asat.*

2126. **sadātmānam** "always the self". 6.15, 28. [*sada* + *ātmānam*]

2127. **sadbhāve** "in the sense of 'truth'; with the meaning of 'real'; to indicate that which exists". 17.26. Also see *sat.*

2128. **sādharmyam** "identification; same nature; unity with (My) nature; the quality of having the same characteristics". 14.2. Also see *dharma.*

2129. **śādhi** "advise (me); direct (me); teach (me)". 2.7.

2130. **sādhibhūtādhidaivam** "together with the *adhibhūta* and the *adhidaiva*; along with the material and divine aspects". 7.30. Also see *adhibhūta, adhidaiva, bhūta, daiva, deva.*

2131. **sādhiyajñam** "along with the true object of worship; along with the ritualistic aspects". 7.30. Also see *adhiyajñaḥ.*

2132. **sādhu** "a person of noble conduct; a righteous person; a good person; a pious person". Also see *sādhubhāve.*

- sādhuḥ "a righteous person". 9.30.
- sādhūnām "of righteous people". 4.8.
- sādhuṣu "in the righteous". 6.9.

2133. **sādhubhāve** "in the sense of auspiciousness; in the meaning of 'goodness'". 17.26. Also see *sādhu.*

2134. **sādhyā** "the Sādhyas". 11.22. [A class of celestial beings. The name literally means "those who are fit to be propitiated."]

2135. **sadoṣam** "defective; having a fault". 18.48. Also see *doṣa.*

2136. **sadṛśa** "like; as; in accordance with; equal to; similar; resembling".

- sadṛśaḥ "like". 16.15.
- sadṛśam "according to; like". 3.33; 4.38.
- sadṛśī "like". 11.12.

2137. **sagadgadam** "with choked voice; in a stammering tone; falteringly". 11.35. [*sa* + *gadgadam*][507]

2138. **sāgaraḥ** "ocean". 10.24.

---

[507] Apte, p. 397, entry for गद्गद,"Stammering, stuttering, faltering"; and –दं "*ind.* In a faltering or stammering tone".

2139. **saḥ** "he; that; that (person)". 1.13, 19, 27; 2.15, 21, 70, 71; 3.6, 7, 12, 16, 21, 42; 4.2, 3, 9, 14, 18 (twice), 20; 5.3, 5, 10, 21, 23 (twice), 24, 28; 6.1, 23, 30, 31, 32, 44, 47; 7.17, 18, 19, 22; 8.5, 10, 13, 19, 20, 22; 9.30 (twice); 10.3, 7; 11.14, 55; 12.14, 15, 16, 17; 13.3, 23, 27, 29; 14.19, 25, 26; 15.1, 19; 16.23; 17.3 (twice), 11; 18.8, 9, 11, 16, 17, 71.

2140. **saha** "with; together with". 1.22; 11.26 (twice); 13.23.

2141. **sahadevaḥ** "Sahadeva". 1.16. [Name of the fourth of the Pāṇḍava brothers. The name means "He who goes with god" or "He who is accompanied by the gods".]

2142. **sahajam** "that which one is born with; innate in one's nature; naturally determined". 18.48.

2143. **sāhaṁkāreṇa** "(action) by one filled with vanity; accompanied by egoism". 18.24. Also see *ahaṁkāra.*

2144. **sahasā** "all of a sudden". 1.13.

2145. **sahasrabāho** "O Thousand-armed One". 11.46. Also see *bāhu.*

2146. **sahasrakṛtvaḥ** "a thousand times". 11.39. Also see *kṛtvā.*

2147. **sahasraśaḥ** "in thousands; by the thousands". 11.5.

2148. **sahasrayugaparyantam** "extending for a thousand *yuga*-s; that whose end comes after a thousand *yuga*-s". 8.17. Also see *yuga, yugasahasrāntām, sūryasahasrasya.*

2149. **sahasreṣu** "in a thousand; among thousands". 7.3.

2150. **sahayajñāḥ** "together with sacrifice". 3.10. Also see *yajña.*

2151. **sainyasya** "of the army (*senā*)". 1.7. Also see *senānīnām, senayoḥ.*

2152. **√ saj** [= **√ sañj**]. See *√ sañj.*

2153. **sajjante** "they are not attached". 3.29. Also see *√ sañj.*

2154. **sajjate** "one is attached". 3.28. Also see *√ sañj.*

2155. **sakhā** "friend; comrade". 4.3; 11.41, 44.

2156. **śākhāḥ** "branches". 15.2. Also see *adhaḥśākham, bahuśākhāḥ.*

2157. **sakhe** "O friend". 11.41.

2158. **sakhīn** "friends; comrades". 1.26.

2159. **sakhyuḥ** "of a friend". 11.44.

2160. **śaknomi** "I am able; I can". 1.30.

2161. **śaknoṣi** "you are able; you can". 12.9.

2162. **śaknoti** "one is able; one can". 5.23.

2163. **sākṣāt** "before the eyes; personally; in person; directly". 18.75.

2164. **sākṣī** "a witness; an onlooker". 9.18.

2165. **sakta** "attached". Also see *asakta, āsaktamanāḥ, avyaktāsakta-cetasām, bhogaiśvaryaprasaktānām, prasaktāḥ, saṅga, √ sañj.*

- saktaḥ "attached". 5.12.
- saktāḥ "attached". 3.25.
- saktam "attached". 18.22.

2166. **śakya** "possible; can be".

- śakyaḥ "possible". 6.36; 11.48, 53, 54.
- śakyam "possible". 11.4; 18.11.

2167. **śakyase** "you are able; you can". 11.8

2168. **śama** "calmness; peace; tranquility; serenity". Also see *aśamaḥ.*

- śamaḥ "calmness; peace". 6.3; 10.4; 18.42.
- śamam "equilibrium". 11.24.

2169. **sama** "same; equal; equally; having a sense of equality; equanimity". Also see *bhīmārjunasamāḥ. samatā, samatvam, sāmya, tulya, tvat-samaḥ.*

- samaḥ "same; equal; equanimity". 2.48; 4.22; 9.29; 12.18 (twice); 18.54.
- samam "same; equal". 5.19.
- samam "in the same position; aligned". 6.13.
- samam "equally". 6.32; 13.27, 28.
- samau "(both) equal; with both in balance". 5.27.
- same "(both) equal; both alike". 2.38.

2170. **sāma** "*Sāmaveda; sāman*; a mantra of the *Sāmaveda*". Also see *Veda.*

- sāma "*Sāma* (*Sāmaveda*)". 9.17.
- sāmavedaḥ "*Sāmaveda*". 10.22.
- bṛhatsāma tathā sāmnāṁ "*Bṛhatsāma* among the *Sāmaveda* chants; the Great Chant among chants". 10.35. [Madhusūdana Sarasvati identifies this as the particular chant called the *Bṛhatsāma*, based on the *Ṛg* mantra 6.46.1 in praise of Indra as the lord of all.[508]]

2171. **samabuddhayaḥ** "those who look upon all things equally; those who view with equanimity; those who have sameness of view; even-minded; impartial". 12.4. Also see *buddhi, samabuddhiḥ.*

2172. **samabuddhiḥ** "one who looks upon all things equally; one who views with equanimity; one who has sameness of view; even-minded; impartial". 6.9. Also see *buddhi, samabuddhayaḥ.*

---

[508] Gambhīrānanda 1998, pp. 634-5.

2173. **samācara** "do; perform". 3.9, 19. [*ā* + *saṁ* + √ *car*. Also see *ācar-*.]

2174. **samācaran** "doing; performing". 3.26. [*ā* + *saṁ* + √ *car*. Also see *ācar-*.]

2175. **samacittatvam** "equanimity; the quality of having a well-balanced mind". 13.9. Also see *citta*.

2176. **samadarśanaḥ** "an eye of evenness for all things[509]; regarding all as the same". 6.29.

2177. **samadarśinaḥ** "look with an equal eye; a person who looks upon all things equally". 5.18.

2178. **samādhi** and √ **samādhā** [Inf. of √ *dhā* with the prefixes *ā* and *saṁ*.] Also see *samāhitaḥ*.

- brahmakarmasamādhinā "by one who is absorbed in work as *Brahman*; by one who has concentration on *Brahman* as the essence of all actions; actions performed with consciousness of *Brahman*; focus on action as consisting of *Brahman*". 4.24.
- samādhau "in *samādhi*; in concentration; in meditation; in deep introspection; in the mind". 2.44, 53.
- samādhātum "to focus on; to fix the mind on". 12.9. [Inf. of √ *dhā* with the prefixes *ā* and *saṁ*.]
- samādhāya "with (the mind) firmly focused; having fixed the mind on; with the (mental) conviction". 17.11.
- samādhisthasya "of one who is established in *samādhi*; of one who is established in meditation; of one who is absorbed in a state of mental repose". 2.54.

2179. **samadhigacchati** "one approaches; one attains". 3.4. Also see *adhigacchati*.

2180. **samaduḥkhasukha** "having equanimity in pain (*duḥkha*) and pleasure (*sukha*)".

- samaduḥkhasukhaḥ "having equanimity in pain and pleasure". 12.13; 14.24.
- samaduḥkhasukham "one who has equanimity in pain and pleasure". 2.15.

2181. **samāgatāḥ** "come together; assembled". 1.23.

2182. **samagra** "the whole; wholly; the entire; completely".

- samagram "whole; entire; in its entirety". 4.23; 7.1; 11.30.
- samagrān "all". 11.30.

---

[509] Swarupananda, p. 152.

2183. **samāḥ** "years". 6.41.

2184. **samāhartum** "to destroy; to annihilate; to dispose of; for devouring[510]; to gather in[511]; gathering the worlds (unto Me)[512]; to consolidate". 11.32. [Inf. of √ *hṛ* with the prefixes *saṁ* and *ā*.]

2185. **samāhitaḥ** "fully collected (mentally); composed; serene; concentrated". 6.7. [Nom. sing. masc. of the past. participial adj. of √ *dhā* with the prefixes *ā* and *saṁ*.] Also see *samādhi* and √ *samādhā*.

2186. **samaloṣṭāśmakāñcanaḥ** "one who looks upon a clod of earth, a stone, and gold with an equal eye". 6.8; 14.24.

2187. **samantāt** "on all sides". 11.17, 30.

2188. **samantataḥ** "completely; in all aspects; on all sides". 6.24.

2189. **samāpnoṣi** "you pervade". 11.40. [*sam* + √ *āp*] Also see *parisamāpyate*.

2190. **samārambhāḥ** "actions that are commenced; enterprises; undertakings". 4.19. Also see *ārambh-*.

2191. **sāmarthyam** "power; capacity; prowess; bravery". 2.36. Also see *asamarthaḥ*.

2192. **samāsataḥ** "briefly; in brief". 13.18. Also see *samāsena*.

2193. **samāsena** "briefly; in brief". 13.3, 6; 18.50. Also see *samāsataḥ*.

2194. **sāmāsikasya** "of the class of compound words; among all compounds". 10.33.

2195. **samatā** "sameness; equality; equanimity; equal-mindedness toward all; even-mindedness". 10.5. Also see *samatvam*.

2196. **samatītāni** "the past; those which have passed away;the departed (beings)". 7.26. Also see *samatītya*.

2197. **samatītya** "after transcending; having crossed over". 14.26. Also see *atītya*, *samatītāni*, *vyatītāni*.

2198. **samatvam** "sameness; equality; equanimity; equal-mindedness toward all; even-mindedness". 2.48. Also see *samatā*.

2199. **samavasthita** "standing assembled; located". Also see *samupasthitam*, *avasthita*.

- samavasthitam "located; dwelling equally in". 13.28.
- samavasthitān "standing assembled; arrayed". 1.28.

2200. **samaveta** "assembled".

- samavetā "assembled". 1.1.

---

[510] Gambhīrānanda 1998, p. 663.

[511] Edgerton, p. 58.

[512] Warrier, p. 365.

- samavetān "assembled". 1.25.

2201. **samāvṛta** "enveloped; covered all over". Also see *āvṛta*.

- mohajālasamāvṛtāḥ "entangled in the snare of delusion; the net of delusion envelops them". 16.16. Also see *moha*.
- yogamāyāsamāvṛtaḥ "veiled by *yogamāyā*; enveloped by the power of illusion; covered by the magic of (my) *yoga*". 7.25. Also see *māyā, yoga*.

2202. **saṁbandhinaḥ** "kinsmen; relatives". 1.34. Also see *bandhuḥ*.

2203. **saṁbhava** "birth; production; creation". Also see *bhāva, bhavaḥ, annasaṁbhavaḥ, ātmasaṁbhāvitāḥ, prakṛtisaṁbhav-, tejoṁśasaṁbhavam*.

- saṁbhavaḥ "birth; creation". 14.3.
- saṁbhavāmi "I am born". 4.6, 8.
- saṁbhavanti "they are produced; they come into existence". 14.4.

2204. **saṁbhāvitasya** "of one so highly esteemed; of a person of well-established reputation". 2.34. Also see *bhāvita*.

2205. **saṁbhūtam** "caused by; come to be; produced by; born of". [√ *bhū*] See *ajñānasaṁbhūtam, aparasparasaṁbhūtam*.

2206. **saṁdṛśyante** "they are seen". 11.27.

2207. **saṁgha** ("group, assembly; combination"). Also see *saṁghātaḥ*.

- avanipālasaṁghaiḥ "with groups of kings". 11.26. Also see *saṁgha*.
- bhūtaviśeṣasaṁghān "groups of various kinds of beings". 11.15. Also see *saṁgha*.
- gandharvayakṣāsurasiddhasaṁghāḥ "groups of *gandharva*-s, *yakṣa*-s, *asura*-s, and Adepts". 11.22. Also see *saṁgha*.
- maharṣisiddhasaṁghāḥ "groups of great sages and Adepts". 11.21. Also see *saṁgha*.
- siddhasaṁghāḥ "groups of Adepts". 11.36. Also see *saṁgha*.
- surasaṁghāḥ "groups of gods". 11.21. Also see *saṁgha*.

2208. **saṁghātaḥ** "a combination; a collection; an assembly". 13.6. Also see *saṁgha*.

2209. **saṁgraheṇa** "with brevity; in summary; briefly". 8.11. Also see *karmasaṁgrahaḥ, lokasaṁgraham*.

2210. **saṁgrāmam** "a battle". 2.33.

2211. **saṁharate** "it withdraws; it draws inwards". 2.58. [*saṁ* + √ *hṛ*]

2212. **samiddhaḥ** "ignited; kindled". 4.37.

2213. **samīkṣya** "having seen; having looked at; contemplating; observing". 1.27. Also see √ *īkṣ*.

2214. **samitiṁjayaḥ** "victorious in war; (possibly the name) Samitiṁjayaḥ". 1.8. [For discussion of variant opinions if this is a name or an epithet, see the entry for Samitiṁjayaḥ in "Who's Who", page 8.]

2215. **saṁjanayan** "producing; causing". 1.12. Also see *prajanaḥ, svajana.*

2216. **saṁjaya** "Saṁjaya; Sañjaya".

- saṁjaya "O Saṁjaya". 1.1.
- saṁjayaḥ "Saṁjaya (said)". 1.2, [24, 47]; 2.1, 9; 11.9, 35, 50; 18.74. [*saṁjaya uvāca* = "Saṁjaya said". A change of speaker is implied before verses 1.24 and 1.47 but is not shown in the Critical Edition text.]

2217. **saṁjāyate** "it is generated; it is created; it arises". 2.62; 13.26; 14.17. Also see *jāyate.*

2218. **-saṁjñ-** "known as; designated". [A word element often used at the end of a compound to indicate a name, designation, or definition.]

- adhyātmasaṁjñitam "designated as spiritual; that which is known as *adhyātma*". 11.1.
- avyaktasaṁjñake "described as unmanifest; designated as the *avyakta*". 8.18.
- karmasaṁjñitaḥ "is called action; that which is designated as *karma*". 8.3.
- sukhaduḥkhasaṁjñaiḥ "designated as joy and sorrow; known as pleasure and pain". 15.5.
- yogasaṁjñitam "designated as *yoga*; known as *yoga*". 6.23.

2219. **saṁjñārtham** "for the sake of knowledge; with a view to introducing them (the leaders); so you may know them". 1.7. Also see *arthaḥ.*

2220. **saṁkalpa** "intention, motive".

- asaṁnyastasaṁkalpaḥ "without renouncing intention (for results); without detaching from the purpose". 6.2. Also see *saṁnyasta.*
- kāmasaṁkalpavarjitāḥ "free from intentions motivated by desire; free from ulterior motives". 4.19.
- saṁkalpaprabhavān "owing their origin to intention; whose origins lie in one's intention". 6.24.
- sarvasaṁkalpasaṁnyāsī "one who has renounced all intention (for results)". 6.4.

2221. **saṁkalpaprabhavān** "owing their origin to intention; whose origins lie in one's intention". 6.24. Also see *prabhava.*

2222. **saṁkara** "putting together; mixture; confusion; miscegenation".

- saṁkaraḥ "mixture". 1.42.

- saṁkarasya "of mixture; of confusion". 3.24.
- varṇasaṁkaraḥ "intermingling of classes; caste mixture". 1.41.
- varṇasaṁkarakārakaiḥ "leading to genealogical impurities; leading to intermingling of blood; causing caste mixture". 1.43.

2223. **śaṁkaraḥ** "**Śaṁkara**". 10.23. [A name of the god Śiva.]

2224. **saṁkhye** "in battle; in war; in the conflict". 1.47; 2.4.

2225. **sāṁkhya** "the path of knowledge; theory; theoretical philosophy; the Sāṁkhya path".[513] Also see *guṇasaṁkhyāne, sāṁkhyayogau.*

- sāṁkhyaiḥ "by those adopting the path of knowledge (Sāṁkhya); by the Sāṁkhyas". 5.5.
- sāṁkhyam "the path of knowledge (Sāṁkhya)". 5.5.
- sāṁkhyānām "of the Sāṁkhyas; for the followers of the Sāṁkhya school; for practitioners of Sāṁkhya; those following the path of philosphical reflection". 3.3.
- sāṁkhye "in theory; in theoretical knowledge; in theoretical or philosophical knowledge; in Sāṁkhya; in the Sāṁkhya school; in the Sāṁkhya system". 2.39; 18.13.
- sāṁkhyena "with analytic thought; with theoretical Sāṁkhya knowledge; by Sāṁkhya". 13.24. [*anye sāṁkhyena yogena karmayogena cāpare* = some by the *yoga* of Sāṁkhya and others by the *yoga* of action]

2226. **sāṁkhyayogau** "the path of knowledge (*Sāṁkhya*) and the path of *Yoga*; the paths of *Sāṁkhya* and *Yoga*". 5.4. Also see *sāṁkhya, yoga.*

2227. **saṁmoha** "thorough delusion; delusion on all sides". Also see *moha,* √ *muh.*

- ajñānasaṁmohaḥ "the delusion of ignorance". 18.72.
- asaṁmohaḥ "lack of confusion; absence of delusion; clarity". 10.4.
- saṁmohaḥ "delusion". 2.63.
- saṁmoham "delusion". 7.27.
- saṁmohāt "from delusion". 2.63.

2228. **saṁmūḍha** "confused; deluded". Also see √ *muh, mūḍh-.*

- dharmasaṁmūḍhacetāḥ "those whose minds are confused about what is right; confused about correct conduct". 2.7.

---

[513] Zaehner (p. 139) rightly points out that "neither the '*Sāṁkhya*' nor the '*Yoga*' of the Gītā corresponds exactly to the 'classical' texts of *Sāṁkhya* and *Yoga* respectively. ... Hence the two terms are legitimately translated as 'theory' and 'practice' respectively."

- guṇasaṁmūḍhāḥ "those who are deluded by the *guṇa*-s". 3.29.
- asaṁmūḍhaḥ "undeluded; not confused". 5.20; 10.3; 15.19.

2229. **sāmnāṁ** "among the *Sāmaveda* chants". 10.35. Also see *Sāma* (*Sāmaveda*).

2230. **saṁniviṣṭaḥaḥ** "entered; located; situated". 15.15.

2231. **saṁniyamyendriyagrāmam** "after restraining all the senses; having restrained the sensory and motor faculties thoroughly". 12.4. Also see *niyamya, indriya, indriyagrāmam.*

2232. √ **saṁnyas** "to renounce; to abandon; to lay aside; to place on; to commit to the care of[514]".

2233. **saṁnyāsa** "renunciation". Also see *karmasaṁnyāsāt, nyāsam.*

- saṁnyāsaḥ "renunciation". 5.2, 6; 18.7.
- saṁnyāsam "renunciation". 5.1; 6.2; 18.2.
- saṁnyāsasya "of renunciation". 18.1.
- saṁnyāsena "by means of renunciation; with renunciation". 18.49.

2234. **saṁnyasanāt** "by renunciation". 3.4.

2235. **saṁnyāsayogayuktātmā** "with the mind well-established in the renunciation (of the fruits of action); one whose mind has become composed by means of Saṁnyāsayoga" 9.28. Also see *ātman, yoga, yogayukta.*

2236. **saṁnyāsī** "a renunciate; a renouncer".

- nityasaṁnyāsī "a person of constant renunciation". 5.3.
- saṁnyāsī "a renunciate; a renouncer". 6.1.
- saṁnyāsinām "for those who renounce". 18.12.
- sarvasaṁkalpasaṁnyāsī "one who has renounced all intentions". 6.4. Also see *saṁkalpa.*

2237. **saṁnyasta** "renounced".

- asaṁnyastasaṁkalpaḥ "without renouncing intention (for results)". 6.2.
- yogasaṁnyastakarmāṇam "one who has abandoned (the bondage of) actions by *yoga*; one who has renounced action through *yoga*; one who has given up the performance of religious rites by *yoga*, i.e., according to the theory of *karmayoga*[515]; one who has dedicated (his) actions (to God) through *yoga*[516]; renouncing (all) works in *yoga*[517]". 4.41. Also see *yoga, karma.*

---

[514] Apte, p. 958, entry for संन्यस्.

[515] Divanji, p. 124, entry #2833.

[516] Gambhīrānanda 1998, p. 328.

[517] Zaehner, p. 198.

2238. **saṁnyasya** "having renounced". 3.30; 5.13; 12.6; 18.57.

2239. **saṁnyasyādhyātmacetasā** "having renounced by means of the mind filled with spiritual wisdom; letting go of things by means of having the mind devoted to the (true) self". 3.30. Also see *cetas*.

2240. **saṁpadam**. See *saṁpat*.

2241. **saṁpadyate** "one attains; one goes to; one becomes identified with[518]". 13.30.

2242. **saṁpaśyan** "seeing; observing, looking at; beholding; realizing; having in view[519]". 3.20. Also see *paśyan*.

2243. **saṁpat** "group of qualities; endowment; heritage[520]; destiny[521]; state[522]".

- saṁpadam "endowment; destiny". 16.3, 4, 5.
- saṁpat "endowment; destiny". 16.5.

2244. **saṁplutodake** "when there is a flood; when there is an inundation". 2.46.

2245. **saṁprakīrtitaḥ** "made widely known; spoken of all over; is designated; is considered to be". 18.4. Also see *kīrti, kīrtayantaḥ, parikīrtitaḥ, prakīrtyā*.

2246. **saṁpratiṣṭhā** "continuance; continued existence; stability; foundation". 15.3. Also see *pratiṣṭh-*.

2247. **saṁpravṛttāni** "(their) coming into existence; (their) appearance; (when they) happen". 14.22. [Contrasted with *nivṛttāni*.] Also see √ *pravṛt*.

2248. **saṁprekṣya** "gazing at; focusing on". 6.13.

2249. **samṛddham** "prosperous". 11.33.

2250. **samṛddhavegāḥ** "with great speed". 11.29 (twice). Also see *vegam*.

2251. **saṁsāra** "Saṁsāra; the circle or course of worldly life; worldly illusion; transmigration; succession of births".[523] Also see *āvṛttim, punarāvartinaḥ, aśubhāt*.

- mṛtyusaṁsārasāgarāt "from the ocean of worldly mortality; from the ocean of death and rebirth". 12.7.
- mṛtyusaṁsāravartmani "in the path of death and rebirth". 9.3.

---

[518] Sharma, Morgan and Pitts, p. 251, vocabulary entry.

[519] Tapasyananda, p. 94; Swarupananda, p. 82, vocabulary entry.

[520] Tapasyananda, pp. 396-9.

[521] Feuerstein and Feuerstein, p. 281, 449. Edgerton's (p. 76) "divine lot" and "demonic lot" have a similar sense of predestination.

[522] Swarupananda, p. 339.

[523] Apte, pp. 941-2, entry for संसारः.

- saṁsāreṣu "in the cycle of existence; in the ceaseless round of existences[524]; in the cycle of births and deaths; in this transmigratory life[525]". 16.19.

2252. **śaṁsasi** "you praise; you advocate". 5.1.

2253. **saṁśaya** "doubt". Also see *saṁśay-, asaṁśaya, chinnasaṁśayaḥ, jñānasaṁchinnasaṁśayam.*
- saṁśayaḥ "doubt". 8.5; 10.7; 12.8.
- saṁśayam "doubt". 4.42; 6.39.
- saṁśayasya "of doubt". 6.39.

2254. **saṁśayātmā** "endowed with a suspicious nature". 4.40. Also see *ātman, saṁśayātmanaḥ.*

2255. **saṁśayātmanaḥ** "the doubter[526]; the doubting self[527]; riven with doubts[528]; one whose mind is full of doubts; endowed with a suspicious nature". 4.40. Also see *ātman, manas, saṁśayātmā.*

2256. **saṁsiddh-** "perfection; full attainment". Also see *siddh-.*
- anekajanmasaṁsiddhaḥ "attaining perfection after several lifetimes; one who has become an adept after undergoing numerous births". 6.45. Also see *janma.*
- saṁsiddhau "toward perfection; toward success; for complete attainment (of something that is sought after)". 6.43.
- saṁsiddhim "perfection; success; complete attainment (of something that is sought after)". 3.20; 8.15; 18.45.
- yogasaṁsiddhaḥ "one who has become an adept by means of *yoga*". 4.38.
- yogasaṁsiddhiṁ "yogic attainment; the adeptness that is the result of *yoga*". 6.37.

2257. **saṁsiddhau** "toward perfection; toward success; for complete attainment (of something that is sought after)". 6.43. Also see *siddhau; saṁsiddhim.*

2258. **saṁsiddhim** "perfection; success; complete attainment (of something that is sought after)". 3.20; 8.15; 18.45. Also see *saṁsiddhau.*

---

[524] Edgerton, p. 78. Edgerton adds a note (p. 101) that in *saṁsāreṣu narādhamān | kṣipāmi*, he believes that *saṁsāreṣu* goes with *kṣipāmi* but that some other translators take *saṁsāreṣu* with *narādhamān* ("the lowest men in the round of existences").

[525] Warrier, p. 524.

[526] Van Buitenen 1981, p. 89.

[527] Warrier, p. 178.

[528] Van Buitenen 1981, p. 89.

2259. **saṁsmṛtya saṁsmṛtya** "remembering again and again; recalling over and over". 18.76, 77. [Repetition indicates distribution.] Also see *smṛt-*.

2260. **saṁsparśa** "contact". Also see *bāhyasparśeṣu, mātrāsparśāḥ, sparśān, sparśanam, spṛśan.*

- brahmasaṁsparśam "contact with *Brahman*". 6.28.
- saṁsparśajā "arising from contact (with objects)". 5.22.

2261. **saṁśritāḥ** "become dependent on; attached to". 16.18. Also see *āśrita, samupāśritaḥ, śritāḥ.*

2262. **saṁstabhyātmānam** "after restraining the (lower) self; after restraining consciousness". 3.43. [*saṁstabhyātmānam ātmanā* = after restraining the (lower) self with the (higher) Self = "pull yourself together"[529]] Also see *ātman.*

2263. **saṁśitavratāḥ** "(those with) determined vows; strivers (*yati*) who firmly adhere to a practice (*vrata*)[530]; firm of resolve[531]; strict in their vows[532]; with severe vows[533]; of accomplished vows[534]; those who have fulfilled their vows[535]". 4.28. Also see *vrata.*

2264. **saṁśuddhakilbiṣaḥ** "purified of all sin". 6.45. Also see *kilbiṣam, śuddh-.*

2265. **saṁtariṣyasi** "you will cross over". 4.36. Also see √ *tṛ*.

2266. **saṁtuṣṭaḥ** "completely contented". 3.17; 12.14, 19. Also see *tuṣṭaḥ, yadṛcchālābhasaṁtuṣṭaḥ.*

2267. **samuddhartā** "a rescuer; a savior; one who raises another up; one who extricates another (from an abyss)". 12.7.

2268. **samudram** "ocean". 2.70; 11.28.

2269. **samupāśritaḥ** "taking recourse to; taking refuge in; being supported by". 18.52. Also see *āśrita, saṁśritāḥ, upāśrita.*

---

[529] Van Buitenen 1981, p. 85.

[530] Minor, p. 171.

[531] Ādidevānanda, p. 179.

[532] Van Buitenen 1981, p. 89. Hill's (p. 143) "men of strict vows" and Edgerton's (p. 26) "with strict vows" are similar.

[533] Gambhīrānanda 1997, p. 216. *Śita* literally means "sharpened" or "whetted".

[534] Sampatkumaran, p. 120.

[535] Apte, p. 940, entry for संशित, lists several alternate meanings including sharp, acute, accomplished, determined, diligent in performing, etc. These lead to several possible translations for the passage. For the expression *saṁśitavrata* Apte gives the specific meaning "one who has fulfilled his vow." Divanji (p. 152, entry #3491) lists this as the meaning.

2270. **samupasthitam** "arisen; has presented itself". 2.2. Also see *samavasthita, sthita.*

2271. **saṁvādam** "speaking together; conversation; dialogue". 18.70, 74, 76. Also see *vādaḥ.*

2272. **saṁvṛttaḥ** "have become (composed in mind)". 11.51.

2273. **samyak** "properly; correctly; appropritately; rightly; truly". 5.4; 8.10; 9.30.

2274. **sāmya** "equanimity; impartiality; the ability to look upon all things with an equal eye". Also see *sama.*

- sāmye "with equanimity; with impartiality; looking upon all things with an equal eye". 5.19.
- sāmyena "as (the vision of) equality[536]; consisting in sameness[537]; as equanimity[538]; through equanimity[539]". 6.33.

2275. **saṁyama** "control; discipline". Also see *niyam-.*

- asaṁyatātmanā "by one who is not self-controlled". 6.36.
- ātmasaṁyamayogāgnau "in the fire of the *yoga* of self-control; in the (internal) fire of yogic restraint; in the fire of the discipline of self-control". 4.27. Also see *agni, yoga.*
- saṁyamāgniṣu "in the fire of self-restraint; in the fire of discipline; in the fire of self-control". 4.26. Also see *agni.*
- saṁyamatām "among disciplinarians". 10.29.
- saṁyamī "the self-controlled person; the one who practices restraint; the *yogī*". 2.69.
- saṁyamya "having restrained or brought under one's control; having controlled". 2.61; 3.6; 6.14; 8.12. [Indec. past part. of √ *yam* with the prefix *saṁ.*]
- saṁyatendriyaḥ "one who has acquired control over the senses". 4.39.

2276. **saṁyamāgniṣu** "in the fire of self-restraint; in the fire of discipline; in the fire of self-control". 4.26. Also see *agni, saṁyama, ātmasaṁyamayogāgnau.*

2277. **saṁyamatām** "among disciplinarians". 10.29. Also see *saṁyama.*

---

[536] Sampatkumaran, p. 165. Rāmānuja interprets the passage as meaning that the *yoga* taught by Kṛṣṇa is a vision of equality everywhere among all selves.

[537] Warrier, p. 242.

[538] Van Buitenen 1981, p. 97; Gambhīrānanda 1998, pp. 458-9.

[539] Tapasyananda's (p. 181) "spiritual communion through equanimity" captures the instrumental *sāmyena.*

2278. **saṁyamī** "the self-controlled person; the one who practices restraint; the *yogī*". 2.69. Also see *saṁyama*.

2279. **saṁyamya** "having restrained or brought under one's control; having controlled". 2.61; 3.6; 6.14; 8.12. [Indec. past part. of √ *yam* with the prefix *saṁ*.] Also see *saṁyama*.

2280. **saṁyatendriyaḥ** "one who has acquired control over the senses". 4.39. Also see *saṁyama*.

2281. **saṁyāti** "it goes along with; it moves". 2.22; 15.8.

2282. **saṁyoga** "connection; contact; union". Also see *yoga*.

- karmaphalasaṁyogam "connection with the result of action; a connection between an act and its fruit". 5.14.
- duḥkhasaṁyogaviyogam "disconnection (*viyoga*) from the connection (*saṁyoga*) with miseries (*duḥkha*); severance of contact with sorrow". 6.23.
- buddhisaṁyogam "reunion with a sense of discrimination". 6.43.
- kṣetrakṣetrajñasaṁyogāt "from the association of the field and the Knower of the field[540]; due to the union of Kṣetra (body) and Kṣetrajña (Spirit)[541]; the coming into contact of the Kṣetra and its knower[542]; due to the union of the body and consciousness". 13.26.
- viṣayendriyasaṁyogāt "from contact between the senses and the objects (of the senses)". 18.38.

2283. **san** "being". 4.6 (twice). [Nom. sing. of the masc. form of the pres. part. adj. *sat*, √ *as*.] Also see *sat*.

2284. **śanaiḥ** "slowly; gradually". 6.25 (twice). [*śanaiḥ śanair* = slowly and gradually]

2285. **sanātana** "eternal; perpetual". Also see *śāśvata, śaśvacchāntim, nitya*.

- sanātanaḥ "eternal". 2.24; 8.20; 11.18; 15.7.
- sanātanāḥ "eternal". 1.40.
- sanātanam "eternal". 4.31; 7.10.

---

540 Gambhīrānanda 1997, p. 555.

541 Sivananda, p. 348.

542 Divanji, pp. 49-50, entry #1120.

2286. **saṅga** "connection; attachment". Also see √ *sañj, asaṅgaśastreṇa, gatasaṅgasya, guṇasaṅgaḥ, jñānasaṅgena, jitasaṅgadoṣāḥ, karmaphalāsaṅgam, karmasaṅga, muktasaṅgaḥ, prasaṅgena, sukhasaṅgena, tṛṣṇāsaṅgasamudbhavam.*

- saṅgaḥ "attachment; contact". 2.47, 62.
- saṅgam "attachment". 2.48; 5.10, 11; 18.6, 9.
- saṅgāt "from attachment; due to attachment". 2.62.

2287. **saṅgarahitam** "free from attachment". 18.23.

2288. **saṅgavarjitaḥ** "having overcome attachment; devoid of attachment". 11.55. Also see *saṅga, saṅgavivarjitaḥ, varjita.*

2289. **saṅgavivarjitaḥ** "having given up attachment; freed from attachment; devoid of attachment". 12.18. Also see *saṅga, saṅgavarjitaḥ, vivarjita.*

2290. √ **sañj** [=√ **saj**] "to connect; to attach; to adhere". See *sajjante, sajjate, sakta, saṅga, sañjayati.*

2291. **sañjayati** "it attaches; it connects". 14.9 (twice). Also see √ *sañj.*

2292. **śaṅkha** "conch". [The shell of a conch is used as a horn.]

- mahāśaṅkham "great conch". 1.15.
- śaṅkhāḥ "conch horns". 1.13.
- śaṅkham "conch". 1.12.
- śaṅkhān "conch horns". 1.18.
- śaṅkhau "two conch horns". 1.14.

2293. **ṣaṇmāsā** "six months".[543] Also see *māsānām.*

- ṣaṇmāsā uttarāyaṇam "six months after the winter solstice; six months when the sun is on the northern path". 8.24.
- ṣaṇmāsā dakṣiṇāyanam "six months after the summer solstice; six months when the sun is on the southern path". 8.25.

2294. **sannyasya**. See *saṁnyasya.*

2295. **santaḥ** "the righteous; good people; pious men". 3.13. Also see *sat.*

2296. **śāntaḥ** "peaceful; pacified; tranquil". 18.53. Also see *aśāntasya. praśānta, śāntarajasam, śāntiḥ.*

---

[543] The ideas in verses 8.24-25 also appear in Upaniṣadic sources. See *Chandogya Up.* 5.3 ff. and *Bṛhadāraṇyaka Up.* 6.2 ff. In the northern hemisphere, for six months after the winter solstice (*ṣaṇmāsā uttarāyaṇam*) there is increasing light as the days get longer, an auspicious trend. This reverses after the summer solstice, when the sun moves on a southern course (*ṣaṇmāsā dakṣiṇāyanam*). Commentators vary widely in their interpretations of these verses.

2297. **śāntarajasam** "*rajas* pacified; having passions calmed". 6.27. Also see *rajas, śāntiḥ.*

2298. **śāntiḥ** "peace". Also see *śāntaḥ.*

- śāntiḥ "peace". 2.66; 12.12; 16.2.
- śāntim "peace". 2.70, 71; 4.39; 5.12, 29; 6.15; 9.31; 18.62.

2299. **sapatnān** "rivals; adversaries; enemies". 11.34. Also see *asapatnam.*

2300. **sapta** "seven". 10.6.

2301. **śaraṇam** "shelter; refuge; rescue". 2.49; 9.18; 18.62, 66.

2302. **sarasām** "of lakes; among lakes". 10.24.

2303. **sarga** "creation; creation of the world; Nature; the universe". Also see *bhūtasargau, visargaḥ.*

- sargaḥ "the worldly cycle; the cycle of births and deaths". 5.19.
- sargāṇām "of all creations; of created things". 10.32.
- sarge "in creation; from birth". 7.27.
- sarge "at creation; at the start of a new creative cycle". 14.2.

2304. **śarīra** "the body". Also see *deha, dehin, dehī, kalevaram, kāya.*

- śarīram "the body; a body". 13.1; 15.8.
- śarīrāṇi "bodies". 2.22.
- śarīre "in the body". 1.29; 2.20; 11.13.

2305. **śārīram** "belonging to the body; with the body; bodily". 4.21; 17.14.

2306. **śarīrastha** "residing in the body; situated in the body".

- antaḥśarīrastham "dwelling deep within the body". 17.6.
- śarīrasthaḥ "residing in the body; situated in the body". 13.31.
- śarīrastham "residing in the body; situated in the body". 17.6.

2307. **śarīravāṅmanobhiḥ** "by the physical body (*śarīra*), speech (*vāk*), or mind (*manas*)". 18.15. Also see *vāc, manas, yatavākkāyamānasaḥ.*

2308. **śarīrayātrā** "sustenance of the body; means of bodily sustenance". 3.8. [*śarīra yā trā*]

2309. **śarīravimokṣaṇāt** "complete liberation from the body". 5.23. Also see *vimokṣ-, mokṣ-.*

2310. **śarīriṇaḥ** "of the embodied; of the soul (possessing a body); of the *ātman*". 2.18. [Gen. sing. of the masc. noun *śarīrin*, the embodied soul.] Also see *dehin.*

2311. **śarma** "ease; happiness; peace". 11.25.

2312. **sarpāṇām** "among serpents; of snakes". 10.28.

2313. **sarva** "all; the entire".

- sarva "O All". 11.40.

- sarvaḥ "all; everyone". 3.5; 11.40.
- sarvāḥ "all". 8.18; 11.20; 15.13.
- sarvaiḥ "by all". 15.15.
- sarvam "all". 2.17; 4.33, 36; 6.30; 7.7, 13, 19; 8.22, 28; 9.4; 10.8, 14; 11.40; 13.13; 18.46.
- sarvān "all". 1.27; 2.55, 71; 4.32; 6.24; 11.15 (twice).
- sarvāṇi "all". 2.30, 61; 3.30; 4.5, 27; 7.6; 9.6; 12.6; 15.16.
- sarvasya "of all; of everyone". 2.30; 7.25; 8.9; 10.8; 13.17; 15.15; 17.3, 7.
- sarve "all". 1.6, 9, 11; 2.12, 70; 4.19, 30; 7.18; 10.13; 11.22, 26, 32, 36; 14.1.
- sarvebhyaḥ "among all". 4.36.
- sarveṣām "of all". 1.25; 6.47.
- sarveṣu "in all". 1.11; 2.46; 8.7, 20, 27; 13.27; 18.21, 54.

2314. **sarvabhāvena** "in every way; in all respects; with one's whole being". 15.19; 18.62.

2315. **sarvabhṛt** "supporting all; it sustains all". 13.14.

2316. **sarvabhūta** "all beings; all creatures". Also see *bhūta, sarvabhūt-*.

- sarvabhūtānām "of all beings". 2.69; 5.29; 7.10; 10.39; 12.13; 14.3; 18.61.
- sarvabhūtāni "all beings". 6.29; 7.27; 9.4, 7; 18.61.
- sarvabhūteṣu "in all beings". 3.18; 7.9; 9.29; 11.55; 18.20.

2317. **sarvabhūtahite** "in the welfare of all beings". 5.25; 12.4. Also see *hita, hitakāmyayā, ahitāḥ*.

2318. **sarvabhūtāśayasthitaḥ** "located in the heart of all beings". 10.20. Also see *āśaya, bhūta, sarvabhūtasth-, sthita*.

2319. **sarvabhūtasth-**. "located in all beings; residing in all creatures". Also see *sarvabhūtāśayasthitaḥ*.

- sarvabhūtastham "located in all beings". 6.29.
- sarvabhūtasthitam "located in all beings". 6.31. Also see *sthita*.

2320. **sarvabhūtātmabhūtātmā** "one who has identified the individual self with the Self of all beings[544]; one whose soul has become the soul of all the created beings[545]; ". 5.7. Also see *ātman, bhūta*.

2321. **sarvadehinām** "of all embodied beings; (of consciousness) of all beings". 14.8. Also see *dehin*.

---

[544] Sharma, Morgan and Pitts, p. 104, vocabulary entry.

[545] Divanji, p. 155, entry #3567.

2322. **sarvadharmān** "all *dharma*-s; all obligations; all duties". 18.66. Also see *dharma*.

2323. **sarvaduḥkhānām** "of all miseries". 2.65.

2324. **sarvadurgāṇi** "all difficult situations; all obstacles". 18.58. Also see *durgatim*.

2325. **sarvadvāra** "all the doors; all the gateways (of the body)". Also see *dvāram, navadvāre*.

- sarvadvārāṇi "all the gateways (of the body)". 8.12.
- sarvadvāreṣu "through all the gateways (of the body)". 14.11.

2326. **sarvagata** "omnipresent; going everywhere; pervading all".

- sarvagataḥ "omnipresent". 2.24.
- sarvagatam "omnipresent". 3.15; 13.32.

2327. **sarvaguhyatamam** "most secret of all". 18.64. Also see guhy-.

2328. **sarvaharaḥ** "all-destroying; he who carries away everything". 10.34.

2329. **sarvajñānavimūḍhān** "deluded about all knowledge; bereft of all knowledge; confusing all knowledge". 3.32. Also see *jñāna*.

2330. **sarvakāmebhyaḥ** "from all longing; from desire of all sorts; for any object of desire". 6.18. Also see *kāma*.

2331. **sarvakarma** "all action". Also see *sarvakarmaphalatyāgam, karma*.

- sarvakarmaṇām "of all actions". 18.13.
- sarvakarmāṇi "all actions". 3.26; 4.37; 5.13; 18.56, 57.

2332. **sarvakarmaphalatyāgam** "renunciation of the fruit of all action; giving up the effects of all rituals[546]". 12.11; 18.2. Also see *sarvakarma, karmaphala, karma, tyāga*.

2333. **sarvakilbiṣaiḥ** "from all sins". 3.13. Also see *kilbiṣam*.

2334. **sarvakṣetreṣu** "in all *kṣetra*; in all fields; in all embodiments of the soul's activity". 13.2. Also see *kṣetram*.

2335. **sarvalokamaheśvaram** "Great Lord of All the Worlds; Great Sovereign of the Entire Universe". 5.29. Also see *īśvara, lokamaheśvara, maheśvara*.

2336. **sarvāṇīndriyakarmāṇi** "all (*sarvāṇi*) the actions (*karmāṇi*) of the sensory and motor organs (*indriya*)". 4.27. Also see *indriya, karma*.

2337. **sarvapāpaiḥ** "from all sins". 10.3. Also see *pāpa, sarvapāpebhyaḥ*.

2338. **sarvapāpebhyaḥ** "from all sins". 18.66. Also see *pāpa, sarvapāpaiḥ*.

2339. **sarvārambhāḥ** "all undertakings". 18.48. Also see *ārambh-*.

---

[546] Bolle, p. 295.

2340. **sarvārambhaparityāgī** "one renouncing all undertakings; relinquishing all (selfish) enterprises; one who abandons all (selfish) initiatives". 12.16; 14.25. Also see *ārambh-*, *parityāgī*, *tyāgī*.

2341. **sarvārthān** "all matters; all things; all objects of knowledge". 18.32. Also see *arthaḥ*.

2342. **sarvaśaḥ** "on all sides; all together; entirely; in every way; in all respects". 1.18; 2.58, 68; 3.23, 27; 4.11; 10.2; 13.29.

2343. **sarvasaṁkalpasaṁnyāsī** "one who has renounced all intentions". 6.4. Also see *saṁkalpa*, √ *saṁnyas*, *saṁnyāsī*.

2344. **sarvāścaryamayam** "wonderful in every way". 1.11. Also see *āścaryavat*.

2345. **sarvataḥ** "on all sides; all around; everywhere".

- sarvataḥ "on all sides". 2.46; 11.16, 17, 40.
- sarvataḥpāṇipādam "with hands and feet on all sides". 13.13.
- sarvataḥśrutimat "with ears on all sides". 13.13.
- sarvatokṣiśiromukham "with eyes, heads, and faces on all sides". 13.13.

2346. **sarvathā** "in every situation; in all respects". 6.31; 13.23.

2347. **sarvatra** "everywhere". 2.57; 6.29[547], 30, 32; 12.4; 13.28, 32; 18.49.

2348. **sarvatraga** "going everywhere; omnipresent".

- sarvatragaḥ "going everywhere; omnipresent". 9.6.
- sarvatragam "going everywhere; omnipresent". 12.3.

2349. **sarvatrāvasthitaḥ** "dwelling everywhere". 13.32.

2350. **sarvatrānabhisnehas** "free from attachment in every situation; free from desire everywhere; unimpassioned on all sides". 2.57. [*sarvatra-an-abhi-snehas*]

2351. **sarvavedeṣu** "in all the Vedas". 7.8. Also see *Veda*.

2352. **sarvavid** "all-knowing; knowing everything; omniscient". 15.19. Also see *sarva*, *-vid*.

2353. **sarvavṛkṣāṇām** "of all trees". 10.26.

2354. **sarvayajñānām** "of all sacrifices". 9.24. Also see *yajña*.

2355. **sarvayoniṣu** "from all wombs; in all species; in all sources of birth". 14.4. Also see *yoni*.

---

[547] In verse 6.29, the CE reads *sarvatra samadarśanaḥ*. Divanji (p. 155, entry # 3553) lists this as a compound (*sarvatrasamadarśanaḥ*).

2356. **sarvendriyaguṇābhāsam** "appearing to have all the attributes of the sense organs; appearing to have the qualities of all the senses[548]; that which has as its reflections the attributes of all the organs of sense[549]; revealing all the senses (i.e., enabling all the senses to function)[550]". 13.14. Also see *guṇa, indriya.*

2357. **sarvendriyavivarjitam** "freed from all the senses; transcending all sense organs; devoid of senses". 13.14. Also see *indriya, sarva, vivarjita.*

2358. **śaśāṅkaḥ** "the moon; one who has the mark of a hare (*śaśa*); the rabbit-marked". 11.39; 15.6. Also see *śaśī.* [Based on seeing the shape or markings of a rabbit in the moon, similar to the "Man in the Moon".]

2359. **saśaram** "with arrow(s)". 1.47.

2360. **śaśi** "the moon; that which contains the rabbit (*śaśa*)". Also see *śaśāṅka.*

- śaśī "the moon". 10.21.
- śaśisūryanetram "having the moon and the sun as eyes". 11.19. Also see *sūrya, netra.*
- śaśisūryayoḥ "the moon and the sun". 7.8. Also see *sūrya.*

2361. **śastra** "weapon". Also see *asaṅgaśastreṇa, nānāśastrapraharaṇāḥ.*

- aśastram "devoid of weapons; unarmed". 1.46.
- śastrabhṛtām "of warriors; among those bearing weapons". 10.31.
- śastrāṇi "weapons". 2.23.
- śastrapāṇayaḥ "warriors with weapons in their hands". 1.46.
- śastrasaṁpāte "collision of the weapons; the clash of arms". 1.20.

2362. **śāstram** "scripture; doctrine; teaching; spiritual science". 15.20; 16.24. Also see *aśāstravihitam, śāstra-.*

2363. **śāstravidhānoktam** "what is prescribed in scripture; that which has been ordained by scripture". 16.24. Also see *śāstravidhim, avidhipūrvakam, śāstram, vidhānoktāḥ, vidhidṛṣṭaḥ, vidhihīnam.*

2364. **śāstravidhim** "scriptural prescription; scriptural injunction; the method prescribed by scripture". 16.23; 17.1. Also see *avidhipūrvakam, śāstram, śāstravidhānoktam, vidhānoktāḥ, vidhidṛṣṭaḥ, vidhihīnam.*

2365. **śaśvacchāntim** "everlasting peace; eternal peace". 9.31. Also see *śāśvata, sanātana, śāntiḥ.*

---

548 This is the sense consistent with Van Buitenen 1981, p. 125.

549 Divanji, p. 156, entry #3593.

550 This is the sense according to Tapasyananda, p. 342.

2366. **śāśvata** "eternal; perpetual; continuing; existing forever". Also see *aśāśvatam, śaśvacchāntim, sanātana, nitya.*

- śāśvatadharmagoptā "protector of imperishable righteousness; defender of eternal *dharma*". 11.18. Also see *dharma.*
- śāśvataḥ "eternal". 2.20.
- śāśvatāḥ "eternal". 1.43.
- śāśvatam "eternal, everlasting". 10.12; 18.56, 62.
- śāśvatasya "of the eternal". 14.27.
- śāśvate "eternal; ongoing". 8.26.
- śāśvatīḥ "many; myriads". 6.41. [Madhusūdana Sarasvati interprets this as years considered according to the standards of Brahmā, and therefore an eternally-long time by human standards.[551]]

2367. **sat** "being; what exists; existent; real; truth". 9.19; 11.37; 13.12; 17.23, 26, 27. Also see *asat, sacchabdaḥ, sadasadyonijanmasu, sadbhāve, san, santaḥ, sataḥ, sati, sattva.*

2368. **sataḥ** "the existent; what exists; the real". Also see *asataḥ, sat.*

- asataḥ "the non-existent; the unreal". 2.16.
- sataḥ "the existent; what exists; the real". 2.16.

2369. **śataśaḥ** "by hundreds; in hundreds". 11.5.

2370. **śaṭhaḥ** "a deceitful person; a wicked person; a rogue". 18.28.

2371. **sati** "in reality; in truth; being so". 18.16. [Loc. sing. neut. of the adj. *sat* used as a noun. *tatraivaṁ sati* = such being the case]

2372. **satkāramānapūjārtham** "for eliciting respect, honor, and reverence". 17.18. [*satkāra + māna + pūjā + artham*] Also see *arthaḥ, pūjā.*

2373. **śatru** "enemy".

- śatrau "toward an enemy; to an enemy". 12.18.
- śatruḥ "enemy". 16.14.
- śatrum "enemy". 3.43.
- śatrūn "enemies". 11.33.

2374. **śatrutve** "in enmity; in hostility". 6.6.

2375. **śatruvat** "like an enemy". 6.6.

---

[551] Gambhīrānanda 1998, pp. 480-1.

2376. **sattva** "*sattva* [one of the three *guṇa*-s]". Also see *āyuḥsattva-balārogyasukhaprītivivardhanāḥ*, *nityasattvasthaḥ*, *guṇa*, *sattv-*, *sāttv-*.

- sattvam "*sattva* [one of the three *guṇa*-s]". 14.5, 6, 9, 10 (3 times), 11; 17.1.
- sattvam "the *sattva* quality; goodness". 10.36. [*asmi sattvaṁ sattvavatām aham* = "I am the *sattva* quality of those possessed of *sattva.*"[552]]
- sattvāt "from *sattva* [*guṇa*]; due to *sattva*". 14.17.
- sattve "in *sattva* [*guṇa*]; in a state of *sattva*". 14.14.

2377. **sattvam** (depending on context:) "something that exists; an entity; an object; a being; existence".

- sattvam "(whatever) object; (whatever) entity; (whatever) being". 10.41. [*yad yad vibhūtimat sattvaṁ śrīmad ūrjitam eva vā*]
- sattvam "(whatever) object; (whatever) entity; (whatever) being". 13.26. [*yāvat saṁjāyate kiṁ cit sattvaṁ sthāvarajaṅgamam*]
- sattvam "(there is no such) entity". 18.40. [*sattvaṁ prakṛtijair muktaṁ yad ebhiḥ syāt tribhir guṇaiḥ*].

2378. **sattvānurūpā** "according to natural constitution of mind; in accordance with their minds[553]; after the pattern of one's own being[554]". 17.3. Also see *rūpa*, *sattva*.

2379. **sattvasamāviṣṭaḥ** "imbued with *sattva*[555]; inspired by *sattva*[556]; one who is possessed all over by the Sattvaguṇa[557]; filled with goodness[558]; man of integrity[559]". 18.10. Also see *āviṣṭa*.

2380. **sattvasaṁśuddhiḥ** "intellectual purity; purity of mind (*sattva*)[560]; purification of the heart[561]; purity of heart[562]; inner purity[563]". 16.1. Also see *śuddh-*.

---

552 Gambhīrānanda 1997, p. 423.
553 Gambhīrānanda 1997, p. 637.
554 Divanji, p. 148, entry #3409.
555 Gambhīrānanda 1997, p. 670.
556 Van Buitenen 1981, p. 139.
557 Divanji, p. 148, entry #3404.
558 Edgerton, p. 84.
559 Bolle, p. 296.
560 Gambhīrānanda 1997, p. 615; Ādidevānanda, p. 505.
561 Divanji, p. 148, entry #3405.
562 Hill, p. 243.
563 Van Buitenen 1981, p. 133.

2381. **sattvasthāḥ** "those established in *sattva* [*guṇa*]; people who conform to *sattva*[564]". 14.18. Also see *sthānam*.

2382. **sattvavatām** "of those possessed of *sattva*; of the courageous[565]". 10.36. [Gen. pl. masc. of the adj. *sattvavat*.]

2383. **sāttvika** "endowed with *sattva* [*guṇa*]; sattvic". Also see *sāttvikapriyāḥ*, *sāttvikī*.

- sāttvikaḥ 17.11; 18.9, 26.
- sāttvikāḥ 7.12; 17.4.
- sāttvikam 14.16; 17.17, 20; 18.20, 23, 37.

2384. **sāttvikapriyāḥ** "favorites of the sattvic person". 17.8. Also see *sāttvika*, *priya*.

2385. **sāttvikī** "sattvic; dominated by *sattva* [*guṇa*]". 17.2; 18.30, 33. Also see *sāttvika*.

2386. **satatam** "always; constantly; continually; all the time; forever". 3.19; 6.10; 8.14; 9.14; 12.14; 17.24; 18.57. Also see *satatayukta*.

2387. **satatayukta** "always yoked; constantly disciplined[566]; always integrated; always having self-control; always composed; always linked; ever steadfast[567]". Also see *satatam*, *yukta*.

- satatayuktāḥ "always yoked; constantly disciplined; constantly practicing; always engaged; ever steadfast". 12.1.
- satatayuktānām "always yoked; constantly disciplined; ever-attached; always connected (with me); ever dedicated (to me); ever steadfast". 10.10.

2388. **satya** "truth". Also see *asatyam*.

- satyam "truth; truthfulness". 10.4; 16.2, 7; 18.65.
- satyam "truthful". 17.15.

2389. **sātyakiḥ** "Sātyaki". 1.17. [The name of a hero fighting on the side of the Pāṇḍavas. See "Who's Who", page 9.] Also see *yuyudhānaḥ*.

2390. **saubhadraḥ** "the son of Subhadrā; Saubhadra; Abhimanyu". 1.6, 18. [Abhimanyu, the son of Arjuna and Subhadrā (Kṛṣṇa's sister).]

---

564 Gambhīrānanda 1997, p. 581.

565 Edgerton (p. 54) and Van Buitenen (1981, p. 139) both translate *'smi sattvaṁ sattvavatām aham* as "I am the courage of the courageous". Edgerton provides a note (p. 98) saying that *sattvavant* is regularly used in the sense of "courageous". He also argues that the rest of the verse deals with Kṣatriya themes.

566 Edgerton, pp. 51, 62.

567 Swarupananda, pp. 224, 276.

2391. **śaucam** "purity". 13.7; 16.3, 7; 17.14; 18.42. Also see *śuciḥ*.

2392. **saukṣmyāt** "due to subtlety". 13.32.

2393. **saumadattiḥ** "Saumadatti; the son of Somadatta; Bhūriśravas". 1.8. [Bhūriśravas was a warrior who fought on the side of the Kauravas. Somadatta was king of the Bāhīkas.

2394. **saumyam** "serene; gracious; mild; gentle". 11.51.

2395. **saumyatvam** "serenity; graciousness; an agreeable nature; mildness; gentleness". 17.16.

2396. **saumyavapuḥ** "in serene form; one who has a gentle bearing". 11.50.

2397. **śauryam** "bravery; valor". 18.43. Also see *śūrāḥ*.

2398. **savijñānam** "along with spiritual wisdom; together with understanding". 7.2. Also see *vijñāna*.

2399. **savikāram** "together with modifications; along with evolutes". 13.6. Also see *vikāra*.

2400. **savyasācin** "O masterful archer; O expert bowman". 11.33. [Literally, "One who can shoot arrows with the left hand" (indicating an ambidextrous archer).]

2401. **śayya** "couch; bed; lying; resting". See *vihāraśayyāsanabhojaneṣu* "while at play (*vihāra*), resting (*śayya*), sitting (*āsana*), or with food (*bhojana*)". 11.42.

2402. **senānīnām** "among the commanders of the army (*senā*)". 10.24. Also see *sainyasya, senayoḥ*.

2403. **senayoḥ** "of the two armies (*senā*)". 1.21, 24, 27; 2.10. Also see *sainyasya, senānīnām*.

2404. **sevate** "one serves; one waits upon; one honors; one obeys". 14.26. Also see *upasevate*.

2405. **sevayā** "by serving; by service; by attendance". 4.34. Also see *yogasevayā*.

2406. **sīdanti** "they are afflicted; they have become weak". 1.29. [√ *sad*] Also see *utsīdeyuḥ*.

2407. **siddha** "perfected one", "Adept". Also see *siddhi*.

- gandharvayakṣāsurasiddhasaṁghāḥ "groups of *gandharva*-s, *yakṣa*-s, *asura*-s, and Adepts". 11.22.
- maharṣisiddhasaṁghāḥ "groups of great Sages and Adepts". 11.21.
- siddhaḥ "an Adept; succesful". 16.14.
- siddhānāṁ "of the perfected ones; of the Adepts; among the accomplished". 7.3; 10.26.
- siddhasaṁghāḥ "assemblies of Adepts". 11.36.

2408. **siddhasaṁghāḥ** "groups of Adepts". 11.36.

2409. **siddhi** "attainment; accomplishment; fulfillment". Also see *asiddhau, naiṣkarmyasiddhim, saṁsiddhau, siddhyasiddhyoḥ.*

- siddhau "in accomplishment; in success". 4.22.
- siddhaye "toward perfection; for accomplisment". 7.3; 18.13.
- siddhiḥ "attainment; accomplishment; fulfillment". 4.12.
- siddhim "attainment; accomplishment; fulfillment". 3.4; 4.12; 12.10; 14.1; 16.23; 18.45, 46, 50.

2410. **siddhyasiddhyoḥ** "in attainment or non-attainment of a desired object". 2.48; 18.26. Also see *siddhi, asiddhau.*

2411. **śikhaṇḍī** "Śikhaṇḍī". 1.17. [Śikhaṇḍī was a warrior fighting on the Pāṇḍava side. For details see p. 9.]

2412. **śikhariṇām** "of peaks; of mountains; among mountain peaks". 10.23.

2413. **siṁhanādam** "a lion's roar; a sound like the roaring of a lion". 1.12.

2414. **śirasā** "with the head". 11.14.

2415. **śiṣya** "a disciple; a pupil".

- śiṣyaḥ "a disciple; a pupil". 2.7.
- śiṣyeṇa "by a disciple; by a pupil". 1.3.

2416. **śītoṣṇasukhaduḥkha** "cold (*śīta*) and heat (*uṣṇa*), pleasure (*sukha*) and pain (*duḥkha*)".

- śītoṣṇasukhaduḥkhadāḥ "giving heat and cold, pleasure and pain; (objects that are) producers of happiness and sorrow through cold and heat[568]". 2.14.
- śītoṣṇasukhaduḥkheṣu "in cold and heat, pleasure and pain". 6.7; 12.18.

2417. **skandaḥ** "Skanda". 10.24. [A name of Kārtikeya, commander of the army of the gods.]

2418. **sma** "definitely not". 2.3. [A particle added to the negative prohibitive particle *mā* to indicate particularly strong disapproval of something.]

2419. **smaran** "remembering; recollecting". 3.6; 8.5, 6. Also see *anusmaran.*

2420. **smarati** "one remembers; one recollects". 8.14. Also see *anusmaret.*

2421. **smṛtā** "it is remembered; it is traditionally known". 6.19.

2422. **smṛtaḥ** "remembered; traditionally known". 17.23.

2423. **smṛtam** "remembered; traditionally known". 17.20, 21; 18.38.

2424. **smṛtibhraṁśāt** "due to failure of memory; due to loss of memory". 2.63.

2425. **smṛtiḥ** "memory". 10.34; 15.15; 18.73. Also see *saṁsmṛtya.*

---

[568] Gambhīrānanda 1998, p. 86.

2426. **smṛtivibhramaḥ** "failure of memory; loss of memory". 2.63.

2427. **snigdhāḥ** "unctuous; oily". 17.8.

2428. **śocati** "grieves; worries". 12.17; 18.54. Also see √ *śuc.*

2429. **śocitum** "to grieve; to worry about". 2.26, 27, 30. Also see √ *śuc.*

2430. **soḍhum** "to endure; to put up with; to tolerate; to bear with; to prevail over; to overcome". [Inf. of √ *sah.*]

- soḍhum "to bear with (an urge); to overcome (an urge); to endure (agitation); to withstand (the force)". 5.23.
- soḍhum "please see fit (to tolerate); pray bear with me[569]; be pleased to show mercy[570]; please (be merciful)". 11.44 [*arhasi ... soḍhum.* Arjuna speaking to Kṛṣṇa.] Also see *arhasi.*

2431. **śokam** "sorrow; grief; melancholy; remorse". 2.8; 18.35. Also see √ *śuc.*

- duḥkhaśokāmayapradāḥ "promoters of misery (*duḥkha*), worries (*śoka*), and diseases (*āmaya*); those which result in discomfort, melancholy, and sickness". 17.9.
- harṣaśokānvitaḥ "filled with (*anvita*) delight (*harṣa*) and grief (*śoka*)". 18.27. Also see *anvita, harṣa.*

2432. **śokasaṁvignamānasaḥ** "with mind disturbed by melancholy (*śoka*); one whose mind is perturbed by grief". 1.47. Also see *vigna, manas, -mānasaḥ.*

2433. **soma** "Soma (a sacred plant); Soma (a beverage); the Moon". [Soma is the name of a sacred plant. Priests and participants at Vedic sacrifices drank a beverage prepared from the plant. Soma was personified as a deity. Soma is also a name for the Moon, which was believed to be the Lord of Herbs, the source of nourishing sap which it bestowed upon plants by night.]

- somaḥ "Soma; the Moon". 15.13.[571] [The moon is implied by context in this verse as the source of life-giving sap for all plants.]

---

[569] Van Buitenen 1981, p. 119.

[570] Edgerton, p. 59.

[571] Bringing out the multiple meanings of the word *soma* in verse 15.13 is a challenge for translators. Edgerton (p. 74) relies on a gloss: "And I nourish all plants, / Becoming the juicy soma (sacred plant and moon, identified)." Hill (p. 239) emphasizes a lunar function without mentioning the moon: "becoming Soma, moisture's essence, I nourish all herbs." Warrier (p. 503) has his translation summarize the commentary by Śaṅkara: "becoming the moon with its essence of sap, I foster all plants and herbs."

- somapāḥ "Soma drinkers". 9.20. [Referring to Brahmins who drink *Soma* at a Vedic sacrifice.]

2434. **śoṣayati** "it dries up". 2.23. Also see *aśoṣya.*

2435. **sparśān** "contacts; sensory objects; (lit.) an object of perception by the sense of touch". 5.27. Also see *bāhyasparśeṣu, mātrāsparśāḥ, nabhaḥspṛśam, saṁsparśa, sparśanam, spṛśan.*

2436. **sparśanam** "the sense of touch; skin". 15.9. Also see *bāhyasparśeṣu, mātrāsparśāḥ, nabhaḥspṛśam, saṁsparśa, sparśān, spṛśan.*

2437. **spṛhā** "expectation; aspiration; desire". 4.14; 14.12. Also see *niḥspṛhaḥ, vigataspṛhaḥ.*

2438. **spṛśan** "touching". 5.8. Also see *bāhyasparśeṣu, mātrāsparśāḥ, nabhaḥ-spṛśam, saṁsparśa, sparśān, sparśanam.*

2439. **śraddhā** "faith; spiritual devotion; trust; confidence". Also see *śraddadhānā.*

- aśraddhayā "without faith; with lack of faith". 17.28. Also see *aśraddadhāna.*
- śraddhā "faith". 17.2, 3.
- śraddhaḥ "faith". 17.3. [*yacchraddhaḥ* = which faith]
- śraddhām "faith". 7.21.
- śraddhāmayaḥ "made of faith". 17.3. [*śraddhā mayaḥ*]
- śraddhāvān "possessing faith; full of faith; endowed with trust". 4.39; 6.47; 18.71.
- śraddhāvantaḥ "(those) endowed with faith; believing". 3.31.
- śraddhāvirahitam "devoid of faith; (performed) without faith". 17.13. [*śraddhā virahitam*]
- śraddhayā "with faith; by faith". 7.22; 12.2; 17.17.
- śraddhayānvitāḥ "those endowed with faith; accompanied with faith; along with faith". 9.23; 17.1. Also see *anvita.* [*śraddhayā + anvitāḥ*]
- śraddhayārcitum "to worship with faith; to honor with faith". 7.21. [*śraddhayā arcitum*]
- śraddhayopetaḥ "one who has arrived at faith; one endowed with faith". 6.37. [*śraddhayā upetaḥ*]

2440. **śraddadhāna** "having faith". Also see *śraddhā.*

- aśraddadhānaḥ "one who has no faith". 4.40.
- aśraddadhānāḥ "those who have no faith". 9.3.
- śraddadhānāḥ "those who have faith; those who trust". 12.20.

2441. **sraṁsate** "it falls; it is falling down; it drops; it is slipping (from my hand)". 1.30.

2442. **śreyaḥ** "well-being, welfare, benefit; good".

- śreyaḥ "benefit; beneficial; what is good; well-being". 1.31; 2.7; 3.2, 11; 16.22. Also see *niḥśreyasakarāu.*
- niḥśreyasakarau "generating (*karau*) the highest bliss (*niḥ-śreyasa*); that which leads to final beatitude; bestowing liberation". 5.2.

2443. **śreyaḥ** "better". 2.5, 31; 3.35; 5.1; 12.12. Also see *śreṣṭhaḥ.* [Nom. sing. neut. of the comp. degree of the adj. *praśasya.*]

2444. **śreyān** "better; more beneficial". 3.35; 4.33; 18.47. Also see *śreṣṭhaḥ.* [Nom. sing. masc. of the comp. degree of the adj. *praśasya.*]

2445. **śreṣṭhaḥ** "the best [leader]; the most excellent [man]". 3.21. [Nom. sing. masc. of the superlative degree of the adj. *praśasya.*] Also see *bharataśreṣṭha, kuruśreṣṭha, śreyaḥ, śreyān.*

2446. **śrībhagavān uvāca** "the Blessed One said; the Illustrious Lord said; Kṛṣṇa said". 2.2, 11, 55; 3.3, 37; 4.1, 5; 5.2; 6.1, 35, 40; 7.1; 8.3; 9.1; 10.1, 19; 11.5, 32, 47, 52; 12.2; 13.1; 14.1, 22; 15.1; 16.1; 17.2; 18.2. Also see *bhagavan.*

2447. **śrīḥ** "beauty; prosperity". 10.34; 18.78.

2448. **śrīmat** "beautiful; glorious; splendid; prosperous". 10.41.

2449. **śrīmatām** "of the weathy; of the well-to-do; of the prosperous". 6.41.

2450. **śritāḥ** "abiding in; resorting to; given shelter to[572]; possessed of". 9.12. Also see *āśrita, saṁśritāḥ.*

2451. √ **sṛj** "to send forth". Also see *sarga, sṛṣṭam, sṛṣṭvā, asṛṣṭānnam.*

- sṛjāmi "I create; I generate; I send forth". 4.7.
- sṛjati "he creates; he generates; he sends forth". 5.14.
- utsṛjāmi "I release; I let go". 9.19.
- utsṛjya "releasing; setting aside; letting go of". 16.23; 17.1.
- visargaḥ "release (of creative force); sending forth". 8.3. Also see *sarga.*
- visṛjāmi "I send forth; I emit; I create". 9.7, 8.
- visṛjan "while releasing; while excreting". 5.9.
- visṛjya "leaving aside; throwing down". 1.47.

2452. **sṛjāmi** "I create; I generate; I send forth". 4.7. Also see √ *sṛj.*

2453. **sṛjati** "he creates; he generates; he sends forth". 5.14. Also see √ *sṛj.*

2454. **śṛṇoti** "one hears". 2.29.

---

[572] Tilak, vol. 2, p. 1048.

2455. **śṛṇu** "(you) hear!; (you) listen!". 2.39; 7.1; 10.1; 13.3; 16.6; 17.2, 7; .18.4, 19, 29, 36, 45, 64.

2456. **śṛṇuyāt** "one may listen". 18.71.

2457. **śṛṇvan** "(while) hearing". 5.8.

2458. **śṛṇvataḥ** "of hearing; of listening". 10.18.

2459. **śroṣyasi** "you will listen; you will hear". 18.58. [*na śroṣyasi* = If you don't listen]

2460. **srotasām** "of rivers; of streams; among flowing waters". 10.31.

2461. **śrotavyasya** "of that which ought to be heard; of instruction to be heard; what is supposed to be revealed[573]". 2.52.

2462. **śrotrādīnīndriyāṇi** "hearing and other sense organs; the group beginning with the sense of hearing". 4.26. Also see *indriya.*

2463. **śrotram** "the sense of hearing". 15.9.

2464. **sṛṣṭam** "created; brought forth". 4.13. Also see *asṛṣṭa,* √ *sṛj.*

2465. **sṛṣṭvā** "having sent forth; having created; having emitted". 3.10. [Indec. past participle of √ *sṛj.*] Also see *–tvā.*

2466. **sṛtī** "two paths; two ways". 8.27.

2467. √ **śru** "to hear". Also see *śṛṇ-, śro-, śrut-, sarvataḥśrutimat.*

2468. **śrutam** "heard". 18.72.

2469. **śrutasya** "of what has been heard; of those instructions already heard". 2.52.

2470. **śrutau** "(both) have been heard". 11.2.

2471. **śrutavān** "I have heard". 18.75.

2472. **śrutiparāyaṇāḥ** "true believers in what they hear[574]; intent on what they hear[575]; one who is solely devoted to, or has full faith in, hearing[576]; regarding what they have heard as the Supreme refuge[577]; devoted to the holy revelation[578]; following Vedic injunctions". 13.25. Also see *śrutivipratipannā, parāyaṇa.*

---

[573] Van Buitenen 1981, p. 79.

[574] Van Buitenen 1981, p. 125.

[575] Miller, p. 116.

[576] Divanji, p. 145, entry #3347.

[577] Sivananda, p. 345.

[578] Edgerton, pp. 67, 100 (note 16). Edgerton's "holy revelation" takes *śruti* as a reference to the Vedas, but he notes that it may mean only "what they hear" as most interpreters understand it. Minor (p. 397) notes Edgerton's translation and concludes that the passage is

2473. **śrutivipratipannā** "that which has become many-sided owing to the hearing (of various views)[579]; tossed about by the conflict of opinions[580]; perplexed by what is heard[581]; averse to traditional lore ('heard' in the Veda)[582]; bewildered by conflicting views of Revelation[583]; getting away from Vedic ritualism". 2.53. Also see *śrutiparāyaṇāḥ*.

2474. **śrutvā** "having heard; after hearing". 2.29; 11.35; 13.25. [Indec. past part. of √ *śru*.] Also see *-tvā*.

2475. **stabdha** "stubborn; obstinate; immovable; arrogant; rude".

- stabdhaḥ "". 18.28.
- stabdhāḥ "". 16.17

2476. **stenaḥ** "a thief". 3.12.

2477. **sthairyam** "steadiness; stability". 13.7. Also see *sthira*.

2478. **sthānam** "place; position; site; basic ground; preservation". 5.5; 8.28; 9.18; 18.62. Also see *antaḥsthāni, matsthāni, matsaṁsthām, prakṛtisthāni, sattvasthāḥ*.

2479. **sthāne** "rightly; appropriately". 11.36.

2480. **sthāṇuḥ** "fixed; static; motionless; immortal". 2.24.

2481. **sthāpaya** "cause (it) to stand; position (it); fix in place". 1.21.

2482. **sthāpayitvā** "having caused to stand". 1.24. [Indec. past. pass. part. of the causal form of √ *sthā-tiṣṭh*.] Also see *–tvā*.

2483. **sthāsyati** "it will remain; it will be fixed". 2.53.

2484. **sthāvarajaṅgamam** "immobile (*sthāvara*) and mobile (*jaṅgama*); inanimate (*sthāvara*) and animate (*jaṅgama*)". 13.26.

2485. **sthāvarāṇām** "among unmoving entities". 10.25.

2486. **sthira** "firm; steady; solid". Also see *asthiram, sthairyam*.

- sthiraḥ "steadfast". 6.13.
- sthirāḥ "substantial (foods); nourishing (foods)". 17.8.

---

probably not referring to the Vedas, but to teachings about spirituality more generally, probably referring to the teachings of the *BG* itself.

[579] Divanji, p. 145, entry #3348. Divanji says that here the word *śruti* does not mean the Vedas.

[580] Swarupananda, p. 60.

[581] Hill, p. 122. Hill's note 5 says that references to *śruti* here and in verses 2.52-53, "must be to the *karmakāṇḍa* of the Veda, whose teaching the *yogin* is expected to transcend."

[582] Edgerton, p. 14. Minor (pp. 81-2) notes Edgerton's interpretation of *śruti* as meaning the Vedas and compares other suggestions.

[583] Bolle, p. 33.

- sthiram "firm; steadily". 6.11; 12.9.
- sthirām "steady; stable". 6.33.

2487. **sthirabuddhiḥ** "one whose intellect has become steady; steady intellect; stabilized intellect". 5.20. Also see *sthiramatiḥ, buddhi.*

2488. **sthiramatiḥ** "one whose intellect has become steady; with steady mind". 12.19. Also *see sthirabuddhiḥ, durmatiḥ, matiḥ.*

2489. **sthita** "standing; staying". Also see *āsthita, avasthita, ākāśasthitaḥ, samupasthitam, sarvabhūtāśayasthitaḥ, sarvabhūtasthitam.*
- sthitaḥ "standing; staying; remaining; established". 5.20; 6.10, 14, 21, 22; 10.42; 18.73.
- sthitāḥ "established". 5.19.
- sthitam "established; staying; located". 5.19; 13.16; 15.10.
- sthitān "standing". 1.26.
- sthitau "(both) standing; (both) staying; both (situated)". 1.14.

2490. **sthitadhīḥ** "one well-grounded in meditation; one well-established in wisdom; one whose intellect has become steady". 2.54, 56. Also see *dhīmat, sthitaprajña.*

2491. **sthitaprajña** "steady wisdom". Also see *prajñā, sthitadhīḥ.*
- sthitaprajñaḥ "a man of steady wisdom; a man (is) of firm judgement (who...); one well-grounded in wisdom". 2.55.
- sthitaprajñasya "a person of steady wisdom; a man of firm judgement; of one well-grounded in wisdom". 2.54.

2492. **sthiti** "position; state; continued existence; permanence".
- sthitiḥ "position; state; stability". 2.72; 17.27.
- sthitim "continued existence; lasting". 6.33.

2493. **sthitvā** "staying; standing firm; fixed". 2.72.

2494. **strī** "women".
- kulastriyaḥ "women of the family". 1.41.
- strīṣu "in women; (when) women". 1.41.
- striyaḥ "women". 9.32.

2495. **stutibhiḥ** "with hymns of praise; with praises". 11.21. Also see *stuvanti, tulyanindāstutiḥ, tulyanindātmasaṁstutiḥ.*

2496. **stuvanti** "they praise". 11.21. Also see *stutibhiḥ, tulyanindāstutiḥ, tulyanindātmasaṁstutiḥ.*

2497. **śubhān** "auspicious; desirable; happy; blessed". 18.71. Also see *aśubhān.*

2498. **śubhāśubham** "auspicious or inauspicious; good and bad". 2.57. Also see *aśubhān*.

2499. **śubhāśubhaparityāgī** "one who relinquishes (judgements between) the auspicious and the inauspicious; renouncing good and evil (objects)[584]". 12.17. Also see *parityāgī, tyāgī, aśubhān*.

2500. **śubhāśubhaphalaiḥ** "by auspicious and inauspicious fruit; the fruits (results) of good or bad actions". 9.28. Also see *phala, aśubhān*.

2501. √ **śuc** "to grieve; to worry about; to be sorry for; to regret". See *anuśoc-, anvaśoc-, aśocyān, śocati, śocitum, śoka-, śucaḥ*.

2502. **śucaḥ** "grieve; worry; lament; feel sorry". 16.5; 18.66. [*mā śucaḥ* = don't worry; do not grieve; have no qualms[585]; be unconcerned[586]] Also see √ *śuc*.

2503. **śucau** "in a pure [location]; in a sacred [space]". 6.11. [*śucau deśe*] Also see *aśucau, śuciḥ*.

2504. **śuciḥ** "a person of pure character; pure". 12.16. Also see *aśuciḥ, śucīnām, śucau, śaucam*.

2505. **śucīnām** "of pure people; of holy people". 6.41. Also see *śuciḥ*.

2506. **śuddh-** "pure; purity". 12.16. See *ātmaśuddhaye, ātmaviśuddhaye, bhāvasaṁśuddhiḥ, saṁśuddhakilbiṣaḥ, sattvasaṁśuddhiḥ, viśuddhātmā, viśuddhayā*.

2507. **śūdra** "Śūdra". [The name of the fourth *varṇa* in the Indo-Āryan social order, consisting of laborers and servants.]

- śūdrāṇām "of the Śūdras". 18.41.
- śūdrāḥ "Śūdras". 9.32.
- śūdrasya "of the Śūdra". 18.44.

2508. **sudurācāraḥ** "a person of very bad conduct". 9.30, Also see *ācāra*.

2509. **sudurdarśam** "very difficult to see; very hard to get a vision of". 11.52.

2510. **sudurlabhaḥ** "very difficult to find; highly difficult to acquire". 7.19. Also see √ *labh, sulabhaḥ, durlabhataram*.

2511. **suduṣkaram** "very difficult to do". 6.34.

2512. **sughoṣamaṇipuṣpakau** "Sughoṣa and Maṇipuṣpaka". 1.16. Also see *maṇi*. [Nakula's conch was named Sughoṣa ("having a soothing sound; Sweet of

---

584 Edgerton, p. 63.

585 Van Buitenen 1981, p. 133.

586 Van Buitenen 1981, p. 143.

Tone[587]"). Sahadeva's conch was named Maṇipuṣpaka ("having gems as flowers; Jewel-Flowered[588]").] Also see *ghoṣaḥ, maṇi, puṣpa.*

2513. **suhṛ-** "friend; companion; (lit.) good heart".

- suhṛdaḥ "friends; companions". 1.27.
- suhṛdaṁ "friend, companion". 5.29.
- suhṛnmitrāryudāsīnamadhyasthadveṣyabandhuṣu "in friends, enemies, neutrals, mediators, despicable persons, and relatives". 6.9.
- suhṛt "friend, companion". 9.18.

2514. **sukham** "happiness; bliss; ease; comfort; pleasures". Also see *antaḥ-sukhaḥ, asukham, āyuḥsattvabalārogyasukhaprītivivardhanāḥ, duḥka, rājyasukhalobhena, samaduḥkhasukha, śītoṣṇasukhaduḥkha.*

- sukham "happiness". 2.66; 4.40; 5.21 (twice); 6.21, 27, 28, 32; 10.4; 13.6; 16.23; 18.36, 37, 38, 39.
- sukham "easily; happily". 5.3, 13. [Used adverbially] Also see *susukham.*
- sukhāni "happiness; bliss; ease; pleasures". 1.32, 33.
- sukhe "in happiness". 14.9.
- sukheṣu "in comforts". 2.56.

2515. **sukhaduḥkhānām** "of happiness and miseries; of pleasure and pain". 13.20.

2516. **sukhaduḥkhasaṁjñaiḥ** "designated as joy and sorrow; known as pleasure and pain". 15.5.

2517. **sukhaduḥkhe** "in happiness and unhappiness". 2.38.

2518. **sukhasaṅgena** "by contact with happiness; attachment to joy". 14.6. Also see *saṅga.*

2519. **sukhasyaikāntikasya** "of absolute happiness; of perfect bliss[589]; of unfailing bliss[590]". 14.27. [*sukhasya ekāntikasya*]

2520. **sukhena** "easily". 6.28.

2521. **sukhī** "a happy person; happy; fortunate". 5.23; 16.14.

2522. **sukhinaḥ** "happy people; happy; fortunate". 1.37; 2.32.

2523. **śuklaḥ** "bright; white". 8.24. [The waxing time of the lunar month.]

2524. **śuklakṛṣṇe** "white (*śukla*) and black (*kṛṣṇa*); bright and dark". 8.26.

2525. **sukṛtaduṣkṛte** "good and bad deeds; virtues and vices". 2.50.

2526. **sukṛtam** "a good deed; virtue;". 5.15. Also see *sukṛt-.*

---

587 Flood and Martin, p. 4.

588 Flood and Martin, p. 4.

589 Van Buitenen 1981, p. 129.

590 Warrier, p. 488.

2527. **sukṛtasya** "well-done; vituous; noble". 14.16.

2528. **sukṛtinaḥ** "doers of good deeds; those who act well; righteous people". 7.16. Also see *sukṛt-, kṛtin.*

2529. **sūkṣmatvāt** "due to subtlety". 13.15.

2530. **sulabhaḥ** "easy to get; of easy access". 8.14. Also see √ *labh, sudurlabhaḥ.*

2531. **śuni** "a dog". 5.18. Also see *śvapāke.*

2532. **suniścitam** "quite definitely; after coming to a definite conclusion; very clearly". 5.1. Also see *niścit-, viniścitaiḥ.*

2533. **sura** "a god". Also see *sura-.*

- suragaṇāḥ "the hosts of gods". 10.2. Also see *gaṇa.*
- surāṇām "of the gods; (over) the gods". 2.8.
- surasaṁghāḥ "assemblies of gods". 11.21. Also see *saṁgha.*
- surendralokam "the abode of the lord of the gods (Indra)". 9.20.

2534. **suragaṇāḥ** "the groups of gods; the hosts of gods; the throngs of gods[591]". 10.2. Also see *gaṇa.*

2535. **śūrāḥ** "brave". 1.4, 9. Also see *śauryam.*

2536. **surasaṁghāḥ** 11.21 "groups of gods".

2537. **surendralokam** 9.20 "the realm of the lord of the gods (Indra)". Also see *loka, ābrahmabhuvanāt, svargalokam.*

2538. **sūrya** "the sun".

- śaśisūryanetram "having the moon and the sun as eyes". 11.19. Also see *śaśi, netra.*
- śaśisūryayoḥ "the moon and the sun". 7.8. Also see *śaśi.*
- sūryaḥ "the sun". 15.6.
- sūryasahasrasya "of a thousand suns". 11.12. Also see *sahasr-.*

2539. **susukham** "very easily". 9.2. Also see *sukham.*

2540. **sūtaputraḥ** "Karṇa; son (*putra*) of a charioteer (*sūta*)". 11.26. Also see *Karṇa.*

2541. **sūtre** "on a thread". 7.7.

2542. **suvirūḍhamūlam** "well-grown (*su-virūḍha*) root (*mūla*); well rooted; firmly rooted; with its root firmly grounded; having its roots firmly fixed". 15.3. Also see *mūla.*

2543. **sūyate** "it produces; it creates; it gives birth to". 9.10. [√ *sū*]

2544. **svabāndhavān** "own kinsmen; own relatives". 1.37. [A variant reading for *sabāndhavān, q.v.*].

---

591 Edgerton, p. 50.

2545. **svabhāvaḥ** "own nature; one's innate nature; inherent nature; natural tendency". 5.14; 8.3. Also see *kārpaṇyadoṣopahatasvabhāvaḥ, svabhāva-.*

2546. **svabhāvaja** "arising out of one's inherent nature; born of innate nature".

- svabhāvajā "born of innate nature". 17.2.
- svabhāvajam "arising out of (their own) inherent nature". 18.42, 43, 44 (twice).
- svabhāvajena "due to (your own) inherent nature". 18.60.

2547. **svabhāvaniyatam** "determined by (one's own) innate nature". 18.47. Also see *niyatam.*

2548. **svabhāvaprabhavaiḥ** "arising out of their innate nature; born of their own nature". 18.41. Also see *prabhava.*

2549. **svacakṣuṣā** "with your own eye". 11.8. Also see *cakṣu.*

2550. **svadhā** "an oblation of food; oblation to the ancestors". 9.16.

2551. **svadharma** "your own duty; duties appropriate to oneself; your prescribed duty; one's own nature; your own path". Also see *dharma, paradharma.*

- svadharmaḥ "your own duty". 3.35; 18.47,
- svadharmam "your own duty". 2.31, 33.
- svadharme "in one's own duty". 3.35.

2552. **svādhyāya** "Vedic study; study on one's own". Also see *vedayajñādhyayanaiḥ.*

- svādhyāyābhyasanam "continued repetitive practice of chanting sacred scriptures; (daily) Vedic recitation; the personal practice of Vedic study". 17.15. Also see *abhyāsa.*
- svādhyāyaḥ "Vedic study". 16.1.
- svādhyāyajñānayajñāḥ "those whose sacrifices consist of Vedic study and the pursuit of knowledge" 4.28.

2553. **svajana** "our own people; our own kinfolk; our kinsmen". Also see *sabāndhavān, prajanaḥ, saṁjanayan.*

- svajanam "our own people". 1.31, 37, 45.
- svajanān "our own people". 1.28.

2554. **svakam** "(his) own". 11.50.

2555. **svakarma** "one's own action".[592] Also see *karma*.

- svakarmanirataḥ "enjoying one's own (appropriate) work; rejoicing in his proper work[593]; content with one's own duty; delighting in one's own special action[594]; engaged in one's own action". 18.45.
- svakarmaṇā "with one's own (appropriate) actions; with one's own duties; by (dedicating) the work that is proper for him". 18.46.

2556. **svam** "(one's) own". 6.13.

2557. **svām** "(my) own". 4.6; 9.8.

2558. **śvapāke** "on a dog-cooker; upon one who eats dog meat; on an outcaste". 5.18. [Term for a group of persons of very low social status.] Also see *śuni*.

2559. **svapan** "sleeping.". 5.8. Also see *svapna*.

2560. **svapna** "sleep". Also see *svapan, nidrā*.

- atisvapnaśīlasya "one who sleeps too much". 6.16.
- svapnam "sleep". 18.35.
- yuktasvapnāvabodhasya "one who regulates one's periods of sleep and waking; a person with balance in sleeping and wakefulness". 6.17.

2561. **svalpam** "very little". 2.40. Also see *alpam*.

2562. **svanuṣṭhitāt** "well-performed". 3.35; 18.47.

2563. **svargadvāram** "gateway to heaven". 2.32. Also see *dvāram*.

2564. **svargalokam** "the world of heaven". 9.21. Also see *loka, ābrahmabhuvanāt, surendralokam*.

2565. **svargam** "heaven". 2.37. Also see *asvargyam*.

2566. **svargaparāḥ** "those who are intent on attainment of heaven; running after heaven". 2.43. Also see *-para*.

2567. **svargatim** "attainment of heaven; going to heaven". 9.20. Also see *gati*.

2568. **śvasan** "breathing". 5.8.

2569. **svasthaḥ** "established in one's own self; self-composed; at ease". 14.24.

2570. **svasti** "Hail![595]; may it be well[596]; let there be prosperity[597]". 11.21. [A benedictory indec. particle expressing auspicious well-wishes.]

---

[592] The saying "tend your own cows" comes to mind in regard to *svakarma*. The sense of that saying is similar to "mind your own business".

[593] Zaehner, 394.

[594] Edgerton, p. 88.

[595] Van Buitenen 1981, p. 115.

[596] Gambhīrānanda 1997, p. 442.

[597] Warrier, p. 358.

2571. **śvaśura** "a father-in-law".

- śvaśurān "fathers-in-law". 1.27.
- śvaśurāḥ "fathers-in-law". 1.34.

2572. **svasyāḥ** "of one's own". 3.33.

2573. **svayā** "by one's own". 7.20. [*prakṛtyā niyatāḥ svayā* = led by their own nature]

2574. **svayam** "personally".

- svayam "oneself; himself". 4.38; 18.75.
- svayam "yourself". 10.13, 15.

2575. **sve** "in (one's) own". 18.45 (twice).

2576. **svena** "with (your) own". 18.60.

2577. **śvetaiḥ** "by white (horses)". 1.14.

2578. **syālāḥ** "brothers-in-law; a wife's brothers". 1.34.[598]

2579. **syandane** "in a chariot". 1.14.

2580. **syām** "I would be; I may be". 3.24; 18.70. [√ *as*]

2581. **syāma** "we would be; we may be; could we be". 1.37. [√ *as*]

2582. **syāt** "it would be; it may be". 1.36; 2.7; 3.17; 10.39; 11.12; 15.20; 18.40. [√ *as*]

2583. **syuḥ** "they would be; they could be; they may be". 9.32. [√ *as*]

T

ट् = Ṭ. त् = T. ठ् = Ṭh. थ् = Th.

2584. **tadā** "then; in that case". 1.2, 21; 2.52, 53, 55; 4.7; 6.4, 18; 11.13; 13.30; 14.11, 14.

2585. **tadanantaram** "thereafter; after that". 18.55. Also see *anantaram, antaram.*

2586. **tadartham** "for the sake of that; with that object". 3.9. Also see *arthaḥ, tadarthīyam.*

2587. **tadarthīyam** "with that end in view". 17.27. Also see *arthaḥ, tadartham.*

2588. **tadātmānaḥ** "those who have identified themselves with that; whose self is that; at one with that; with the self directed toward that". 5.17. Also see *ātman.*

---

[598] The Critical Edition reads *syālāḥ*. Vulgate readings include *śyālāḥ*, with same meaning.

2589. **tadbhāvabhāvitaḥ** "transformed into that state of being[599]; one who is actuated by the sentiment of identity with it[600]; colored by that image". 8.6. [*smaran bhāvam ... sadā tadbhāvabhāvitaḥ* = "a person always becomes whatever being he thinks of"[601]] Also see *bhāva, bhāvita.*

2590. **tadbuddhayaḥ** "with intellect directed toward that; one who is thinking of that object alone[602]". 5.17.

2591. **tadvat** "like that; likewise". 2.70.

2592. **tadvidaḥ** "those who know this". 13.1. Also see *-vid.*

2593. **taiḥ** "by these; by those; by them". 3.12; 5.19; 7.20 (twice).

2594. **tam** "that; him; to him". 2.1, 10; 4.19; 6.2, 23, 43; 7.20 (twice); 8.6 (twice), 10, 21, 23; 9.21; 10.10; 13.1; 15.1, 4; 17.12; 18.46, 62.

2595. **tām** "that". 7.21; 17.2.

2596. **tamas** "the *guṇa* of *tamas*; darkness; sloth". [Sometimes used as a technical term as one of the three *guṇa*-s, and at other times in a general sense as "darkness" or "sloth".]

- tamaḥ
    - ajñānajaṁ tamaḥ "the darkness arising from ignorance". 10.11. [Used in a simile of light driving away darkness.]
    - "the *guṇa* of *tamas*" 14.5, 8, 9, 10 (three times); 17.1.
    - tamodvāraiḥ "gateway to darkness; the door to the state of *tamas*". 16.22.
- tamasā (*tamasāvṛtā*) "covered by *tamas*, slothful". 18.32. Also see *āvṛta.*
- tamasaḥ
    - tamasaḥ parastāt "located beyond darkness". 8.9.
    - tamasaḥ param "beyond darkness". 13.17.
    - ajñānaṁ tamasaḥ phalam "the fruit of *tamas* is ignorance". 14.16.
    - pramādamohau tamaso bhavato 'jñānam eva ca "negligence, delusion, and ignorance arise from *tamas*". 14.17.
- tamasi "in the *guṇa* of *tamas*". 14.13, 15.

2597. **tāmasa** "having the characteristic of *tamas*".

- tāmasaḥ 18.7, 28.
- tāmasāḥ 7.12; 14.18; 17.4.

---

[599] Sargeant, p. 354.

[600] Divanji, p. 63, entry #1407.

[601] Van Buitenen 1981, p. 101.

[602] Divanji, p. 62, entry #1406.

- tāmasam 17.13, 19, 22; 18.22, 25, 39.
- tāmasapriyam "that which is liked by a person characterized by *tamas*". 17.10. Also see *priya*.
- tāmasī 17.2; 18.32, 35.

2598. **tamodvāraiḥ** "gateway to darkness; the door to the state of *tamas*". 16.22. Also see *tamas, dvāram*.

2599. **tāni** "those; these; them". 2.61; 4.5; 9.7, 9; 18.19.

2600. **tān** "those; these; them". 1.7 (twice), 27; 2.14; 3.29, 32; 4.11, 32; 7.12, 22; 16.19; 17.6.

2601. **tanniṣṭhāḥ** "those who have faith in it; well-established in that; founded on it[603]; whose steadfastness is in that[604]; deeply devoted to Him[605]". 5.17. Also see *niṣṭhā*.

2602. **tanum** "the body; outward form". 7.21; 9.11.

2603. √ **tap** "to shine; to blaze, to give out heat; to suffer pain; to hurt; to mortify the body; to undergo penance". Also see *paraṁtapa, pratapanti, pratāpavān, tapas-, tapo-*.

2604. **tapāmi** "I shine; I give heat". 9.19.

2605. **tapantam** "heating; burning". 11.19.

2606. **tapas** "aceticism; spiritual austerity; spiritual exertion; penance; heating; burning". Also see *atapaskāya, jñānatapasā, tap-, yajñadānatapaḥkarma, yajñadānatapaḥkriyāḥ, yajñatapasām, yajñatapaḥkriyāḥ*.

- tapaḥ "austerity; *tapas*". 7.9; 10.5; 16.1; 17.5, 7, 14, 15, 16, 17, 18, 19, 28; 18.5, 42.
- tapaḥsu "in austerities; in acts of *tapas*". 8.28.
- tapasā "by austerity; by *tapas*". 11.53.
- tapasi "in austerity; in *tapas*". 17.27.

2607. **tapasvibhyaḥ** "(superior to) those who practice austerities". 6.46.

2608. **tapasviṣu** "in ascetics". 7.9. [*tapaś cāsmi tapasviṣu* = I am the austerity in ascetics]

2609. **tapasyasi** "you practice austerity; you undergo penance". 9.27.

2610. **tapobhiḥ** "by austerities; by *tapas*". 11.48.

---

[603] Van Buitenen 1981, p. 91.

[604] Swarupananda, p. 130.

[605] Tapasyananda, p. 154.

2611. **tapoyajñāḥ** "those who offer sacrifice in the form of austerities; offering performance of austerities". 4.28. Also see *tapas, yajña*.

2612. **taptam** "suffered; undergone; practiced". 17.17, 28.

2613. **tapyante** "they suffer; they endure; they undergo; they practice". 17.5.

2614. **taranti** "they cross (over)". 7.14. Also see √ *tṛ*.

2615. **tariṣyasi** "you will cross over". 18.58. Also see √ *tṛ*.

2616. **tāsām** "of them; their". 14.4.

2617. **tasmāt** "from that; therefore". 1.37; 2.18, 25, 27, 30, 37, 50, 68; 3.15, 19, 41; 4.15, 42; 5.19; 6.46; 8.7, 20, 27; 11.33, 44; 16.21, 24; 17.24; 18.69 (twice).

2618. **tasmin** "in that". 14.3.

2619. **tasya** "of that; of him; his". 1.12; 2.57, 58, 61, 68; 3.17, 18; 4.13; 6.3, 6, 30, 34, 40; 7.21 (twice), 22[606]; 8.14; 11.12; 15.2; 18.7, 15. [For 7.21, *tasya tasya* = "of each one of them". For 7.22, see footnote on variant reading *tasyāḥ*.]

2620. **tasyāḥ** "of that". 7.22.[607]

2621. **tasyām** "in that". 2.69.

2622. **tat** "that". 1.10, 46; 2.7, 17, 57 (twice), 67; 3.1 ("then"), 2, 21 (three times); 4.16, 34, 38; 5.1, 5, 16; 6.21; 7.1, 23, 29; 8.1, 6, 11, 21, 28; 9.26, 27; 10.39 (twice), 41 (twice); 11.4, 42, 45, 49; 13.2, 3 (twice), 12 (twice), 13, 15 (twice), 16, 17, 26; 14.7, 8; 15.4, 5, 6 (twice), 12; 17.17, 18, 19, 20, 21, 22, 23, 25, 28; 18.5, 20, 21, 22, 23, 24, 25, 37 (twice), 38 (twice), 39, 40, 45, 60, 77.

2623. **tāta** "O dear one; O my son; dear boy". 6.40. [A term of affection between seniors and juniors.]

2624. **tataḥ** "then; from that; than that; therefore; thereafter". 1.13, 14; 2.33, 36, 38; 6.22, 26 (twice), 43, 45; 7.22; 11.4, 9, 14, 40; 12.9, 11; 13.28, 30; 14.3; 15.4; 16.20, 22; 18.55, 64. [Sense depends on context.]

2625. **tatam** "pervaded". 2.17; 8.22; 9.4; 11.38; 18.46.

2626. **tathā** "so; also; in that way; in the same manner; likewise; thus". 1.8, 26, 34 (twice); 2.1, 13, 22, 26, 29; 3.25, 38; 4.11, 28, 29, 37; 5.24; 6.7; 7.6; 8.25; 9.6, 32, 33; 10.6, 13, 35; 11.6, 15, 23, 26, 28, 29, 34, 46, 50; 12.18; 13.18, 29, 32, 33; 14.10, 15; 15.3; 16.21; 17.7, 26; 18.14, 50, 63. [Often paired with *yathā* to make similes or comparisons.] Also see *tathaiva, tathāpi*.

2627. **tathaiva** "even thus, as well; in that very way; also". 1.8, 34; 2.29; 4.11; 11.29, 46. [*tathā* + *eva*]

---

[606] For the word *tasya* in 7.22a, see the footnote on the entry for the word *rādhanam*.

[607] For the word *tasyāḥ* in 7.22a, see the footnote on the entry for the word *rādhanam*.

2628. **tathāpi** "thus yet; still". 2.26. [*tathā + api*]

2629. **tathāsaktaḥ** "likewise detached". 3.25. [*tathā asaktaḥ*]

2630. **tatpara** "that supreme". Also see *para.*

- tatparaḥ "devoted to that". 4.39.
- tatparam "that supreme; that which is beyond". 5.16; 11.37.

2631. **tatparāyaṇāḥ** "those engaged in pursuit of that". 5.17. Also see *parāyaṇa.*

2632. **tatprasādāt** "through his grace". 18.62. Also see *prasad.*

2633. **tatra** "there; in that matter; in regard to these". 1.26; 2.13, 28; 6.12, 43; 8.18, 24, 25; 11.13; 14.6; 18.4, 16, 78.

2634. **tatsamakṣam** "so in company; in the presence of others". 11.42.

2635. **tattva** "that-ness; reality; truth". Also see *atattvārthavat, tattvadarśin, tattvajñānārthadarśanam, tattvataḥ, tattvavid.*

- tattvam "the truth; the essence; the true nature; the real meaning". 18.1.
- tattvena "in reality; in essence; essentially". 9.24 (*na tu mām abhijānanti tattvenātaḥ* = "but they do not know me as I really am" *or* "though they do not really recognize me"[608]); 11.54 (*tattvena praveṣṭum* = essentially joined with; "joined in essence"[609]).

2636. **tattvadarśin** "one who sees the truth; one who perceives the essence (of reality)". Also see *tattva, tattvavid.*

- tattvadarśibhiḥ "by the seers of truth[610]; by enlightened persons; by those who have realized the essence (of reality); those who see the principles[611]". 2.16.
- tattvadarśinaḥ "those who have realized the truth[612]; enlightened seers; enlightened sages; those who have realized the essence (of reality)". 4.34.

---

[608] Van Buitenen 1981, p. 107.

[609] In the line *jñātuṁ draṣṭuṁ ca tattvena praveṣṭum,* Van Buitenen (1981, p. 121) treats the three verbs as completely separate ideas, translating them as "Only through exclusive *bhakti* can I be seen thus, Arjuna, and known as I really am, and entered into", which connects *tattvena* with *jñātum.* Gambhīrānanda (1997, p. 526) connects *tattvena* with the two items *jñātuṁ draṣṭuṁ ca* rather than with *praveṣṭum,* e.g., "able to be known and seen in reality, and also entered into". Bolle (1979, pp. 145, 299) also parses the phrase *jñātuṁ draṣṭuṁ ca tattvena* as "I can be known and seen … as I really am".

[610] Gambhīrānanda 1997, p. 54.

[611] Van Buitenen 1981, p. 75.

[612] Gambhīrānanda 1997, p. 222.

2637. **tattvajñānārthadarśanam** "seeing the object to be achieved by knowledge of the truth; awareness of the goal of true knowledge; perception of the object of the knowledge of reality". 13.11. [Liberation is the real object according to Śaṅkara.[613]] Also see *arthaḥ, tattva, jñāna.*

2638. **tattvataḥ** "really; truly; in essence; in fact; as things really are; a thing in its essence *or* the essential truth; a thing as it really is". [Indec. adv.] Also see *tattvataḥ* used as a noun.

- tattvataḥ "truly; in truth; really; in essence; as in fact it is[614]". 4.9. [*evaṁ yo vetti tattvataḥ* = "He who thus knows truly"[615]]
- tattvataḥ "truly; in truth; really; in reality". 7.3. [*māṁ vetti tattvataḥ* = "knows me as I really am" *or* "really knows me"[616]]
- tattvataḥ "truly; in truth; really; in reality". [*yo vetti tattvataḥ* = "one who knows truly"] 10.7.
- tattvataḥ "truly; in truth; really; in reality". 18.55 (twice).

2639. **tattvataḥ** "(away) from reality; (away) from truth". 6.21 (*vetti yatra na caivāyaṁ sthitaś calati* = "established wherein he never moves from the Reality[617]"). [The neut. noun *tattva* with the suffix *–tas*, having the sense of the abl. case termination.] Also see *tattvataḥ* used as an indec. adv.

2640. **tattvavid** "a knower of truth; the knower of reality[618]; one who knows the essential nature; a knower of the facts[619]; he who knows the principles[620]". 3.28; 5.8. Also see *tattva, tattvadarśin.* Also see suffix *-vid.*

2641. **tau** "(both of) those; (both of) them; (both of) these two". 2.19; 3.34.

2642. **tava** "of you; your". 1.3; 2.36 (twice); 4.5; 10.42; 11.15, 16, 20, 28, 29, 30, 31, 36, 41, 47, 51; 18.73.

2643. **tāvāt** "that much; to that extent". 2.46.

2644. **tayā** "by that; thereby". 2.44; 7.22.

2645. **tayoḥ** "of the two; of both". 3.34; 5.2.

---

[613] Gambhīrānanda 1997, p. 526.

[614] Van Buitenen 1981, p. 87.

[615] Gambhīrānanda 1997, p. 181.

[616] Van Buitenen 1981, p. 99.

[617] Sivananda, p. 140.

[618] Gambhīrānanda 1997, p. 247.

[619] Gambhīrānanda 1997, p. 160.

[620] Van Buitenen 1981, pp. 84-5.

2646. **te** "they; to you; your; by you". [A pronoun with multiple meanings.]

- te "they; they (all); those; these". 1.33; 2.6; 3.11, 13, 31; 5.19, 22; 7.12, 14, 28, 29, 30; 8.17; 9.20, 21, 23, 24, 29, 32; 10.10; 12.2, 4, 20; 13.25, 34; 16.8, 17. [Nom. pl. masc. of the pronoun *tad.*]
- te "to you; for you". 1.7; 2.39; 4.3, 16, 34; 7.2; 8.11; 9.1; 10.1, 19; 11.8, 31, 37, 39 (twice), 40 (twice), 49; 18.63, 65. [Dat. sing. of the pronoun *yuṣmad.*]
- te "of you; your". 2.7, 34, 47 (twice), 52, 53; 3.1, 8; 10.14; 11.3, 23, 25, 27; 16.24; 18.59, 64, 72. [Gen. sing. of the pronoun *yuṣmad.*]
- te "by you". 18.67. [Used with sense of inst. sing.]

2647. **tejas** "splendor; resplendence; brilliance; lustre; glow; glory; light; spiritual or physical radiance; heroic prowess; might; strength of character".

- svatejasā "with (your) own splendor; with (your) own brilliance". 11.19.
- tejaḥ "light; brilliance; splendor". 7.9, 10; 10.36; 15.12 (twice); 16.3; 18.43.
- tejasvinām "of the brilliant; of the splendid". 7.10; 10.36. [*tejasvin* = one who is brave, powerful, or brilliant. *tejas tejasvinām* = the glory of the glorious, the might of the mighty, the splendor of the splendid, etc.]
- tejobhir "with (hot) brilliance; with radiance; with glory". 11.30.
- tejomayam "glorious; self-resplendent; full of light; completely pervaded by lustre; abounding in radiance". 11.47.
- tejoṁśasaṁbhavam "born from a fraction (*aṁśa*) of (My) light; born from a part of my power; arising from a portion of (My) splendor". 10.41. Also see *aṁśa, saṁbhava.*
- tejorāśiṁ "a mass of brilliance; a heap of glory; radiant on all sides". 11.17.

2648. **tena** "by that; by this; by him". 3.38; 4.24; 5.15; 6.44; 11.1, 46; 17.23; 18.70.

2649. **teṣām** "of those; of them; their". 5.16; 7.17, 23; 9.22; 10.10, 11; 12.1, 5, 7; 17.1, 7.

2650. **teṣu** "in them; in those". 2.62; 5.22; 7.12; 9.4, 9, 29; 16.7.

2651. **tīkṣṇa** "sharp, pungent[621]". 17.9. See *kaṭvamlalavaṇātyuṣṇatīkṣṇarūkṣa-vidāhinaḥ.*

2652. **tiṣṭh-** "stand; remain firm; abide". Also see *anutiṣṭhanti, ātiṣṭha, avatiṣṭh-, pratiṣṭh-, uttiṣṭha.*

- tiṣṭhantam "abiding". 13.27.
- tiṣṭhanti "they stay; they dwell". 14.18.

---

[621] Rāmānuja's commentary (Ādidevānanda, p. 530) notes that foods may be *tīkṣṇa* (sharp) due to extremes of temperature, either very hot or very cold.

- tiṣṭhasi "you stand; you abide; you exist". 10.16.
- tiṣṭhati "one stays; one resides; one remains". 3.5; 13.13; 18.61.

2653. **titikṣasva** "tolerate; endure with courage". 2.14.

2654. **toyam** "water". 9.26.

2655. √ **tṛ** "to cross".

- atitaranti "they cross beyond". 13.25. [*ati* + √ *tṛ*]
- saṁtariṣyasi "you will cross over". 4.36. [*saṁ* + √ *tṛ*]
- taranti "they cross (over)". 7.14.
- tariṣyasi "you will cross over". 18.58.
- vyatitariṣyati "it will cross over". 2.52. [*vi* + *ati* + √ *tṛ*]

2656. **traiguṇa** "the three *guṇa*-s".

- nistraiguṇyaḥ "one who is free from the three *guṇa*-s; one who transcends the three *guṇa*-s". 2.45.
- traiguṇyaviṣayā "the spheres of action of the three *guṇa*-s; their subject matter pertains to the three *guṇa*-s.". 2.45. Also see *viṣaya*. [*traiguṇyaviṣayā vedā* = the Vedas have the three *guṇa*-s as their subject matter]

2657. **trailokyarājyasya** "for the sake of dominion over the three worlds; for the sovereignty of the three worlds; of the kingdom of the three worlds". 1.35. Also see *loka, lokatraya, rājya*.

2658. **traividyāḥ** "those versed in the three Vedas; those conversant with the Vedic rituals". 9.20. Also see *trayīdharmam, vidyā*.

2659. **trayam** "triad; a group of three" 16.21. Also see *lokatraya*.

2660. **trāyate** "it protects; it guards against". 2.40.

2661. **trayīdharmam** "the Vedic ritual; the course of duties prescribed by the three Vedas[622]; the Law of the Vedas[623]". 9.21. Also see *dharma, traividyā*.

2662. **tribhiḥ** "by three". 7.13; 16.22; 18.40. [Referring to the three *guṇa*-s.]

2663. **tridhā** "in three ways; of three types". 18.19.

2664. **trīn** "the three". 14.20, 21 (twice). [Referring to the three *guṇa*-s.]

2665. **triṣu** "in the three (worlds)". 3.22.

2666. **trividhā** "threefold; having three types". Also see *-vidhā*.

- trividhā "threefold". 17.2; 18.18.
- trividhaḥ "threefold". 17.7, 23; 18.4, 18.

---

[622] Divanji, pp. 66-7, entry #1499.

[623] Van Buitenen 1981, p. 107.

- trividham "threefold". 16.21; 17.17; 18.12, 29, 36.

2667. **tṛptiḥ** "satisfaction; satiation". 10.18. Also see *ātmatṛptaḥ, nityatṛptaḥ, jñānavijñānatṛptātmā.*

2668. **tṛṣṇāsaṅgasamudbhavam** "the source (*samudbhavam*) of craving (*tṛṣṇā*) and passion (*āsaṅga*)[624]; born of (*samudbhavam*) hankering (*tṛṣṇā*) and attachment (*āsaṅga*)[625]; arising from (*samudbhavam*) thirst (*tṛṣṇā*) and attachment (*saṅga*)[626]; that which results from greed and attachment[627]". 14.7. Also see *-udbhava.*

2669. **tu** "but; however; also; indeed". 1.2, 7, 10; 2.5, 12, 14, 16, 17, 39, 64; 3.7, 13, 17, 28, 32, 42 (twice); 5.2, 6, 14, 16; 6.6, 16, 35, 36, 45; 7.5, 12, 18, 23, 26, 28; 8.16, 20, 22, 23; 9.1, 13, 24, 29; 10.40; 11.8, 54; 12.3, 6, 20; 13.25; 14.8, 9, 14, 16; 15.17; 17.1, 7, 12, 21; 18.6, 7, 11, 12, 16, 21, 22, 24, 34, 36.

2670. **tulyaḥ** "alike; similar; the same; equal". 14.25 (twice). Also see *sama.*

2671. **tulyanindāstutiḥ** "alike in criticism (*nindā*) or praise (*stutis*); indifferent to blame or praise[628]; one who looks upon censure and eulogy with an equal eye[629]". 12.19. Also see *tulyanindātmasaṁstutiḥ*, √ *nind, stutibhiḥ, stuvanti.*

2672. **tulyanindātmasaṁstutiḥ** "alike in criticism (*nindā*) or praise (*stuti*); one who looks upon censure and eulogy with an equal eye[630]". 14.24. Also see *ātman, tulyanindāstutiḥ*, √ *nind, stutibhiḥ, stuvanti.*

---

[624] Warrier, p. 474. Śaṅkara's commentary reads *āsaṅga* explicitly (तृष्णाऽऽसङ्गसमुद्भवं). Warrier's translation says that *rajas* is the source of *tṛṣṇā* and *āsaṅga,* not vice versa. That is the way Tilak (vol. 2, p. 1126) understands it, translating as, "Desire and Attachment arise from this constituent."

[625] Gambhīrānanda (1997, p. 574) parses the compound as *tṛṣṇā-āsaṅga-samudbhavam.* This word division is consistent with Śaṅkara's commentary, which reads *āsaṅga* explicitly (see Warrier, p. 474, तृष्णाऽऽसङ्गसमुद्भवं). Madhusūdana's commentary follows Śaṅkara in reading *āsaṅga* (Gambhīrānanda 1998, p. 757).

[626] Sargeant (p. 569) parses the compound as *tṛṣṇā-saṅga-samudbhavam.* This word division is consistent with Rāmānuja's commentary, which defines *saṅga* explicitly (see Ādidevānanda, p. 466).

[627] Divanji, p. 65, entry #1469.

[628] Sargeant, p. 526.

[629] Divanji, p. 65, entry #1460.

[630] Divanji, p. 65, entry #1459.

2673. **tulyapriyāpriyaḥ** "who maintains equality with both the favored (*priya*) and the unfavored (*apriya*); one in whose eyes things liked and not liked are equal[631]". 14.24. Also see *priya.*

2674. **tumula** "tumultuous". 1.13, 19.

2675. **tūṣṇīm** "calm; quiet". 2.9.

2676. **tuṣṭaḥ** "contented; satisfied". 2.55. Also see *saṁtuṣṭaḥ.*

2677. **tuṣṭiḥ** "contentment; satisfaction". 10.5.

2678. **tuṣyanti** "they are contented". 10.9.

2679. **tuṣyati** "one is contented". 6.20.

2680. **tvā** "to you; you". 2.2; 11.21[632]; 18.66.

2681. **tvadanyaḥ** "other than you". 6.39. [*tvad anyaḥ*]

2682. **tvadanyena** "by other than you". 11.47, 48. [*tvad anyena*]

2683. **tvak** "skin". 1.30.

2684. **tvam** "you". 2.11, 12, 26, 27, 30, 33, 35; 3.8, 41; 4.4, 5, 15; 10.15, 16, 41; 11.3, 4, 18 (four times), 33, 34, 37, 38 (twice), 39, 40, 43, 49; 18.58.

2685. **tvām** "you". 2.7 (twice), 35; 10.13, 17; 11.16, 17, 19, 21 (twice[633]), 22, 24, 26, 32, 42, 44, 46; 12.1; 18.59.

2686. **tvaramāṇāḥ** "rushing; making haste". 11.27.

2687. **tvatprasādāt** "through your grace; due to your favor; from your kindness". 18.73. Also see *prasad.*

2688. **tvatsamaḥ** "equal to you; like you". 11.43. Also see *sama.*

2689. **tvattaḥ** "from you". 11.2.

2690. **tvayā** "by you". 6.33; 11.1, 20, 38; 18.72.

2691. **tvayi** "in you". 2.3.

2692. **tyāga** "renunciation; relinquishment; abandonment". Also see *parityāgaḥ, parityāgī, parityajya, tyāgaphalam, √ tyaj.*

- tyāgaḥ "renunciation; relinquishment". 16.2; 18.4, 9.
- tyāgam "renunciation; relinquishment". 18.2, 8.
- tyāgasya "of renunciation; of relinquishment". 18.1.
- tyāgāt "from renunciation; from relinquishment". 12.12.

---

[631] Divanji, p. 65, entry #1461.

[632] In verse 11.21a, the Critical Edition reads *amī hi tvā surasaṁghā.* Vulgate editions read *amī hi tvāṁ surasaṁghā.* If the Critical Edition reading *tvā* is followed, there is only one instance of *tvām* in verse 11.21. The issue of how to interpret *tvā* in verse 11.21 (with sense *tvām*) is noted in Gambhīrānanda 1998, p. 656.

[633] For a possible two instances of *tvāṁ* in verse 11.21, see the note on *tvā* for verse 11.21.

- tyāge "in renunciation; in relinquishment". 18.4.

Compounds:

- karmaphalatyāgaḥ "renunciation of the fruit of action". 12.12. Also see *karmaphala.*
- sarvakarmaphalatyāgam "renunciation of the fruit of all action". 12.11; 18.2. Also see *karmaphala.*

2693. **tyāgaphalam** "the fruit of abandonment; the result of renunciation". 18.8.

2694. **tyāgī** "the renouncer; one who has renounced; the man of renunciation". 18.10, 11.

Compounds:

- karmaphalatyāgī "one who renounces the fruit of action". 18.11.
- sarvārambhaparityāgī "one renouncing all undertakings; relinquishing all (selfish) enterprises; one who abandons all (selfish) initiatives". 12.16; 14.25.
- śubhāśubhaparityāgī "one who relinquishes (judgements between) the auspicious and the inauspicious; renouncing good and evil (objects)[634]". 12.17. Also see *parityāgī.*

2695. √ **tyaj** "to renounce; to relinquish; to abandon". See *atyāginām, parityajya, tyāg-, tyaj-, tyāj-, tyakt-.*

2696. **tyajan** "having abandoned; having relinquished". 8.13.

2697. **tyajati** "one leaves aside; one renounces". 8.6.

2698. **tyajet** "one should abandon; one should relinquish; one should give up". 16.21; 18.8, 48.

2699. **tyājyam** "should be relinquished; should be abandoned". 18.3 (twice), 5.

2700. **tyaktajīvitāḥ** "who have given up their lives; who have sacrificed their lives; (many) surrendering life". 1.9. Also see √ *jīv.*

2701. **tyaktasarvaparigrahaḥ** "one who has given up accepting all kinds of gifts; one who has given up all need to possess; one who has renounced all possessions". 4.21. Also see *parigraha, sarva.*

2702. **tyaktum** "to renounce; to abandon". 18.11.

2703. **tyaktvā** "having abandoned; after abandoning; having given up; after giving up; after letting go; after leaving aside". 1.33; 2.3, 48, 51; 4.9, 20; 5.10, 11, 12; 6.24; 18.6, 9, 51. Also see *–tvā.*

---

[634] Edgerton, p. 63.

U

उ = U. ऊ = Ū.

2704. **ubhau** "both". 2.19; 5.2; 13.19.

2705. **ubhayavibhraṣṭaḥ** "fallen from both; a failure either way[635]". 6.38.

2706. **ubhayoḥ** "of both". 1.21, 24, 27; 2.10, 16; 5.4.

2707. **ubhe** "both". 2.50.

2708. **uccaiḥ** "loudly, at a high pitch". 1.12. [Used in the compound *vinadyoccaiḥ* = *vinadya* + *uccaiḥ*) "roaring loudly". *Vinadya* = "sounding forth; bellowing" = Indec. past part. of √ *nad* with the prefix *vi.* Used here in the context of a lion's roar.]

2709. **uccaiḥśravasam** "Uccaiḥśravasa".10.27. [The name of Indra's white horse, who emerged when the ocean was churned by the gods and the demons.]

2710. **ucchiṣṭam** "that which is left over after being enjoyed; leftover food; garbage; that which is abandoned as useless or rejected". 17.10.

2711. **ucchoṣaṇam** "drying up; whithering; dessicating". 2.8.

2712. **ucyate** "it is said (to be)". 2.25, 48, 55, 56; 3.6, 40; 6.3 (twice), 4, 8, 18; 8.1, 3; 13.12, 17, 20 (twice); 14.25; 15.16; 17.14, 15, 16, 27, 28; 18.23, 25, 26, 28. [√ *vac*] Also see *abhidhīyate, procyate.*

2713. **udāhṛta** "is said to be; stated; described; designated".

- udāhṛtaḥ "said to be". 15.17.
- udāhṛtam "said to be". 13.6; 17.19, 22; 18.22, 24, 39.

2714. **udāhṛtya** "having said; after chanting". 17.24. [*tasmād om ity udāhṛtya*]

2715. **udapāne** "in a well; in a water reservoir". 2.46.

2716. **udara** "belly; stomach".

- anekabāhūdaravaktranetram "endowed with many arms, bellies, mouths [or faces], and eyes". 11.16. Also see *aneka, bahu, vaktra, netra.*
- bahūdaram "having many bellies". 11.23. Also see *bahu.*
- vṛkodaraḥ "Wolf-belly". 1.15. [Epithet of Bhīma, who was said to have an enormous appetite.]

2717. **udārāḥ** "having exemplary character; worthy of praise; noble". 7.18.

---

[635] Van Buitenen 1981, pp. 97, 165, section 28[6], note 8, "failing both in gainful acting and in reaching *brahman*—lost like a torn-off cloud".

2718. **udāsīna** "neutral; detached; impartial; indifferent; (lit.) sitting apart". Also see *madhyastha.*

- suhṛnmitrāryudāsīnamadhyasthadveṣyabandhuṣu "in friends, enemies, neutrals, mediators, despicable persons, and relatives". 6.9.
- udāsīnavad "like a neutral person". 9.9, 14.23.
- udāsīnaḥ "neutral". 12.16.

2719. **udbhava** "origin; origination; coming into being". 10.34. Also see *bhavaḥ.*

2720. **-udbhava** "source of; origin of" [Used as an enclitic affix.]

- amṛtodbhavam "born from (the ocean of) ambrosial nectar". 10.27.
- bhūtabhāvodbhavakaraḥ "what brings all objects into being;". 8.3.
- brahmākṣarasamudbhavam "*Brahman* springs from the Imperishable[636]; (the Vedas (*brahman*) originate from the syllable *om* (the imperishable)[637]". 3.15.
- brahmodbhavam "that which is born out of *brahman*". 3.15.
- dehasamudbhavān "the origin of the body[638]; (constituents) which give the body its existence[639]; that spring from the body[640]; which arise in the body[641]; that which arises from the body[642]; that come from bodily existence[643]". 14.20.
- kāmakrodhodbhavam "arising from desire and anger". 5.23.
- karmasamudbhavaḥ "arises out of action; is born from *karma*". 3.14.
- rajoguṇasamudbhavaḥ "arising from *rajoguṇa;* having the *guṇa rajas* as the source". 3.37.

---

636 Edgerton, p. 19.

637 The context of the verse is Vedic ritual action. Thus, "this *brahman* itself issues from the Syllable OM" in Van Buitenen 1981, p. 83. Here *brahman* refers to the Vedas.

638 Gambhīrānanda 1997, p. 583. The interpretation here is that the *guṇa*-s are "the origin of the body" or "the seed of the birth of the body".

639 Zaehner, p. 356. Zaehner notes that the "compound more naturally reads, 'which arise from the body', but it is the constituents that give existence to the body not vice versa."

640 Edgerton, p. 71. Edgerton adds a note on the ambiguity of how this compound can be translated (p. 100, note 1 on chapter 14).

641 Ādidevānanda, pp. 475-6. The interpretation here is that the *guṇa*-s "arise in the body", i.e., spring from Prakṛti transformed into the form of the body.

642 Divanji, p. 73, entry #1644.

643 Bolle, p. 273.

- tṛṣṇāsaṅgasamudbhavam "the source (*samudbhavam*) of craving (*tṛṣṇā*) and passion (*āsaṅga*)[644]; born of (*samudbhavam*) hankering (*tṛṣṇā*) and attachment (*āsaṅga*)[645]; arising from (*samudbhavam*) thirst (*tṛṣṇā*) and attachment (*saṅga*)[646]; that which results from greed and attachment[647]". 14.7.

2721. **uddeśataḥ** "succinctly; in summary; for example; a brief statement". 10.40.
2722. **uddharet** "one should uplift; one should raise; one should liberate". 6.5.[648]
2723. **uddiśya** "with expectation for; aiming at; pointing to". 17.21.
2724. **udvijate** "one feels upset; one feels disquiet; one is troubled; one trembles" 12.15 (twice).
2725. **udvijet** "one should be upset; one should feel disquiet; one should be troubled; one should tremble". 5.20.
2726. **udya** "raised; lifted; prepared for".
    - divyānekodyatāyudham "with numerous divine weapons raised (for battle)". 11.10. Also see *divya.*
    - raṇasamudyame "in raising (this) battle; in undertaking (this) battle; in preparation on the battlefield". 1.22.
    - udyamya "having raised; having lifted; having taken up". 1.20.
    - udyatāḥ "prepared for; intent on; ready". 1.45.
2727. **ugra** "terrible; terrifying; fierce".
    - ugrāḥ "terrible; fierce (rays)". 11.30.
    - ugraiḥ "by fierce (austerities); by strenuous (austerities)". 11.48

---

[644] Warrier, p. 474. Śaṅkara's commentary reads *āsaṅga* explicitly (तृष्णाऽऽसङ्गसमुद्भवं). Warrier's translation says that *rajas* is the source of *tṛṣṇā* and *āsaṅga,* not vice versa. That is the way Tilak (vol. 2, p. 1126) understands it, translating as, "Desire and Attachment arise from this constituent."

[645] Gambhīrānanda (1997, p. 574) parses the compound as *tṛṣṇā-āsaṅga-samudbhavam.* This word division is consistent with Śaṅkara's commentary, which reads *āsaṅga* explicitly (see Warrier, p. 474, तृष्णाऽऽसङ्गसमुद्भवं). Madhusūdana's commentary follows Śaṅkara in reading *āsaṅga* (Gambhīrānanda 1998, p. 757).

[646] Sargeant (p. 569) parses the compound as *tṛṣṇā-saṅga-samudbhavam.* This word division is consistent with Rāmānuja's commentary, which defines *saṅga* explicitly (see Ādidevānanda, p. 466).

[647] Divanji, p. 65, entry #1469.

[648] Van Buitenen's (1981, p. 93) translation of *uddhared ātmanātmānaṁ nātmānam avasādayet* as "Let him by himself save himself and not lower himself" captures the sense of freeing something by lifting it up.

- ugrakarmāṇaḥ "(doers of) terrible deeds". 16.9.
- ugram "terrifying; fierce (form)". 11.20.
- ugrarūpaḥ "(in this) terrifying form". 11.31. Also see *rūpa*.

2728. **ukta** "said; stated". [√ *vac*] Also see *śāstravidhānoktam, vidhānoktāḥ*.

- uktaḥ "said". 1.24; 8.21; 13.22.
- uktāḥ "said". 2.18.
- uktam "said". 11.1, 41; 12.20; 13.18; 15.20.

2729. **uktvā** "having spoken; after speaking; having said; after saying" 1.47; 2.9 (twice); 11.9, 21, 50. [Indec. past part. of √ *vac*.] Also see *–tvā*.

2730. **ulbena** "by a membrane". 3.38. [*yathā* + *ulbena* + *āvṛtaḥ* = just as (an embryo) is covered by a membrane]

2731. **unmiṣan** "while opening the eyes". 5.9. Also see *nimiṣan*.

2732. **upadekṣyanti** "they will teach; they will impart". 4.34.

2733. **upadhāraya** "understand; you should understand; regard as". 7.6; 9.6. Also see *dhārayan*.

2734. **upadraṣṭā** "observer; onlooker; impartial witness". 13.22. Also see *draṣṭā*.

2735. **upahanyām** "I would kill; I would destroy". 3.24. Also see *hanyuḥ*. [*upa* + √ *han*]

2736. **upaiṣyasi** "you will go to; you will arrive at; you will attain". 9.28. [*upa* + √ *i*]

2737. **upaiti** "one reaches; one goes to; one attains". 6.27; 8.10, 28. [*upa* + √ *i*]

2738. **upajāyante** "they arise; they are produced". 14.2. Also see *jāyante*.

2739. **upajāyate** "it arises; it is produced". 2.62, 65; 14.11. Also see *jāyate*.

2740. **upajuhvati** "one offers as an oblation". 4.25. [*upa* + √ *hu*] Also see *juhvati*.

2741. **upalabhyate** "can be perceived; is attainable". 15.3. Also see √ *labh*.

2742. **upalipyate** "it is tainted; it is smeared; it is polluted". 13.32 (twice). Also see √ *lip*.

2743. **upamā** "a simile". 6.19.

2744. **upapadyate** "it approaches; it arrives at; it takes place; it is proper; it is suitable; it is befitting". 2.3; 6.39; 13.18; 18.7.

2745. **upapannam** "has come; has arrived; has happened". 2.32.

2746. **uparamate** "it rests; it becomes tranquil; it gets withdrawn; it attains quietude". 6.20. Also see *ramate, ramanti*.

2747. **uparamet** "one should withdraw (from objects other than the self); one should be serene; one should abstain; one should turn away from (the objects of the sense organs)". 6.25.

2748. **uparatam** "(one who has) turned away; having desisted (from the fight); fled (from the battle); retired (from the field)". 2.35.

2749. **upasaṁgamya** "having approached". 1.2.

2750. **upāsate** "they worship; they serve; they honor; they revere; they venerate". 9.14, 15; 12.2, 6; 13.25. Also see *paryupāsate*.

2751. **upasevate** "one enjoys; one abides in". 15.9 Also see *sevate*.

2752. **upāśrita** "depending upon; having resorted to; taking refuge in; being supported by". Also see *āśrita, samupāśritaḥ*.

- upāśritāḥ "those who take shelter in; those who depend on; attached to". 4.10; 16.11.
- upāśritya "after resorting to; after taking refuge in; after depending on". 14.2; 18.57.
- samupāśritaḥ "taking recourse to; taking refuge in; being supported by". 18.52.

2753. **upāviśat** "he sat". 1.47.

2754. **upaviśyāsane** "sitting on a (suitable) seat". 6.12. Also see *āsana*.

2755. **upayānti** "they go to; they reach". 10.10. Also see *yānti*.

2756. **upāyataḥ** "by employment of the proper means". 6.36.

2757. **upeta** "having reached; arrived at; having come to; having attained; endowed with; possessed of". [*upa* + √ *i*]

- upetaḥ "having reached; having attained". 6.37.
- upetāḥ "having reached; having attained". 12.2.

2758. **upetya** "approaching; coming near to; reaching; attaining". 8.15, 16. [*upa* + √ *i*]

2759. **uragān** "snakes; serpents". 11.15.

2760. **ūrdhvam** "upward; thereafter".

- adhaś cordhvam "below and above; down and upward". 15.2.
- ata ūrdhvam "from now on; henceforth". 12.8.
- ūrdhvam "upward". 14.18.

2761. **ūrdhvamūlam** "with roots above; having its root upwards". 15.1. Also see *mūla*.

2762. **ūrjitam** "vigorous; energetic; powerful; glorious". 10.41.

2763. **ūru** "thigh". See *bahubāhūrupādam* "having many (*bahu*) arms (*bāhu*), thighs (*ūru*), and feet (*pādam*)". 11.23.

2764. **uśanā** "Uśanas". 10.37. [Name of a Vedic sage, also known as Śukra, the preceptor of the Daityas.]

2765. **uṣitvā** "having dwelled". 6.41. [√ *vas*]

2766. **ūṣmapāḥ** "the *Ūṣmapa*-s; the souls of departed ancestors". [A class of ancestor spirits (*manes*) belived to drink the steam arising from hot food.[649]]

- coṣmapāś (*ca ūṣmapāś*) "and the spirits of the ancestors". 11.22.

2767. **uṣṇa** "hot". 17.9. See *kaṭvamlalavaṇātyuṣṇatīkṣṇarūkṣavidāhinaḥ, śītoṣṇasukhaduḥkha*.

2768. **uta** "truly; and; also; or; but". 1.40; 14.9, 11. [Indec. particle used to add emphasis or express a guess.]

2769. **utkrāmantam** "going out; leaving; departing". 15.10.

2770. **utkrāmati** "it goes out; it leaves; it departs". 15.8.

2771. **utsādanārtham** "that aims at injuring others[650]; to effect another's downfall[651]". 17.19. Also see *arthaḥ*. [*parasya utsādanārtham*]

2772. **utsādyante** "they are destroyed; they sink down". 1.43.

2773. **utsannakuladharmāṇām** "of those whose family traditions are lost; for men who have cast aside their family Laws[652]". 1.44. Also see *dharma, kuladharmāḥ*.

2774. **utsīdeyuḥ** "they would perish; they would sink down". 3.24. [*ud* + √ *sad*] Also see *sīdanti*.

2775. **utsṛjāmi** "I release; I let go". 9.19. Also see √ *sṛj*.

2776. **utsṛjya** "releasing; setting aside; letting go of". 16.23; 17.1. Also see √ *sṛj*.

2777. **uttama** "highest; supreme; best; excellent". Also see *anuttama, puruṣottama* [*puruṣa + uttama*].

- uttamaḥ "the supreme". 15.17, 18.
- uttamam "the best; excellent; supreme". 4.3; 6.27; 9.2; 14.1; 18.6.

2778. **uttamāṅgaiḥ** "with heads". 11.27. [*uttama-aṅga* = the highest limb]

2779. **uttamaujāḥ** "Uttamaujas". 1.6. [Name of a warrior, meaning "One of great strength" or "One of great power".] Also see *ojas*.

2780. **uttamavidām** "of those who know the highest; of those who have the highest knowledge; of the best enlightened ones". 14.14. Also see *vid-*.

---

[649] Divanji, p. 35, entry #807.

[650] Warrier, p. 541.

[651] Van Buitenen 1981, p. 137.

[652] Van Buitenen 1981, p. 73.

2781. **uttarāyaṇam** "the northern path". 8.24. [*ṣaṇmāsā uttarāyaṇam* = six months after the winter solstice; six months when the sun is on the northern path]
2782. **uttiṣṭha** "arise!; get up!". 2.3, 37; 4.42; 11.33. Also see *tiṣṭh-*.
2783. **utthitā** "risen". 11.12.
2784. **uvāca** "said". 1.1, 2, 25, [21, 24, 28, 47[653]]; 2.1 (twice), 2, 4, 9, 10, 11, 54, 55; 3.1, 3, 10, 36, 37; 4.1, 4, 5; 5.1, 2; 6.1, 33, 35, 37, 40; 7.1; 8.1, 3; 9.1; 10.1, 12, 19; 11.1, 5, 9, 15, 32, 35, 36, 47, 50, 51, 52; 12.1, 2; 13.1; 14.1, 21, 22; 15.1; 16.1; 17.1, 2; 18.1, 2, 73, 74.

V

व् = V.

2785. **vā** "or". 1.32; 2.6 (twice), 20 (twice), 26, 37 (twice); 6.32 (twice); 8.6; 10.41; 11.41; 15.10 (twice); 17.19, 21; 18.15 (twice), 24, 40 (twice).
2786. √ **vac** "to speak". See *ucyate, ukta, uktvā, uvāca, vac-, vak-, vāk-*.
2787. **vacaḥ** "word; speech; statement; command". 2.10; 10.1; 11.1; 18.64.
2788. **vacanam** "word; speech; statement; opinion; command". 1.2; 11.35; 18.73.
2789. **vācyam** "to be spoken; fit to be spoken of". 18.67. Also see *avācyavādān*.
2790. **vada** "tell; state; instruct". 3.2.
2791. **vādaḥ** "discourse". 10.32. Also see *saṁvādam, pravadatām*.
2792. **vadanaiḥ** "with mouths". 11.30.
2793. **vadanti** "they speak; they say". 8.11. Also see *pravadanti*.
2794. **vadasi** "you say". 10.14.
2795. **vadati** "some say; one speaks". 2.29.
2796. **vādinaḥ** "those who advance this doctrine; holders of this view; declaring". 2.42. Also see *anahaṁvādī, brahmavādinām, vedavādaratāḥ*.
2797. **vadiṣyanti** "they will speak". 2.36.
2798. **vaḥ** "you; of you; your; to you". 3.10, 11, 12.
2799. **vahāmi** "I carry; I bear the burden". 9.22.
2800. **vahniḥ** "fire". 3.38. Also see *agni*.

---

[653] Some editions add explicit *uvāca* lines in verses 1.21, 1.24, 1.28, and 1.47 to indicate changes of speaker that are implied in the text.

2801. **vainateyaḥ** "Vainateya; the son of Vinatā; Garuḍa". 10.30. [Garuḍa, the King of Birds, is the vehicle of Viṣṇu.]

2802. **vairāgya** "indifference toward the objects of sense perception; dispassion; detachment; renunciation".[654] Also see *rāga*.

- vairāgyam "dispassion; detachment". 13.8; 18.52.
- vairāgyeṇa "with dispassion; with detachment; with renunciation". 6.35. [*abhyāsena tu kaunteya vairāgyeṇa ca gṛhyate* = "with practice (*abhyāsena*) and with dispasssion (*vairāgyeṇa*)..."; compare *YS* 1.12.]

2803. **vairiṇa** "enemy". Also see *nirvairaḥ*.

- nityavairiṇā "by the perpetual enemy". 3.39. Also see *nitya*.
- vairiṇam "enemy". 3.37.

2804. **vaiśvānaraḥ** "Vaiśvānara; the universal fire; the fire of digestion[655]". 15.14. [Name of the digestive fire, located in the gastric region. The sense in this verse is as the fire of life or the digestive fire. In other contexts the word could refer to general consciousness (in Vedanta) or a name for the Supreme Being.]

2805. **vaiśya** "Vaiśya". [The name of the third *varṇa* in the Indo-Āryan social order, consisting of traders and agriculturalists.]

- brāhmaṇakṣatriyaviśām "of the Brāhmaṇas, the Kṣatriyas, and the Vaiśyas". 18.41. Also see *Brāhmaṇa, Kṣatriya*.
- vaiśyāḥ "Vaiśyas". 9.32.
- vaiśyakarma "the natural duties of the Vaiśyas". 18.44. Also see *karma*.

2806. **vajram** "the Vajra". 10.28. [Name of the weapon of Indra, identified with the thunderbolt.]

2807. **vāk** "speech". Also see *śarīravāṅmanobhiḥ, yatavākkāyamānasaḥ, vāṅmayam*.

- vācam "speech". 2.42.
- vāk "speech". 10.34

2808. **vakṣyāmi** "I will speak; I will explain". 7.2; 8.23; 10.1; 18.64. Also see *pravakṣ-*.

2809. **vaktra** "face; mouth; (lit.) talker".

- anekabāhūdaravaktranetram "endowed with many arms, bellies, mouths [or faces], and eyes". 11.16. Also see *aneka, bahu, udara, netra*.

---

[654] *Vairāgya* is a critical factors for success in overcoming the dualities of mind. Compare Patañjali's *Yogasūtra* 1.12: *abhyāsa-vairāgyābhyāṁ tan-nirodhaḥ* = By practice and dispassion, restraint of these (modifications of the mind is achieved).

[655] Apte, p. 892, entry for वैश्वानरः, meaning 2.

- anekavaktranayanam "endowed with many mouths [or faces] and eyes". 11.10. Also see *aneka, nayana.*
- bahuvaktranetram "endowed with numerous mouths [or faces] and eyes". 11.23. Also see *bahu, netra.*
- dīptahutāśavaktram "with face shining like a blazing fire; with mouth like a blazing fire consuming oblations". 11.19. Also see *dīpta, hutāśa.*
- vaktrāṇi "mouths". 11.27, 28, 29.

2810. **vaktum** "to speak, to tell, to describe". 10.16.

2811. **vākyam** "speech; sentence; statement". 1.21; 2.1; 17.15.

2812. **vākyena** "by the statement". 3.2.

2813. **vāṅmayam** "relating to speech; vocal". 17.15. Also see *vāk.*

2814. **vara** "O best (of embodied souls)". 8.4. [*dehabhṛtāṁ vara*]

2815. **varjita** "freed from; having overcome". Also see *vivarjita.* See *kāma-saṁkalpavarjitāḥ* (4.19); *saṅgavarjitaḥ* (11.55).

2816. **varṇa** "*varṇa;* social class; color". [Indian society was divided into four primary social classes called *varṇa*-s. The word also means "color".]

- ādityavarṇam "the color of the sun; radiant like the sun". 8.9.
- anekavarṇam "many-colored; having many complexions; (lit.) not a single color". 11.24.
- cāturvarṇyam "the four social classes". 4.13.
- nānāvarṇākṛtīni "having various colors and shapes". 11.5.
- varṇasaṁkaraḥ "mixing of the social orders; intermingling of the *varṇa*-s". 1.41.
- varṇasaṁkarakārakaiḥ "due to the production of intermixture of the social orders; due to that which is a cause of the mixture of the *varṇa*-s". 1.43.

2817. **varṣam** "rain'. 9.19.

2818. **vārṣṇeya** "O scion of the Vṛṣṇi clan". 1.41; 3.36. [For the Vṛṣṇi, see page 9.] Also see *vṛṣṇīnām.*

2819. **vartamānaḥ** "existing; acting; living". 6.31; 13.23.

2820. **vartamānāni** "the living; existing things; the present". 7.26.

2821. **vartante** "they act; they operate; they work". 3.28; 5.9; 14.23.

2822. **vartate** "it acts; it lives; it abides; it stays near at hand". 5.26; 6.31; 16.23.

2823. **varte** "I move; I engage in action". 3.22.

2824. **varteta** "it would exist; it would act; it would function". 6.6.

2825. **vartetātmaiva** [*varteta ātmā eva*] "the self itself acts; the self itself would become engaged; the self itself would exist". 6.6. Also see *ātman.*

2826. **varteyam** "engage in action; move; behave; be occupied with". 3.23.

2827. **vartma** "path; route". 3.23; 4.11. See *vartmānuvartante.*

2828. **vartmānuvartante** "they follow (My) path". 3.23; 4.11. [*mama vartmānuvartante* = "they follow my path".[656]] Also see *anuvartante, mṛtyusaṁsāravartmani.*

2829. **varuṇaḥ** "Varuṇa". 10.29; 11.39. [In the Epic Period, chiefly considered as the god of the oceans and waters.]

2830. **vāsaḥ** "dwelling; residing". 1.44.

2831. **vaśam** "control; subordination; being under direction". 3.34; 6.26. Also see *vaśāt, vaśe, vaśī, avaśa, vaśyātmanā, ātmavaśyaiḥ.*

2832. **vāsāṁsi** "clothes; clothing". 2.22.

2833. **vaśāt** "due to will; from the power; under the control of". 9.8.

2834. **vasavaḥ** "the Vasus". 11.22. Also see *vasu.*

2835. **vāsavaḥ** "Vāsava; Indra". 10.22. [An epithet of Indra.[657]]

2836. **vaśe** "under control". 2.61. Also see *vaśam.*

2837. **vaśī** "one who has self-control; self-directed". 5.13. Also see *vaśam.*

2838. **vasu** "the Vasus". [A group of eight Vedic gods.]

- vasavaḥ "the Vasus". 11.22.
- vasūn "the Vasus". 11.6.
- vasūnām "of the Vasus, among the Vasus". 10.23.

2839. **vāsudeva** "Vāsudeva". [Epithet of Kṛṣṇa.]

- vāsudevaḥ "son of Vasudeva". 7.19; 10.37; 11.50.
- vāsudevasya "of Vāsudeva". 18.74.

2840. **vāsukiḥ** "Vāsuki". 10.28. [Name of a king of the Nāgas, a class of semi-divine beings having the form of serpents.]

2841. **vaśyātmanā** "by one whose (lower) self is under control; by one who has acquired control over oneself". 6.36. [*vaśya* + *ātmanā*] Also see *ātman, ātmavaśyaiḥ.*

2842. **vayam** "we". 1.37, 45; 2.12.

---

[656] Verse 3.23c is repeated in 4.11c.

[657] Hopkins, p. 171, says that the epithet Vāsava implies that Indra was the lord or first of the Vasus.

2843. **vāyu** "wind; air; Vāyu (the god of wind)"

- vāyoḥ "of the wind". 6.34. [*nigrahaṁ manye vāyor iva suduṣkaram* = I consider it is as difficult to do as control of the wind]
- vāyuḥ "the wind". 2.67 (here suggesting a storm or strong wind); 9.6; 15.8.
- vāyuḥ "air (one of the five gross elements of Indian philosophy)". 7.4.
- vāyur "Vāyu (the God of Wind)". 11.39.

2844. **Veda** "the Veda; the Vedas". Also see *Ṛk, Sāma, Yajuḥ, brahmaṇaḥ* "of the Veda" (4.32); *brahmavādinām* (17.24), *brahmodbhavam* (3.15), *chandāṁsi, śabdabrahmātivartate, sarvavedeṣu, śrutiparāyaṇāḥ, śrutivipratipannā, traividyāḥ, trayīdharmam, veda-, vedā-.*

- vedaiḥ "by the Vedas; with the help of the Vedas". 11.53; 15.15.
- vedāḥ "the Vedas". 2.45; 17.23.
- vedānām "among the Vedas". 10.22.
- vede "in the Vedas (taken collectively); in scripture". 15.18.
- vedeṣu "in the Vedas". 2.46; 8.28.

2845. **veda** "knows; know". 2.21, 29; 4.5; 7.26 (twice); 15.1.

2846. **vedāntakṛt** "maker of the Vedānta; author of the Vedānta; the founder of the Vedāntic school of thought". 15.15. [The Vedānta texts are the "end of the Vedas", i.e., the Upaniṣads.]

2847. **vedavādaratāḥ** "those engaged in Vedic ritualism; those who delight in the letter of the Veda." 2.42. Also see *vedavid, vādinaḥ, ratāḥ.*

2848. **vedavid** "knower of the Vedas; one who knows the Vedas". Also see *vedavādaratāḥ, -vid.*

- vedavidaḥ "Those conversant with the Vedas". 8.11.
- vedavid "knower of the Vedas". 15.1, 15.

2849. **vedayajñādhyayanaiḥ** "by the Vedas, performance of rituals, and studies; by means neither of the Vedas, sacrifices, studies[658]; neither through the study of the Vedas, nor by sacrifices[659]; study of the Vedas and of sacrifices[660]". 11.48. Also see *svādhyāya, veda, yajña.*

2850. **veditavyam** "object of knowledge; that which should be known". 11.18.

2851. **veditum** "to know". 18.1.

2852. **vedyaḥ** "He who should be known". 15.15.

---

658 Warrier, p. 377.

659 Ādidevānanda, p. 389.

660 Divanji, p. 138, entry #3177; Gambhīrānanda 1997, p. 466.

2853. **vedyam** "that which should be known". 9.17; 11.38.

2854. **vegam** "forceful surge; driving force; strong impetus". 5.23. Also see *ambuvegāḥ, anudvegakaram, harṣāmarṣabhayodvegaiḥ, samṛddhavegāḥ.*

2855. **vepamānaḥ** "trembling". 11.35.

2856. **vepathuḥ** "trembling". 1.29.

2857. **vettā** "the knower". 11.38.

2858. **vettha** "you know". 4.5; 10.15.

2859. **vetti** "one knows; one thinks; one comprehends; one considers". 2.19; 4.9; 6.21; 7.3; 10.3, 7; 13.1. 23; 14.19; 18.21, 30.

2860. **vibhakta** "divided".

- avibhaktam "undivided; unfragmented". 13.16; 18.20.
- pravibhaktam "divided; distributed". 11.13.
- pravibhaktāni "divided; distributed". 18.41.
- vibhaktam "divided". 13.16.
- vibhakteṣu "in the divided; in separate beings; in the fragmented ones". 18.20.

2861. **vibhāvasau** "in flame; in the sun". 7.9. Also see *agni.*

2862. **vibhu** "all-pervading; omnipresent; lord".

- vibhuḥ "The One Who Pervades; The Lord". 5.15.
- vibhum "The One Who Pervades; The Lord". 10.12.

2863. **vibhūti** "something in which the divine is manifested in a special way; manifestation of glory; glorious manifestations; manifest power; ubiquity". Also see √ *bhū.*

- ātmavibhūtayaḥ "special manifestations of the self; self-manifestations; the forms in which one's self has become manifest in a special way". 10.16, 19.
- vibhūteḥ "of glorious manifestation". 10.40.
- vibhūtibhiḥ "by special manifestations; with glorious attributes". 10.16.
- vibhūtim "special manifestation". 10.7, 18.
- vibhūtimat "having *vibhūti*; having mighty power; glorious". 10.41. [Nom. sing. neut. form of the adj. *vibhūtimat.*]
- vibhūtīnāṁ "of my glorious manifestations". 10.40.

2864. **vicakṣaṇāḥ** "the learned ones; men of discernment". 18.2.

2865. **vicālayet** "one should disturb; one should cause to waver; one should discourage". 3.29.

2866. **vicālyate** "one is disturbed; one wavers; one is shaken; one is moved; one is affected by". 6.22; 14.23.

2867. **vicetasaḥ** "those who have lost their sense of discrimination". 9.12.

2868. –**vid** (suffix). "knowing (something); a knower of (something)" See *ahorātra-vidaḥ, akṛtsnavidaḥ, brahmavid, evaṁvidhaḥ, kṛtsnavid, sarvavid, tadvidaḥ, tattvavid, uttamavidām, vedavid, viditvā, yajñavidaḥ.*

2869. **vidadhāmi** "I grant (unwavering faith)[661]; I make (that faith steadfast)[662]; I confirm[663]; I strengthen[664]". 7.21. Also see *dadhāmi.*

2870. **vidāhina** "causing a burning sensation, causing great heat, causing inflammation[665]". 17.9. See *kaṭvamlalavaṇātyuṣṇatīkṣṇarūkṣavidāhinaḥ.*

2871. **viddhi** "(you) know; understand; realize". 2.17; 3.15, 32, 37; 4.13, 32, 34; 6.2; 7.5, 10, 12; 10.24, 27; 13.2, 19 (twice), 26; 14.7, 8; 15.12; 17.6, 12; 18.20, 21.

2872. **-vidhā** "type; kind; mode; manner".

- bahuvidhā "many types". 4.32.
- caturvidhā "four types". 7.16; 15.14.
- dvividhā "two types; two categories; twofold". 3.3.
- evaṁvidhaḥ "in this way; in this form; in this aspect". 11.53, 54.
- nānāvidhāni "various types; several categories". 11.5.
- pṛthagvidhā "various types". 10.5; 18.14, 21.
- trividhā "three types; three categories; threefold". 16.21; 17.2, 7, 17, 23; 18.4, 12, 18 (twice), 29, 36.
- vividhā "various types; several". 13.4; 17.25; 18.14.

2873. **vidhānoktāḥ** "as prescribed in the scriptures; mentioned in the prescribed rules (for ceremonies)". 17.24. Also see *avidhipūrvakam, śāstravidhim, śāstravidhānoktam, vidhidṛṣṭaḥ, vidhihīnam.*

2874. **vidheyātmā** "the self-controlled man; a self-disciplined one; the self-controlled; one who can regulate his heart; governing one's self". 2.64. Also see *ātman.*

---

[661] Miller, p. 76.

[662] Ādidevānanda, p. 261. For the simple rendering as "I make" also see Sivananda, p. 168.

[663] Zaehner, p. 252.

[664] Gambhīrānanda 1997, pp. 331-2.

[665] Apte p. 856, entry for विदाहः.

2875. **vidhidṛṣṭaḥ** "as recognized by scriptural rules; as prescribed in the scriptures". 17.11. Also see *avidhipūrvakam, dṛṣṭim, śāstravidhim, śāstra-vidhānoktam, vidhānoktāḥ, vidhihīnam.*

2876. **vidhihīnam** "not conforming to scripture; devoid of prescribed form". 17.13. Also see *avidhipūrvakam, śāstravidhim, śāstravidhānoktam, vidhānoktāḥ, vidhidṛṣṭaḥ.*

2877. **vidhīyate** "it is fit for (*samādhi*); it is ordained; it is granted; it is enjoined[666]". 2.44. Also see *anuvidhīyate.*

2878. **viditātmanām** "one who knows the self; proficient in the mystery of *ātman*". 5.26. Also see *ātman.*

2879. **viditvā** "after knowing; having known". 2.25; 8.28. [Indec. past. part of √ *vid.*] Also see *-tvā.*

2880. **vidmaḥ** "we know". 2.6.

2881. **viduḥ** "they know; they understand". 4.2; 7.29, 30 (twice); 8.17; 10.2, 14;.13.34; 16.7; 18.2.

2882. **vidvān** "the wise; a wise person; a learned person". 3.25, 26. Also see *avidvāṁsaḥ.*

2883. **vidyā** "knowledge; science". Also see *adhyātmavidyā, rājavidyā, traividyā.*

2884. **vidyām** "may I know; can I know". 10.17.

2885. **vidyānām** "among sciences". 10.32.

2886. **vidyāt** "one should know; it should be known; let it be known". 6.23; 14.11.

2887. **vidyate** "it is". 2.16 (twice), 31, 40; 3.17; 4.38; 6.40; 8.16; 16.7.

2888. **vidyāvinayasaṁpanne** "in one endowed with (*saṁpanne*) learning (*vidyā*) and cultivation (*vinaya*); in one endowed with knowledge and good manners". 5.18. Also see *saṁpat.*

2889. **vigata** "gone away; departed; free from; having been dispelled; vanished".

- vigatabhīḥ "having become free of fear; having dispelled fear". 6.14.
- vigataḥ "gone away; departed; vanished". 11.1.
- vigatajvaraḥ "free from the fever (of ignorance); one whose mental distress has gone away". 3.30.
- vigatakalmaṣaḥ "freed from sin; sin having gone away". 6.28. Also see *kalmaṣa.*

---

[666] Van Buitenen 1981, p. 79.

- vigataspṛhaḥ "free from longings; desire gone away". 2.56; 18.49. Also see *spṛhā, niḥspṛhaḥ*.
- vigatecchābhayakrodhaḥ "desire, fear, and anger having gone away". 5.28.

2890. **vigatecchābhayakrodhaḥ** "one who is free of desire (*icchā*), fear (*bhaya*), and anger (*krodha*)". 5.28.

2891. **vigna** "trouble; obstacle".
- anudvignamanāḥ "one whose mind is not troubled; not perturbed mentally; not distressed". 2.56. Also see *-manāḥ, manas*.
- śokasaṁvignamānasaḥ "with mind disturbed by melancholy; one whose mind is perturbed by grief". 1.47. Also see *śoka, manas, -mānasaḥ*.

2892. **viguṇaḥ** "of inferior quality; deficient in quality; lacking in merit; imperfect". 3.35; 18.47.

2893. **vihāra** "movements; activity; recreation; diversions".
- vihāraśayyāsanabhojaneṣu "while at play (*vihāra*), resting (*śayya*), sitting (*āsana*), or with food (*bhojana*)". 11.42.
- yuktāhāravihārasya "one whose food and movements are regulated[667]; a person with balanced diet (*āhāra*) and regimens (*vihāra*)". 6.17. Also see *yukta*.

2894. **vihāya** "abandoning; leaving aside; casting off". 2.22 (twice), 71.

2895. **vihita** "ordained; granted; bestowed; given; provided".
- aśāstravihitam "that which is not prescribed by scriptures; not in accordance with guidelines in the scriptures". 17.5. Also see *śāstram*.
- vihitān "were ordained; given; provided". 7.22.
- vihitāḥ "were ordained; were created; were done". 17.23.

2896. **vijānataḥ** "of one who realizes; for one who knows; to a wise person". 2.46. [*vi* + √ *jñā*]

2897. **vijānītaḥ** "they (both) realize; (the two of them) know". 2.19. [*vi* + √ *jñā*]

2898. **vijānīyām** "I should understand; I should comprehend". 4.4. [*vi* + √ *jñā*] [*katham etad vijānīyām* = How am I to understand this?]

2899. **vijaya** "victory". Also see *anantavijayam, jayaḥ*.
- vijayaḥ "victory". 18.78.
- vijayam "victory". 1.32.

---

667 Gambhīrānanda 1998, p. 417.

2900. **vijitātmā** "one who has self-control; one of controlled mind". 5.7. Also see *ātman, jitātman.*

2901. **vijitendriyaḥ** "one who has control over one's senses". 6.8. Also see *indriya, jitendriyaḥ.*

2902. **vijñāna** "discriminating wisdom; direct insight; understanding". Also see *jñāna, avijñeyam, vijñātum, vijñāya.*

- jñānavijñānanāśanam "destroyer of material and spiritual wisdom; destroyer of knowledge and discrimination". 3.41. Also see *nāśanam.*
- jñānavijñānatṛptātmā "contented with practical and spiritual knowledge; one whose soul is satisfied by knowledge and spiritual insight". 6.8.
- jñānaṁ te 'haṁ savijñānam "I will explain to you this knowledge, along with spiritual wisdom". 7.2.
- jñānaṁ vijñānasahitaṁ "knowledge, along with spiritual insight". 9.1.
- jñānaṁ vijñānam "knowledge, spiritual awareness". 18.42.

2903. **vijñātum** "to know; to understand". 11.31. [With the sense of "to experience (you)".] Also see *vijñāna, jñātum.*

2904. **vijñāya** "after understanding; after knowing". 13.18. Also see *vijñāna.*

2905. **vikampitum** "to shake; to tremble; to waver". 2.31. [*na vikampitum arhasi* = "do not waver"[668] or "you should not tremble"] Also see *arhasi, avikampena.*

2906. **vikāra** "change, modification; evolution; evolute".

- avikāryaḥ "immutable; incapable of undergoing any change". 2.25.
- nirvikāraḥ "not changed". 18.26.
- savikāram "together with modifications; along with evolutes". 13.6.
- vikārān "modifications; evolutes; evolutions". 13.19.
- yadvikāri "that from which it has evolved; of what it is a transformation". 13.3. [Nom. sing. of the neut. form of the comp. adj. *yadvikārin.*]

2907. **vikarmaṇaḥ** "of improper action; of undesirable action; about prohibited action". 4.17. Also see *karma.*

2908. **vikarṇaḥ** "Vikarṇa". 1.8. [A Kaurava warrior, the third son of King Dhṛtarāṣṭra.]

2909. **vikrāntaḥ** "one who performs heroic deeds; powerful; striding boldly". 1.6.

2910. **vīkṣante** "they see; they view; they gaze at; they observe". 11.22. Also see *√ īkṣ.*

2911. **vilagnāḥ** "stuck or pressed hard, sticking fast". 11.27.

---

[668] Van Buitenen 1981, p. 77.

2912. **vimatsaraḥ** "free from jealousy; free from envy". 4.22.

2913. **vimohayati** "it deludes". 3.40. Also see √ *muh, vimuhyati, vimūḍh-, ajñānavimohitāḥ*

2914. **vimokṣ-** Also see *mokṣ-, vimuc-, vimuk-, vimuñc-.*

- śarīravimokṣaṇāt "complete liberation from the body". 5.23. Also see *vimokṣ-, mokṣ-.*
- vimokṣāya "to complete release; to final liberation". 16.5.
- vimokṣyase "you will be completely released; you will have final liberation". 4.32.

2915. **vimṛśya** "having considered; after thinking over". 18.63.

2916. **vimucya** "abandoning; relinquishing; freed from". 18.53. Also see *mucyante,* √ *muc.*

2917. **vimūḍhaḥ** "deluded; confused". 6.38.

2918. **vimūḍhāḥ** "the deluded; those who are confused". 15.10.

2919. **vimūḍhabhāvaḥ** "state of delusion; confused state; deluded state of being". 11.49.

2920. **vimūḍhātmā** "deluded self; confused self; one whose self is overcome with delusion". 3.6. Also see *ātman.*

2921. **vimuhyati** "one becomes deluded, one is confused, is perplexed". 2.72. Also see *vimūḍh-, mūḍh-, vimohayati.*

2922. **vimukta** "released; absolutely liberated". Also see *vimokṣ-, mukt-,* √ *muc.*

- vimuktaḥ "released". 9.28; 14.20; 16.22.
- vimuktāḥ "released". 15.5.

2923. **vimuñcati** "he gets rid of; he gives up". 18.35. Also see √ *muc.*

2924. **vinā** "without". 10.39.

2925. **vinadyoccaiḥ** (*vinadya* + *uccaiḥ*) "loudly sounding; roaring loudly". 1.12. [*vinadya* = "sounding forth; bellowing" = Indec. past part. of √ *nad* with the prefix *vi.* Used here in the context of a lion's roar.]

2926. **vinaṅkṣyasi** "you will perish". 18.58. Also see *avinaś-, avināś-, naśy-, vinaś-, vināś-.*

2927. **vināśa** "destruction; perishing". Also see *avinaś-, avināś-, naśy-, vinaś-.*

- vināśaḥ "destruction; failure; lost". 6.40.
- vināśam "destruction". 2.17.
- vināśāya "for the destruction". 4.8. Also see *nāśāya.*

2928. **vinaśyati** "perishes". 4.40; 8.20. Also see *vinaṅkṣyasi, praṇaś-, naśyati, avinaś-, avināś-.*

2929. **vinaśyatsu** "perishing". 13.27. Also see *vinaṅkṣyasi, naśyati, avinaś-, avināś-.*

2930. **vindāmi** "I find; I attain; I obtain; I get". 11.24.

2931. **vindate** "one finds; one attains; one obtains; one gets". 5.4.

2932. **vindati** "one finds; one attains; one obtains; one gets". 4.38; 5.21; 18.45, 46.

2933. **viniścitaiḥ** "by conclusive (arguments); by well-settled (views); with definite (reasons)". 13.4. Also see *suniścitam, niścit-.*

2934. **vinivartante** "(objects of the senses) cease to attract". 2.59. Also see *nivartate, vinivṛttakāmāḥ.*

2935. **vinivṛttakāmāḥ** "those for whom desires have thoroughly ceased; those devoid of (worldly) desires; those who abstain from desires". 15.5. Also see √ *nivṛt, kāma, vinivartante.*

2936. **viniyamya** "after controlling completely; having regulated well". 6.24. Also see *niyamya.*

2937. **viniyatam** "well-regulated; well-disciplined". 6.18. Also see *niyatam.*

2938. **viparīta** "opposite; contrary; reverse; wrong; adverse; perverse".

- viparītam "unrightful (action); wrong; perverse". 18.15.
- viparītān "opposite; contrary; perverted". 18.32.
- viparītāni "adverse (omens); inauspicious; perverse". 1.31.

2939. **viparivartate** "it revolves; it moves about in a circle; it evolves". 9.10.

2940. **vipaścitaḥ** "of the wise". 2.60. [*puruṣasya vipaścitaḥ* = of the person of wisdom] Also see *avipaścitaḥ.*

2941. **virāṭaḥ** "Virāṭa". King of the Matsyas. He gave shelter to the Pāṇḍavas, who lived incognito in his court during the thirteenth year of their exile. He fought on the side of the Pāṇḍavas during the Mahābharata war. 1.4, 17.

2942. **vīryavān** "virile; strong; vigorous; brave; valient". 1.5, 6. Also see *anantavīryam, anantavīryāmitavikramaḥ.*

2943. **viṣādam** "dejection; sadness; grief; sorrow; depression of spirits; despair". 18.35. Also see *viṣīd-.*

2944. **viṣādī** "habitually in a dejected mood; pessimistic in nature; subject to depression". 18.28. Also see *viṣīd-.*

2945. **viśāla** "wide; broad; expansive, vast".

- dīptaviśālanetram "endowed with blazing wide eyes". 11.24. Also see *dīpta, netra.*
- viśālam "vast, wide". 9.21.

2946. **viṣam** "poison". 18.37, 38.

2947. **viṣame** "in this danger; at this critical time; in this difficult situation". 2.2.

2948. **viśanti** "they enter". 8.11; 9.21; 11.21, 27, 28, 29 (twice). Also see *praviśanti.*

2949. **visargaḥ** "release (of creative force); sending forth". 8.3. Also see √ *sṛj, sarga.*

2950. **viśate** "one enters". 18.55.

2951. **viṣaya** "(specific) object (of the senses)".

- traiguṇyaviṣayā "the spheres of action of the three *guṇa*-s". 2.45. Also see *triguṇa.*
- viṣayāḥ "the objects (of the senses)". 2.59.
- viṣayān "the objects (of the senses)". 2.62, 64; 4.26; 15.9; 18.51 (*viṣayāṁs*).
- viṣayapravālāḥ "the objects (of the senses) as sprouting shoots" 15.2. Also see *pravālāḥ.*
- viṣayendriyasaṁyogāt "from contact between the senses and the objects (of the senses)". 18.38. Also see *indriya.*

2952. **viśeṣa** "specific; various; varieties".

- kriyāviśeṣabahulām "abounding in (many) specific rites; replete with various ritual acts". 2.43. Also see *kriyā.*
- bhūtaviśeṣasaṁghān "groups of various kinds of beings; hosts of various beings". 11.15. Also see *bhūta.*

2953. **viṣīdan** "despairing; desponding; being sad; feeling dejected". 1.28. Also see *viṣād-.*

2954. **viṣīdantam** "despairing; despondent; dejected". 2.1, 10. Also see *viṣād-.*

2955. **viśiṣṭāḥ** "distinguished ones; outstanding ones; excellent". 1.7.

2956. **viśiṣyate** "one excels; one is outstanding; has special importance; is best of all; is more excellent". 3.7; 5.2; 6.9; 7.17; 12.12.

2957. **vismaya** "astonishment; amazement; wonder; surprise".

- vismayaḥ "astonishment; amazement; wonder; surprise". 18.77.
- vismayāviṣṭaḥ "awestruck with astonishment; possessed by wonder; filled with amazement". 11.14. Also see *āviṣṭa.*

2958. **vismitāḥ** "astonished; surprised; in wonder". 11.22.

2959. **Viṣṇu** "Viṣṇu". [The god Viṣṇu.] Also see *prabhaviṣṇu.*

- viṣṇo "O Viṣṇu". 11.24, 30.
- ādityānām ahaṁ viṣṇuḥ "of the Ādityas I am Viṣṇu". 10.21.

2960. **visṛjāmi** "I send forth; I emit; I create". 9.7, 8. Also see √ *sṛj.*

2961. **visṛjan** "while releasing; while excreting". 5.9. Also see √ *sṛj.*

2962. **visṛjya** "leaving aside; throwing down". 1.47. Also see √ *sṛj.*

2963. **viṣṭabhya** "supporting; sustaining". 10.42.

2964. **vistaraḥ** "expansion; elaboration". 10.40.

2965. **vistāram** "expansion". 13.30.

2966. **vistarasya** "of expansion; of elaboration". 10.19.

2967. **vistaraśaḥ** "in detail; extensively". 11.2; 16.6.

2968. **vistareṇa** "in detail; extensively". 10.18.

2969. **viṣṭhitam** "fixed variously; established; pervading; situated; residing in; present in". 13.17.

2970. **viśuddhātmā** "with the (lower) self purified; with the mind purified; pure in mind; one whose heart is purified". 5.7. Also see *ātman, ātmaśuddhaye, ātmaviśuddhaye, śuddh-*.

2971. **viśuddhayā** "with pure". 18.51. Also see *śuddh-*.

2972. **viśvam** ("universe; all")

- viśvam "the universe". 11.19, 38.
- viśvam "universal; all". 11.47. [Used as an adj. qualifying the nom. sing. neut. noun *rūpam*.]
- viśvamūrte "O One who has assumed the form of the Universe; O Embodiment of All; O One who has all forms; O Universal Form". 11.46.
- viśvarūpa "O One who has the Universe as his form; O Universal Form". 11.16.
- viśvasya "of the universe; of all". 11.18, 38.
- viśveśvara 11.16 "O Lord of the Universe; O Lord of All".

2973. **viśvamūrte** "O One who has assumed the form of the Universe; O Embodiment of All; O One who has all forms; O Universal Form; embodied in all[669]". 11.46. Also see *avyaktamūrtinā, mūrtayaḥ, viśva*.

2974. **viśvarūpa** "O One who has the Universe as his form; O Universal Form". 11.16. Also see *rūpa, viśva*.

2975. **viśvatomukha** "facing in all directions; having faces everywhere". [*viśvataḥ* ("everywhere; on all sides"+ *mukha* ("face").]

- viśvatomukhaḥ 10.33.
- viśvatomukham 9.15; 11.11.

2976. **viśve** "the Viśvedevas". 11.22. [An abbreviated form of the term *viśvedevāḥ*, a group of Vedic gods.]

---

669 Van Buitenen 1981, p. 119.

2977. **viśveśvara** "O Lord of the Universe; O Lord of All". 11.16. Also see *īśvara, viśva.*

2978. **vītarāgabhayakrodha** "free of attachment (*rāga*), fear (*bhaya*), and anger (*krodha*)".

- vītarāgabhayakrodhaḥ "one who is free of attachment, fear, and anger". 2.56.
- vītarāgabhayakrodhāḥ "those who are free of attachment, fear, and anger". 4.10.

2979. **vītarāgāḥ** "free from attachments". 8.11. Also see *rāga.*

2980. **vitatāḥ** "spread out; revealed; expounded". 4.32.

2981. **vitteśaḥ** "Vitteśa; Lord of Wealth". 10.23. Also see *īśa.* [An epithet of Kubera.]

2982. **vivardhanāḥ** "promoters; causing increase". See *āyuḥsattvabalārogyasukha-prītivivardhanāḥ.*

2983. **vivarjita** "freed from; having overcome; devoid of". Also see *varjita.*

- kāmarāgavivarjitam "freed from desire (*kāma*) and attachment (*rāga*)". 7.11.
- saṅgavivarjitaḥ "freed from attachment (*saṅga*)". 12.18.
- sarvendriyavivarjitam "freed from all the senses (*sarvendriya*); transcending all sense organs; devoid of senses". 13.14.

2984. **vivasvata** "Vivasvat; the Sun god".

- vivasvān "the Sun god". 4.1.
- vivasvate "to the Sun god". 4.1
- vivasvataḥ "of the Sun god". 4.4.

2985. **vividhā** "having various types". Also see *-vidhā.*

- vividhāḥ "various". 17.25; 18.14.
- vividhaiḥ "with various types". 13.4.

2986. **viviktadeśasevitvam** "the quality of having made a secluded (*vivikta*) place (*deśa*) one's residence; living in solitude". 13.10. Also see *viviktasevī, deśe.*

2987. **viviktasevī** "one who has made a secluded place one's residence; one who lives in solitude". 18.52. Also see *viviktadeśasevitvam.*

2988. **vivṛddha** "well developed; augmented; increased".

- vivṛddham "dominant; augmented; increased". 14.11.
- vivṛddhe "when dominant". 14.12, 13.

2989. **viyoga** "disconnection; disunion". See *duḥkhasaṁyogaviyogam, kāma-krodhaviyuktānām, rāgadveṣaviyuktaiḥ, saṁyoga.*

2990. **vraja** "take (refuge); turn (to Me); go to (Me)". 18.66. [*mām ekaṁ śaraṇaṁ vraja* = "turn to Me, your only refuge"[670]. √ *vraj*]

2991. **vrajeta** "he walks; one would move (through life); he behaves". 2.54. [*vrajeta kim* = lit. "how does he walk?" This has the sense, "How does he behave in life in general?"[671]]

2992. **vrata** "vow".

- aśucivratāḥ "those of impure vows". 16.10.
- brahmacārivrate "in the vow of a celibate". 6.14.
- devavratāḥ "those who are dedicated to the gods". 9.25.
- dṛḍhavratāḥ "with firm resolve; those who are unyielding in the observance of vows; steady; persevering". 7.28; 9.14.
- pitṛvratāḥ "those dedicated to the forefathers; those who observe vows with a view to propitiate the manes[672]". 9.25.
- saṁśitavratāḥ "(those with) determined vows". 4.28. [multiple possible meanings, see *saṁśitavratāḥ*.]

2993. **vṛjinam** "sin". 4.36.

2994. **vṛkodaraḥ** "Wolf-belly". 1.15. [Epithet of Bhīma, who was said to have an enormous appetite.] Also see *Bhīma, udara.*

2995. **vṛṣṇīnām** "of the Vṛṣṇi; among members of the Vṛṣṇi branch of the Yādava clan". 10.37. [For the Vṛṣṇi, see page 9.] Also see *vārṣṇeya.*

2996. **vyadārayat** "it tore open". 1.19.

2997. **vyādhi** "disease".

- janmamṛtyujarāvyādhiduḥkhadoṣānudarśanam "contemplation (*anudarśana*) of the fault (*doṣa*) consisting of the miseries (*duḥkha*) of birth (*janma*), death (*mṛtyu*), old age (*jarā*), and disease (*vyādhi*)". 13.8. Also see *janma, mṛtyu, jarā, duḥkha, doṣa.*

2998. **vyāharan** "chanting; uttering; muttering; repeating in a low tone". 8.13.

2999. **vyakta** "manifested". Also see *avyakta.*

- vyaktamadhyāni "manifest in the middle (state); (their) middles are manifest". 2.28. Also see *madhya.*
- vyaktayaḥ "manifestions; things which are manifest". 8.18.
- vyaktim "(having come into) manifestation". 7.24.

---

670 Zaehner, p. 400.

671 Tapasyananda, p. 64. Compare the English expression, "Does he walk the walk or talk the talk?"

672 Divanji, p. 88, entry # 2000.

- vyaktim "manifestation". 10.14. [With sense of "true identity".]

3000. **vyāmiśreṇa** "mixed up; confusing; ambiguous; contradictory". 3.2. Also see *miśram.*

3001. **vyanunādayan** "causing a loud sound; causing to resound; causing to reverberate". 1.19. [*vi* + *anu* + *nādayan*]

3002. **vyapāśritya** "taking refuge in; after taking shelter". 9.32. Also see *āśrita.*

3003. **vyapetabhīḥ** "free from (*vyapeta*) fear (*bhīs*); gone away from fear". 11.49. [*vi* + *apa* + √ *i* + *bhīs*] Also see *gatavyathaḥ.*

3004. **vyāptam** "pervaded; permeated". 11.20.

3005. **vyāpya** "pervading; permeating". 10.16.

3006. **vyāsaḥ** "Vyāsa". 10.13, 37. Also see *vyāsaprasādāt.* [Vyāsa was the sage traditionally credited as the compiler of the Vedas as well as the *Mahābhārata,* of which the *BG* is a part. The name means editor, arranger, or compiler. He is the son of the sage Parāśara and Satyavatī. He fathered Dhṛtarāṣṭra, Pāṇḍu, and Vidura.]

3007. **vyāsaprasādāt** "through the grace of Vyāsa". 18.75. Also see *prasad, vyāsaḥ.*

3008. **vyathā** "fear; distress; trembling". 11.49. [*mā te vyathā* = "don't tremble" or "be not afraid"[673].] Also see *gatavyathaḥ, pravyathita.*

3009. **vyathanti** "they tremble; they are disturbed; they are distressed; they are afflicted". 14.2. Also see *gatavyathaḥ, pravyathita.*

3010. **vyathayanti** "they trouble; they afflict; they distress". 2.15. Also see *gatavyathaḥ, pravyathita.*

3011. **vyathiṣṭhāḥ** "tremble; hesitate; be distressed; be grieved". 11.34. [*mā vyathiṣṭhā* = "do not hesitate!"[674]] Also see *gatavyathaḥ, pravyathita.*

3012. **vyatītāni** "have elapsed; have passed away". 4.5. Also see *atītya, samatītya.*

3013. **vyatitariṣyati** "it will cross over". 2.52. Also see √ *tṛ.*

3014. **vyāttānanam** "with mouth wide open". 11.24. [*vyātta* (opened) + *ānanam* (mouth, face)]

3015. **vyavasāyaḥ** "enterprise; determination; effort; stratagem". 10.36; 18.59. Also see *avyavasāyinām, vyavasāyātmikā, vyavasita, vyavasthita.*

3016. **vyavasāyātmikā** "of the nature of a fixed determination; resolute; one-pointed". 2.41, 44. Also see *ātman, avyavasāyinām, vyavasāyaḥ.*

---

673 Swarupananda, p. 272.

674 Sargeant, p. 486.

3017. **vyavasita** "determination to do a particular thing". Also see *vyavasāyaḥ, vyavasthita.*

- vyavasitaḥ "resolve; determination". 9.30.
- vyavasitāḥ "resolved; determined; setting out to (do); prepared for". 1.45.

3018. **vyavasthita** "determined to do a particular thing; steadfast". Also see *vyavasāyaḥ, vyavasita, avasthita.*

- vyavasthitān "organized; arranged; steadfast". 1.20.
- vyavasthitau "are at work; are engaged". 3.34.
- jñānayogavyavasthitiḥ "steadfast in the discipline of knowledge". 16.1.
- kāryākāryavyavasthitau "in determining what to do and what not to do; distinguishing what should and should not be done". 16.24.

3019. **vyudasya** "getting rid of; casting off; rejecting". 18.51.

3020. **vyūḍha** "deployed; mobilized; arranged strategically (for battle)".

- vyūḍham "deployed". 1.2.
- vyūḍhām "deployed". 1.3.

Y

य् = Y.

3021. **yā** "which; that which". 2.69; 18.30, 32, 50.

3022. **yābhiḥ** "those by which". 10.16.

3023. **yacchraddhaḥ** "which faith". 17.3. Also see *śraddhā.*

3024. **yadā** "when". 2.52, 53, 55, 58; 4.7 (twice); 6.4, 18; 13.30; 14.11, 14, 19. [In verse 4.7, the repetition *yadā yadā* means "whenever".]

3025. **yādasām** "of water deities". 10.29.

3026. **yadā yadā** "whenever". 4.7. Also see *yadā.*

3027. **yādava** "O Yādava; O member of the family of Yadu". 11.41. [For the Yādavas see page 10.]

3028. **yadi** "if". 1.38, 46; 2.6; 3.23; 6.32; 11.4, 12.

3029. **yadṛcchālābhasaṁtuṣṭaḥ** "content with whatever gain; one who is satisfied with what one gets by chance; contented with anything that comes his way[675]". 4.22. Also see *lābham, saṁtuṣṭaḥ, tuṣṭaḥ.*

3030. **yadṛcchayā** "on its own; spontaneously; by chance". 2.32.

---

[675] Van Buitenen 1981, p. 87.

3031. **yādṛk** "like what; of what appearance". 13.3.

3032. **yadvat** "as; in which way; in like manner". 2.70.

3033. **yadvikāri** "that from which it has evolved; of what it is a transformation". 13.3. Also see *vikāra*.

3034. **yaḥ** "who; one who; which". 2.19 (twice), 21, 57, 71; 3.6, 7, 12, 16, 17, 42; 4.9, 14, 18 (twice); 5.3, 5, 10, 23, 24 (twice), 28; 6.1, 30, 31, 32, 33, 47; 7.21 (twice); 8.5, 9, 13, 14, 20; 9.26; 10.3, 7; 11.55; 12.14, 15 (twice), 16, 17 (twice); 13.1, 3, 23, 27, 29; 14.23 (twice), 26; 15.1, 17, 19; 16.23; 17.3, 11; 18.11, 16, 55, 67, 68, 70, 71.

3035. **yāḥ** "those which". 14.4.

3036. √ **yaj** "to sacrifice; to worship". Also see *ijyate, ijyayā, iṣṭaḥ, iṣṭvā, juhvati, madyājin, yajantaḥ, yajante, yajanti, yajña, yakṣye, yaṣṭavyam.*

3037. **yajantaḥ** "sacrificing; worshipping". 9.15. [√ *yaj.*]

3038. **yajante** "they worship; they make sacrifice". 4.12[676]; 9.23; 16.17; 17.1, 4 (twice). [√ *yaj.*]

3039. **yajanti** "they worship". 9.23. [√ *yaj.*]

3040. **yajña** "a sacrifice; a sacrificial ritual; performance of a ritual". Also see √ *yaj, adhiyajñaḥ, ayajñasya, dravyayajñāḥ, jñānayajña, japayajñaḥ, juhoṣi, juhvati, kratuḥ, madyājin, nāmayajñaiḥ, sahayajñāḥ, sarva-yajñānām, tapoyajñāḥ, vedayajñādhyayanaiḥ, yajñ-, yogayajñāḥ.*

- yajñaḥ "a sacrifice; performance of a ritual". 3.14; 9.16; 16.1; 17.7, 11; 18.5,
- yajñāḥ "sacrifices; rituals".4.32; 17.23.
- yajñaiḥ "with performance of sacrifices". 9.20.
- yajñam "a sacrifice; a ritual". 4.25 (twice); 17.12, 13.
- yajñānām "of sacrifices; among sacrifices". 10.25.
- yajñāt "due to sacrifice; from sacrifice". 3.14; 4.33.
- yajñāya "for the sake of sacrifice; as dedication to the Supreme". 4.23.
- yajñe "in the sacrifice; in the ritual". 3.15; 17.27.
- yajñena "with the (help of the visible) sacrifice". 4.25.
- yajñeṣu "in rituals". 8.28.

3041. **yajñabhāvitāḥ** "propitiated by the performance of sacrifices". 3.12. Also see *bhāvita.*

3042. **yajñadānatapaḥkarma** "actions (*karma*) related to rituals (*yajña*), donations (*dāna*), and austerities (*tapas*); acts of sacrifice, charity, and penance". 18.3, 5.

---

[676] In 4.12, "*yajanta iha*" is *sandhi* for "*yajante iha*". Divanji (p. 118, entry #2703) lists this as *yajantaḥ.*

Also see *yajñadānatapaḥkriyāḥ, yajñatapasām, yajñatapaḥkriyāḥ, yajña, dāna, tapas, karma.*

3043. **yajñadānatapaḥkriyāḥ** "activities (*kriyā*) related to rituals (*yajña*), donations (*dāna*), and austerities (*tapas*); acts of sacrifice, charity, and penance". 17.24. Also see *yajñadānatapaḥkarma, yajñatapasām, yajñatapaḥkriyāḥ, yajña, dāna, tapas, kriyā.*

3044. **yajñakṣapitakalmaṣāḥ** "whose sins have been destroyed through sacrifice". 4.30.

3045. **yajñārthāt** "done as an offering to the divine; as part of a ritual; for the sake of making a sacrifice". 3.9. Also see *arthaḥ.*

3046. **yajñaśiṣṭa** "remnants of sacrifice". Also see *yajña.*

- yajñaśiṣṭāmṛtabhujaḥ "one who experiences immortality from the remnants of the sacrifice; one who eats the ambrosial remnants of the sacrifice; one who eats the nectar of the remnant of the food offered at a sacrifice".[677] 4.31.
- yajñaśiṣṭāśinaḥ "those who eat the remnants (of food offered at) a sacrifice". 3.13.

3047. **yajñatapaḥkriyāḥ** "rituals and acts of austerities; ceremonies such as that relating to a sacrifice or a penance[678]". 17.25. Also see *tapas, kriyā, yajñadānatapaḥkarma, yajñadānatapaḥkriyāḥ, yajñatapasām.*

3048. **yajñatapasām** "of rituals and austerities". 5.29. Also see *tapas, yajñadānatapaḥkarma, yajñadānatapaḥkriyāḥ, yajñatapaḥkriyāḥ.*

3049. **yajñavidaḥ** "those who are conversant with sacrifices; those who practice sacrifices". 4.30. Also see *yajña, –vid.*

3050. **yajñāyācarataḥ** "undertaking for sacrifice". 4.23. Also see *ācar-, yajña.* [*yajñāyācarataḥ karma* = undertaking action for sacrifice]

3051. **yajuḥ** "*Yajurveda; yajus;* a mantra of the *Yajurveda*". 9.17. Also see *Veda.*

3052. **yakṣa** "Yakṣa; gnome". [A type of semidivine entity, minions of Kubera, the god of Wealth.]

- gandharvayakṣāsurasiddhasaṁghāḥ "groups of *gandharva*-s, *yakṣa*-s, *asura*-s, and *siddha*-s". 11.22.
- yakṣarakṣāṁsi "*Yakṣa*-s and *Rakṣa*-s". 17.4.

---

[677] Divanji, p. 118, entry # 2714, glosses this as "One who eats the nectar of, i.e., the remnant of the food offered at, a sacrifice."

[678] Divanji, p. 118, entry #2709.

- yakṣarakṣasām "among the *Yakṣa*-s and *Rakṣa*-s". 10.23.

3053. **yakṣye** "I will sacrifice". 16.15. Also see √ *yaj*.

3054. **yam** "which; whom". 2.15, 70; 6.2, 22; 8.6 (twice), 21.

3055. **yām** "that which". 2.42; 7.21 (twice).

3056. **yamaḥ** "Yama; the god of death; the Great Regulator; Discipline". 10.29; 11.39.

3057. **yān** "those which". 2.6.

3058. **yānti** "they go; they follow; they attain". 3.33; 4.31; 7.23 (twice), 27; 8.23; 9.7, 25 (four times), 32; 13.34; 16.20. Also see *upayānti*.

3059. **yantrārūḍhāni** "mounted on a machine". 18.61.

3060. **yaśaḥ** "fame; reputation". 10.5; 11.33. Also see *ayaśaḥ*.

3061. **yasmāt** "from which; due to which; because". 12.15; 15.18.

3062. **yasmin** "in which". 6.22; 15.4.

3063. **yaṣṭavyam** "it ought to be done; what ought to be done as duty[679]; to be sacrificed[680]; to be offered; to be performed for its own sake[681]". 17.11. Also see *ijyate*. [√ *yaj*]

3064. **yasya** "of which; of whom; whose". 2.61, 68; 4.19; 8.22; 15.1; 18.17 (twice).

3065. **yasyām** "in which". 2.69.

3066. **yāsyasi** "you will come to; you will go; you will get; you will fall into". 2.35; 4.35. [√ *yā*]

3067. **yat** "who; which; that which; in which; what; whether". 1.45; 2.6, 7, 8, 67; 3.21 (three times); 4.16, 35; 5.1, 5, 21; 6.21, 42; 7.2; 8.11 (three times), 17, 28; 9.1, 27 (five times); 10.1, 14, 39 (twice), 41 (twice); 11.1, 7, 37, 41, 42, 47, 52; 13.2, 3 (twice), 11, 12 (twice); 14.1; 15.6, 8 (twice), 12 (three times); 17.3, 10, 12, 15, 18, 19, 20, 21, 22, 28; 18.8, 9, 15, 21, 22, 23, 24, 25, 37, 38, 39, 40, 59, 60.

3068. **yatacetasām** "of those who control their thoughts; of those with disciplined minds". 5.26. Also see *yatacitt-*, *yatātman*.

3069. **yatacittasya** "of a person with a disciplined mind; one who has brought his mind under restraint". 6.19. Also see *citta*.

3070. **yatacittātmā** "with disciplined mind and self; with disciplined mind and consciousness; one who has brought his mind and heart under restraint; with mind and body under control". 4.21; 6.10. Also see *ātman*, *citta*, *yatātm-*.

---

[679] Tapasyananda, p. 416.

[680] Sargeant, p. 644.

[681] Swarupananda, p. 354.

3071. **yatacittendriyakriyaḥ** "the workings of mind and senses are under control[682]; controlling the activities of the mind and the senses[683]; one who has brought under restraint the actions of the mind and the senses[684]". 6.12. Also see *citta, indriya.*

3072. **yataḥ** "from where; whence; that from which; from whom". 6.26 (twice); 13.3; 15.4; 18.46. [In 6.26, the repeated *yatah yataḥ* = from wherever, from all situations]

3073. **yatamānaḥ** "striving". 6.45.

3074. **yatantaḥ** "striving; making an earnest effort". 9.14; 15.11 (twice).

3075. **yatanti** "they strive; they make earnest effort". 7.29.

3076. **yatatā** "by one who perseveres". 6.36.

3077. **yatataḥ** "striving; making an earnest effort". 2.60.

3078. **yatatām** "of persons striving". 7.3.

3079. **yatate** "one strives; one makes effort". 6.43.

3080. **yatati** "one strives; one makes effort". 7.3.

3081. **yatātman** "self-controlled; self-restrained". Also see *asaṁyatātmanā, ātman, kāmātmānaḥ, mahātmān, niyatātmabhiḥ, prayatātmanaḥ, yata-cetasām, yatātmavān.* [*yata* + *ātman*]

- yatātmā "with self under control; controlling himself". 12.14.
- yatātmānaḥ "whose selves are restrained; controlling themselves". 5.25.

3082. **yatātmavān** "with self-control; with self restraint". 12.11. Also see *ātman, yatātman.* [Nom. sing. masc. of *yatātmavat.*]

3083. **yatavākkāyamānasaḥ** "controlling speech (*vāk*), body (*kāya*), and mind (*manas*)". 18.52. Also see *-mānasaḥ, śarīravāṅmanobhiḥ.*

3084. **yatayaḥ** "ascetics; austere yogis; self-controlled ones". 4.28; 8.11. Also see *yatīnām.*

3085. **yātayāmam** "(food that is) stale; which is spoiled; that over which a night has passed away'. 17.10.

3086. **yatendriyamanobuddhiḥ** "well-regulated senses, motor organs, mind, and intellect; one who has the senses, mind, and intellect under control". 5.28. Also see *indriya, manas, buddhi.*

---

[682] Van Buitenen 1981, p. 95.

[683] Warrier, p. 227.

[684] Divanji, p. 119, entry #2729.

3087. **yathā** "just as; just like; just how". 1.11; 2.13, 22; 3.25, 38 (twice); 4.11, 37; 6.19; 7.1; 9.6; 11.3, 28, 29, 53; 12.20; 13.32, 33; 18.45, 50, 63. [Often paired with *tathā* to make similes or comparisons.] Also see *anyathā, ayathāvat, yathāvat.*

3088. **yathābhāgam** "according to assignment; according to divisions". 1.11. [*yathā + bhāgam*] Also see *guṇakarmavibhāga.*

3089. **yathādarśaḥ** "just as a mirror". 3.38. [*yathā + ādarśaḥ*]

3090. **yathaidhāṁsi** "just as fuel". 4.37. [*yathā + edhāṁsi*]

3091. **yathākāśasthitaḥ** "just as abiding in space". 9.6. [*yathā + ākāśa + sthitaḥ*]

3092. **yathāttha** "just as you say". 11.3. [*yathā + āttha*]

3093. **yathāvat** "as a thing is; appropriate". 18.19. Also see *yathā.* [*yathā + vat*]

3094. **yathecchasi** "just as you wish". 18.63. [*yathā + icchasi*]

3095. **yathoktam** "as stated". 12.20. Also see *ukta.* [*yathā + uktam*]

3096. **yatholbenāvṛtaḥ** "just as (an embryo) is covered by a membrane". 3.38. [*yathā + ulbena + āvṛtaḥ*]

3097. **yāti** "one goes to; one reaches; one attains". 6.45; 8.5, 8, 13, 26; 13.28; 14.14; 16.22.

3098. **yatīnām** "of ascetics; of austere yogis; of self-controlled ones". 5.26. Also see *yatayaḥ.*

3099. **yatra** "where; that in which". 6.20 (twice), 21; 8.23; 18.36, 78 (twice).

3100. **yatprabhāvaḥ** "the powers he is endowed with; of what kind of prowess". 13.3. Also see *apratimaprabhāva, prabhāva.*

3101. **yauvanam** "youth". 2.13.

3102. **yāvān** "of what kind; as much; that much". 2.46; 18.55.

3103. **yāvat** "so that; as much". 1.22 ("so that"); 13.26 ("as much; any").

3104. **yayā** "by which". 2.39; 7.5; 18.31, 33, 34, 35.

3105. **ye** "those which; those who". 1.7, 23; 3.13, 31, 32; 4.11; 5.22; 7.12 (twice), 14, 29, 30; 9.22, 23, 29, 32; 11.22, 32; 12.1 (twice), 2, 3, 6, 20; 13.34; 17.1, 5.

3106. **yena** "by which; with what; by whom". 2.17; 3.2; 4.35; 6.6; 8.22; 10.10; 12.19; 18.20, 46.

3107. **yenakenacit** "by anything whatever". 12.19. [*yena kenacit*]

3108. **yeṣām** "of whom; among those who; those which". 1.33; 2.35; 5.16, 19; 7.28; 10.6.

3109. **yoddhavyam** "to be fought; it is incumbent to fight". 1.22.

3110. **yoddhukāmān** "those desirous of fighting; pugnacious[685]". 1.22. Also see *kāma*.

3111. **yodhāḥ** "warriors; fighters". 11.32.

3112. **yodhamukhyaiḥ** "with the principal warriors" 11.26. Also see *mukhyam*.

3113. **yodhavīrān** "heroic warriors; battle heroes". 11.34.

3114. **yoga**[686] "union; spiritual practice; discipline; yogic power". Also see *saṁyoga, yogayukta, abhyāsayoga, ātmasaṁyamayogāgnau, ātmayogāt, ayogataḥ, bhaktiyogena, brahmayogayuktātmā, buddhisaṁyogam, buddhiyoga, duḥkhasaṁyogaviyogam, dhyānayogaparaḥ, jñanayoga, karmaphalasaṁyogam, karmayoga, kṣetrakṣetrajñasaṁyogāt, niryogakṣema, sāṁkhyayogau, saṁnyāsayogayuktātmā, viṣayendriyasaṁyogāt, yoktavyaḥ, yuj-, yukt-, yuñj-.*

- yogaiḥ "by *yoga*; with *yoga*". 5.5.
- yogaḥ "*yoga*". 2.48, 50; 4.2, 3; 6.16, 17, 23, 33, 36.
- yogam "*yoga*". 2.53; 4.1, 42; 5.1, 5; 6.2, 3, 12, 19; 7.1; 9.5 (yogic power); 10.7 (yogic power), 18 (yogic power); 11.8 (yogic power); 12.11 (*madyogam*); 18.75.
- yogasya "of *yoga*". 6.44.
- yogāt "from *yoga*; from the yogic path". 6.37.
- yogāya "to *yoga*". 2.50.
- yoge "in *yoga*; in practice". 2.39.

3115. **yogabalena** "with the strength of discipline; with the strength that comes from the practice of *yoga*; with the power of *yoga*". 8.10. Also see *bala*.

---

[685] Bolle, p. 304.

[686] For discussion of what *yoga* means, see the Theme Guide for *Yoga as Spiritual Discipline* on page 294. For three specific definitions of *yoga*, see verses 2.48, 2.50, and 6.23. For "practice" as an underlying concept see the word *yoktavyaḥ* ("should be practiced" or "should be concentrated on") in verse 6.23. Sometimes *yoga* has a sense more like "divine power" or "yogic power" as in 9.5, 10.7, 10.18, and 11.8. Śaṅkara's commentary on verse 10.7 (Warrier, p. 325) says that "... by *Yoga* is meant omniscience and power due to mastery of Yogic attainments" (योगैश्वर्यसामर्थ्यं सर्वज्ञत्वं योगजं योगः उच्यते). Śaṅkara's commentary on verse 10.18 (Warrier, p. 332) says in that case *yoga* means "the unique power of Yogic lordliness" (योगैश्वर्यशक्तिविशेषं).

3116. **yogabhraṣṭaḥ** "one who has strayed from discipline; the man who has fallen from the path of *yoga*; failed yogin[687]". 6.41.

3117. **yogadhāraṇām** "well-established in yogic meditation". 8.12.

3118. **yogakṣemam** "fulfillment and maintenance of well-being; acquisition of that which is not in one's possession and the preservation of that which is[688]". 9.22. Also see *kṣema, niryogakṣemaḥ.*

3119. **yogamāyāsamāvṛtaḥ** "veiled by *yogamāyā*; enveloped by the power of illusion; covered by the magic of (my) *yoga*". 7.25. Also see *māyā, samāvṛta, yoga.*

3120. **yogārūḍhaḥ** "one who has attained the height of *yoga*; one who has ascended (the ladder) of *yoga*". 6.4. [i.e., one who is an adept in *yoga*.]

3121. **yogārūḍhasya** "of one who has attained the height of *yoga*; of one who has ascended (the ladder) of *yoga*". 6.3. [i.e., of one who is an adept in *yoga*.]

3122. **yogasaṁjñitam** "designated as *yoga*; known as *yoga*". 6.23. [*duḥkha-saṁyogaviyogaṁ yogasaṁjñitam* = one should understand *yoga* as disconnection from misery]

3123. **yogasaṁnyastakarmāṇam** "one who has abandoned (the bondage of) actions by *yoga*; one who has renounced action through *yoga*; one who has given up the performance of religious rites by *yoga* i.e., according to the theory of *karmayoga*[689]; one who has dedicated (his) actions (to God) through *yoga*[690]; renouncing (all) works in *yoga*[691]". 4.41. Also see *karma*, √ *saṁnyas, saṁnyasta.*

3124. **yogasaṁsiddhaḥ** "one who has become an adept by means of *yoga*". 4.38.

3125. **yogasaṁsiddhim** "yogic attainment; the adeptness that is the result of *yoga*". 6.37.

3126. **yogasevayā** "with the practice of *yoga*". 6.20. Also see *sevayā.*

3127. **yogasthaḥ** "well-established in *yoga*; one who has his mind fixed in *yoga*". 2.48.

3128. **yogavittamāḥ** "the best knowers of *yoga*". 12.1.

3129. **yogayajñāḥ** "those who offer sacrifice in the form of *yoga*; those with austerities of *yoga*". 4.28. Also see *yajña.*

---

687 Van Buitenen 1981, p. 97.

688 Divanji, p. 123, entry #2823.

689 Divanji, p. 124, entry #2833.

690 Gambhīrānanda 1998, p. 328.

691 Zaehner, p. 198.

3130. **yogayukta** "disciplined in *yoga*; engaged in *yoga*". Also see *yoga, yukta*.

- abhyāsayogayuktena "controlled by (constant) practice; engaged in the *yoga* of practice; disciplined by the practice of *yoga*; yoked by the *yoga* of practice". 8.8.
- brahmayogayuktātmā "one whose self is well-established in union with *Brahman*; the state of being in union with *Brahman*; one whose mind has acquired Brahmayoga[692]; his spirit yoked with the *yoga* of *brahman*[693]". 5.21.
- saṁnyāsayogayuktātmā "with the mind well-established in the renunciation (of the fruits of action); one whose mind has become composed by means of Saṁnyāsayoga". 9.28.
- yogayuktaḥ "employing *yoga* equipped with *yoga*; one who practices *yoga*; a follower of the path of *yoga*". 5.6, 7; 8.27.
- yogayuktātmā "one who has disciplined the (lower) self with *yoga*; one whose mind is composed by the practice of *yoga*". 6.29.

3131. **yogayuktātmā** "one who has disciplined the (lower) self with *yoga*; one whose mind is composed by the practice of *yoga*". 6.29. Also see *ātman, yogayukta, yuktātmā*.

3132. **yogena** "by means of *yoga*; by discipline".

- abhyāsayogena "by the *yoga* of practice". 12.9.
- bhaktiyogena "by the practice of devotion". 14.26. [The *yoga* consisting of the practice of spiritual devotion.]
- ananyayogena "without means of another discipline; without using another *yoga*; by the *yoga* consisting of concentration on only one ideal". 13.10.
- jñānayogena "by the *yoga* of knowledge; by the discipline of knowledge". 3.3.
- karmayogena "by the practice of action". 3.3; 13.24.
- yogena "by *yoga*". 10.7; 12.6; 13.24.
- yogenāvyabhicāriṇyā "by unswerving discipline". 18.33. Also see *avyabhicār-*.

---

692 Divanji, p. 102, entry #2340.

693 Van Buitenen 1981, p. 93.

3133. **yogeśvara** "Lord of *yoga*; master of *yoga*". Also see *īśvara*.

- mahāyogeśvaraḥ "the great Lord of *yoga*". 11.9.
- yogeśvara "O Lord of *yoga*". 11.4.
- yogeśvaraḥ "the Lord of *yoga*". 18.78.
- yogeśvarāt "from the Lord of *yoga*". 18.75.

3134. **yogin** "a practitioner of *yoga*; a practitioner of the study to become renounced; a *yogin*".

- yogī "a yogin". 5.24; 6.1, 2, 8, 10, 15, 28, 31, 32, 45, 46 (three times); 8.25, 27, 28; 12.14.
- yogin "O yogin". 10.17. [Referring to Kṛṣṇa.]
- yoginaḥ "yogins (nom. pl.); of a yogin (gen. sing.)". 4.25; 5.11; 6.19; 8.14, 23; 15.11.
- yoginam "a yogin". 6.27.
- yoginām "of yogins". 3.3; 6.42, 47.

3135. **yoktavyaḥ** "must be yoked[694]; should be practiced; should be concentrated on". 6.23. [√ *yuj*]

3136. **yoni** "womb; source; origin; generating cause".

- duḥkhayonayaḥ "origins of misery; sources of sorrow". 5.22. Also see *duḥkha*.
- etadyonīni "originating from that (these two types of Nature); having this as their source". 7.6. [The two sources are the higher and lower Natures.]
- mūḍhayoniṣu "among the stupid species". 14.15. Also see *mūḍha*.
- pāpayonayaḥ "of inferior origin; of inauspicious birth; born of sin". 9.32. Also see *pāpa*.
- sadasadyonijanmasu "in births taking place in good and bad species of beings; births in good and evil wombs". 13.21. Also see *sat, asat, janma*.
- sarvayoniṣu "from all wombs; in all species; in all sources of birth". 14.4. Also see *sarva*.
- yoniḥ "womb". 14.3, 4.
- yonim "line of birth; species". 16.20.
- yoniṣu "into the wombs; into the species". 16.19.

3137. **yotsyamānān** "those who are about to fight". 1.23.

---

[694] Van Buitenen's (1981, p. 95) "*yoga* must be yoked" brings out the wordplay in *yoktavyo yogaḥ* (verse 6.23). The idea is that *yoga* must be pursued with determination. The idea could also be rendered as "*yoga* should be practiced".

3138. **yotsye** "I will fight". 2.9; 18.59. [√ *yudh*. *na yotsya iti* = "I will not fight". Sandhi changes *e* to *a*, producing *yotsya*.] Also see *pratiyotsyāmi*.

3139. **yuddha** "battle; combat; war".

- yuddham "battle". 2.32.
- yuddhāt "as a result of battle; than (a righteous) war". 2.31.
- yuddhāya "for battle". 2.37, 38.
- yuddhe "in the battle; in war". 1.23, 33; 18.43.

3140. **yuddhaviśāradāḥ** "skilled in military science; skilled in battle; skillful fighters". 1.9.

3141. **yudhāmanyuḥ** "Yudhāmanyu". 1.6. [A warrior allied with the Pāṇḍavas. The name means "very brave".]

3142. **yudhi** "in battle". 1.4.

3143. **yudhiṣṭhiraḥ** "Yudhiṣṭhira; Steady in Battle". 1.16. [Name of the eldest of the five Pāṇḍava brothers.] See "Who's Who", page 10.

3144. **yudhya** "fight!". 8.7.

3145. **yudhyasva** "fight!". 2.18; 3.30; 11.34.

3146. **yuga** [a cosmic time period; an age or cycle]

- sahasrayugaparyantam "extending for a thousand *yuga*-s; that whose end comes after a thousand *yuga*-s". 8.17.
- yugasahasrāntām "ending after a thousand *yuga*-s". 8.17. Also see *sahasr-*.
- yuge yuge "in age after age". 4.8.

3147. **yugapat** "simultaneously, at once". 11.12.

3148. √ **yuj** "to join; to unite; to yoke; to harness; to endow with; to employ; to direct; to turn one's mind to; to meditate on". Also see *yuj-*, *yukt-*, *yuñj-*, *niyojayasi*, *niyojitaḥ*, *niyokṣyati*, *prayujyate*, *prayuktaḥ*.

3149. **yujyasva** "join; engage; yoke yourself; be ready for". 2.38, 50. [Imp. 2nd pers. sing. of √ *yuj*, used in the sense of "to take to" or "to prepare oneself for"]

- yuddhāya yujyasva "join the battle!" or "engage in the struggle!". 2.38.
- yogāya yujyasva "join yourself to *yoga*" or "engage in *yoga*". 2.50.

3150. **yujyate** "it is employed or is used (17.26); is united with (10.7)". 10.7; 17.26. [Pass. 3rd pers. sing. of √ *yuj*, used in the sense of to be joined with or be established in something.] Also see *prayujyate*.

3151. **yukta** "disciplined; having a composed mind; fixed in *yoga*; endowed with; accompanied by". Also see *ayukta, buddhiyukta, dambhāhaṁkārasaṁyuktāḥ, kāmakrodhaviyuktānām, nityayukta, prāṇāpānasamāyuktaḥ, prayuktaḥ, rāgadveṣaviyuktaiḥ, satatayukta, yogayukta.*

- yuktaḥ "a well-disciplined person; one who has a well-regulated mind; a *yogin*". 2.61; 3.26; 4.18; 5.8, 12, 23; 6.8, 14, 18. Verses 4.18, 5.23, 6.8, and 6.18 provide definitions of a *yuktaḥ* that make the term virtually synonymous with *yogin.*
- yuktaḥ "endowed with; accompanied by". 2.39; 7.22; 8.10; 18.51.
- yuktaiḥ "by well-disciplined people". 17.17.

3152. **yuktaceṣṭasya** "of one who is moderate in actions; of one whose movements are under control". 6.17. Also see *ceṣṭāḥ.*

3153. **yuktacetasaḥ** "those with well-regulated minds; those who are mentally disciplined". 7.30. Also see *yuktātmā.*

3154. **yuktāhāravihārasya** "one whose food and movements are regulated[695]; a person with balanced diet (*āhāra*) and regimens (*vihāra*)". 6.17. [*yukta-āhāra-vihārasya*]

3155. **yuktasvapnāvabodhasya** "one who regulates one's periods of sleep and waking; a person with balance in sleeping and wakefulness". 6.17. Also see *svapna.*

3156. **yuktatamaḥ** "the best *yogin*". 6.47.

3157. **yuktatamāḥ** "the best *yogins*". 12.2

3158. **yuktātmā** "one who has a composed mind; one who has a well-regulated mind". Also see *ātman, yuktacetasaḥ.*

- brahmayogayuktātmā "well-established in union with *Brahman*; one whose self is yoked in union with *Brahman*". 5.21. Also see *brahma.*
- saṁnyāsayogayuktātmā "one whose mind has become composed by means of Saṁnyāsayoga". 9.28. Also see *saṁnyas-.*
- yogayuktātmā "one who has disciplined the (lower) self with *yoga*; one whose mind is composed by the practice of *yoga*". 6.29. Also see *yoga.*
- yuktātmā "one who has a composed mind; one who has a well-regulated mind". 7.18.

3159. **yukte** "yoked". 1.14.

---

695 Gambhīrānanda 1998, p. 417.

3160. **yuktvā** "having been joined; after connecting with; having united (yourself with Me); having yoked (yourself to Me)[696]; having integrated[697]; having disciplined (thyself)[698]; having regulated (one's mind)[699]". 9.34. [Indec. past part. of √ *yuj*.] Also see *–tvā*.

3161. **yuñjan** "practicing (*yoga*); engaging in (*yoga*); practicing discipline; disciplining himself; keeping steadfast; regulating (one's life);". 6.15, 28; 7.1. [Nom. sing. of the present participial adj. *yuñjat*, √ *yuj*.]

3162. **yuñjataḥ** "(of) the practicing one; of the one engaged in *yoga*; of the yoked; of the disciplined". 6.19. [Gen. sing. of the present participial adj. *yuñjat*, √ *yuj*.]

3163. **yuñjīta** "should practice (*yoga*); should yoke himself; should discipline himself; should keep (the mind) steady". 6.10. [√ *yuj*]

3164. **yuñjyāt** "one should practice; let one practice (*yoga*)". 6.12. [√ *yuj*]

3165. **yuyudhānaḥ** "Yuyudhāna". 1.4. ["Eager to fight", an epithet for Sātyaki, a warrior allied with the Pāṇḍavas.]

3166. **yuyutsavaḥ** "determined to fight; eager to fight". 1.1. Also see *yuyutsūm*.

3167. **yuyutsūm** "determined to fight; eager to fight". 1.28. Also see *yuyutsavaḥ*.

---

[696] Van Buitenen's translation (1981, p. 107) of the hemistich is "you shall come to me, having thus yoked yourself to me as your highest goal."

[697] Gambhīrānanda (1997, p. 398) translates Śaṅkara's commentary on *yuktvā* as "by concentrating your mind". Zaehner (pp. 286-9) dismisses Śaṅkara's view and says that *yuktvā* refers to the "integrated self" (connecting it with *ātmānam*), consistent with his view of *yoga* as "integration" of the personality of the practitioner. Rāmānuja's commentary says that in this verse *ātman* stands for the mind, so Ādidevānanda (pp. 322-4) translates the idea as "engaging your mind in this manner".

[698] Edgerton, p. 49.

[699] Divanji, p. 122, entry #2795, notes that *yuj* can mean "to join" but also "to regulate one's mind", adding that the latter meaning applies here.

Theme Guides

The *Bhagavadgītā* does not follow a strictly linear teaching scheme, and important topics come up in more than once place. It is essential to step back and see how core ideas run through the work as a whole.

This section includes brief introductions to key themes, listing verses that can be read as a group to understand a specific idea. If the book is used in connection with a class or seminar, each session can be based on a single Theme Guide, with group discussion of the material. The approach is to encourage reading the primary source material rather than secondary analysis.

Theme Guide

Yoga as Spiritual Discipline

In verse 18.75 Saṁjaya sums up his narrative by saying, "this *yoga* has been described by the Lord of *Yoga*" (*yogaṁ yogeśvarāt*). What does *yoga* mean in the *BG*? What is a *yogin*? There are no simple answers for these questions. The word *yoga*, and terms related to it, occur many times in the text with varying meanings depending on context.

Today, many people think of *yoga* primarily as a form of physical exercise, with some meditative aspects. That is not the meaning in the *BG*, where *yoga* most often means a type of spiritual discipline or control. Some modern practitioners think of *yoga* as something like a practice undertaken to promote integration of the personality, but this is not the meaning in the *BG* which is transpersonal in essence.

The *BG* refers to specific types of *yoga*, such as *karmayoga*, *bhaktiyoga*, or *jñānayoga*, that will appeal to people of varying personality types. Sometimes, as in verses 2.39-40, *yoga* has the sense of "practice" as opposed to theoretical knowledge (*sāṁkhya*). For "practice" as an underlying concept see the word *yoktavyaḥ* ("should be practiced" or "should be yoked to") in verse 6.23. In a few verses, *yoga* is used with a sense more like *spiritual power* or *yogic power*.[700]

Originally, *yoga* may have meant *joining* or *connection*, but later it was used for methods of control or restraint by which union with the highest spiritual reality could be attained.[701] That later understanding underlies Patañjali's definition of *yoga* as control of the mind.[702] Most modern commentators derive the word *yoga* from the Sanskrit root *yuj*, in the sense *to join*. However, Pāṇini's *dhātupāṭha* actually lists three different forms of the root *yuj*.[703] Root 4-68, *yuja samādhau*,

---

[700] For *yoga* as "yogic power" see 9.5, 10.7, 10.18, and 11.8. Śaṅkara's commentary on verse 10.7 as translated by Warrier (p. 325) says that "... by *Yoga* is meant omniscience and power due to mastery of Yogic attainments" (योगैश्वर्यसामर्थ्यं सर्वज्ञत्वं योगजं योगः उच्यते). Śaṅkara's commentary on verse 10.18 as translated by Warrier (p. 332) says in that case *yoga* means "the unique power of Yogic lordliness" (योगैश्वर्यशक्तिविशेषं).

[701] Hill, pp. 40-41, and p. 159, note 1.

[702] *YS* 1.2: *yogaścittavṛttinirodhaḥ*.

[703] Katre, pp. 1188 (4-68, *yuja samādhau*), 1193 (7-7, *yujir yoge*), and 1199 (10-264, *yuja ... saṁyamane*); Vasu, p. 59* (root index). In commenting on the first verse of Patañjali's *Yogasūtra*, Vyāsa's *Yogasūtrabhāṣya* explains *yoga* as *samādhi* (योगः समाधिः), which is consistent with the meaning *samādhau*.

means *to meditate*; root 7-7, *yujir yoge*, means *to join*; and root 10-264, *yuja ... saṁyamane*, means *to control*. Even if modern linguists would not agree that these are three distinct roots, the fact that early grammarians classified them as such suggests awareness of *polysemy*—the ability of a word to take many different meanings. For example, in verse 6.23, wordplay such as *duḥkhasaṁyogaviyogam* ("disconnection from connection with suffering") is based on an underlying meaning of being yoked to something. In verse 5.21, Hill translates *brahmayogayuktātmā* as "his self controlled by contemplating *Brahman*", understanding *yoga* as contemplation.[704] In verse 10.7, we have *yoga* referring to Kṛṣṇa's divine power.

Leaving grammatical considerations aside, three verses provide practical definitions of *yoga* from different points of view:

- 2.48: *samatvaṁ yoga ucyate* = *yoga* is said to be equanimity.
- 2.50: *yogaḥ karmasu kauśalam* = *yoga* is skill in action.
- 6.23: *taṁ vidyād duḥkhasaṁyogaviyogaṁ yogasaṁjñitam* = one should understand that disconnection (*viyogam*) from connection with misery as *yoga*. That state is described in verses 6.20-23.

A *yogin* is a practitioner of *yoga*. A contemporary understanding of the term might be a well-disciplined or well-integrated person (*yuktaḥ*), but that misses the sense of an active spiritual seeker who is employing specific practices to reach a transpersonal goal. Verses 4.18, 5.23, 6.8, and 6.18 provide definitions of a *yuktaḥ* that make that word virtually synonymous with *yogin*. Related words can be found by looking for elements such as *yog-*, *yuj-*, *yukt-*, and *yuñj-*. Important compound words include *bhaktiyoga, brahmayoga, buddiyoga, jñanayoga, karmayoga*, and *sāṁkhyayoga*.

Verses related to this theme

- 2.39-40: Wisdom in theory (*sāṁkhya*) is contrasted to wisdom in practice (*yoga*). Even a little of this discipline is beneficial.
- 2.48: *Yoga* is said to be equanimity of mind (*samatvaṁ yoga ucyate*).
- 2.49-51: After becoming well-established in *yoga*, perform all action. *Yoga* is skill in action (*yogaḥ karmasu kauśalam*).
- 2.53: When your wisdom is unwavering you will attain union (*yoga*) with your true Self.
- 2.61: Having controlled the senses the disciplined one (*yuktaḥ*) should remain intent on Me.

[704] Hill, pp. 41, 152.

- 2.66: For an undisciplined person (*ayuktaḥ*) there is neither wisdom nor spiritual devotion.
- 3.26: A wise person should inspire by performing all actions in a well-disciplined (*yuktaḥ*) manner.
- 4.18: One who can see non-action in action, and action in non-action, is a well-disciplined person (*yuktaḥ*).
- 4.38: There is nothing as purifying as knowledge. In time, one well-accomplished in *yoga* (*yoga-saṁsiddhaḥ*) finds that (knowledge) in one's own self.
- 5.6-12: The nature of *karmayoga* is explained. Using this method, setting aside attachment to the results of action, a disciplined person (*yuktaḥ*) attains peace.
- 5.19: The worldly cycle is overcome by those whose minds are established in equanimity, the ability to view all things with an equal eye (*sāmya*). This restates the definition of *yoga* as "sameness" (*samatvam*) that was given in verse 2.48.
- 5.21: A person without attachment to external objects attains happiness in the Self. That person, in communion with *Brahman* (*brahmayogayuktātmā*), finds imperishable happiness.
- 5.23-4: One who can withstand an urge arising from passion and anger is a well-disciplined person (*yuktaḥ*). The *yogin* identified with *Brahman* attains liberation in *Brahman*.
- 6.3-4: Action is the means for the wise person who desires to attain the height of *yoga*. After one attains the height of *yoga*, serenity is the means for the same person. When one is not attached to objects of the senses and actions, and has renounced intents (for any fruits of actions), then that person is described as having attained the height of *yoga* (*yogārūḍhaḥ*).
- 6.7-8: Characteristics of a well-integrated person (*yuktaḥ*) are described. That person is called a *yogin*.
- 6.10-29: The characteristics and practices of the *yogin* are described.
- 6.23: Disconnection from connection with misery (*duḥkha-saṁyoga-viyogam*) is known as *yoga*.
- 6.29: With the self disciplined by *yoga* (*yogayuktātmā*), one sees oneself residing in all beings, and all beings in oneself, regarding all everywhere as the same.
- 6.33: Arjuna uses the word *sāmyena* to characterize the *yoga* Kṛṣṇa teaches. This repeats the word *sāmya* that was used in verse 5.19.

Translators render the idea of *sāmyena* "as (the vision of) equality[705]; consisting in sameness[706]; as equanimity[707]; or "through equanimity",[708] all of which restate the definition of *yoga* in verse 2.48: *samatvaṁ yoga ucyate* = *yoga* is said to be equanimity.

- 6.46-7: A *yogin* is superior to those who practice austerities, to persons of knowledge, and to persons of action. Therefore, become a *yogin.* Moreover, of all *yogins,* one who is devoted to Me is the best *yogin.*
- 7.1: Hear how practicing *yoga* with mind attached to Me you will know Me completely.
- 7.16-18: Four types of persons are devoted to Me. Of these, the best is the wise one (*jñānī*) who is one-pointedly dedicated to Me. With self well-regulated (*yuktātmā*), that one is established in Me as the highest goal.
- 8.8: Meditating, with mind not straying, engaged in continuous practice of *yoga* (*abhyāsayogayuktena*), one attains the Supreme Consciousness (*paramaṁ puruṣam*).
- 8.10: At the time of death, focusing the life force with yogic power (*yukto yogabalena*), one attains the Supreme Consciousness (*paraṁ puruṣam*).
- 8.14: I am easily accessible to that ever-dedicated *yogin* (*nityayuktasya yoginaḥ*) who constantly remembers Me.
- 8.27-28: Therefore, always be engaged in *yoga.* On knowing this, the *yogin* goes beyond that fruit of righteousness that is spelled out in the Vedas, in sacrifices, in austerieties, and even in charity. One attains the supreme, primal abode.
- 9.14: Those of firm vows, ever steadfast (*nitya-yuktaḥ*), worship Me.
- 9.28: Well-established in renunciation (*saṁnyāsayogayuktātmā*), liberated, you will attain Me.
- 9.34: Having united (*yuktvā*) yourself with Me, you will truly attain Me.
- 10.7: One who knows in truth this glorious manifestation and *yoga* of Mine is united with unshakable *yoga.*

---

705 Sampatkumaran, p. 165. Rāmānuja interprets the passage as meaning that the *yoga* taught by Kṛṣṇa is a vision of equality everywhere among all selves.

706 Warrier, p. 242.

707 Van Buitenen 1981, p. 97; Gambhīrānanda 1998, pp. 458-9.

708 Tapasyananda's (p. 181) "spiritual communion through equanimity" captures the instrumental *sāmyena.*

- 10.10: To those who are constantly in communion (*satatayuktānām*) with Me, who worship Me with love, I give that *yoga* of wisdom (*buddhiyogam*) by which they come to Me.
- 12.1-2: Who has the best knowledge of *yoga* (*yogavittamāḥ*)? Those who are ever joined (*satatayuktāḥ*) in worshipping You in manifest form or those who worship the imperishable Unmanifest? Those who are always joined (*nityayuktāḥ*) in worshipping Me are the best *yogins* (*yuktatamāḥ*).
- 12.11: Kṛṣṇa refers to *madyogam* ("My *yoga*"). This may simply mean the type of *karmayoga* that Kṛṣṇa teaches and practices (verses 3.22-25). Śaṅkara takes *madyoga* as meaning casting off all action onto God. Alternatively, Rāmānuja takes *madyoga* as meaning *bhaktiyoga*, the practice of devotion.
- 18.51-3: Characteristics of one fit for identity with *Brahman* are described. These include being endowed with (*yuktaḥ*) pure wisdom and being engaged in the practice of meditation (*dhyāna-yoga-paraḥ*).
- 18.57: Taking recourse in the *yoga* of discriminating wisdom (*buddhiyogam*), let your mind be continuously focused on Me.
- 18.75: Saṁjaya sums up his narrative by saying, "this *yoga* has been described by the Lord of *Yoga*" (*yogaṁ yogeśvarāt*).

Theme Guide

Overcoming the Duality of Attraction and Aversion

Overcoming dualities is a core theme of the *Bhagavadgītā*. Attraction (*rāga, icchā*) and aversion (*dveṣa*) underlie more specific dualities such as pleasure and pain (*sukha* and *duḥka*) or success and failure (*siddha* and *asiddha*). Attraction and aversion are symptoms of attachment (*saṅga*). The *Bhagavadgītā* recommends reducing attachment and developing an attitude of equanimity (*sama*), which results in a feeling of peace (*śānti*).

Several synonyms for the concepts of attraction and aversion are used. Finding the best English words to capture the basic duality is challenging. Verse 7.27 uses the compound *icchā-dveṣa* (desire and dislike), which means the same thing as the compound *rāga-dveṣa*. One pole is *rāga* (*icchā*) which may be translated as desire, attraction, or longing. The other pole is *dveṣa*, which may be translated as hatred, aversion, or dislike. The word *dveṣa* is from the root *dviṣ*, which means to hate or be hostile to something. The following verses can be read as a group to see the duality of attraction and aversion ("longing and loathing") as a key theme.

Verses related to this theme

- 2.45: A person should become free of dualities (*nirdvandva*), firmly established in one's true Self.
- 2.48: *Yoga* is defined as "equanimity" (*samatvam*) in both success and failure (*siddhyasiddhyoḥ samo bhūtvā samatvaṁ yoga ucyate*).
- 2.50: *Yoga* is further defined as "skill in actions" (*yogaḥ karmasu kauśalam*). The practitioner casts off both good and evil deeds (*jahātīta ubhe sukṛta-duṣkṛte*). This must be interpreted in light of verse 2.49 which emphasizes that the motives for action must not be based on desire for fruit (*phala*). That is, one must perform action motivated by a sense of duty, not motivated by desire or hatred.
- 2.57: One who is without attachment neither rejoices nor dislikes (*nābhinnandati na dveṣṭi*) whatever is encountered.
- 2.64: One attains tranquility (*prasādam*) by detaching from desire and aversion (*rāga-dveṣa-viyuktaiḥ*).
- 2.71: One who is free from desire (*niḥspṛhaḥ*) attains peace.
- 3.34: "Longing and loathing" (*rāga-dveṣa*) are enemies, and one should not come under their power.

- 4.22: Content with whatever is gained, transcending duality (*dvandvātīta*), one is not bound even having performed action.
- 5.3: True renunciation, as practiced by the perpetual renouncer (*nitya-saṁnyāsī*) is that of someone who has freed themself from the pairs of opposites, neither hating nor desiring *(dveṣṭi na kāṅkṣati*).
- 5.23: One who can withstand the impulses of desire (*kāma*) and anger (*krodha*) is a disciplined and happy person.
- 5.25-26: For those detached from desire and anger (*kāmakrodha-viyuktānām*), the bliss of *Brahman* (*brahma-nirvāṇam*) lies near.
- 7.27-28: Liberated persons overcome the pairs of opposites that arise out of desire and aversion (*icchā-dveṣa-samutthena*).
- 9.29: Kṛṣṇa says that he is the same in all beings, and that none is disliked or dear to Him (*na me dveṣyo 'sti na priyaḥ*).
- 12.17: The devotee who neither hates nor rejoices, not mourning or longing for things, is beloved by Kṛṣṇa.
- 12.18-19: God loves a person who is able to remain the same (*sama*) in regard to friends and enemies, honor and dishonor, cold and heat, pleasure and displeasure, censure and praise. That person maintains equanimity (*sama*), is free from attachment (*saṅga-vivarjita*), and is contented with anything.
- 13.6: Desire and aversion (*icchā, dveṣaḥ*) and pleasure and pain (*sukham, duḥkham*) are listed as pairs of opposites.
- 14.22: The liberated person does not act due to attachment, neither negatively by loathing (*dveṣṭi*) nor positively by craving (*kāṅkṣati*). These two responses are "the pairs" that are transcended by the liberated (compare 7.27 and 5.3).
- 14.23-25: A person is considered to have transcended the *guṇa*-s when able to remain neutral, maintaining an attitude of equality in the face of dualities.
- 15.5: Being free from attachment and being free from dualities are two of the characteristics of spiritual development.
- 18.10: The renouncer (*tyāgī*) neither hates disagreeable action nor is attached to agreeable action.
- 18.23: Being free from attachment (*saṅgarahitam*), without desire or hatred (*a-rāga-dveṣataḥ*), is *sāttvic*.
- 18.51: One becomes fit for oneness with *Brahman* (18.53) by casting off attraction and hatred (*rāga-dveṣau vyudasya*).

Theme Guide

Karmayoga: Action as Spiritual Practice

The way of works (*karmayoga*) is balanced against other methods such as the way of knowledge (*jñānayoga*) and the way of devotion to God (*bhaktiyoga*). Different commentators stress one or another of these paths in their own interpretations of what is most essential in the text.

One essential idea behind *karmayoga* is that, "Although the body acts, the Self is not the doer" (verse 3.27). In this thought, one recognizes that all activity exists only in Nature (*Prakṛti*) and is essentially different from the Consciousness (*Puruṣa*) that witnesses the activity. In addition to recognizing that all action exists only in the realm of Nature, two other essential aspects of *karmayoga* are renunciation of the fruits of action (e.g., 2.51) and dedicating actions to the Divine (e.g., 3.30).

The text assumes a belief in reincarnation. Since action (*karma*) done during life will affect one's next birth, avoiding the harmful after-effects of action was a subject of great concern. Some people felt that the best approach was to not perform action at all. Others said that complete avoidance of action was impossible and undesirable, and that the better way was to perform action but renounce the fruits of that action, recognizing that all action takes place only within the operations of Nature (*Prakṛti*). The mental attitude of performing action in a spirit of selfless service with no attachment to results is the key to *karmayoga*. It transforms every action into a sacrifice (*yajña*) offered to the Divine. Action done in this way has no harmful effect on rebirth.

Action is a valid spiritual path that is suitable for many people. Examples are given of great leaders such as Janaka and others who attained spiritual fulfillment while remaining engaged in the world. These examples remind us that this text was intended for an audience of "regular people" and not just for a spiritual elite.

Verses related to this theme

- 2.38-39: One should not begin battle unless you can view victory and defeat as the same. Endowed with wisdom you will get rid of the bondage of action.
- 2.47: Your duty is confined to action alone, and not to the fruits of action. Do not be motivated by the fruits of action, and have no attachment to inaction.

- 2.48: After becoming well-established in *yoga*, after letting go of all attachments, maintaining equilibrium in success or failure, perform action. Equanimity is considered the best *yoga* (*samatvaṁ yoga ucyate*).
- 2.49: Action (motivated merely by desire) is inferior to (action done with) wisdom. Seek shelter in wisdom. Those attached to the results of their actions are pitiful.
- 2.50: In this world, one endowed with wisdom (*buddhi*) transcends both virtues and vices. Therefore, adopt the *yoga* of wisdom. *Yoga* is skill in action (*yogaḥ karmasu kauśalam*).
- 2.51: Relinquishing the fruits of action, those endowed with wisdom become free from the bondage of births and attain a state of freedom from suffering.
- 3.1-7: These verses summarize the question of why action must be undertaken even if it can have negative consequences. The path of knowledge (*jñānayoga*) is suitable for those who are drawn to philosophy. The path of action (*karmayoga*) is suitable for *yogins*. One does not transcend action simply by not acting. No one can ever remain without action. Everyone is forced to act by the *guṇa*-s of Nature (*Prakṛti*). One who outwardly controls the motor organs but inwardly broods on the objects of the senses is a hypocrite. But one who, having controlled the senses with the mind, initiates action with the motor organs without attachment—that person excels.
- 3.8: Perform your assigned duty because action is superior to non-action. Without action you cannot even maintain your own body.
- 3.9: All actions in this world cause bondage, except those done as a divine offering (*yajñārthāt*), free from attachment. Perform action as a divine offering, free from attachment (*tadarthaṁ karma kaunteya muktasaṅgaḥ samācara*).
- 3.17-19: For one who delights only in the Self (*ātman*), who is contented with the Self, and who is satisfied only with the Self, there is nothing that must be done. That person has nothing to gain either with performance or non-performance of action. Therefore always perform obligatory action without attachment. One who performs action without attachment attains the Supreme.
- 3.20-26: Examples are given of great leaders such as Janaka and others who attained spiritual fulfillment by action alone. Great leaders must set a good example, and God Himself is an example of tireless action. But in all cases the wise must act with detachment.

- 3.27-29: In all respects, all actions are performed by the *guṇa*-s of Nature. A person whose mind is deluded by vanity thinks, "I am the doer." But a person who knows the truth about the activity of the *guṇa*-s is not attached, thinking, "the *guṇa*-s operate on the *guṇa*-s." Unwise people who do not understand these things become attached to the actions of the *guṇa*-s.
- 3.30-31: After surrendering all actions to God by keeping the mind on the Self (or on spirituality), take action! People who always practice this teaching of Mine, with devotional faith and without disrespect, are liberated from the bondage of actions.
- 3.33: Beings behave according to their nature. Of what use is repression?
- 4.12: Those desiring fulfillment of their actions worship the gods because accomplishment arising from action comes quickly in the human world.
- 4.13-19: Although God is the creator of human society and many other things, God is not bound by action and has no desire for the result of any action. Having understood this, you should perform action in the same way. One who sees non-action in action, and action in non-action, is wise. That wise person is well-disciplined (*yuktaḥ*), performing all actions. One whose undertakings are free from ulterior motives, and whose *karma* is burned in the fire of knowledge (*jñānāgni*), is called wise.
- 4.20-23: That person who abandons attachment to fruits of action never really acts. The entire action evaporates for one who is free from attachment and who performs action in the spirit of sacrifice (*yajña*).
- 4.33: Sacrifice consisting of knowledge (*jñānayajña*) is better than material sacrifice. All works find their consummation in wisdom.
- 4.37: Just as fire burns wood to ashes, so does the fire of wisdom reduce all works to ashes.
- 4.41-42: Actions do not bind one who has renounced (the fruits of) actions, whose doubts have been removed by knowledge, and is well established in realization of the Self (*ātmavantam*). The chapter concludes with the command, "get up, Arjuna" (*uttiṣṭha bhārata*). In context, this is a command to engage in one's rightful duties.
- 5.1-12: Arjuna asks a question about why both renunciation of action (*saṁnyāsa*) and detached performance of action (*karmayoga*) are being recommended. Much of the chapter deals with clarification of ideas concerning action and non-action that were of great interest at

the time the text was written. The technical term *saṁnyāsa* is central to the discussion. The entire chapter refines key ideas of *karmayoga*.

- 5.21: The person having no attraction to external objects of the senses attains happiness in the Self (*ātman*). That person is well established in union with *Brahman* and attains immortal bliss.
- 6.1-4: One who does work that must be done without attachment to results is a true *yogin*, not the person who doesn't perform the fire ceremony or do his or her work. Action is the means for the wise person who desires to attain the height of *yoga*. After attaining the height of *yoga*, serenity (*śamaḥ*) is the means for the same person.
- 6.18: When the disciplined mind is well established in the self (*ātmani*) alone, free from all desires and longings, such a person is considered to be a real *yogī*.
- 8.3: The release of creative force that causes the origination of material beings is called action (*karma*).
- 9.27-28: Whatever you do, make it an offering to God. Thus you will be liberated from the bondage of actions, consisting of good and bad results. And liberated, well-established in renunciation, you will attain God.
- 12.6-7: God is the savior from the ocean of worldly mortality for those who serve God, surrendering all actions to God, intent on God, meditating on God with single-minded practice.
- 12.10-11: Even if you are not able to do other spiritual practices, become a doer of actions for the sake of God alone. While doing actions in this way you will achieve perfection. If you are unable to do even this, relinquish the fruits of all actions with self-control.
- 12.12: Relinquishment of the fruits of action is better than meditation. Peace comes soon after relinquishment.
- 13.24: Some people realize the Self through the self by meditation on the Self. Others (realize the Self) by the *yoga* of knowledge (*jñānayoga*), and others by the *yoga* of action (*karmayoga*).
- 13.29: One who realizes that all actions are taken by Nature alone, and that one's true Self is actionless, that person truly sees.
- 14.12-13: When *rajas* predominates, initiation of actions appears. Inactivity is a sign that *tamas* predominates.
- 14.16: The fruit of noble action is pure and *sattvic*. The fruit of *rajas* is misery. The fruit of *tamas* is ignorance.
- 18.1-12: Some wise people say that all action is to be abandoned as evil. Other say that certain kinds of action, such as acts of sacrifice,

charity, and austerity should not be abandoned. These verses summarize a debate over the right way to practice *tyāga* (relinquishment) and *saṁnyāsa* (renunciation) and reaffirm that inaction is not the solution to the problem of residual *karma*.

- 18.16-17: A person of imperfect understanding sees oneself alone as the agent (of action), but this is not the correct perspective. A person who is not egoistic and whose mind is not colored by ulterior motives is not bound (by the consequences of action).
- 18.23-28: Actions and agents are classified according to the *guṇa*-s.
- 18.46: By dedicating to the Divine the duty that is appropriate for oneself, a person finds fulfillment.
- 18.47-49: Better is one's own duty, even if lacking in merit, than another's duty performed well. One performing the duty enjoined by one's own inherent nature does not incur sin. One must not abandon one's natural duty. One who has an unattached understanding everywhere, who is self-controlled and free from longing, attains the highest success in (true) non-action.
- 18.57: Surrender all actions to God and be devoted to God.
- 18.59-60: Nature will compel you to act. Bound by your own *karma*, arising out of your own nature, you will do even what you do not wish to do.

Theme Guide

Bhaktiyoga: Devotion as Spiritual Practice

The *BG* is a decidedly theistic text. Although it is of great importance in the *BG*, the theme of devotion to God is introduced only gradually before reaching a dramatic climax with the vision of God's Universal Form in chapter 11. The way of devotion to God (*bhaktiyoga*) is balanced against other methods such as the way of works (*karmayoga*) and the way of knowledge (*jñānayoga*). Different commentators stress one or another of these paths in their own interpretations of what is most essential in the text.

Devotion (*bhakti*, √ *bhaj*) involves a loving and continuous awareness of the role of the Divine in our lives. Close attention to the vocabulary of the text shows that practices based on loving devotion (√ *bhaj*) are always regarded highly, but practices that may involve religious formalism (√ *yaj*) must be considered with regard to motive.[709]

Verses related to this theme

- 2.61: After controlling all the senses, the disciplined one (*yuktaḥ*, the *yogin*) should stay intent on Me (*matparaḥ*).
- 3.30: Fight only after surrendering all actions to Me, keeping the mind on the Self, becoming free from longing and personalizing.
- 3.31-32: Persons practicing these teachings endowed with devotional faith (*śraddhāvantaḥ*) and without disrespect (*anasūyantaḥ*) are liberated from the bondage of actions.
- 6.47: Of all *yogins*, the one who, inwardly absorbed in Me, endowed with faith, is devoted to Me—I consider that person to be the best *yogin*.
- 7.1: Practicing *yoga* with mind fixed on Me (*mayy āsaktamanāḥ*) you will know Me completely.
- 7.3: Among thousands of human beings, rarely does anyone comprehend Me.

[709] See the Concordance for vocabulary examples of √ *bhaj* (to serve; to be devoted to; to worship) and √ *yaj* (to sacrifice; to worship). Religious sacrifice (*yajña*, √ *yaj*), is covered in the Theme Guide for *The Best Type of Worship* on page 328.

- 7.17: Among virtuous people, the best type is the wise one who is dedicated to Me. I am dear to the wise one, and the wise one is dear to Me.
- 7.18: The wise one is My own Self, established in Me alone as the highest goal.
- 7.19: Upon completion of many births, the wise one resorts to Me, thinking "Vāsudeva is everything." Such a great soul is very hard to find.
- 7:21-23: To any devotee who wants to faithfully worship any form, I grant unwavering faith in that alone. Endowed with that faith, the devotee seeks a deity's favor, and obtains what is desired, actually granted by Me. But the results of those who worship the gods are only temporary. My devotees, on the other hand, surely go to Me.
- 8.7: Meditate on Me at all times and engage in action. With mind and intellect surrendered in Me you will truly attain Me.
- 8.14: I am easily accessible to that ever-dedicated *yogin* who constantly remembers Me, keeping the mind on no other object (*ananyacetāḥ*).
- 8.15-16: Having come to Me, those great souls are not subjected to rebirth. The worlds below Me dissolve and return again, but having come to Me, there is no rebirth.
- 9.13: Great souls of a divine nature are devoted to Me single-mindedly (*ananyamanasaḥ*).
- 9.22: For those persons who are devoted to Me, meditating on nothing else, in eternal communion with Me—for them, I take full charge of the fulfillment and maintenance of their well-being.
- 9.26: One who offers Me with devotion a leaf, a flower, a fruit, or water, that sincere offering I accept from one whose soul is pure.
- 9.27-28: Whatever you do, make it an offering to Me. Thus you will be liberated from the bondage of actions and will attain Me.
- 9.29: I am the same toward all beings. For Me, there is none unlikeable, none dear. But those who worship Me with devotion, they abide in Me, and I also abide in them.
- 9.30-31: Even if a person of evil conduct is devoted to Me alone, that person should be considered as noble, having the right resolve. That person quickly becomes righteous and attains eternal peace. Know for certain, My devotee never perishes.
- 9.32-33: Truly, anyone taking shelter in Me, even those who might be of inauspicious birth, as well as women, merchants, and manual

laborers, they too will attain the supreme goal. So also for holy people and devoted sages. Having come to this ephemeral, unhappy world, worship Me!

- 9.34: With mind on Me, be devoted to Me. Performing sacrifice for Me, bow before Me. By being solely devoted to Me, uniting yourself with Me, you will truly attain Me.
- 10.8: I am the origin of all. From Me everything proceeds. Realizing that, the wise worship Me with deep devotion.
- 10.10-11: To those who are constantly in communion with Me, who worship Me with love, I give that *yoga* of wisdom by which they come to Me. For the sake of granting grace to those persons, I, located in their innermost self, destroy the darkness arising out of ignorance with the shining lamp of knowledge.
- 11.53-54: [These verses follow the vision of the Universal Form.] I cannot be seen in this way by means of the Vedas, nor by austerities, nor by charity, nor by sacrifices. My true nature can be known, seen, and entered into in essence only by single-minded devotion.
- 12.2: Those who focus their minds on Me, ever worshipping Me, endowed with faith, are the best *yogins*.
- 12.6-7: I am the savior from the ocean of worldly mortality for those who serve Me, surrendering all actions to Me, meditating on Me, whose minds abide in Me.
- 12.8: Fix your mind on Me alone. From now on you will dwell in Me alone.
- 12.9-11: If you are not able to focus your mind on Me steadily, use one of the other recommended practices that will keep you in connection with Me.
- 12:13-20: My devotees, who exhibit many good qualities, are dear to Me. This series of verses achieves the effect of a litany by repetition of the construction "(that one) is dear to Me" (*sa me priyaḥ*).
- 14.26: One who serves Me with the unswerving practice of devotion, transcending the *guṇa*-s, is fit for identification with *Brahman*.
- 18.46: That from which beings are manifested, That by which all this is pervaded—worshipping That with one's own duty, a person finds fulfillment.
- 18.55-58: With devotion, a person comes to know Me in reality. Then, having known Me, one enters Me thereupon. Mentally surrendering all actions to Me, devoted to Me, let your mind be continuously focused on Me. With My grace you will overcome all obstacles.

- 18.61-62: God resides in the heart of all beings, causing all beings to whirl around as if mounted on a machine by *māyā*. Seek shelter in God alone. Through God's grace you will attain supreme peace, the eternal abode.
- 18.65: With mind on Me, be devoted to Me. Thus you will come to Me alone. I promise this to you. You are dear to Me.
- 18.66: Relinquishing all *dharmas*, take shelter in Me alone. I will liberate you from all sins. Don't worry.

Theme Guide

Jñānayoga: Knowledge as Spiritual Practice

The way of knowledge (*jñānayoga*) is balanced against other methods such as the way of works (*karmayoga*) and the way of devotion to God (*bhaktiyoga*). Different commentators stress one or another of these paths in their own interpretations of what is most essential in the text.

An obvious question is, "knowledge of what?" Some commentators think it refers to knowledge of God, while others think it refers to knowledge of the true Self (*ātman*), or to the non-difference between the Self (*ātman*) and the absolute ground of being (*Brahman*).

The word *jñāna* is from the root *jña*, which means to know. Comparisons with the Greek concept of *gnosis* suggest interesting philosophical parallels. Vocabulary words that are helpful in identifying this theme include *jñāna* (knowledge), *jñānin* (the person who has knowledge), *vijñāna* (special knowledge or direct insight), *jñānayoga* (the spiritual discipline of knowledge), and *jñānayajña* (a sacrifice consisting of knowledge). The distinction between *jñāna* and *vijñāna* is not agreed upon by all commentators. The sense of these terms changed over time. As used in this text, *vijñāna* appears to be a special type of knowledge corresponding to direct insight or true understanding of something in a way that is more practical or experiential than ordinary knowledge. Verses in which both *jñāna* and *vijñāna* are mentioned make it clear that the terms are not synonymous.

The word *prajñā* is used in some verses. Often translated as "wisdom", the concept is a special type of knowing. The root *vid*, which also means to know, is the basis of words such as *vidyā* (knowledge, science) and *avidyā* (ignorance) which are also important in the text.

Words related to knowledge occur very often. The verses listed here only highlight major ideas.

Verses related to jñāna

- 3.39-40: Even the knowledge of the knowers is covered over by the eternal enemy, with the form of desire (*kāmarūpeṇa*). The abode of the eternal enemy is the senses (*indriya*), the mind (*manas*), and the higher intelligence (*buddhi*). With these it obscures knowledge in one who has a body. These verses are based on the Sāṁkhya understanding of how an embodied personality comes into existence.

- 4.9-10: Whoever knows the truth of God's nature is freed from rebirth and goes to God. Also see 7.19; 10.3; 14.1-2 ff.
- 4.19: One who has consumed their *karma* in the fire of knowledge (*jñānāgni*) is called a sage (*paṇḍit*). Verse 4.37 repeats the simile in which the fire of knowledge (*jñānāgniḥ*) reduces all *karma* to ashes.
- 4.23: The *karma* completely melts away for one who is free from attachment, who is liberated, whose thought is established in knowledge (*jñānāvasthitacetasaḥ*), and who does *karma* only as a sacrifice.
- 4.27: The fire of the *yoga* of self-restraint is kindled in knowledge (*jñānadīpite*). Some people offer all actions of the senses and vital energy into this fire. Also see verse 10.11 (*jñānadīpena*).
- 4.28: Ascetics of severe vows offer sacrifice consisting of study of scriptures and the pursuit of knowledge (*svādhyāyajñānayajñāḥ*).
- 4.33: A sacrifice of knowledge (*jñānayajñaḥ*) is better than material sacrifice.
- 4.34: By showing respect, asking questions, and doing service, those who have knowledge (*jñāninaḥ*), who perceive truth (*tattvadarśinaḥ*), will teach that knowledge (*jñānam*) to you.
- 4.35: Having known this (*yaj jñātvā*) you will not fall into delusion again and will see all beings in yourself, and also in God.
- 4.36: Even if you were the most evil of evildoers, you would cross over all wickedness by the boat of knowledge (*jñānaplavena*).
- 4.37: As fire reduces wood to ashes, the fire of knowledge (*jñānāgni*) reduces all *karma* to ashes. Verse 4.19 repeats this simile.
- 4.38: No purifier equal to knowledge is found here in this world. One who is perfected in *yoga* finds that knowledge in the Self (or in oneself).
- 4.39: One who possesses faith attains knowledge. Devoted to that, having attained knowledge (*jñānaṁ labdhvā*), one quickly attains supreme peace.
- 4.40: A person who is ignorant (*ajñaḥ*) and without faith is destroyed and without happiness, in this world and the next.
- 4.41-42: One must cut doubt away with the sword of knowledge and resort to *yoga*.
- 5.15-17: God does not receive either the good or evil of anyone. People are deluded by ignorance. However, for those in whom ignorance of the Self is destroyed by knowledge, that knowledge, like the sun, reveals the Supreme. Those whose minds are absorbed in that (i.e., the

Supreme), whose evils have been shaken off by knowledge (*jñāna*), attain freedom from rebirth.

- 6.46: The *yogin* is superior to those who have knowledge (*jñānibhyaḥ*), as well as to ascetics and to ritualists. Therefore be a *yogin.*
- 7.16-19: Four kinds of people worship God: the distressed, those who desire wealth, those who desire knowledge (*jijñāsuḥ*), and the person of knowledge (*jñānī*). Of these, the person of knowledge (*jñānī*) who is of single devotion (*ekabhaktiḥ*) is best. At the end of many births, the person of wisdom gives themself to God.
- 10.11: Out of compassion, God—dwelling within the inmost self of His devotees—dispels the darkness born of ignorance with the shining lamp of wisdom (*jñānadīpena*). Also see verse 4.27 (*jñānadīpite*).
- 13.2: Knowledge of the "field" and the "knower of the field" (*kṣetrakṣetrajñayor jñanam*) is (true) knowledge.
- 13.7-11: This series of verses describes what knowledge is said to be (*jñānam iti proktam*). Ignorance (*ajñānam*) is what is contrary to that.
- 13.12: That which should be known (*jñeyam*) is the beginningless supreme *Brahman,* which is said to be neither existent nor non-existent. Knowing that, one attains immortality.
- 13.17: This is said to be the light of lights, beyond darkness. It is knowledge, the object of knowledge, and the goal that is attainable through knowledge, seated in the heart of all (*jñānaṁ jñeyaṁ jñānagamyaṁ hṛdi sarvasya viṣṭhitam*).
- 14.6: *Sattva guṇa* is free from impurity, illuminating, and healthful. It binds by attachment to the good and by attachment to knowledge (*jñānasaṅgena*).
- 14.11: When the light of knowledge shines through all the gates of the body, then it should be known that *sattva guṇa* is predominant.
- 15.7-10: A fragment of the Lord (*Īśvara*) is the eternal soul in the world of the living, drawing to itself the senses and mind. This indwelling Lord moves from body to body, presiding over the senses and mind, experiencing the objects of the senses. The deluded do not perceive Him, but those who have the eye of knowledge (*jñānacakṣuṣaḥ*) can perceive Him.
- 15.19: One who, undeluded, knows (*jānāti*) Me as the Supreme Being (*puruṣottamam*), that person, all-knowing (*sarvavit*), worships Me with all their being.

- 18.20-22: These three verses classify knowledge according to the *guṇa*-s. Knowledge that perceives one imperishable Being in all beings, undivided in separate beings, has the nature of *sattva*.
- 18.50: Learn how one who has attained perfection also attains *Brahman*, the highest state of knowledge (*niṣṭhā jñānasya yā parā*).

Verses related to jñānayoga

- 3.3: In this world, God has taught two spiritual practices: the *yoga* of knowledge" (*jñānayoga*) practiced by the Sāṁkhyas, and the *yoga* of action (*karmayoga*) practiced by the Yogins.
- 16.1: One of the attributes of persons who are endowed with divine nature is that they are steadfast in (*vyavasthitiḥ*) the *yoga* of knowledge (*jñānayoga*). Some translators interpret the compound as steadfast in (*vyavasthitiḥ*) the separate functions of *Jñāna* and *Yoga*.[710]

Verses related to jñānayajña

- 9.15: Some people worship the divine by a knowledge-sacrifice (*jñānayajñena*) either as One or in manifold forms.
- 18.70: Those who study the *Bhagavadgītā* worship the Divine by means of a knowledge-sacrifice (*jñānayajñena*).

Verses related to vijñāna

- 3.41: *jñāna-vijñāna-nāśanam* = "destroyer of material and spiritual wisdom; destroyer of knowledge and discrimination".
- 6.8: *jñāna-vijñāna-tṛptātmā* = "contented with practical and spiritual knowledge; one whose soul is satisfied by knowledge and spiritual insight".
- 7.2: *jñānaṁ te 'haṁ savijñānam* = "I will explain to you this knowledge, along with spiritual wisdom".
- 9.1: Kṛṣṇa will reveal the most secret knowledge, along with spiritual insight (*jñānaṁ vijñāna-sahitam*). Having known this (*jñātvā*), you will be released from evil.
- 18.42: Knowledge and spiritual awareness (*jñānaṁ vijñānam*) are listed separately among duties.

---

[710] E.g., Divanji, p. 60, entry #1352.

Verses related to verb form vi + jñā

- 11.31: *vijñātum* "to know; to understand". [With sense of "to experience (you)".]
- 13.18: *vijñāya* "after understanding; after knowing".

Verses related to pra + jñā

- 2.54-68: Discussion of the "person of steady wisdom" (*sthitaprajñaḥ*). *Sthitaprajñaḥ* could be translated as "one of steady wisdom", "one of firm judgement", "one well-grounded in wisdom", etc. The word *prajñā* (wisdom) is used repeatedly in this section, e.g., 2.57, 58, 61, 67, 68.
- 2.11: *prajñāvādān* "wise words". Commentators and translators vary in their understanding of the phrase *prajñāvādāṁś ca bhāṣase* ("You speak wise words"). In context the statement is ironic. Arjuna is speaking *as if* he were wise, but he does not understand the situation properly. The sense is something like "you pay lip service to wisdom" or "you speak words that are fit to be spoken by the wise (yet you do not understand properly)."

Verses related to root vid

- 7.29-30: Whoever seeks to win release from old age and death, putting trust in God, they know (*viduḥ*) *Brahman* in its wholeness, as well as what pertains to the Self (*ātman*) and to *karma*. At death, with steadfast thought, they know (*viduḥ*) God.
- 9.2: This royal knowledge (*rājavidyā*) is a supreme purifier. It can be understood as if were before your very eyes (*pratyakṣāvagamam*), is righteous, easy to practice, and imperishable.[711]
- 11.18: Kṛṣṇa is the supreme object of knowledge (*paramaṁ veditavyam*), identifiable as the Primeval Consciousness (*sanātanas tvaṁ puruṣo mato me*).

---

[711] Evidence that was directly perceptible (*pratyakṣa*) was one of the standards of proof that would have been acceptable even to the materialist philosophers of the period.

Theme Guide

Controlling the Lower Self by the Higher Self

The word *ātman* (the self) is used with a variety of meanings in the *BG*, but rarely in a purely philosophical sense. Sometimes the text plays between use of the word as a reflexive pronoun ("oneself")—referring to the empirical self that must be controlled—and the concept of an eternal higher self (the *ātman*). Depending on context, references to the self also may have the sense of "the heart", "the mind", or "the physical body". Many of the verses in this group pose a challenge for translators who must try to sort out which meaning of *ātman* is intended, and how to convey possible wordplay in English. Some translators rely on capitalization to distinguish the higher *Self* from the lower *self*.

Self-discipline is urged again and again throughout the text. A wordplay construction of controlling "the self by the self" occurs several times in the text with the sense that the lower self is to be controlled by calling upon the higher self. Examples of this verbal pattern can be found by looking for the instrumental singular *ātmanā* ("by the self").

Verses related to this theme

- 2.55: When one is content in one's self alone, with the self, that person is considered to be well-grounded in wisdom. (*ātmany evātmanā tuṣṭaḥ sthitaprajñas tadocyate*)
- 3.43: After restraining the (lower) self with the (higher) Self, kill desire. Van Buitenen's translation of *saṁstabhyātmānam ātmanā* as "pull yourself together" captures the idea well.[712]
- 6.5-6: These two verses use the word *ātman* seven times. The effect of the sound repetition is striking in the Sanskrit, but can become muddled in English translations.

  uddhared ātmanātmānaṁ nātmānam avasādayet ।
  ātmaiva hy ātmano bandhur ātmaiva ripur ātmanaḥ ॥ 6.5 ॥
  bandhur ātmātmanas tasya yenātmaivātmanā jitaḥ ।
  anātmanas tu śatrutve vartetātmaiva śatruvat ॥ 6.6 ॥
- 6.20: That place where, seeing the self through the self, one is contented in the self. (*yatra caivātmanātmānaṁ paśyann ātmani tuṣyati*)

---

[712] Van Buitenen 1981, p. 85.

- 10.15: Only You know Yourself, by Yourself, O Supreme *Puruṣa*. (*svayam evātmanātmānaṁ vettha tvaṁ puruṣottama*)
- 13.24: Some people realize the self in the self through the self by meditation. (*dhyānenātmani paśyanti ke cid ātmānam ātmanā*)
- 13.28: One who sees the Lord as truly residing everywhere equally, does not harm the self with the self. Thereafter one attains the supreme goal.

  samaṁ paśyan hi sarvatra samavasthitam īśvaram ।
  na hinasty ātmanātmānaṁ tato yāti parāṁ gatim ॥ 13.28 ॥

Theme Guide

Body and the Indwelling Spirit

According to the *Bhagavadgītā*, an eternal, unchanging Self makes use of a series of ever-changing physical bodies to have certain experiences. The Western terminology of "body and soul" overlaps with these ideas, but Indian philosophy has its own doctrines about how this duality works. The physical body (the *deha* or *śarīra*) is a transient manifestation that exists within Nature (*Prakṛti*). The eternal Consciousness (*Puruṣa* or *ātman*) exists independently of the body, a notion rejected by materialist philosophers.

In Indian tradition, the body itself can be used as an instrument of spiritual practice. Physical methods such as *haṭha yoga* are not discussed in detail in the *Bhagavadgītā*, but there are passing references to them in the text. Verses on regulation of vital energies of the body (*prāṇa*) are consistent with more detailed descriptions of similar yogic practices in other sources (e.g., 4.27-30; 5.27-28; 8.9-13; 10.9; 15.14; 18.33).

The body's senses (*indriya*), mind (*manas*), and higher intellect (*buddhi*) are the basis of craving and anger (3.39-40). These physical attributes delude the embodied soul (*dehinam*) by covering wisdom (*jñāna*). Although complete liberation from the body (*śarīravimokṣaṇa*) is a goal of spiritual practice (5.23), neglect of the physical body during life is unwise. One should do those actions necessary for the proper sustenance of the body (3.8). The text adopts a moderate approach toward physical asceticism. It speaks against extreme physical practices that are injurious to the body (17.5-6).

One way to understand the dichotomy between the body and the Self is to look for references to the physical body. The Sanskrit words *deha* and *śarīra*, which both refer to the physical body, are used often in the text. The indwelling entity that makes use of a body is often called the *dehin* ("possessor of a *deha*") or the *śarīrin* ("possessor of a *śarīra*"). These are used as virtual synonyms for the more familiar Vedantic term *ātman* (the Self) and the Sāṁkhyan term *puruṣa* (Consciousness or the conscious entity).

Verses related to this theme

- 1.29: Arjuna's body (*śarīre* = in the body) trembles and he becomes weak when he thinks of the terrible battle that will come.

- 2.13: Just as the embodied soul (*dehinaḥ*) passes through childhood, youth, and old age in this body, in the same way it attains another body. (*dehāntaraprāptiḥ* = acquisition of another body)
- 2.18-30: These bodies (*dehāḥ*), which come to an end, belong to an embodied Self that is eternal, indestructible, and immeasurable. The *śarīrin* is "the embodied", referring to the soul possessing a body. In Vedantic terms, the *śarīrin* is the *ātman*.
- 2.58-9: When one withdraws the sense organs from their external objects, like a tortoise withdraws its limbs, one's wisdom become well-grounded. The objects of the senses cease to attract an embodied person (*dehinaḥ*), though inner longing may continue. Even these longings cease to operate after one perceives the Supreme. This model of yogic withdrawl of the senses (*indriyas*) from their objects is based on the traditional model of *buddhi, ahaṁkāra*, and *manas* within an embodied person.
- 3.8. Perform your assigned duty, because action is superior to non-action. Without action you cannot even maintain your own body. (*śarīrayātrā* = *śarīra yā trā* = sustenance of the body, means of bodily sustenance)
- 3.39-40: The senses (*indriya*), mind (*manas*), and the higher intellect (*buddhi*) are the basis of craving and anger. They delude the embodied soul (*dehinam*) by covering wisdom (*jñāna*). Even *buddhi*, the higher intellect, is not immune to the influence of the senses, just as it is fooled by the influence of the ego (*ahaṁkāra*; see 3.27).
- 4.9: After death, one who truly knows God is not born again. That person comes to God.
- 4.21: Expecting nothing, with a disciplined mind and heart, free from all possessiveness, one does not incur sin while the body alone performs action. This summarizes the doctrine of *karmayoga*. (*śārīram* = belonging to the body, bodily)
- 5.13: After having renounced all actions mentally, a self-controlled embodied person (*dehī*) rests comfortably in the city of nine gates (*nava-dvare*), neither truly doing, nor causing anything to be done. The "city of nine gates" is symbolic of the body: two eyes, two ears, two nostrils, mouth, anus, and genitals. Like a wise ruler in a city with well-guarded gates, one works, but does not identify with those works.

- 5.23: One who can withstand an urge arising from passion and anger, in this world prior to release from the body (*śarīravimokṣaṇāt*) is a disciplined (*yuktaḥ*) and happy person.
- 6.40-44: The process of reincarnation is described. Upon rebirth, one regains union with that same wisdom that was achieved in the previous embodiment (*paurvadehikam*) and is instinctively carried on to continue spiritual practice.
- 8.2: Arjuna asks "who is the basis of sacrifice (*adhiyajñya*), and how (is He so), in this body (*dehe*). The technical term "basis of sacrifice" (*adhiyajñya*) refers to the divinity who oversees and is the focus of a religious sacrifice.
- 8.4: God answers the question raised in 8.2 by saying that He is the basis of sacrifice in the body (*dehe*). In this verse God calls Arjuna the "Best of Embodied Beings" (*dehabhṛtāṁ vara*), reflecting the subject of their conversation.
- 8.9-13: Through continuous meditation, with mind not straying, one attains the Supreme Consciousness (*paramaṁ puruṣam*). At the time of death, with unwavering mind, one attains that Consciousness. One who passes away and relinquishes the body while well-established in yogic meditation attains the supreme state.
- 11.7: The entire universe is located within the body of God (*dehe*).
- 11.13: The universe, while divided in many forms, is located within the body of God (*śarīre*).
- 11.15: All types of beings, including the lesser gods, are contained within the body of God (*dehe*).
- 12.5: Spiritual practice is more difficult for those whose minds are directed toward the Unmanifest because an unmanifest goal is hard to obtain by embodied souls (*dehavadbhiḥ*). Material beings find it easier to focus on something concrete rather than an abstraction.
- 13.1: This body (*śarīram*) is called the *kṣetra* ("field"). One who knows this is called the *kṣetrajña* ("field-knower"). The technical terms *kṣetra* and *kṣetrajña* are based on the Sāṁkhya duality of *Prakṛti* (Nature) and *Puruṣa* (Consciousness). All of chapter 13 discusses the nature of this dualism.
- 13.14: While appearing to have all the qualities of the senses, Consciousness transcends all the senses (*indriyas*). Truly unattached, it supports everything. Beyond the *guṇa*-s, it is the experiencer of the *guṇa*-s. This is Sāṁkhya philosophy in a nutshell.

- 13.21-22: Consciousness (*Puruṣa*), located in Nature (*Prakṛti*), experiences the *guṇa*-s that exist in Nature. Attachment to the *guṇa*-s is the cause of its births taking place in various species. In the body (*dehe*), Consciousness is called by various names, including the Supreme Self (*puruṣaḥ paraḥ*).
- 13.31: Being without beginning and transcending the *guṇa*-s, this imperishable Supreme Self neither acts nor is contaminated by action, even though residing in the body (*śarīrasthaḥ*).
- 13.32: Just as space, due to its subtlety, is not contaminated though omnipresent, so also the Self (*ātman*) is not contaminated though dwelling in the body (*dehe*). Here the Vedantic term *ātman* is used to refer to the Self.
- 14.5: Nature's three *guṇa*-s (*sattva, rajas,* and *tamas*) bind the imperishable, embodied Consciousness (*dehinam*) in the body (*dehe*).
- 14.6-8: Each of the three *guṇa*-s binds the embodied Consciousness (*dehinam*) in a distinctive way.
- 14.11: When the light of knowledge (*jñāna*) shines through all the gates of the body (*dehe*) then one may know that *sattva* is predominant.
- 14.14: When an embodied being (*dehabhṛt*) dies with a preponderance of *sattva,* then it attains the pure worlds of those who have the highest knowledge.
- 14.20: Transcending the three *guṇa*-s that are the origin of the body (*dehasamudbhavān*), the embodied one (*dehī*) attains immortality, liberated from the afflictions of birth, death, and old age. Translations of the compound *dehasamudbhavān* vary: the origin of the body[713]; (constituents) which give the body its existence[714]; that spring from the body[715]; which arise in the body[716]; that which arises from the body[717]; that come through bodily existence.[718]

---

[713] Gambhīrānanda 1997, p. 583. The interpretation here is that the *guṇa*-s are "the origin of the body" or "the seed of the birth of the body".

[714] Zaehner, p. 356. Zaehner notes that the "compound more naturally reads, 'which arise from the body', but it is the constituents that give existence to the body not vice versa."

[715] Edgerton, p. 71. Edgerton adds a note on the ambiguity of how this compound can be translated (p. 100, note 1 on chapter 14).

[716] Ādidevānanda, pp. 475-6. The interpretation here is that the *guṇa*-s "arise in the body", i.e., spring from Prakṛti transformed into the form of the body.

[717] Divanji, p. 73, entry #1644.

[718] Bolle, p. 273.

- 15.8: When the Lord (*Īśvara*) adopts a body (*śarīram*) or abandons it, He takes these (senses and mind) along as He goes, much as the wind carries fragrance from a source (such as a flower).
- 15.9: Presiding over hearing, sight, touch, taste, and smell, as well as the mind (*manas*), He enjoys the objects of the senses.
- 15.14: Becoming the fire of life (*vaiśvanara*) dwelling in the body (*deham*) of all living beings, the Lord in union with the two types of vital energy (*prāṇa* and *apāna*) digests food.
- 15.15: The Lord is located in the heart of all.
- 16.18-20: Clinging to ego, power, arrogance, lust, and anger, malicious people hate Me in their own bodies and in those of others (*ātmaparadeheṣu*). Persons of such a hateful nature are reincarnated in lower types of birth.
- 17.2-4: The natural faith of embodied persons (*dehinām*) varies according to their predominating *guṇa*.
- 17.5-6: The text discourages extreme physical asceticism that tortures the body and the Divine Spirit "dwelling deep within the body" (*antaḥ-śarīrastham*).
- 17.14: Reverence for the gods, for the twice-born, for the teachers (*gurus*), and the wise, and having purity, honesty, control of the senses, and non-violence (*ahiṁsā*) are declared to be bodily austerity (*śārīram tapas*).
- 18.11: It is not possible for embodied persons (*dehabhṛtā*) to relinquish action completely. But one who relinquishes the fruits of action is called a relinquisher (*tyāgī*).
- 18.13-15: Whatever action a person initiates by the physical body (*śarīra*), speech (*vāc*), or mind (*manas*) has five causes.

Words related to this theme

- *ātman* "the Self".
- *deha* "the physical body; the body".
- *dehabhṛt* "the bearer of a body; the embodied entity; the embodied being".

- *dehin* "the embodied; the embodied essence; an embodied soul; the *ātman* within a body; the embodied person; the consciousness within a body; the soul".[719]
- *śarīra* "the body".
- *śarīrastha* "residing in the body; situated in the body".
- *śarīrin* "the embodied soul".

---

[719] The translation of *dehinaḥ* as "soul" is an interpretation of the more literal meaning "the embodied" or "that which has a body". The same terminology is also used in 2.30 (*dehi*), 3.40 (*dehinam*), 12.5 (*dehavadbhiḥ*). Elsewhere in the text, sometimes the word *ātman* is used to refer to the Higher Self, but at other times it is used to mean *one* or *oneself*, e.g., 6.7 (*jitātmanaḥ*), 7.18 (*yuktātmā*), 7.19 (*mahātmā*), 8.15 (*mahātmānaḥ*), 11.12 (*mahātmanaḥ*), 11.20 (*mahātman*), 11.24 (*pravyathitāntarātmā*), 11.37 (*mahātman*), 11.50 (*mahātmā*), 16.9 (*naṣṭātmānaḥ*), 18.74 (*mahātmanaḥ*). In 7.5 and 15.7 the term *jīvabhūta* (individual empirical consciousness) is used.

Theme Guide

The Guṇas and Material Nature

Sattva, rajas, and *tamas* are the three *guṇa*-s, the fundamental strands or dispositions of material Nature. Frequent mention of them shows that the author of the *Bhagavadgītā* was familiar with Sāṁkhya philosophy, a dualistic system in which Consciousness (*Puruṣa*) is considered eternally distinct from material Nature (*Prakṛti*). Classical Sāṁkhya philosophy does not have a role for a Supreme Lord (*Īśvara*) presiding above *Puruṣa* and *Prakṛti.* The *Bhagavadgītā* adapts Sāṁkhya ideas to its own theistic framework, setting Kṛṣṇa above all other things.

The *guṇa*-s operate at the material level of existence. The *Bhagavadgītā* encourages us to reduce our attachment to the purely material realm, increasing our focus on the spiritual dimension of things. This is consistent with the Vedantic teaching that what is most real about us is the eternal aspect that transcends our mortal existence. By identifying with our higher Self (the *ātman*), we obtain detachment from the constant flux of the *guṇa*-s, allowing us to recognize the stable and unifying reality that is hidden by them. This higher vantage point frees us to take appropriate action in the world with an untroubled mind.

Verses related to this theme

- 2.45: Vedic religion deals with material ends determined by the three *guṇa*-s (*traiguṇya viṣayā vedāḥ*). It is better to be beyond the influence of the three *guṇa*-s (*nistraiguṇyo bhavārjuna*).
- 3.5: No one can remain free from action because we are all compelled to act by the forces of Nature (*prakṛtijair guṇaiḥ*).
- 3.27: All actions are performed by the *guṇa*-s of Nature. A person whose mind is deluded by vanity thinks, "I am the doer."
- 7.4-7: Eightfold Nature (the material world of *Prakṛti*) is the lower nature of God, sustained by His higher nature (the consciousness of *Puruṣa*), which consists of living beings (individual empirical consciousness). God is the source of both. These verses do not explicitly mention the *guṇa*-s, but the literate reader would have recognized underlying Sāṁkhya thinking in which the *guṇa*-s exist within the material realm. Kṛṣṇa is above both His lower and higher "natures", thus transcending the *guṇa*-s entirely. Compare 15.7.
- 7.12-14: The world, deluded by these states composed of the three *guṇa*-s, does not recognize Me as imperishable (and) beyond (the

guṇa-s). This divine *māyā* of Mine, composed of the three *guṇa*-s, is difficult to overcome. Only those who take refuge in Me cross this *māyā*.

- 7.24-25: Though I am unmanifest, those of inadequate understanding view Me as having manifestation, not knowing My supreme state, imperishable and unexcelled. Veiled by My *yogamāyā*, I cannot be seen clearly by everybody. This deluded world does not know Me as unborn and imperishable.
- 13.21-23: Attachment to the *guṇa*-s is the cause of auspicious and inauspicious rebirth. One who knows *Puruṣa, Prakṛti*, and the nature of the *guṇa*-s is not born again.
- 14.3: Great Nature ("the great *Brahman*") is like a womb to Me. I place therein the germ of creation, out of which everything comes into being. Here, *Brahman* seems to refer to *Prakṛti*.
- 14.5-18: The three *guṇa*-s, born of *Prakṛti*, bind the immortal soul to the body, each in their own way.
- 14.19-20: When an embodied person realizes that the *guṇa*-s alone are the agents in all actions, then one attains "My state" (*mad-bhāvam*). Having transcended the *guṇa*-s, one is completely delivered (*vimuktaḥ*) from the miseries of birth, death, and old age. Compare verse 18.17.
- 14.21-25: The characteristics of one who has transcended the *guṇa*-s are described.
- 14.26-27: One who serves Me through unswerving devotion transcends the *guṇa*-s and attains fitness to become *Brahman*, "for I am the foundation of *Brahman*" (*brahmaṇo hi pratiṣṭhāham*).
- 15.10: Deluded people who identify with the *guṇa*-s do not recognize the indwelling Self when it enters or leaves the body, or when it experiences objects though the body, but those endowed with the eye of wisdom can perceive this.
- 17.1-22: Types of faith, foods, types of worship, austerities, and gifts are classified according to the *guṇa*-s.
- 18.7-10: Various ways of renouncing actions are classified according to the *guṇa*-s.
- 18.19-39: Knowledge, actions, agents, intellect, the power of determination, and pleasures are classified according to the *guṇa*-s.
- 18.40: No being anywhere is free from the three *guṇa*-s of *Prakṛti*.
- 18.41-44: Duties of the social classes are classified according to the *guṇa*-s. Compare verse 18.60.

Theme Guide

Dharma: Personal Nature and Social Justice

The word *dharma* is virtually untranslatable. The underlying meaning is "that which sustains", but the specific sense depends on context. *Dharma* can mean "that which is right", either from the point of view of one's individual nature, the social contract, or religious law. In verse 9.21, where there is a reference to "the law of the three Vedas" (*trayīdharmam*), *dharma* has the sense of "doctrine" or orthodox tradition. In many passages it can be understood as "duty", which is determined by one's situation. What is "right" for one person may be "wrong" for another.

Individual people have distinctive personalities and social responsibilities. All things have their "own *dharma*" (*svadharma*) that defines their nature (*svabhāva*). In philosophy, a *dharma* is an essential quality that makes a thing be what it is. The *dharma* of fire is to burn. The *dharma* of water is to cool. To expect fire to cool or water to burn would violate their differing natures. One's *dharma* (*svadharma*) and one's nature (*svabhāva*) determine what actions (*karma*) are natural for someone. These terms come together in verse 18.47, which says, "Better is one's own duty (*svadharmaḥ*), even if lacking in merit, than another's performed well. One performing the duty enjoined by one's nature (*svabhāvaniyatam karma kurvan*) does not incur sin."

Normative social responsibilities (*varṇāśrama dharma*) were based on social class (*varṇa*) and stage of life (*āśrama*). At the time the *BG* was written, Indian society was divided into four primary classes with distinct functions in the community. In addition, social roles change as people grow older. A young student may grow up and raise a family, then adopt a more solitary and contemplative life in retirement and old age.

Verses related to this theme

- 1.1: The first word of the *BG* is *dharma*, establishing the setting for the battle "on the field of righteousness" (*dharmakṣetre*).
- 1.40: With the destruction of the family, the eternal tradition of righteousness is destroyed. When these traditions are lost, sin truly overcomes the entire family. (*dharme naṣṭe* = when tradition perishes. *adharma* = injustice, unrighteousness, lawlessness, conduct that is against the dictates of religion.)
- 1.41: When overcome by injustice (*adharmābhibhavāt*) the purity of family lineage is destroyed.

- 1.43-44: People who destroy social and family traditions commit great evil. (*jātidharmāḥ* = traditions of society. *jati* = group of people, community of professions. *kuladharmāḥ* = family traditions.)
- 2.7: Arjuna says that he is confused about his duty (*dharma-saṁmūḍhacetāḥ*) and asks for guidance.
- 2.31-33: Battle is discussed from the point of view of a warrior's personal duty (*svadharma*). Verse 2.31 says you must consider your own duty when faced with battle (*svadharmam api cāvekṣya*). Do you have a duty to fight? If so, for a warrior there is nothing better than a righteous battle *(dharmyāddhi yuddhāc chreyo'nyat*). Verse 2.33 clarifies that engaging in conflict incurs no sin if such conflict is *dharmyam* ("as prescribed by the laws of duty" or "righteous"). On the contrary, failing to do one's duty (*svadharma*) in such a situation would be inappropriate.
- 2.40: Even a little of this wisdom (*dharmasya*) guards against great fear.
- 3.35: Better is one's own duty (*svadharmaḥ*), even if lacking in merit, than another's duty performed well. This idea is repeated in verse 18.47.
- 4.7-8: From time to time Kṛṣṇa incarnates "for re-establishment of righteousness" (*dharmasaṁsthāpanārthāya*). (*dharmasya glāniḥ* = decline of *dharma*. *abhyutthānam adharmasya* = rise of *adharma*)
- 4.13: Kṛṣṇa says he is the creator of the system of four classes (*cāturvarṇyaṁ mayā sṛṣṭam*).
- 7.11: In beings, Kṛṣṇa is that desire which is not opposed to *dharma*. (*dharmāviruddhaḥ* = not contrary to ethical principles)
- 9.2: Kṛṣṇa says that the doctrine he teaches is conducive to righteousness (*dharmyam*).
- 9.3: Those who have no faith in this doctrine (*dharmasya*) return to the cycle of death and rebirth.
- 9.21: Kṛṣṇa contrasts His teaching with Vedic doctrine, the law of the three Vedas (*trayīdharmam*).
- 9.30-31: Even an evil person who beomes dedicated to God and has the right resolve quickly becomes righteous. The term (*dharmātmā*), which could be translated as *virtuous*, has the sense of being identical with *dharma* or having a *dharmic* nature.
- 11.18: Kṛṣṇa is praised as the protector of eternal righteousness (*śāśvatadharmagoptā*).

- 12.20: Kṛṣṇa describes His teaching as the ambrosial nectar of righteousness (*dharmyāmṛtam*).
- 14.2: Kṛṣṇa says that those who have become "identified with My nature" (*mama sādharmyam*) escape the cycle of dissolution and rebirth.
- 14.27: Kṛṣṇa says that he is the substratum of eternal *dharma*.
- 18.31-32: Inability to correctly discriminate between right and wrong (*dharmam adharmam ca*) is due to the influence of *rajoguṇa* and *tamoguṇa*.
- 18.34: Three traditional Hindu aims of life are mentioned together: duty (*dharma*), enjoyment (*kāma*), and material prosperity (*artha*).
- 18.41-44: The talents and duties of the four classes arise from their inherent nature (*svabhāva*) and are determined by the *guṇa*-s.
- 18.45: Contented with one's own duty (*sve sve karmaṇi*), one obtains complete fulfillment.
- 18.46: A person finds fulfillment by worshipping "That by which everything is pervaded" with one's own duty (*svakarmaṇā tam abhyarcya*).
- 18.47: Better is one's own duty (*svadharmaḥ*), even if lacking in merit, than another's performed well. This idea is repeated in verse 3.35. One performing the duty enjoined by one's nature (*svabhāvaniyatam karma kurvan*) does not incur sin.
- 18.48: One must not abandon one's naturally determined duty (*sahajaṁ karma*), even if imperfect. All undertakings are covered with imperfection, as fire is covered by smoke.
- 18.66: Relinquishing all *dharmas*, take shelter in Me alone.
- 18.70: The *Bhagavadgītā* is described as "a righteous dialogue" (*dharmyaṁ saṁvadam*).

Theme Guide

The Best Type of Worship

Only the simplest practices are needed to realize the spiritual doctrine taught in the *BG.* In this text, the purpose of worship is to identify fully with the Divine. The methods are easy to do and can be done by anyone regardless of background. The highest type of worship is to simply dedicate ourselves to the Divine, performing all actions as sacrificial offerings. In striving to divinize our lives in this way, we ourselves become the ultimate offering. Close attention to the vocabulary of the text shows that practices based on loving devotion (√ *bhaj*) are always regarded highly, but practices that may involve religious formalism (√ *yaj*) must be considered with regard to motive.[720]

The emphasis on simplicity of spiritual practice and ease of access by anyone are in sharp contrast to the complex Vedic ritual practices that were performed with the intention of achieving worldly benefits and temporary entry to lower heavens. The criticism seems directed at the Purvamīmāṁsā school, which emphasizes the use of specific rituals to attain enjoyments on earth and happiness in heaven.[721] The *BG* does not reject the Vedas themselves, but criticizes those who understand them only as a means to achieving limited rewards. The criticism of Vedic ritualism is intended to draw a distinction with the simpler devotional approach of the *BG.*[722]

Verses related to this theme

- 2.42-44: Delighting in the mere words of the Vedas (*veda-vāda-ratāḥ*), the unwise (*avipaścitaḥ*) utter flowery words (*puṣpitāṁ vācam*), saying there is nothing else. Their attachment to worldly aims leads to new births and makes their minds unfit for meditation.
- 3.9: All actions in the world result in bondage except those performed as offerings to the divine (*yajñārthāt*). One should perform action as a

---

[720] See the Concordance for vocabulary examples of √ *bhaj* ("to serve; to be devoted to; to worship") and √ *yaj* ("to sacrifice; to worship"). Devotion (*bhakti*, √ *bhaj*), is covered in the Theme Guide for *Bhaktiyoga* on page 306.

[721] The Purvamīmāṁsā connection is mentioned by Sivananda (p. 39) and Tapasyananda (p. 78).

[722] *BG* 9.20 refers to the "knowers of the three Vedas" (*traividyāḥ*) and *BG* 9.17 mentions the *Ṛg, Sāma,* and *Yajur* Vedas. This may suggest that only those three were recognized at the time the *BG* was written.

divine offering, free from attachment. This key idea is essential to correct performance of *karmayoga*. Compare this with verse 18.46, which says that one finds fulfillment by worshipping the divine with one's own duty (*svakarmaṇā*).

- 3.10-16: The traditional transactional model of Vedic sacrifice (*yajña*) is described.
- 4.11: So long as one is open to God, God responds accordingly regardless of different traditions and cultures. There is no single "right" way to approach God.
- 4.12: Those seeing fulfillment of their actions in this world worship the gods for that reason.
- 4.23: *Karma* evaporates for one who performs action in the spirit of *yajña*, dedicating all things to God.
- 4.24: The verse uses the image of offering an oblation into a fire to make the point that the Divine is in all things. *Brahman* is the instrument of offering, *Brahman* is the oblation offered into the fire of *Brahman* by *Brahman*. *Brahman* alone is attained by one who comprehends (every) action as *Brahman*.
- 4.25-31: A variety of spiritual practices are mentioned, showing that no single path is expected of everyone. Different people will choose methods that suit them. But those who have no spiritual practice cannot enjoy even this world, let alone the next. Verse 4.28 mentions the pursuit of spiritual knowledge as a type of worship. For the concept of worship through knowledge (*jñānayajña*) also see verses 4.33, 9.15, and 18.70.
- 4.32-33: Many different types of rituals (*bahuvidhā yajñā*) are specified in orthodox Vedic religion, but all of them arise out of action (and therefore result in bondage). Sacrifice consisting of knowledge (*jñānayajñaḥ*) is superior to material sacrifice. All bondage of action is eliminated with knowledge. For the concept of worship through knowledge (*jñānayajña*) also see verses 4.28, 9.15, and 18.70.
- 5.29: Kṛṣṇa says He is the supreme recipient of all sacrifices and austerities (*yajñatapasām*) and the supreme friend of all beings.
- 8.28: Having come to a higher understanding, the spiritual practitioner (*yogin*) goes beyond seeking the benefits of meritorious action (*puṇyaphalam*) that are spelled out in the Vedas, in sacrifices, in austerities, and in giving donations.

- 9.2: The spiritual knowledge taught in the *BG* is an excellent purifier, understandable by direct realization, conducive to righteousness (*dharmyam*), and very easy to do (*susukhaṁ kartum*).
- 9.15: One method for worship is by the ritual offering of knowledge (*jñānayajñena*). For the concept of worship through knowledge (*jñānayajña*) also see verses 4.28, 4.33, 18.70.
- 9.16: Kṛṣṇa identifies Himself with all aspects of traditional religious ritual. He is the ritual itself, the sacrifice, the things used as offerings, the chanting, the fire into which oblations are given, and so on. Compare verse 4.24 which has a similar idea.
- 9.20-21: Those who worship with sacrifices desiring heavenly benefits attain them, but the benefits are only temporary. When their merit is exhausted, they return to the cycle of death and rebirth.
- 9.22-25: God provides for the needs of those who dedicate themselves fully to the Divine. Even those devotees who faithfully worship the Divine in other forms receive benefits, for there is only one pervading Divine who receives all worship. Those dedicated to the gods or other spiritual beings will attain them, but those who are dedicated to Me will attain Me (in My most pure form).
- 9.26-28: Only the simplest of rituals are needed, so long as they are offered with devotion. Whatever you do, whatever you eat, whatever oblations you make, whatever gifts you give, whatever austerieties you practice—make it an offering to God.
- 10.10-11: To those who are constantly in communion with Me, who worship Me with love (*bhajatāṁ prītipūrvakam*), I give that *yoga* of wisdom (*buddhiyoga*) by which they come to Me.
- 10.17: One can know the Divine by constantly keeping it in mind, in various forms. Verses 10.18-42 provide examples of the pervasive nature of the Divine.
- 10.25: Among sacrifices I am the sacrifice of repetitive prayer (*japayajñaḥ*). It is noteworthy that in contrast with the complex and sometimes expensive sacrifices of traditional rituals, here Kṛṣṇa identifies Himself with one of the simplest and most basic mental practices in the life of a spiritual practitioner.
- 11.48: The direct experience of divinity cannot be achieved by study of the Vedas and performance of sacrifices (*vedayajñādhyayanaiḥ*).
- 11.52-55: Direct mystical perception of the Divine is a rare gift that cannot be achieved by the Vedas, by austerities, by donations, or by sacrifices. It can be achieved by single-minded devotion.

- 12.1-5: The Divine can be worshipped in either manifest form or unmanifest form. For incarnated beings, understanding an unmanifest goal is difficult. Both approaches ultimately can reach the same objective. Abstract, impersonal thinking is hard for most people, but when coupled with control of the senses and adopting an attitude of equanimity to all beings, it results in attainment of the Divine.
- 16.1: Traditional religious practices such as performance of sacrifices (*yajñaḥ*), donations, study of religious texts, and austerities are included in a list of practices that are characteristic of a person imbued with the divine quality (*saṁpadaṁ daivīm*).
- 16.17: Self-centered people, full of vanity and lust for wealth, hypocritically make sacrifices in name only (*yajante nāmayajñaiḥ*) without regard to prescribed procedure.
- 17.1-4: Arjuna asks about the state of people who deviate from scriptural injunctions but offer sacrifice full of faith (*ye śāstravidhim utsṛjya yajante śraddhayānvitāḥ*). Kṛṣṇa replies that the natural faith of an embodied person is determined by the form of their natural constitution of mind. Whatever type of faith one has, the person truly is just that.
- 17.11-13: Types of sacrifice (*yajñaḥ*) are classified according to the *guṇa*-s.
- 17.23-28: The traditional mantra *oṁ tat sat* is noted in connection with the making of sacrifices and other religious duties.
- 18.3-6: Arjuna asks if sacrifices, charity, and austerities (*yajñadāna-tapaḥkarma*) should be given up. Kṛṣṇa replies that those acts should not be given up, and must be done, for they are purifiers of the wise. But they should be done after relinquishing attachment to the fruits of those actions.
- 18.70: Study of the *BG* is a way of worshipping the divine through a sacrifice of knowledge (*jñānayajña*). For the concept of worship through knowledge (*jñānayajña*) also see verses 4.28, 4.33, and 9.15.

Theme Guide

"Becoming" Kṛṣṇa as an End to Rebirth

BG 8.6 says that whatever being or state (*bhāva*) one meditates on at the time of death will determine the state after death. *BG* 8.7 expands on this idea, saying that those who focus on Kṛṣṇa (as Vāsudeva) will attain Him. This theme is one of the core doctrinal messages of the *Bhagavadgītā*. The following verses show the development of this idea in the *BG*. The translation of many of these verses depends on understanding the doctrine as a whole, and the use of the word *bhāva* in other passages of the text.

For possible precursors of this idea see:

- *Muṇḍaka Upaniṣad* 3.2.4 entry into the abode that is *Brahman* (*brahmadhāma*).
- *Kaṭhopaniṣad* 3.9 the supreme place of Viṣṇu (*āpnoti tad viṣṇoḥ paramam*).
- *Śatapata Brāmaṇa* 1.2.5, where the highest place of Viṣṇu is like an eye fixed in the heaven, seen only by the wise.[723]

Verses related to this theme

- 2.51: The wise are freed from the bondage of rebirth and "attain a state" (*padam gacchanti*, lit., "go to a place") that is free from suffering (*anāmayam*).
- 4.9: One who knows Kṛṣṇa "in essence" (*tattvataḥ*) does not attain rebirth. Instead, "one comes to Me" (*mām eti*).[724]
- 4.10: Those who have "identified with Me" (*manmayā mām*) have attained "My essential state" (*mad-bhāvam āgatāḥ*). Many have attained this state. The expression *mad-bhāvam* is also used in 8.5, 10.6, 13.18, and 14.19. These five verses could be reviewed as a group. Zaehner translates *mad-bhāvam* as "my own mode of being".[725]
- 5.29: One who realizes Kṛṣṇa as the Lord of the worlds will attain peace (*śāntim*). Compare 9.31.

---

[723] Hill, p. 11.

[724] The R. K. Sharma translation of this passage (Sharma, Morgan and Pitts, p. 83) includes a gloss that, "Here, individual consciousness fully identifies itself with the absolute or supreme consciousness."

[725] Zaehner, p. 185.

- 6.15: The *yogin* attains peace and supreme *nirvāṇa* by "abiding in Me" (*mat-saṁsthām*). Compare 7.29, which equates knowing Kṛṣṇa with completely knowing *Brahman*, which gives liberation from old age and death. Compare 10.3 which says that the one who truly knows Kṛṣṇa is liberated from all sin. Compare 12.6-7 where Kṛṣṇa is the savior from the ocean of the world of mortality.
- 6.30: One should strive to see Kṛṣṇa everywhere, and everything in Him. Compare 9.14.
- 6.31: The *yogin* who worships Kṛṣṇa as residing in all beings abides in (*vartate*) Kṛṣṇa, with the sense "is in Me". Compare 9.34.
- 6.47: Of all *yogin*-s, the best *yogin* is one "abiding in Me" (*mad-gatenā*) with faith. The expression *mad-gatenā* literally means "having gone to Me" or "having attained Me". Compare 12.2.
- 7.1: By attaching the mind to Him and depending on Him you will know Him completely.
- 7.3: It is rare for anyone to really comprehend who Kṛṣṇa is. (Compare 7.19, 7.24, 9.11-13, 10.14)
- 7.13-14: Failure to recognize Him is due to delusion by the *guṇa*-s. *Māyā* can be crossed over only by taking refuge in Him. (Compare 7.25-26)
- 7.15: Wrongdoers do not resort to Kṛṣṇa and are drawn to "demonic states of being" (*āsuraṁ bhāvam*). The devilish mode of being is described in 16.6-20.
- 7.18: The person of wisdom (*jñānī*) is established in (*āsthitaḥ*) Kṛṣṇa as the highest goal (*gatim*).
- 7.19: After many births, the wise person resorts to Kṛṣṇa; such people are hard to find.
- 7.23: The worshippers of the gods go to the gods; the devotees of Kṛṣṇa "go to Me" (*yānti mām*).
- 7.24: The ignorant do not know Kṛṣṇa's supreme state (*paraṁ bhāvam*). *Bhāvam* could be translated here as "state" or "form". The expression *paraṁ bhāvam* is used again in 9.11.
- 7.30: Those who know Him as the basis of all things will know Him even at the time of death. This establishes that the practice of visualization of Him during life creates the conditions that will apply at the time of death. This affects interpretation of the word *sadā* in verse 8.6.
- 8.5: At the time of death, whoever takes the final journey meditating on Kṛṣṇa alone "attains My state" (*mad-bhāvaṁ yāti*). The verb *yāti* is often translated as "one attains" but also means "one goes".

- 8.6: The *bhāva* held at the time of death determines where one goes (*eti*) after death. The verb "one goes" could also mean "one attains". Consider Zaehner's translation "Whatever state a man may bear in mind when in the end he casts his mortal frame aside, even to that state does he accede, for ever does that state make him grow into itself."[726] For the idea that whatever faith a person has, so that person is, see 17.3.
- 8.7: One should keep Kṛṣṇa in mind at the time of death in order to go to Him. For interpretation of the word *sadā* in 8.6 see 7.30. A similar idea is expressed in 9.25.
- 8.12-13: Describes the process of dying while repeating the mantra *oṁ* and meditating on Kṛṣṇa. The person who does this attains the supreme state, which is emancipation.
- 8.14: Kṛṣṇa is easily accessible to the *yogin* who recollects Him without interruption, with one-pointed mind.
- 8.15: "Having come to Me" (*mām upetya*) there is no rebirth.
- 8.16: The verse contrasts the fact that there is no rebirth after "one has attained Me" (*mām upetya*) with what happens "up to the abode of Brahmā" (*ā brahmabhuvanāt*), where rebirth does take place. The verse assumes the existence of other abodes or states that are attained by worship of other gods.
- 8.21: Kṛṣṇa's unmanifested state is the supreme goal (*paramām gatim*). After attaining the abode (*dhāma*) of Kṛṣṇa there is no return to the cycles of birth and death. The word *dhāma* is used for Kṛṣṇa's abode again in 10.12, 11.38, and 15.6. The general meaning of *dhāma* is a dwelling place or domain.
- 8.28: The *yogin* goes beyond the fruits obtained by other means and attains "the supreme, primal abode" (*yogī paraṁ sthānam upaiti cādyam*).
- 9.3: Those who do not believe in this doctrine do not attain Kṛṣṇa and return to the path of mortality (the cycle of birth and death).
- 9.4: All beings are pervaded by Me and located in Me.
- 9.11-12: The ignorant do not recognize Kṛṣṇa's "true Being" (*paraṁ bhāvam*) dwelling in His embodied form (*tanum āśritam*). The verse contrasts physical form (*tanum*) with real nature or true state (*bhāva*). The expression *paraṁ bhāvam* was used before in 7.24.
- 9.20-21: Performers of Vedic rituals go to "the abode of the Lord of the gods (Indra's heaven)" (*surendra-lokam*), but upon exhausting their

---

[726] Zaehner, p. 262.

merits, return to the cycle of birth and death. The passage is noteworthy because of the reference to worshipping "Me" (*mām*) by proxy. (Compare 9.23-24 for worship by proxy.)

- 9.22: Those persons who are devoted to Me, meditating on nothing else, are in eternal communion with Me (*nitya-abhi-yuktānām*).
- 9.25: Restates the idea that the worshippers of the gods go to the gods, but those dedicated to Kṛṣṇa "attain Me".
- 9.27-28: By offering everything you do to Kṛṣṇa you will be liberated and will attain Him. Compare 9.34, 11.54-55, and 12.8 (which says that by fixing your mind on Kṛṣṇa you will dwell in Him alone).
- 9.29: The worshipper of Kṛṣṇa abides in Him, and vice versa.
- 9.32: Even those who would normally be excluded from Vedic rituals, including women and those of low birth, can take refuge in Kṛṣṇa. This reflects the non-Vedic background of the Kṛṣṇa faith.
- 10.5: All "states of existence originate" (*bhavanti bhāvā bhūtānām matta eva*) from Him. Zaehner translates this as "dispositions of contingent beings."[727]
- 10.6: The seven sages and the four Manus are "co-existent with Me" (*mad-bhāva*).
- 10.10: Kṛṣṇa gives the *yoga* of wisdom (*buddhiyoga*) to those who are devoted to Him, and it is by that *yoga* that "they come to Me" (*mām upayānti*). The verb "to go" is used again for this idea. Zaehner's "draw nigh to Me" captures the sense of *upayānti*.
- 10.12: Kṛṣṇa is the supreme abode (*paraṁ dhāma*). The expression *paraṁ dhāma* is used again in 11.38.
- 11.25: The epithet *jagannivāsa*, which means "Refuge of the Worlds" or "Abode of the World" is used three times in this chapter and not elsewhere in the text. Compare 11.37, 11.45.
- 11.38: Kṛṣṇa is the supreme abode (*paraṁ dhāma*). The expression *paraṁ dhāma* was used before in 10.12.
- 11.54: One can enter into Kṛṣṇa in essence (*tattvena praveṣṭum*) through single-minded devotion.
- 13.18: The devotee who has gained correct knowledge qualifies for "identification with Me" (*madbhāvāyopapadyate*).
- 13.21-23: Attachment to the *guṇa*-s is the cause of auspicious and inauspicious rebirth. One who knows *Puruṣa, Prakṛti,* and the nature of the *guṇa*-s is not born again.

---

[727] Zaehner, p. 293.

- 13.30: When one perceives that the plurality of beings abide in one source, that person becomes one with *Brahman* (*brahma saṁpadyate*). Note that in 13.30 and throughout chapter 13 the omnipresent reality is referred to as *Brahman*, but in three verses of this chapter "the Lord" is mentioned, reflecting the theistic emphasis of the *BG*. See 13.22 "the Great Lord" (*maheśvara*); 13.27 "the Supreme Lord" (*parameśvara*); and 13.28 "the Lord" (*īśvara*).
- 14.2: Those who become "identified with My nature" (*mama sādharmyam*) are neither reborn at the time of creation, nor affected at the time of the dissolution.
- 14.19: When one sees only the *guṇa*-s as acting, and knows what transcends the *guṇa*-s, that person will "attain identification with Me" (*madbhāvam adhigacchati*).
- 14.26: The person who serves Kṛṣṇa with one-pointed devotion is fit for "identification with *Brahman*" (*brahma-bhūyāya*), literally "becoming *Brahman*" as in Zaehner.[728]
- 15.6: Having attained "my supreme abode" (*dhāma paramam mama*) none return (to the cycle of birth and death).
- 15.19: The person who knows Kṛṣṇa as the Supreme *Puruṣa* is all-knowing and devoted to Him "in all respects" (*sarva-bhāvena*). Zaehner notes that *sarva-bhāvena* can mean both "with all his being" and "all his love", pointing to possible wordplay here.[729] The expression *sarva-bhāvena* is used again in 18.62.
- 16.20: The ignorant ones take birth after birth and "do not attain Me" (*mām aprāpyaiva*).
- 18.55: With devotion one can be aware in reality (*tattvataḥ*) of who Kṛṣṇa is. After knowing Him fully, one "enters" (*viśate*) Him soon thereafter. As the *BG* moves to a conclusion the key theme of identifying completely with Kṛṣṇa is emphatically summarized in multiple verses.
- 18.56: One should dedicate oneself fully to Him. This results in gaining the "eternal, imperishable state" (*śāśvataṁ padam avyayam*).
- 18.57: Let your mind be continuously focused on Him.
- 18.58: If you do not have complete focus on Him you will perish.
- 18.62: Seek refuge in Him with "all your being" (*sarva-bhāvena*) or "all your love", repeating the possible wordplay of 15.19. "Through His grace

---

[728] Zaehner, p. 357.

[729] Zaehner, p. 368.

you will attain absolute peace and eternal abode" (*sthānam prāpsyasi śāśvatam*).

- 18.65: Be with mind dedicated to Me so "you will come to Me" (*mām eṣyasi*). You are dear to Me.
- 18.66: Relinquishing all *dharma*-s, take shelter in Me alone. This results in liberation from all sins. Don't worry.
- 18.68: One who imparts this secret to My devotees, having absolute devotion in Me, surely "will come to Me alone" (*mām eva eṣyati*).

Transliteration

This book includes some text in Devanāgarī, one of the Indian writing systems used for Sanskrit. When making direct quotations from sources that use other transliteration methods, in most cases I reproduce their texts as I find them, sometimes adding italics to normalize references to Sanskrit terms. In all other cases, I standardize transliteration according to this system:[730]

अ	a	आ	ā	इ	i	ई	ī	उ	u
ऊ	ū	ए	e	ऐ	ai	ओ	o	औ	au
ऋ	ṛ	ॠ	ṝ	ऌ	ḷ	ॡ	ḹ		
				◌ँ	m̐	◌ं	ṁ[731]	◌ः	ḥ
क	ka	ख	kha	ग	ga	घ	gha	ङ	ṅa
च	ca	छ	cha	ज	ja	झ	jha	ञ	ña
ट	ṭa	ठ	ṭha	ड	ḍa	ढ	ḍha	ण	ṇa
त	ta	थ	tha	द	da	ध	dha	न	na
प	pa	फ	pha	ब	ba	भ	bha	म	ma
		य	ya	र	ra	ल	la	व	va
		श	śa	ष	ṣa	स	sa	ह	ha

[730] The sections on Transliteration and Pronunciation are adapted with permission from Morgan 2011, pp. xix-xxiv.

[731] Using *ṁ* as specified by the International Standards Organization (ISO) 15919 standard, rather than *ṃ* as in the older International Alphabet of Sanskrit Transliteration (IAST) standard.

Pronunciation

The Sanskrit language is most often written in the Devanāgarī writing system, which has a larger number of letters than English. The sounds are arranged in a logical system in which vowels combine with consonants to form syllables. Long vowels (*ā, ī, ū, ṝ, ḹ*) are held for a longer duration than short vowels (*a, i, u, ṛ, ḷ*).

Vowels and aftersounds

a	अ	like the *a* in *about* or the *u* in *but* or *sum.*
ā	आ	like the *a* in *father* or *tar,* held twice as long as short *a.*
i	इ	like the *i* in *it* or *pin* or *bit.*
ī	ई	like the *i* in *pique* or *police* or *magazine,* or the *ee* in *week,* held twice as long as short *i.*
u	उ	like the *u* in *push* or *bush.*
ū	ऊ	like the *u* in *rule* or *rude* or the *oo* in *fool,* held twice as long as short *u.*
ṛ	ऋ	like the *ri* in *rich* or *rim,* or the *re* in *pretty* ("*pṛdy*"), but more like the French *ru.*
ṝ	ॠ	like the *rea* in *reach.* Held twice as long as short *ṛ.*
ḷ	ऌ	no good English equivalent, but like the *lry* in *revelry* or the *le* in *table,* but in some regions more like *lree* and in other regions more like *lruu.*
ḹ	ॡ	[not used in this text]
e	ए	like the *e* in *they* or *prey,* or like the *a* in *made.* This is a dipthong.
ai	ऐ	like the *ai* in *aisle,* or the *i* in *bite.* This is a single dipthong, not two vowels.
o	ओ	like the *o* in *go* or *home.* This is a dipthong.
au	औ	like the *ow* in *cow,* or the *ou* in *found,* or the *au* sounds in *sauerkraut.* This is a single dipthong, not two vowels.
ḥ	◌ः	*visarga* is a final breathing aftersound similar to *h,* uttered in the articulating position of the preceding vowel and echoing that vowel. *Gajaḥ* (गजः elephant) sounds somewhat like "*gajaha*", *guruḥ* (गुरुः, teacher) sounds like "*guruhu*", etc.

ṁ ं *anusvāra* indicates that the vowel is to be pronounced with a resonant nasal aftersound with open mouth, like the *n* in the French word *bon*. The sound is influenced by whatever consonant follows the *anusvāra*.

m̐ ँ *anunāsika* is a type of nasal sound following a vowel. It is represented by the *candrabindu* diacritical mark.

Twenty-five consonants fall into five groups based on the part of the mouth in which the sound is produced. The consonant groups begin at the throat (guttural consonants), and move forward to the lips (labial consonants). Sanskrit has both aspirated and unaspirated consonants. All aspirated consonants (*kh, gh, ch, jh, ṭh, ḍh, th, dh, ph, bh*) are pronounced with a slight expulsion of air accompanying the consonant, but not strongly distinct from it. For example, in the word *dot* the *t* sound ends abruptly (त्), but in the word *pot* there is a slight aspiration of the *t* sound, suggesting the sound *th* (थ्).

Gutturals are pronounced with the sound coming from the throat:

k क् like the *k* in *kite* or *kid*, or the *c* in French *coup*
kh ख् like the *kh* in *Eckhart* or *workhorse*
g ग् like the *g* in *give* or *gate* or *go*
gh घ् like the *gh* in *dig-hard* or *dog-house*
ṅ ङ् like the *n* in *sing*

Palatals are pronounced from the palate:

c च् like the *ch* in *chair* or *chill* or *church*
ch छ् like the *ch* in *staunch heart* or Churchill
j ज् like the *j* in *joy* or *jump*
jh झ् like the *j* sound followed by *h* ("*geh*") *hedgehog* or *lodgehouse*
ñ ञ् like the Spanish *ñ* in *cañon* or *piñata*

Cerebrals are pronounced with the tip of the tongue touching the roof of the mouth in a retroflex position:

ṭ ट् like the *t* in *tub*, but with the tongue more retroflex
ṭh ठ् like the *t* in *light hearted*, but with the tongue more retroflex
ḍ ड् like the *d* in *dynamite* or *dove* or *red*, but with the tongue more retroflex
ḍh ढ् like the *d* in *red hot*, but with the tongue more retroflex
ṇ ण् like the *n* in *tint* or *under*, or in *rna* [prepare to say the *r* and say *na*], but with the tongue more retroflex

Dentals are pronounced with the tongue forward against the teeth or at the point where the teeth join the roof of the mouth:

t त् like the *t* in *dot* but with the tongue touching the teeth

th थ् like the *t* in *torn* or *tool* or the first *t* in the French *tout* but with the tongue touching the teeth

d द् like the *d* in *lude* but with the tongue touching the teeth

dh ध् like the *d* in *red hot* but with the tongue touching the teeth

n न् like the *n* in *nut* or *no* but with the tongue touching the teeth

Labials are pronounced with lips first closed and then open, with sound coming from the front of the mouth:

p प् like the *p* in *pine* or *pin* or *pub*

ph फ् like the *ph* in *uphill* but sometimes more like *pharmacy*

b ब् like the *b* in *bird* or *but*

bh भ् like the *bh* in *abhor* or *rub hard*

m म् like the *m* in *mother* or *mum*

Semivowels

y य् *y* as in *yes* or *yellow*

y र् *r* as in *run* or *rum*

l ल् *l* as in *light* or *love* or *lug*

v व् *v* as in *vine* or *vote*

Sibilants

ś श् *sh* as in *shoot* or *shove,* or the German word *sprechen,* but with the tongue in a palatal position

ṣ ष् *sh* as in *shine* or *crashed,* but with the tongue more retroflex (cerebral) position

s स् *s* as in *such* or *suit*

Aspirate

h ह् *h* as in *home* or *hope*

Typographic Conventions

1. Some words that are used as technical terms in the text have no exact English translation, and so are left untranslated. Sanskrit words appearing within the context of English text are shown in lower-case italics, e.g., *ātman, dharma, karma,* and *buddhi.* Proper names (such as Arjuna and Kṛṣṇa) and a few terms that are anglicized forms of Sanskrit words are not italicized unless special attention is being drawn to them.
2. Since the concept of capitalization does not exist in Devanāgarī, generally I do not capitalize Sanskrit terms, with the exception of proper names and words that have special importance, e.g., *Brahman.* The names of meters are treated as proper names and capitalized but not put into italics, e.g., Anuṣṭubh and Triṣṭubh.
3. Transliteration generally follows the method used in the digital version of the Critical Edition, which often preserves *anusvāra,* transliterated here as *ṁ.* For example, in 2.45 the Critical Edition reads निर्द्वंद्वो in Devanāgarī and *nirdvaṁdvo* in transliteration. The phoneme for *anusvāra* has several allophones. Sometimes for clarity I replace *anusvāra* with the nasal of the corresponding class, standardizing the nasals as follows:
    a. Guttural: e.g., ṁk = ṅk
    b. Palatal: e.g., ṁc = ñc
    c. Cerebral: e.g., ṁṭ = ṇṭ
    d. Dental: e.g., ṁt = nt
    e. Labial: e.g., ṁp = mp
4. Use of *anusvāra* (ं, transliterated as *ṁ*) at the end of a line is standardized as labial *m* (म्).
5. *Anusvāra* is retained when it is used as part of a prefix, unless the prefix is followed by a labial, in which case the *anusvāra* converts to a labial *m.* E.g., *saṁnyāsa* and *saṁgati* retain *anusvāra,* but *saṁbandha* changes to *sambandha.*
6. There are two nasal sounds in Sanskrit, *anusvāra* (ं, transliterated as *ṁ*) and the *anunāsika* (ँ, transliterated as m̐, using the *candrabindu* diacritical mark).[732] In the electronic text of the Critical Edition, *anunāsika* is found in only four verses (4.39, 6.41, 18.17, 18.71).

---

[732] Kale, p. 5.

7. In transliteration I generally separate *ca* for clarity, e.g., विराटश्च (*virāṭaśca*) becomes *virāṭaś ca* in verse 1.4.
8. A single apostrophe (*avagraha,* ऽ) represents omission of a short *a* (अ). Double apostrophes (double *avagraha,* ऽऽ) represent omission of a long *ā* (आ), e.g.: tadā'nalaśikhā dīrghā jāyate vāyunā''hatā ॥ HP 3.65 ॥
9. *Daṇḍa* (।) and double *daṇḍa* (॥) show the ends of half-verses and full verses respectively.

Abbreviations

√, verbal root (*dhātu*)

abl., ablative

acc., accusative

act., active

adj., adjective

adv., adverb

BCE, Before the Common Era (= BC, Before Christ)

BG, *Bhagavadgītā*

CE, Common Era (= AD, *Anno Domini*)

dat., dative

der., derivative, derived from

etc., *et cetera*

fem., feminine

fut., future

gen., genitive

ifc., *in fine compositi*, at the end of a compound, indicating use as the last member of a compound

imp., imperative

indec., indeclinable

indic., indicative

inf., infinitive

inst., instrumental

interrog., interrogative

irreg., irregular

lit., literal, literally

loc., locative

masc., masculine

MBh., *Mahābhārata*

mid., middle

neut., neuter

nom., nominative

opt., optative

p., past

pl., plural

pres., present

q.v., quod vide, "which see", indicating a cross-reference

RV, Ṛgveda

sing., singular

voc., vocative

YS, Yogasūtra of Patañjali

Index to First Words of Verses

उपैति शान्तरजसं ब्रह्मभूतमकल्मषम्	6.27c
उभयोरपि दृष्टोऽन्तस्त्वनयोस्तत्त्वदर्शिभिः	2.16c
उभौ तौ न विजानीतो नायं हन्ति न हन्यते	2.19c
उवाच पार्थ पश्यैतान्समवेतान्कुरूनिति	1.25c
ऊर्ध्वं गच्छन्ति सत्त्वस्था मध्ये तिष्ठन्ति राजसाः	14.18a
ऊर्ध्वमूलमधःशाखमश्वत्थं प्राहुरव्ययम्	15.1a
ऋतेऽपि त्वा न भविष्यन्ति सर्वे; येऽवस्थिताः प्रत्यनीकेषु योधाः	11.32c
ऋषिभिर्बहुधा गीतं छन्दोभिर्विविधैः पृथक्	13.4a
एकं सांख्यं च योगं च यः पश्यति स पश्यति	5.5c
एकत्वेन पृथक्त्वेन बहुधा विश्वतोमुखम्	9.15c
एकमप्यास्थितः सम्यगुभयोर्विन्दते फलम्	5.4c
एकया यात्यनावृत्तिमन्ययावर्तते पुनः	8.26c
एकाकी यतचित्तात्मा निराशीरपरिग्रहः	6.10c
एकोऽथ वाप्यच्युत तत्समक्षं; तत्क्षामये त्वामहमप्रमेयम्	11.42c
एतच्छ्रुत्वा वचनं केशवस्य; कृताञ्जलिर्वेपमानः किरीटी	11.35a
एतज्ज्ञानमिति प्रोक्तमज्ञानं यदतोऽन्यथा	13.11c
एतत्क्षेत्रं समासेन सविकारमुदाहृतम्	13.6c
एतद्धि दुर्लभतरं लोके जन्म यदीदृशम्	6.42c
एतद्बुद्ध्वा बुद्धिमान्स्यात्कृतकृत्यश्च भारत	15.20c
एतद्यो वेत्ति तं प्राहुः क्षेत्रज्ञ इति तद्विदः	13.1c
एतद्योनीनि भूतानि सर्वाणीत्युपधारय	7.6a
एतन्मे संशयं कृष्ण छेत्तुमर्हस्यशेषतः	6.39a
एतस्याहं न पश्यामि चञ्चलत्वात्स्थितिं स्थिराम्	6.33c
एतां दृष्टिमवष्टभ्य नष्टात्मानोऽल्पबुद्धयः	16.9a
एतां विभूतिं योगं च मम यो वेत्ति तत्त्वतः	10.7a
एतान्न हन्तुमिच्छामि घ्नतोऽपि मधुसूदन	1.35a
एतान्यपि तु कर्माणि सङ्गं त्यक्त्वा फलानि च	18.6a
एतैर्विमुक्तः कौन्तेय तमोद्वारैस्त्रिभिर्नरः	16.22a
एतैर्विमोहयत्येष ज्ञानमावृत्य देहिनम्	3.40c
एवं ज्ञात्वा कृतं कर्म पूर्वैरपि मुमुक्षुभिः	4.15a
एवं त्रयीधर्ममनुप्रपन्ना; गतागतं कामकामा लभन्ते	9.21c
एवं परंपराप्राप्तमिमं राजर्षयो विदुः	4.2a
एवं प्रवर्तितं चक्रं नानुवर्तयतीह यः	3.16a
एवं बहुविधा यज्ञा वितता ब्रह्मणो मुखे	4.32a
एवं बुद्धेः परं बुद्ध्वा संस्तभ्यात्मानमात्मना	3.43a
एवं सततयुक्ता ये भक्तास्त्वां पर्युपासते	12.1a
एवंरूपः शक्य अहं नृलोके; द्रष्टुं त्वदन्येन कुरुप्रवीर	11.48c
एवमुक्तो हृषीकेशो गुडाकेशेन भारत	1.24a
एवमुक्त्वा ततो राजन्महायोगेश्वरो हरिः	11.9a

छित्त्वैनं संशयं योगमातिष्ठोत्तिष्ठ भारत	4.42c
छिन्नद्वैधा यतात्मानः सर्वभूतहिते रताः	5.25c
जघन्यगुणवृत्तस्था अधो गच्छन्ति तामसाः	14.18c
जन्म कर्म च मे दिव्यमेवं यो वेत्ति तत्त्वतः	4.9a
जन्मबन्धविनिर्मुक्ताः पदं गच्छन्त्यनामयम्	2.51c
जन्ममृत्युजरादुःखैर्विमुक्तोऽमृतमश्नुते	14.20c
जन्ममृत्युजराव्याधिदुःखदोषानुदर्शनम्	13.8c
जयोऽस्मि व्यवसायोऽस्मि सत्त्वं सत्त्ववतामहम्	10.36c
जरामरणमोक्षाय मामाश्रित्य यतन्ति ये	7.29a
जहि शत्रुं महाबाहो कामरूपं दुरासदम्	3.43c
जातस्य हि ध्रुवो मृत्युर्ध्रुवं जन्म मृतस्य च	2.27a
जिज्ञासुरपि योगस्य शब्दब्रह्मातिवर्तते	6.44c
जितात्मनः प्रशान्तस्य परमात्मा समाहितः	6.7a
जीवनं सर्वभूतेषु तपश्चास्मि तपस्विषु	7.9c
जीवभूतां महाबाहो ययेदं धार्यते जगत्	7.5c
जोषयेत्सर्वकर्माणि विद्वान्युक्तः समाचरन्	3.26c
ज्ञातुं द्रष्टुं च तत्त्वेन प्रवेष्टुं च परंतप	11.54c
ज्ञात्वा शास्त्रविधानोक्तं कर्म कर्तुमिहार्हसि	16.24c
ज्ञानं कर्म च कर्ता च त्रिधैव गुणभेदतः	18.19a
ज्ञानं ज्ञेयं ज्ञानगम्यं हृदि सर्वस्य विष्ठितम्	13.17c
ज्ञानं ज्ञेयं परिज्ञाता त्रिविधा कर्मचोदना	18.18a
ज्ञानं तेऽहं सविज्ञानमिदं वक्ष्याम्यशेषतः	7.2a
ज्ञानं यदा तदा विद्याद्विवृद्धं सत्त्वमित्युत	14.11c
ज्ञानं लब्ध्वा परां शान्तिमचिरेणाधिगच्छति	4.39c
ज्ञानं विज्ञानमास्तिक्यं ब्रह्मकर्म स्वभावजम्	18.42c
ज्ञानं विज्ञानसहितं यज्ज्ञात्वा मोक्ष्यसेऽशुभात्	9.1c
ज्ञानमावृत्य तु तमः प्रमादे सञ्जयत्युत	14.9c
ज्ञानयज्ञेन चाप्यन्ये यजन्तो मामुपासते	9.15a
ज्ञानयज्ञेन तेनाहमिष्टः स्यामिति मे मतिः	18.70c
ज्ञानयोगेन सांख्यानां कर्मयोगेन योगिनाम्	3.3c
ज्ञानविज्ञानतृप्तात्मा कूटस्थो विजितेन्द्रियः	6.8a
ज्ञानाग्निः सर्वकर्माणि भस्मसात्कुरुते तथा	4.37c
ज्ञानाग्निदग्धकर्माणं तमाहुः पण्डितं बुधाः	4.19c
ज्ञानेन तु तदज्ञानं येषां नाशितमात्मनः	5.16a
ज्ञेयं यत्तत्प्रवक्ष्यामि यज्ज्ञात्वामृतमश्नुते	13.12a
ज्ञेयः स नित्यसंन्यासी यो न द्वेष्टि न काङ्क्षति	5.3a
ज्यायसी चेत्कर्मणस्ते मता बुद्धिर्जनार्दन	3.1a
ज्योतिषामपि तज्ज्योतिस्तमसः परमुच्यते	13.17a
झषाणां मकरश्चास्मि स्रोतसामस्मि जाह्नवी	10.31c

त्रिभिर्गुणमयैर्भावैरेभिः सर्वमिदं जगत्	7.13a
त्रिविधं नरकस्येदं द्वारं नाशनमात्मनः	16.21a
त्रिविधा भवति श्रद्धा देहिनां सा स्वभावजा	17.2a
त्रैगुण्यविषया वेदा निस्त्रैगुण्यो भवार्जुन	2.45a
त्रैविद्या मां सोमपाः पूतपापा; यज्ञैरिष्ट्वा स्वर्गतिं प्रार्थयन्ते	9.20a
त्वत्तः कमलपत्राक्ष माहात्म्यमपि चाव्ययम्	11.2c
त्वदन्यः संशयस्यास्य छेत्ता न ह्युपपद्यते	6.39c
त्वमक्षरं परमं वेदितव्यं; त्वमस्य विश्वस्य परं निधानम्	11.18a
त्वमव्ययः शाश्वतधर्मगोप्ता; सनातनस्त्वं पुरुषो मतो मे	11.18c
त्वमादिदेवः पुरुषः पुराण;स्त्वमस्य विश्वस्य परं निधानम्	11.38a
दंष्ट्राकरालानि च ते मुखानि; दृष्ट्वैव कालानलसंनिभानि	11.25a
दण्डो दमयतामस्मि नीतिरस्मि जिगीषताम्	10.38a
ददामि बुद्धियोगं तं येन मामुपयान्ति ते	10.10c
दम्भाहंकारसंयुक्ताः कामरागबलान्विताः	17.5c
दम्भो दर्पोऽतिमानश्च क्रोधः पारुष्यमेव च	16.4a
दया भूतेष्वलोलुप्त्वं मार्दवं ह्रीरचापलम्	16.2c
दर्शयामास पार्थाय परमं रूपमैश्वरम्	11.9c
दातव्यमिति यद्दानं दीयतेऽनुपकारिणे	17.20a
दानं दमश्च यज्ञश्च स्वाध्यायस्तप आर्जवम्	16.1c
दानक्रियाश्च विविधाः क्रियन्ते मोक्षकाङ्क्षिभिः	17.25c
दानमीश्वरभावश्च क्षत्रकर्म स्वभावजम्	18.43c
दिवि सूर्यसहस्रस्य भवेद्युगपदुत्थिता	11.12a
दिव्यं ददामि ते चक्षुः पश्य मे योगमैश्वरम्	11.8c
दिव्यमाल्याम्बरधरं दिव्यगन्धानुलेपनम्	11.11a
दिशो न जाने न लभे च शर्म; प्रसीद देवेश जगन्निवास	11.25c
दीयते च परिक्लिष्टं तद्दानं राजसं स्मृतम्	17.21c
दुःखमित्येव यत्कर्म कायक्लेशभयात्त्यजेत्	18.8a
दुःखेष्वनुद्विग्नमनाः सुखेषु विगतस्पृहः	2.56a
दूरेण ह्यवरं कर्म बुद्धियोगाद्धनंजय	2.49a
दृष्ट्वा तु पाण्डवानीकं व्यूढं दुर्योधनस्तदा	1.2a
दृष्ट्वा हि त्वां प्रव्यथितान्तरात्मा; धृतिं न विन्दामि शमं च विष्णो	11.24c
दृष्ट्वाद्भुतं रूपमिदं तवोग्रं; लोकत्रयं प्रव्यथितं महात्मन्	11.20c
दृष्ट्वेदं मानुषं रूपं तव सौम्यं जनार्दन	11.51a
दृष्ट्वेमान्स्वजनान्कृष्ण युयुत्सून्समवस्थितान्	1.28c
देवद्विजगुरुप्राज्ञपूजनं शौचमार्जवम्	17.14a
देवा अप्यस्य रूपस्य नित्यं दर्शनकाङ्क्षिणः	11.52c
देवान्देवयजो यान्ति मद्भक्ता यान्ति मामपि	7.23c
देवान्भावयतानेन ते देवा भावयन्तु वः	3.11a
देशे काले च पात्रे च तद्दानं सात्त्विकं स्मृतम्	17.20c

न च मां तानि कर्माणि निबध्नन्ति धनंजय	9.9a
न च शक्नोम्यवस्थातुं भ्रमतीव च मे मनः	1.30c
न च श्रेयोऽनुपश्यामि हत्वा स्वजनमाहवे	1.31c
न च संन्यसनादेव सिद्धिं समधिगच्छति	3.4c
न चातिस्वप्नशीलस्य जाग्रतो नैव चार्जुन	6.16c
न चाभावयतः शान्तिरशान्तस्य कुतः सुखम्	2.66c
न चाशुश्रूषवे वाच्यं न च मां योऽभ्यसूयति	18.67c
न चास्य सर्वभूतेषु कश्चिदर्थव्यपाश्रयः	3.18c
न चैतद्विद्मः कतरन्नो गरीयो; यद्वा जयेम यदि वा नो जयेयुः	2.6a
न चैनं क्लेदयन्त्यापो न शोषयति मारुतः	2.23c
न चैव न भविष्यामः सर्वे वयमतः परम्	2.12c
न जायते म्रियते वा कदा चि;न्नायं भूत्वा भविता वा न भूयः	2.20a
न तदस्ति पृथिव्यां वा दिवि देवेषु वा पुनः	18.40a
न तदस्ति विना यत्स्यान्मया भूतं चराचरम्	10.39c
न तद्भासयते सूर्यो न शशाङ्को न पावकः	15.6a
न तु मां शक्यसे द्रष्टुमनेनैव स्वचक्षुषा	11.8a
न तु मामभिजानन्ति तत्त्वेनातश्च्यवन्ति ते	9.24c
न त्वत्समोऽस्त्यभ्यधिकः कुतोऽन्यो; लोकत्रयेऽप्यप्रतिमप्रभाव	11.43c
न त्वेवाहं जातु नासं न त्वं नेमे जनाधिपाः	2.12a
न द्वेष्टि संप्रवृत्तानि न निवृत्तानि काङ्क्षति	14.22c
न द्वेष्ट्यकुशलं कर्म कुशले नानुषज्जते	18.10a
न प्रहृष्येत्प्रियं प्राप्य नोद्विजेत्प्राप्य चाप्रियम्	5.20a
न बुद्धिभेदं जनयेदज्ञानां कर्मसङ्गिनाम्	3.26a
न मां कर्माणि लिम्पन्ति न मे कर्मफले स्पृहा	4.14a
न मां दुष्कृतिनो मूढाः प्रपद्यन्ते नराधमाः	7.15a
न मे पार्थास्ति कर्तव्यं त्रिषु लोकेषु किंचन	3.22a
न मे विदुः सुरगणाः प्रभवं न महर्षयः	10.2a
न योत्स्य इति गोविन्दमुक्त्वा तूष्णीं बभूव ह	2.9c
न रूपमस्येह तथोपलभ्यते; नान्तो न चादिर्न च संप्रतिष्ठा	15.3a
न विमुञ्चति दुर्मेधा धृतिः सा पार्थ तामसी	18.35c
न वेदयज्ञाध्ययनैर्न दानै;र्न च क्रियाभिर्न तपोभिरुग्रैः	11.48a
न शौचं नापि चाचारो न सत्यं तेषु विद्यते	16.7c
न स सिद्धिमवाप्नोति न सुखं न परां गतिम्	16.23c
न हि कल्याणकृत्कश्चिद्दुर्गतिं तात गच्छति	6.40c
न हि कश्चित्क्षणमपि जातु तिष्ठत्यकर्मकृत्	3.5a
न हि ज्ञानेन सदृशं पवित्रमिह विद्यते	4.38a
न हि ते भगवन्व्यक्तिं विदुर्देवा न दानवाः	10.14c
न हि देहभृता शक्यं त्यक्तुं कर्माण्यशेषतः	18.11a
न हि प्रपश्यामि ममापनुद्या;द्यच्छोकमुच्छोषणमिन्द्रियाणाम्	2.8a

भीष्मद्रोणप्रमुखतः सर्वेषां च महीक्षिताम्	1.25a
भीष्ममेवाभिरक्षन्तु भवन्तः सर्व एव हि	1.11c
भीष्मो द्रोणः सूतपुत्रस्तथासौ; सहास्मदीयैरपि योधमुख्यैः	11.26c
भुञ्जते ते त्वघं पापा ये पचन्त्यात्मकारणात्	3.13c
भूतग्रामः स एवायं भूत्वा भूत्वा प्रलीयते	8.19a
भूतग्राममिमं कृत्स्नमवशं प्रकृतेर्वशात्	9.8c
भूतप्रकृतिमोक्षं च ये विदुर्यान्ति ते परम्	13.34c
भूतभर्तृ च तज्ज्ञेयं ग्रसिष्णु प्रभविष्णु च	13.16c
भूतभावन भूतेश देवदेव जगत्पते	10.15c
भूतभावोद्भवकरो विसर्गः कर्मसंज्ञितः	8.3c
भूतभृन्न च भूतस्थो ममात्मा भूतभावनः	9.5c
भूतानि यान्ति भूतेज्या यान्ति मद्याजिनोऽपि माम्	9.25c
भूमिरापोऽनलो वायुः खं मनो बुद्धिरेव च	7.4a
भूय एव महाबाहो शृणु मे परमं वचः	10.1a
भूयः कथय तृप्तिर्हि शृण्वतो नास्ति मेऽमृतम्	10.18c
भोक्तारं यज्ञतपसां सर्वलोकमहेश्वरम्	5.29a
भोगैश्वर्यप्रसक्तानां तयापहृतचेतसाम्	2.44a
भ्रामयन्सर्वभूतानि यन्त्रारूढानि मायया	18.61c
भ्रुवोर्मध्ये प्राणमावेश्य सम्य;क्स तं परं पुरुषमुपैति दिव्यम्	8.10c
मच्चित्तः सर्वदुर्गाणि मत्प्रसादात्तरिष्यसि	18.58a
मच्चित्ता मद्गतप्राणा बोधयन्तः परस्परम्	10.9a
मत्कर्मकृन्मत्परमो मद्भक्तः सङ्गवर्जितः	11.55a
मत्त एवेति तान्विद्धि न त्वहं तेषु ते मयि	7.12c
मत्तः परतरं नान्यत्किंचिदस्ति धनंजय	7.7a
मत्प्रसादादवाप्नोति शाश्वतं पदमव्ययम्	18.56c
मत्स्थानि सर्वभूतानि न चाहं तेष्ववस्थितः	9.4c
मदनुग्रहाय परमं गुह्यमध्यात्मसंज्ञितम्	11.1a
मदर्थमपि कर्माणि कुर्वन्सिद्धिमवाप्स्यसि	12.10c
मद्भक्त एतद्विज्ञाय मद्भावायोपपद्यते	13.18c
मद्भावा मानसा जाता येषां लोक इमाः प्रजाः	10.6c
मनः संयम्य मच्चित्तो युक्त आसीत मत्परः	6.14c
मनःप्रसादः सौम्यत्वं मौनमात्मविनिग्रहः	17.16a
मनःषष्ठानीन्द्रियाणि प्रकृतिस्थानि कर्षति	15.7c
मनसस्तु परा बुद्धिर्यो बुद्धेः परतस्तु सः	3.42c
मनसैवेन्द्रियग्रामं विनियम्य समन्ततः	6.24c
मनुष्याणां सहस्रेषु कश्चिद्यतति सिद्धये	7.3a
मन्त्रोऽहमहमेवाज्यमहमग्निरहं हुतम्	9.16c
मन्मना भव मद्भक्तो मद्याजी मां नमस्कुरु	9.34a
मन्मना भव मद्भक्तो मद्याजी मां नमस्कुरु	18.65a

यथा नदीनां बहवोऽम्बुवेगाः; समुद्रमेवाभिमुखा द्रवन्ति	11.28a
यथा प्रकाशयत्येकः कृत्स्नं लोकमिमं रविः	13.33a
यथा प्रदीप्तं ज्वलनं पतंगा; विशन्ति नाशाय समृद्धवेगाः	11.29a
यथा सर्वगतं सौक्ष्म्यादाकाशं नोपलिप्यते	13.32a
यथाकाशस्थितो नित्यं वायुः सर्वत्रगो महान्	9.6a
यथैधांसि समिद्धोऽग्निर्भस्मसात्कुरुतेऽर्जुन	4.37a
यथोल्बेनावृतो गर्भस्तथा तेनेदमावृतम्	3.38c
यदक्षरं वेदविदो वदन्ति; विशन्ति यद्यतयो वीतरागाः	8.11a
यदग्रे चानुबन्धे च सुखं मोहनमात्मनः	18.39a
यदहंकारमाश्रित्य न योत्स्य इति मन्यसे	18.59a
यदा ते मोहकलिलं बुद्धिर्व्यतितरिष्यति	2.52a
यदा भूतपृथग्भावमेकस्थमनुपश्यति	13.30a
यदा यदा हि धर्मस्य ग्लानिर्भवति भारत	4.7a
यदा विनियतं चित्तमात्मन्येवावतिष्ठते	6.18a
यदा संहरते चायं कूर्मोऽङ्गानीव सर्वशः	2.58a
यदा सत्त्वे प्रवृद्धे तु प्रलयं याति देहभृत्	14.14a
यदा हि नेन्द्रियार्थेषु न कर्मस्वनुषज्जते	6.4a
यदादित्यगतं तेजो जगद्भासयतेऽखिलम्	15.12a
यदि भाः सदृशी सा स्याद्भासस्तस्य महात्मनः	11.12c
यदि मामप्रतीकारमशस्त्रं शस्त्रपाणयः	1.46a
यदि ह्यहं न वर्तेयं जातु कर्मण्यतन्द्रितः	3.23a
यदिच्छन्तो ब्रह्मचर्यं चरन्ति; तत्ते पदं संग्रहेण प्रवक्ष्ये	8.11c
यदृच्छया चोपपन्नं स्वर्गद्वारमपावृतम्	2.32a
यदृच्छालाभसंतुष्टो द्वंद्वातीतो विमत्सरः	4.22a
यद्गत्वा न निवर्तन्ते तद्धाम परमं मम	15.6c
यद्यदाचरति श्रेष्ठस्तत्तदेवेतरो जनः	3.21a
यद्यद्विभूतिमत्सत्त्वं श्रीमदूर्जितमेव वा	10.41a
यद्यप्येते न पश्यन्ति लोभोपहतचेतसः	1.38a
यद्राज्यसुखलोभेन हन्तुं स्वजनमुद्यताः	1.45c
यया तु धर्मकामार्थान्धृत्या धारयतेऽर्जुन	18.34a
यया धर्ममधर्मं च कार्यं चाकार्यमेव च	18.31a
यया स्वप्नं भयं शोकं विषादं मदमेव च	18.35a
यष्टव्यमेवेति मनः समाधाय स सात्त्विकः	17.11c
यस्तु कर्मफलत्यागी स त्यागीत्यभिधीयते	18.11c
यस्त्वात्मरतिरेव स्यादात्मतृप्तश्च मानवः	3.17a
यस्त्विन्द्रियाणि मनसा नियम्यारभतेऽर्जुन	3.7a
यस्मात्क्षरमतीतोऽहमक्षरादपि चोत्तमः	15.18a
यस्मान्नोद्विजते लोको लोकान्नोद्विजते च यः	12.15a
यस्मिन्स्थितो न दुःखेन गुरुणापि विचाल्यते	6.22c

यो मामजमनादिं च वेत्ति लोकमहेश्वरम् 10.3a
यो मामेवमसंमूढो जानाति पुरुषोत्तमम् 15.19a
यो यो यां यां तनुं भक्तः श्रद्धयार्चितुमिच्छति 7.21a
यो लोकत्रयमाविश्य बिभर्त्यव्यय ईश्वरः 15.17c
योऽन्तःसुखोऽन्तरारामस्तथान्तर्ज्योतिरेव यः 5.24a
योऽयं योगस्त्वया प्रोक्तः साम्येन मधुसूदन 6.33a
योगं योगेश्वरात्कृष्णात्साक्षात्कथयतः स्वयम् 18.75c
योगयुक्तो मुनिर्ब्रह्म नचिरेणाधिगच्छति 5.6c
योगयुक्तो विशुद्धात्मा विजितात्मा जितेन्द्रियः 5.7a
योगसंन्यस्तकर्माणं ज्ञानसंछिन्नसंशयम् 4.41a
योगस्थः कुरु कर्माणि सङ्गं त्यक्त्वा धनंजय 2.48a
योगारूढस्य तस्यैव शमः कारणमुच्यते 6.3c
योगिनः कर्म कुर्वन्ति सङ्गं त्यक्त्वात्मशुद्धये 5.11c
योगिनामपि सर्वेषां मद्गतेनान्तरात्मना 6.47a
योगिनो यतचित्तस्य युञ्जतो योगमात्मनः 6.19c
योगी युञ्जीत सततमात्मानं रहसि स्थितः 6.10a
योगेनाव्यभिचारिण्या धृतिः सा पार्थ सात्त्विकी 18.33c
योगेश्वर ततो मे त्वं दर्शयात्मानमव्ययम् 11.4c
योत्स्यमानानवेक्षेऽहं य एतेऽत्र समागताः 1.23a
रक्षांसि भीतानि दिशो द्रवन्ति; सर्वे नमस्यन्ति च सिद्धसंघाः 11.36c
रजः सत्त्वं तमश्चैव तमः सत्त्वं रजस्तथा 14.10c
रजसस्तु फलं दुःखमज्ञानं तमसः फलम् 14.16c
रजसि प्रलयं गत्वा कर्मसङ्गिषु जायते 14.15a
रजस्तमश्चाभिभूय सत्त्वं भवति भारत 14.10a
रजस्येतानि जायन्ते विवृद्धे भरतर्षभ 14.12c
रजो रागात्मकं विद्धि तृष्णासङ्गसमुद्भवम् 14.7a
रसवर्जं रसोऽप्यस्य परं दृष्ट्वा निवर्तते 2.59c
रसोऽहमप्सु कौन्तेय प्रभास्मि शशिसूर्ययोः 7.8a
रस्याः स्निग्धाः स्थिरा हृद्या आहाराः सात्त्विकप्रियाः 17.8c
राक्षसीमासुरीं चैव प्रकृतिं मोहिनीं श्रिताः 9.12c
रागद्वेषवियुक्तैस्तु विषयानिन्द्रियैश्चरन् 2.64a
रागी कर्मफलप्रेप्सुर्लुब्धो हिंसात्मकोऽशुचिः 18.27a
राजन्संस्मृत्य संस्मृत्य संवादमिममद्भुतम् 18.76a
राजविद्या राजगुह्यं पवित्रमिदमुत्तमम् 9.2a
रात्रिं युगसहस्रान्तां तेऽहोरात्रविदो जनाः 8.17c
रात्र्यागमे प्रलीयन्ते तत्रैवाव्यक्तसंज्ञके 8.18c
रात्र्यागमेऽवशः पार्थ प्रभवत्यहरागमे 8.19c
रुद्राणां शंकरश्चास्मि वित्तेशो यक्षरक्षसाम् 10.23a
रुद्रादित्या वसवो ये च साध्या; विश्वेऽश्विनौ मरुतश्चोष्मपाश्च 11.22a

वीतरागभयक्रोधः स्थितधीर्मुनिरुच्यते 2.56c
वीतरागभयक्रोधा मन्मया मामुपाश्रिताः 4.10a
वृष्णीनां वासुदेवोऽस्मि पाण्डवानां धनंजयः 10.37a
वेत्तासि वेद्यं च परं च धाम; त्वया ततं विश्वमनन्तरूप 11.38c
वेत्ति यत्र न चैवायं स्थितश्चलति तत्त्वतः 6.21c
वेत्ति सर्वेषु भूतेषु तज्ज्ञानं विद्धि राजसम् 18.21c
वेदवादरताः पार्थ नान्यदस्तीति वादिनः 2.42c
वेदानां सामवेदोऽस्मि देवानामस्मि वासवः 10.22a
वेदाविनाशिनं नित्यं य एनमजमव्ययम् 2.21a
वेदाहं समतीतानि वर्तमानानि चार्जुन 7.26a
वेदेषु यज्ञेषु तपःसु चैव; दानेषु यत्पुण्यफलं प्रदिष्टम् 8.28a
वेदैश्च सर्वैरहमेव वेद्यो; वेदान्तकृद्वेदविदेव चाहम् 15.15c
वेद्यं पवित्रमोंकार ऋक्साम यजुरेव च 9.17c
वेपथुश्च शरीरे मे रोमहर्षश्च जायते 1.29c
व्यपेतभीः प्रीतमनाः पुनस्त्वं; तदेव मे रूपमिदं प्रपश्य 11.49c
व्यवसायात्मिका बुद्धिः समाधौ न विधीयते 2.44c
व्यवसायात्मिका बुद्धिरेकेह कुरुनन्दन 2.41a
व्यामिश्रेणैव वाक्येन बुद्धिं मोहयसीव मे 3.2a
व्यासप्रसादाच्छ्रुतवानेतद्गुह्यमहं परम् 18.75a
व्यूढां द्रुपदपुत्रेण तव शिष्येण धीमता 1.3c
शक्नोतीहैव यः सोढुं प्राक्शरीरविमोक्षणात् 5.23a
शक्य एवंविधो द्रष्टुं दृष्टवानसि मां यथा 11.53c
शनैः शनैरुपरमेद्बुद्ध्या धृतिगृहीतया 6.25a
शब्दादीन्विषयांस्त्यक्त्वा रागद्वेषौ व्युदस्य च 18.51c
शब्दादीन्विषयानन्य इन्द्रियाग्निषु जुह्वति 4.26c
शमो दमस्तपः शौचं क्षान्तिरार्जवमेव च 18.42a
शरीरं यदवाप्नोति यच्चाप्युत्क्रामतीश्वरः 15.8a
शरीरयात्रापि च ते न प्रसिध्येदकर्मणः 3.8c
शरीरवाङ्मनोभिर्यत्कर्म प्रारभते नरः 18.15a
शरीरस्थोऽपि कौन्तेय न करोति न लिप्यते 13.31c
शान्तिं निर्वाणपरमां मत्संस्थामधिगच्छति 6.15c
शारीरं केवलं कर्म कुर्वन्नाप्नोति किल्बिषम् 4.21c
शाश्वतस्य च धर्मस्य सुखस्यैकान्तिकस्य च 14.27c
शीतोष्णसुखदुःखेषु तथा मानावमानयोः 6.7c
शीतोष्णसुखदुःखेषु समः सङ्गविवर्जितः 12.18c
शुक्लकृष्णे गती ह्येते जगतः शाश्वते मते 8.26a
शुचीनां श्रीमतां गेहे योगभ्रष्टोऽभिजायते 6.41c
शुचौ देशे प्रतिष्ठाप्य स्थिरमासनमात्मनः 6.11a
शुनि चैव श्वपाके च पण्डिताः समदर्शिनः 5.18c

सर्वतःपाणिपादं तत्सर्वतोक्षिशिरोमुखम्	13.13a
सर्वतःश्रुतिमल्लोके सर्वमावृत्य तिष्ठति	13.13c
सर्वत्रगमचिन्त्यं च कूटस्थमचलं ध्रुवम्	12.3c
सर्वत्रावस्थितो देहे तथात्मा नोपलिप्यते	13.32c
सर्वथा वर्तमानोऽपि न स भूयोऽभिजायते	13.23c
सर्वथा वर्तमानोऽपि स योगी मयि वर्तते	6.31c
सर्वद्वाराणि संयम्य मनो हृदि निरुध्य च	8.12a
सर्वद्वारेषु देहेऽस्मिन्प्रकाश उपजायते	14.11a
सर्वधर्मान्परित्यज्य मामेकं शरणं व्रज	18.66a
सर्वभूतस्थमात्मानं सर्वभूतानि चात्मनि	6.29a
सर्वभूतस्थितं यो मां भजत्येकत्वमास्थितः	6.31a
सर्वभूतात्मभूतात्मा कुर्वन्नपि न लिप्यते	5.7c
सर्वभूतानि कौन्तेय प्रकृतिं यान्ति मामिकाम्	9.7a
सर्वभूतानि संमोहं सर्गे यान्ति परंतप	7.27c
सर्वभूतेषु येनैकं भावमव्ययमीक्षते	18.20a
सर्वमेतदृतं मन्ये यन्मां वदसि केशव	10.14a
सर्वयोनिषु कौन्तेय मूर्तयः संभवन्ति याः	14.4a
सर्वसंकल्पसंन्यासी योगारूढस्तदोच्यते	6.4c
सर्वस्य चाहं हृदि संनिविष्टो; मत्तः स्मृतिर्ज्ञानमपोहनं च	15.15a
सर्वस्य धातारमचिन्त्यरूप;मादित्यवर्णं तमसः परस्तात्	8.9c
सर्वाणीन्द्रियकर्माणि प्राणकर्माणि चापरे	4.27a
सर्वारम्भपरित्यागी गुणातीतः स उच्यते	14.25c
सर्वारम्भपरित्यागी यो मद्भक्तः स मे प्रियः	12.16c
सर्वारम्भा हि दोषेण धूमेनाग्निरिवावृताः	18.48c
सर्वार्थान्विपरीतांश्च बुद्धिः सा पार्थ तामसी	18.32c
सर्वाश्चर्यमयं देवमनन्तं विश्वतोमुखम्	11.11c
सर्वेऽप्येते यज्ञविदो यज्ञक्षपितकल्मषाः	4.30c
सर्वेन्द्रियगुणाभासं सर्वेन्द्रियविवर्जितम्	13.14a
सहजं कर्म कौन्तेय सदोषमपि न त्यजेत्	18.48a
सहयज्ञाः प्रजाः सृष्ट्वा पुरोवाच प्रजापतिः	3.10a
सहसैवाभ्यहन्यन्त स शब्दस्तुमुलोऽभवत्	1.13c
सहस्रयुगपर्यन्तमहर्यद्ब्रह्मणो विदुः	8.17a
सांख्ययोगौ पृथग्बालाः प्रवदन्ति न पण्डिताः	5.4a
सांख्ये कृतान्ते प्रोक्तानि सिद्धये सर्वकर्मणाम्	18.13c
सात्त्विकी राजसी चैव तामसी चेति तां शृणु	17.2c
साधिभूताधिदैवं मां साधियज्ञं च ये विदुः	7.30a
साधुरेव स मन्तव्यः सम्यग्व्यवसितो हि सः	9.30c
साधुष्वपि च पापेषु समबुद्धिर्विशिष्यते	6.9c
सिंहनादं विनद्योच्चैः शङ्खं दध्मौ प्रतापवान्	1.12c

Concordancing Methodology

The concordance includes all words that appear in the Critical Edition of the text. Each entry is numbered to make referencing easy. The format used for this concordance is designed to supplement two Devanāgarī concordances based on the Vulgate text:

- G. A. Jacob. *A Concordance to the Principal Upaniṣads and Bhagavadgītā.* 1891. Reprint: Motilal Banarsidass Publishers Pvt. Ltd.: Delhi, 1963.
- P. C. Divanji. *Critical Word-Index to the Bhagavadgītā.* Samarth Bharat Press: Poona, 1945. This excellent concordance is based on the Vulgate, but is also useful when working with the Critical Edition. Variant readings, including the Kāśmīr recension, are included. Part I includes 3,865 "Primary Word-Units" found in the Vulgate text. These Primary Word-Units include compounds as distinct words, arranged according to the first word of a compound. The indexes of Part II are in Devanāgarī and do not cite verse numbers where the compound forms are located, merely pointing back to the Primary Word-Units themselves. Part II includes 1,102 "Secondary Word-Units" in which the constituent parts of compounds are considered individually, with cross-references to the compound forms listed in Part I. Part II also includes an index of 296 "Tertiary Word-Units" in which compounds listed as "Secondary Word-Units" are further decomposed into their constituent members. The "Tertiary Word-Units" are then further subdivided into an index of 36 "Quaternary Word-Units" in the same manner.

Word indexes that are less extensive than the two cited above include:

- Annie Besant and Bhagavan Das. *The Bhagavad Gītā: With Samskṛit [sic] Text, free translation into English, a word-for-word translation, and an Introduction on Samskṛit [sic] Grammar.* Theosophical Publishing Society: London and Benares, 1905. The word index that appears on pp. 335-348 of that 1905 edition was republished as an Appendix in volume 2 of Bal Gangadhar Tilak, *Śrīmad Bhagavadgītā Rahasya.* 1935.

- W. Douglas P. Hill. *The Bhagavadgītā.* Oxford University Press: London, 1928.
- Swāmī Gambhīrānanda. *The Bhagavad-Gītā: With the commentary of Śaṅkarācārya.* Advaita Ashrama: Calcutta, 1997.
- Kees W. Bolle. *The Bhagavadgītā.* University of California Press: Berkeley, 1979.

The following example shows the indexing method used in this concordance. In the sample entry below, four references to the word *saṁkalpa* ("intention") are grouped under one entry, arranged in English alphabetical order for the transliterated Sanskrit word. The corresponding Primary Word-Unit index numbers in the Divanji concordance are shown in **boldface** to illustrate that the words are widely separated from one another in the Divanji concordance, which lists the four entries in Sanskrit alphabetical order based on the first word of the compounds in which they appear.[733]

saṁkalpa (intention, motive)

- asaṁnyastasaṁkalpaḥ "without renouncing intention (for results); without detaching from the purpose". 6.2. **[Divanji #488]**
- kāmasaṁkalpavarjitāḥ "free from intentions motivated by desire". 4.19. **[Divanji #976]**
- saṁkalpaprabhavān "that which owes its origin to intention; originating from intention". 6.24. **[Divanji #3374]**
- sarvasaṁkalpasaṁnyāsī "one who has renounced all intention (for results)". 6.4. **[Divanji #3580]**

In contrast with this simple list, Divanji's Secondary Word-Units index for *saṁkalpa* reads as follows:[734]

951. सङ्कल्प—सङ्कल्पप्रभवान्—[विग्रहपद्धत्यै 'प्रभव' (१) शब्दो द्रष्टव्यः] ।

This entry correctly notes the compound *saṁkalpaprabhavān* but does not list the other three compounds. However, there is also an entry for *saṁkalpa* in the Tertiary Word-Units index as follows:[735]

---

[733] Cross-references to Divanji entries are given in footnotes for some entries in this concordance when a Divanji translation is cited or some other annotation on a word is noted.

[734] Divanji, p. 289, entry #951.

[735] Divanji, p. 319, entry #263.

263. सङ्कल्प—(१) कामसङ्कल्प । (२) सन्नयस्तसङ्कल्प । (३) सर्वसङ्कल्प ।—(१) काम–सङ्कल्पवर्जिताः । (२) असन्नयस्तसङ्कल्पः । (३) सर्वसङ्कल्पसन्नयासी ।

This entry notes three more compounds: *kāmasaṁkalpavarjitāḥ*, *asaṁnyastasaṁkalpaḥ*, and *sarvasaṁkalpasaṁnyāsī*. But since the fourth compound (*saṁkalpaprabhavān*) was already listed as a Secondary Word-Unit, it does not appear in this list of Tertiary Word-Units. This example shows that all the words are there in the Divanji concordance, but finding them would challenge the average reader of the *BG*.

Treatment of Compounds

This edition uses a simplified method for locating significant words found within compounds or combined with a prefix. Word elements can be found by referring to a primary entry that lists all references to a word regardless of grammatical form or position within compounds. Entries of this type, which cluster words together based on some underlying grammatical similarity, are shown with a special **bold typeface** to distinguish them from entries that only point to a single word form. An example is the following entry for the word *ari*, which means "enemy". This word occurs three times in the text, but never with the same spelling. It is spelled *ari*, *āry*, and *āri* depending on its position in compounds and the effect of *sandhi* with adjoining words.

42. ari ("enemy")

- arisūdana "O Destroyer of the Enemy". 2.4.
- mitrāripakṣayoḥ "toward friend or enemy sides". 14.25.
- suhṛnmitrāryudāsīnamadhyasthadveṣyabandhuṣu "in friends, enemies, neutrals, mediators, despicable persons, and relatives". 6.9.

For another example, the entry for the stem *guh-* shows all references to the word *guhya*, which means "secret". These include the compounds *rājaguhyaṁ* (in verse 9.2) and *sarvaguhyatamaṁ* (in verse 18.64), both of which would be missed if only the beginning of a word was indexed.

The method of indexing used in this concordance results in some words appearing more than once, sometimes as individual words standing on their own, and sometimes as members of a grouped entry that brings them together with related words. This redundancy serves the goal of making it easy for the average reader to find words based on more than one lookup strategy. For example, the word *sarvasaṁkalpasaṁnyāsī* might interest the reader because it includes the concept of intention (*saṁkalpa*), or because it describes a renouncer (*saṁnyāsī*). The word therefore appears in both of those concept groups, even though it does not begin with either of the two words.

In compiling the concordance, "false positives" have been removed from grouped entries. This is an obvious thing to do, but it requires human judgement to accurately parse compounds. For example, a computer search for the word fragment "*rahas-*" in the digital source text will find two valid references to words meaning "secret" (*rahasyam* and *rahasi*), but will also find two false positives (*cak**rahas**tam* and *p**rahas**ann*) that have no connection with the underlying idea of "secret". False positives of this type have been omitted in the concordance.

References

Ādidevānanda, Svāmi. n.d. *Śrī Rāmānuja Gītā Bhāṣya.* Translated by Svāmi Ādidevānanda. Mylapore, Madras: Sri Ramakrishna Math.

Apte, Vaman Shivram. 1965, Fourth Edition. *The Practical Sanskrit-English Dictionary.* Delhi: Motilal Banarsidass.

Besant, Annie, and Bhagavan Das. 1905. *The Bhagavad Gītā: With Samskṛit Text, free translation into English, a word-for-word translation, and an Introduction on Samskṛit Grammar.* London and Benares: Theosophical Publishing Society.

Bhattacharyya, Narendra Nath. 2001. *A Dictionary of Indian Mythology.* New Delhi: Munshiram Manoharlal Publishers Pvt. Ltd.

Bolle, Kees W. 1979. *The Bhagavadgītā.* Berkeley: University of California Press.

Bucknell, Roderick S. 1994; Reprint, 2004. *Sanskrit Manual.* Delhi: Motilal Banarsidass Publishers Pvt. Ltd.

Chidbhavananda, Swami. 1997. *The Bhagavad Gita.* Tirupparaitturai: Sri RamakrishnaTapovanam.

Divanji, P. C. 1945. *Critical Word-Index to the Bhagavadgītā.* Poona: Samarth Bharat Press.

Edgerton, Franklin. 1944; Reprint, 1995. *The Bhagavad Gītā.* Cambridge: Harvard University Press.

Feuerstein, Georg, and Brenda Feuerstein. 2011. *The Bhagavad-Gītā.* Boston: Shambhala Publications, Inc.

Flood, Gavin, and Charles Martin. 2012. *The Bhagavad Gita.* New York: W. W. Norton & Company, Inc.

Gambhīrānanda, Swāmī (translator). 1997, Fourth Reprint. *The Bhagavad-Gītā: With the commentary of Śaṅkarācārya.* Calcutta: Advaita Ashrama.

Gambhīrānanda, Swāmī (translator). 1998, First Edition. *Bhagavad-Gītā with the Annotation Gūḍhārtha Dīpikā by Madhusūdana Sarasvati.* Calcutta: Advaita Ashrama.

Gambhīrānanda, Swāmī (translator). 1989, Second Revised Edition in two volumes. *Eight Upaniṣads: With the Commentary of Śaṅkarācārya.* Calcutta: Advaita Ashrama.

Gotshalk, Richard. 1985. *Bhagavad Gītā: Translation and Commentary.* Delhi: Motilal Banarsidass.

Hill, W. Douglas P. 1928. *The Bhagavadgītā.* London: Oxford University Press.

Hopkins, E. Washburn. 1915; Reprint, 1969. *Epic Mythology.* New York: Biblo and Tannen.

Jacob, G.A. 1891; Reprint, 1999. *A Concordance to the Principal Upaniṣads and Bhagavadgītā.* Delhi: Motilal Banarsidass Publishers Pvt. Ltd.

Kale, M. R. 1894; Reprint, 1972. *A Higher Sanskrit Grammar.* Delhi: Motilal Banarsidass Publishers Private Limited.

Katre, Sumitra M. (translator). 1987. *Aṣṭādhyāyī of Pāṇini.* Austin: University of Texas Press.

Macdonell, Arthur Anthony. 1929. *A Practical Sanskrit Dictionary.* Reprint. New Delhi: Munshiram Manoharlal Publishers Pvt. Ltd.

Marjanovic, Boris. 2004, Second Edition. *Abhinavagupta's Commentary on the Bhagavad Gita: Gītārtha-saṁgraha.* Varanasi: Indica Books.

Miller, Barbara Stoler. 1986. *The Bhagavad-Gita: Krishna's Counsel in Time of War.* New York: Bantam Dell, Random House, Inc.

Minor, Robert N. 1982. *Bhagavad-Gītā: An Exegetical Commentary.* Columbia: South Asia Books.

Monier-Williams, Monier. 1899. *A Sanskrit-English Dictionary.* Reprint. Motilal Banarsidass.

Morgan, Les. 2011. *Croaking Frogs: A Guide to Sanskrit Metrics and Figures of Speech.* Pacifica: Mahodara Press.

—. 2017. *Translating the Bhagavadgītā: A Workbook for Sanskrit Students.* Pacifica: Mahodara Press.

Ryder, Arthur W. 1929. *The Bhagavad-Gita.* Chicago: University of Chicago Press.

Sampatkumaran, M. R. 1985. *The Gītābhāṣya of Rāmānuja.* Bombay: Anantacharya Indological Research Institute.

Sankaranarayanan, P. 1996. *Śrī Viṣṇusahasranāma Stotram.* Mumbai: Bharatiya Vidya Bhavan.

Sargeant, Winthrop. 1994. *The Bhagavad Gītā.* Revised. Albany: State University of New York Press.

Sharma, Ram Karan, Les Morgan, and Carol Pitts. 2015, First Edition. *Bhagavadgītā.* Edited by Les Morgan. Mahodara Press.

Sivananda, Swami. 1995. *The Bhagavad Gita.* Tenth Edition. Shivanandanagar: The Divine Life Society.

Smith, John. 2009. *The Mahābhārata.* London: Penguin Books.

Sörensen, S. 1904; Reprint, 2006. *An Index to Names in the Mahābhārata.* Delhi: Motilal Banarsidass Publishers Pvt. Ltd.

Stutley, Margaret. 2003. *The Illustrated Dictionary of Hindu Iconography.* First Indian Edition. New Delhi: Munshiram Manoharlal Publishers Pvt. Ltd.

Sukthankar, Vishnu, SK Belwalkar, and PL Vaidya. 1933-1972. *Mahābhārata.* Poona: Bhandarkar Oriental Research Institute.

Swarupananda, Swami. 1989. *Srimad Bhagavad Gita.* Reprint. Calcutta: Advaita Ashrama.

Tapasyananda, Swami. n.d. *Śrīmad Bhagavad Gītā.* Mylapore, Madras: Sri Ramakrishna Math.

Tilak, Bal Gangadhar. 1935; Reprint, 2002. *Śrīmad Bhagavadgītā Rahasya.* Delhi: D. K. Publishers Distributors Pvt. Ltd.

Tokunaga, Muneo, and John Smith. 2005. *Mahābhārata, Electronic text of the Critical Poona Edition.* Poona: Bhandarkar Oriental Research Institute (BORI). http://bombay.oriental.cam.ac.uk/john/mahabharata/. Accessed October 5, 2005.

Upadhaya, K. N. 1971; Reprint, 1998. *Early Buddhism and the Bhagavadgītā.* Delhi: Motilal Banarsidass Publishers Private Ltd.

Van Buitenen, J. A. B. 1981. *The Bhagavadgītā in the Mahābhārata.* Chicago: The University of Chicago Press.

—. 1975. *The Mahābhārata: 2. The Book of the Assembly Hall; 3. The Book of the Forest.* Chicago: The University of Chicago Press.

Vasu, Śrīśa Chandra (translator). 1891; Reprint, 1997. *The Aṣṭādhyāyī of Pāṇini.* Two volumes. New Delhi: Motilal Banarsidass Publishers Pvt. Ltd.

Venkateswaran, R. J. 1991. *Dictionary of Bhagavad Gita.* Delhi: Sterling Publishers Pvt. Ltd.

Vireśwarānanda, Swāmī. 1972. *Śrīmad Bhagavad Gītā: Text, Translation of the Text and of the Gloss of Śrīdhara Swāmī.* Madras: Sri Ramakrishna Math.

Warrier, A. G. Krishna. 1983. *Śrīmad Bhagavad Gītā Bhāṣya of Śrī Śaṅkarācārya.* Chennai: Sri Ramakrishna Math.

Wilson, Horace Hayman. 1868. *Vishṇu Purāṇa: A System of Hindu Mythology and Tradition.* London: Trübner & Co.

Zaehner, R. C. 1969. *The Bhagavad-Gītā.* Oxford: Oxford University Press.

About the Author

Les Morgan is the author of *Croaking Frogs: A Guide to Sanskrit Metrics and Figures of Speech* (2011), and *Translating the Bhagavadgītā: A Workbook for Sanskrit Students* (2017). His *Study Guide to the Bhagavadgītā: With Practical Concordance* (2017) is a companion volume to Ram Karan Sharma's *Bhagavadgītā*, which he edited. Other current projects include a translation of the Gaṇeśa Sahasranāma and preparation of a study guide for the Sāṁkhyakārikā of Īśvarakṛṣṇa.

Since 2005 he has been collaborating with R. K. Sharma to produce a concordance of poetic images in the *Mahābhārata* and *Rāmāyaṇa* and has co-presented with R. K. Sharma on that project at the University of California and at the 15th World Sanskrit Conference in New Delhi (2012). As a technologist, he has a special interest in corpus linguistics and digital texts. He is the co-developer of the Vidyut Input Method Editor (IME), used for entry of Devanāgarī on Windows computers. He provides a web site where recordings of spoken Sanskrit are provided free of charge (*mywhatever.com/sanskrit*). He is the developer of the first bilingual software used in spaceflight by NASA on the International Space Station, with interfaces in both English and Russian.

Other recent publications as an Editor and book designer include Nancy Jaicks Alexander's *Just Enough* (2010), Lori A. Hedderman's *Preparing Your Children For Goodbye: A Guidebook For Dying Parents* (2011) and *Remembering Together: A Guidebook for Meaningful Conversations With Your Aging Parents* (2016), Carol Pitts' *Spiritual Freedom in the Brahma Sūtras* (2012), Peter Frentzel's *Tao Te Ching: The Inner Journey* (2013), and Joanne Lynn's *MediCaring Communities: Getting What We Want and Need in Frail Old Age At An Affordable Cost* (2016).

He is the founder of Growth House, Inc. (*growthhouse.org*), an organization that provides education on end-of-life issues. He serves as a Senior Consultant to the Center for Elder Care and Advanced Illness, specializing in health care policy and information technology.

Made in the USA
Middletown, DE
30 January 2021

32715548R00225